BIBLIOTECA DELL' «ARCHIVUM ROMANICUM»
Serie I: Storia, Letteratura, Paleografia

464

GIUSEPPE GAZZOLA

MONTALE, THE MODERNIST

LEO S. OLSCHKI EDITORE
MMXVI

CASA EDITRICE LEO S. OLSCHKI
Viuzzo del Pozzetto, 8
50126 Firenze
www.olschki.it

ISBN 978 88 222 6482 4

ACKNOWLEDGEMENTS

This book has been a long time in the making. Its primal scene dates back to the meetings with the late Franco Croce, in his studio-attic in Palazzo Croce-Bermondi in Genoa, where, every time I mentioned a supposed objective correlative from *Ossi di seppia* or *Le occasioni*, he would admonish me: "It is an allegory, not a symbol". Almost twenty years have passed since our meetings, and I hope I finally understand what he meant. Along the way, I have been immeasurably helped and supported by a variety of distinguished teachers, colleagues and friends, whom it is a pleasure to acknowledge here.

My gratitude goes out, first and most importantly, to my teachers: Theodore Cachey, Jr. and John P. Welle at the University of Notre Dame; Giuseppe Mazzotta and Paolo Valesio at Yale. My colleagues at Stony Brook University deserve special thanks for their engagement, useful discussions, and support: I salute with deep gratitude Lisa Diedrich, Victoria Hesford, Luigi Fontanella, Peter Manning, Irene Marchegiani, Celia Marshik, Mario Mignone, and Kathleen Wilson; I am grateful as well to the students of Eugenio Montale and of Italian modernisms in my graduate and undergraduate classes at Stony Brook, for providing endless opportunities for discovery.

Colleagues from different institutions have kindly read and commented on the manuscript, in whole or part: I am grateful to David Bénéteau, Mimmo Cangiano, Pedro Capelo, Peter Carravetta, Rocco Rubini, Emily Setina, and Paola Sica. An unexpected conversation with David Quint was essential in determining the direction of the book; Millicent Marcus's opinion of its title was fundamental to its final form. Ernesto Livorni, Olaf Müller, Tullio Pagano and Massimo Riva have been generous intellectual interlocutors over the years.

My family in India, in Italy, and in the United States has unswervingly supported me along the way; I am bound to them by love and appreciation. The book is dedicated to my partner of "fine distinction and steadfast love", Ayesha Ramachandran, and to Zazie and Viola, who keep things real indeed.

The Italian Department at Brown University, welcoming me as a Visiting Assistant Professor in Fall 2012, granted me the time and leisure to start the project; the Humanities Institute at Stony Brook, appointing me as a fellow in the Spring of 2015, greatly facilitated the task of concluding it. This book is published with the generous support of the Humanities Institute at Stony Brook, and with a Research Initiative Grant for Faculty in the Fine Arts, Humanities, and Lettered Social Sciences (*FAHSS*).

I am grateful to the Yale University Art Gallery and its Editorial Assistant for Publications and Editorial Services, Julianna White, for permitting the reproduction of Gaudier-Brzeska's *Portrait of Ezra Pound* (1914).

Early versions of chapter 3 have previously appeared as "Lo sforzo sincretico degli *Ossi brevi*," in ed. Daniela Rapattoni, *Scrittori liguri verso il terzo millennio*, Pisa-Roma, Fabrizio Serra Editore, 2010, pp. 95-102, and as *Padre Dante e padre Mediterraneo: Nuove considerazioni sull'influenza dantesca nella poesia del giovane Eugenio Montale*, «Italian Poetry Review», IX, 2014, pp. 229-242. An abridged version of chapter 6 appeared as *Postmodern Montale*, «Forum Italicum Online», Vol. 50, n. 1, http://foi.sagepub.com/content/early/2016/08/19/0014585816662444.abstract. I am grateful for their permission to reproduce some parts in this book.

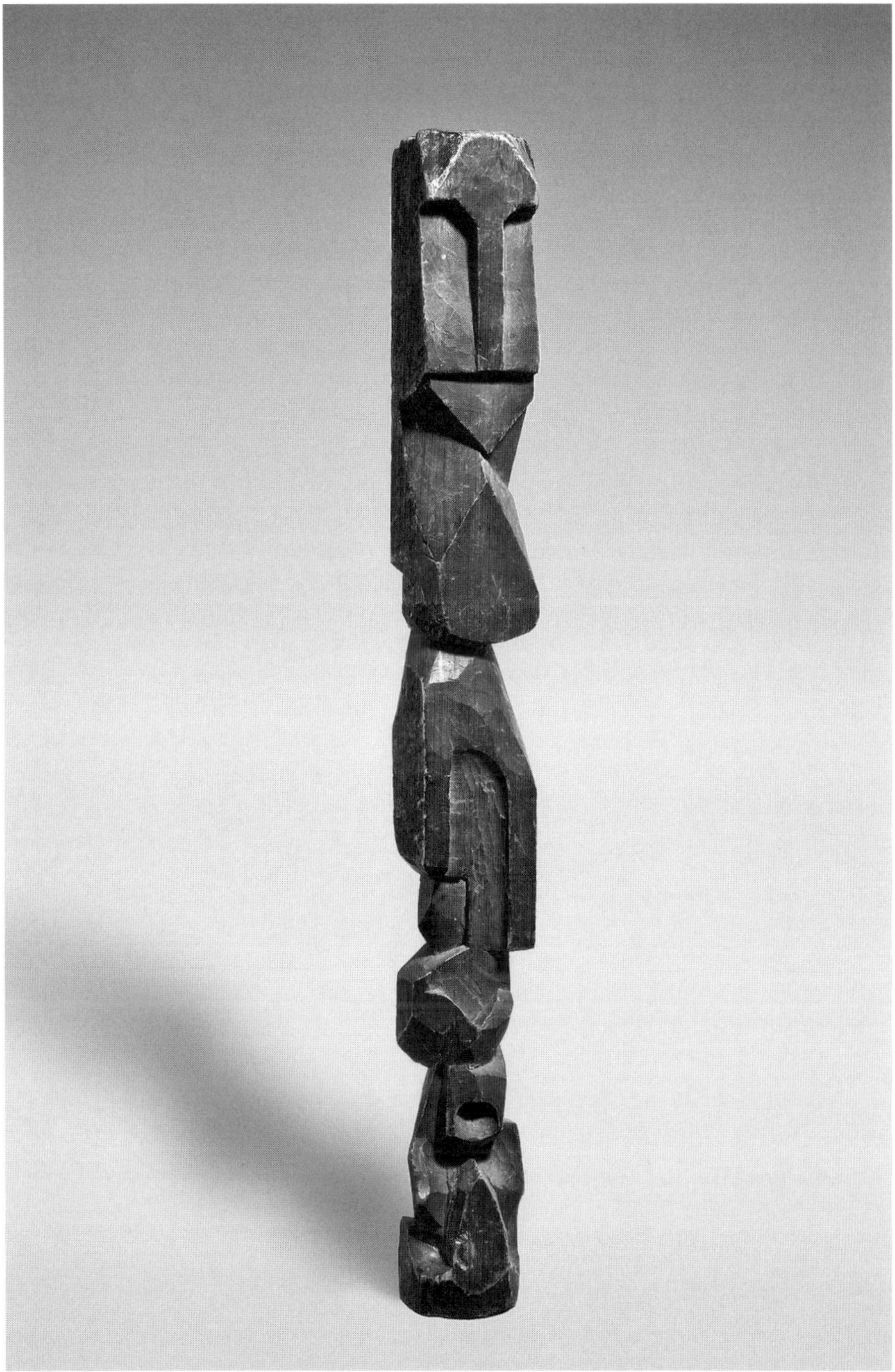

Henri Gaudier-Brzeska, *Portrait of Ezra Pound*, 1914. Wood, 28 1/2 × 3 × 3 in. (72.39 × 7.62 × 7.62 cm). Yale University Art Gallery, Purchase Director's Fund, 1961.23. Photo courtesy Yale University Art Gallery.

Chapter I

BEGINNINGS

1. The Heads of Janus

The quest for origins – poetic, personal, philosophical – defines the poetry of Eugenio Montale. From the early, unpublished poems looking for the definition of a lyric "I" to the verses composing the first book, *Ossi di seppia* (1925), which explore the poetic landscape of his native Liguria in search of sources, and the "non-stories stories" included in the book *Farfalla di Dinard* (1956), which begin a fictional autobiography returning again to the point of departure, Montale sought both to recover and to imagine a myth of origin that would shape his oeuvre. Even the collection of articles *Fuori di casa* (1969), which in compliance with its title gathers Montale's travel narratives, begins with a piece on the Cinque Terre ("Le Cinque Terre", PR 233), the place where Eugenio spent the summers of his childhood, as if to confirm the intuition of Italo Calvino that "una spiegazione generale del mondo e della storia deve innanzitutto tener conto di com'era situata casa nostra".[1] In all of Montale's works the locales of the Riviera di Levante – that part of the Riviera that extends from Genoa to the Cinque Terre and Portovenere – represent both the point of departure of his poetry and the original milestone against which he kept measuring the progress of his literary career. Later, after World War II and the consumption of the Ligurian landscape due to the speculative building boom of the 1950s and

---

[1] I. Calvino, *La strada di San Giovanni. Romanzi e racconti*, III, Milano, Mondadori 1997, p. 7: "A general explanation of the world and of history must, first and foremost, consider the position where our home was located". See also T.S. Eliot, *Four Quartets*, in T.S. Eliot, *The Complete Poems and Plays, 1909-1950*, New York, Harcourt, 1980, p. 129: "Home is where one starts from". J. Varner Gunn in *Autobiography: Towards a Poetic of Experience*, Philadelphia, University of Pennsylvania Press, 1982, p. 9, needs a more articulated sentence to express the same concept: "When the autobiographer brings a life 'to language,' he or she always adumbrates a perspective from somewhere – namely, from a world whose meanings and codes and even whose burden of unintelligibility serve to locate and ground that perspective".

1960s, Montale would refuse to return physically to the region where he was born, yet he kept returning there in memory and imagination, remaining faithful in spirit to a place that he could see by then only in his dreams.[2]

Montale's early interest in eco-criticism is, of course, a consequence of his modernist position – of his belonging in a Weltanschauung born from the convergence of the philosophical crisis that invested positivism and idealism at the turn of the century, the scientific innovations of the period, and the apocalyptic sentiments common in Europe after the shock created by the mechanized war. Such beliefs and life-experiences connect Montale's thought with the work of the major European modernist authors of his generation; and yet, precisely by virtue of his rootedness in an original landscape, the Genoese poet is capable of maintaining a stunning individuality, recognized in his citation for the Nobel prize in 1975.

Montale's originality is linked, not only by way of semantics, to his myth of origin. A fitting emblem for such a myth of origin is the figure of Janus, the pagan divinity representing the threshold of space and time, and also the legendary founder of Genoa, who transmitted to the city his ability to look simultaneously in two different directions.

Janus's cult begins in Rome, where he was a revered figure from the sixth century B.C. Represented with two faces,[3] since he could look into the future as well as at the past, Janus was celebrated as the god of beginnings. These celebrations occurred at the beginning of the year, through the month of January that bears his name, at the beginning of each month, and at the beginning of each day. As the god of transitions, he was invoked at births and deaths, and at the beginning of journeys and new enterprises. The temple dedicated to him in the Forum had two gates, each facing the direction of his two heads, and the building itself was configured as an expanded threshold, marking the passage from past to future, from youth to old age, ultimately coming to represent the journey of an individual life:

> Omnis habet geminas, hinc atque hinc, ianua frontis,
> e quibus haec populum spectat, at illa larem;

---

[2] See E. Montale, "Genova nei ricordi di un esule" (1968), SM 2879: "resto attaccato allo scoglio dove sono nato, resto fedele a un paesaggio che vedo solo in sogno perché i suoi abitanti lo hanno reso irriconoscibile" ("I remain attached to the reef where I was born, I remain faithful to a landscape that I see only in my dreams because its inhabitants have transformed it beyond recognition").

[3] "Biceps", "double headed", is the epithet generally associated to him. See Ovid, *Fas.* I, 65-66: "Iane biceps, anni tacite labentis origo, / sulus de superis qui tua terga vides" ("Two headed Janus, you who give origin to the year that silently passes, the only one among the gods who can see his back").

utque sedens primi vester prope limina tecti
ianitor egressus introitusque videt,
sic ego perspicio caelestis ianitor aulae
Eoas partes Hesperiasque simul.[4]

Eoa and Hesperia in this prosopopoeia indicate East and West, the place where the sun rises and where it sets; they represent at once the beginning and the end of the day, and the beginning and the end of human life. Janus's trope thus spans a geographical distance (the distance between East and West) and the passage of time (the time the sun employs to cover said distance, or the time of human life). As he spatializes time, Janus also measures the effect of time in space, explaining how the passage of time acts upon the composition of the phenomenal world, allowing the four elements to proceed from chaos to a naturally ordered reality:

me Chaos antiqui (nam sum res prisca) vocabant:
aspice, quam longi temporis acta canam.
lucidus hic aer et quae corpora restant,
ignis, aqua et tellus, unus acervus erat.
ut semel haec rerum secessit lite suarum
inque novas abiit massa soluta domos,
flamma petit altum, propior locus aera cepit,
sederunt medio terra fretumque solo.
Tunc ego, qui fueram globus et sine imagine moles,
in faciem redii dignaque membra deo.[5]

As Ovid's exposition suggests, Janus emerged at the worlds' beginning, when the four elements separated to generate a world of order and harmony. A powerful myth of genesis, whose characteristics made him all the more suitable to humanize as a foundational hero, Janus also represents the human-in-process, entangled in time and space, imagining and shaping his own beginning as he looks back to the past and forward to his future. The story of Janus points therefore to the mythologization of human life

---

4 Ovid, *Fas.* I, 135-140: "Every threshold has two heads, on one side and the other, of which one faces the public and the other the Lares; and just as a door-keeper, sitting at the door, sees who enters and exits, so I, the door-keeper of the celestial courts, see at once towards East and West".

5 Ovid, *Fas.* I, 103-111: "The ancients called me Chaos, since I am a being of old; consider the very long ages of which I speak. Back then bright air and the other three bodies, fire, water, earth, were all piled together. Once, through the discord of its elements, the mass unfastened, and went in diverse ways to seek new homes, fire went up high, air filled the space nearby, while earth and sea sank in the middle. At that point I, until that time a shapeless lump, assumed the face and formed the limbs of a god".

as passage – a conceptual process whose consequences for poetry and philosophy would interest Montale throughout his whole life.

If, in the Roman pantheon, Janus testified to the common origin of time and space, at the beginning of what we call early modernity he was transformed by Genoese historians from a primeval divinity into the historical figure of the founder of the city, who thus become one with the city itself. At the moment of the Genoese Republic's great splendor, when its galleys scurried all corners of the Mediterranean Sea, its historian, Jacobus Doria, decided to dignify the origin of the city with a foundational story that captured its political and military greatness. Helped by the assonance between the name of the city in Latin, Ianua, and Ianus, he forged a connection between the two by making Janus the historical founder of the city.[6] Making a clear connection between the city, its maritime and commercial prerogatives, and Ovid's representation of Janus, Jacobus created a link between the Roman god and the land he meant to celebrate, extolling its function as a threshold between land and sea, between East and West:

> Ianua a Iano dicitur. Hec Ianua, id est porta, primus ingressus, primus introitus, quia Ianus est deus principiorum, cui antiqui omnem exitum et introitum consecraverunt. Unde sicut porta est introitus et exitus cuislibet domus, ita civitas nostra est introitus et exitus totius Lon[go]bardie. Vel dicitur Ianua a Iano deo principiorum, qui pingitur habere duas facies, scilicet ante et retro, sic civitas Ianue prospicit ante mare, et retro terram; et dicitur, habere duas faculas, id est duas portas, oriens et occidens, sic civitas Ianue habet duas portas, videlicet portam maris, et portam terre.[7]

---

[6] See C. Benes, *Urban Legends. Civic identity and the Classical Past in Northern Italy, 1250-1350*, University Park, Pennsylvania State University Press, 2011. The origin of the name "Genoa" is thought to derive instead from an Indo-European root word, either *geneu- ("knee") or *genu- ("mouth"); in the former case, the name would be a reference to the shape of the coast, which formed a safe natural harbor; in the latter, it would indicate the mouth of the river Bisagno (incidentally, the place where Montale's poem *La foce*, later renamed *Incontro*, is set). An alternative, more recent theory links the name "Genoa" to the Etruscan word "Kainua", meaning "New city". See P. Melli, *Genova preromana*, Genova, Fratelli Frilli, 2007. A specific critique of the figure of Janus is in Augustine of Hippo, *De Civitate Dei* VII 7-9.

[7] Jacobus Doria, *Annales Januenses*, 8: "Genoa receives its name from Ianus. This (word) Ianua means threshold, first access, first entrance, since Ianus is the god of beginnings, to whom the ancients dedicated every entrance and every exit. As a threshold represents the entrance and the exit to anyone's house, our city represents the entrance and the exit of all of Northern Italy. And since Genoa receives its name from Janus, god of the beginnings, who is depicted having two faces, in the front and in the back, the city overlooks the sea before and the land behind. As Janus is believed to have two faces, i.e. two gates, to the east and to the west, so the city of Genoa has two gates: namely, the one that leads to the sea, and the one that leads to the land". For a recent analysis of the city of Genoa as a threshold between land and sea, inspired by this passage, see M. Quaini, *L'ombra del paesaggio: Orizzonti di un'utopia conviviale*, Reggio Emilia, Diabasis, 2006, pp. 21-22.

He thereby created a propitious mythical foundation for the contemporary and successive development of Genoa as a place of commercial exchange, a point of departure for merchants and explorers, and the birthplace of the mechanisms of financial capitalism.[8] This is the threshold city that Montale, in his turn, will define as "città buonsensaia e commerciale" ("a commercial city where practical sense prevails").[9]

Another Jacobus reinforced the connection between the Roman divinity and the city that, by then, had become the ruler of the Mediterranean. Jacobus de Voragine, as the toponymy of his name suggests, was born in a small town on the Ligurian coast (present day Varazze), and was appointed Archbishop of Genoa in 1292. By then, a respected author because of his *Legenda Aurea*, he distinguished among three different Januses in his own history of the city:

> Notandum est quod tres fuisse Iani dicuntur. Primus est Ianus, qui de partibus orientis in Ytaliam venit et ibi primo regnavit. Secundus est quidam princeps, qui fuit civis Troiae, qui post destructionem Troiae ad Ytaliam venit. Tertius est rex Epyrotarum, qui Romam venit et post mortem suam Romani ipsum deificaverunt et tamquam deum coluerunt.[10]

In Jacobus's account the first king erected the city of Genoa, the second improved it, and the third was honored in the city for his important role in Roman civilization. The Archbishop here rationalizes the city's mythic foundations with a euhemerist explanation that amplifies the overlap between human, historical experience and the process of mythmaking – a process that Montale himself adopts in his mythic representations of Ligurian and Genoese experiences. The shores and the vegetable gardens of the region, in Montale's writing, were visited by other classical divinities: Pan and Triton, for example, who – exactly like Janus – had to adapt and transform to represent adequately a myth of origin that impacted the very origin of the myth.[11]

---

8 See the chapter "The First (Genoese) Systemic Cycle of Accumulation", in G. Allegri, *The Long Twentieth Century*, London, Verso, 1994, pp. 109-128.

9 See E. Montale, "Il successo", (1950), PR 59.

10 Jacopo da Varagine, *Cronaca della città di Genova dalle origini al 1297*, ed. Stefania Bertini Guidetti, Genoa, ECIG, 1995, p. 342: "We need to notice that there were three Januses. The first is Janus, who came to Italy from the East and reigned there first. The second is a Prince, who was a citizen of Troy and came to Italy after the destruction of that city. The third is the king of the Epyrotes, who came to Rome and after whose death the Romans deified and venerated as a god". See also p. 388.

11 See E. Montale, "Là fuoriesce il Tritone..." (OV 35), and "La riviera di Ciceri (e la mia)" (1970), AMS 1459: "Anche in quegli orti il dio Pan faceva capolino; ma doveva rimpic-

If Genoese historians had already exploited the symbolic potential of the Janus figure, by the nineteenth-century, Nietzsche's *The Birth of Tragedy* (1871) would identify the two heads of Janus with Apollo and Dionysus in order to explain the inherent dichotomy of Greek drama – thereby amplifying the mythic potentials of the Janus story to serve new ends. Now, on the threshold of modernism, the figure of the two-headed god who looks at the past and in the future, to the East and the West, becomes an emblem of the unity of space and time that characterizes modernity. Janus is therefore a powerful emblem for a book on modernism, a moment in which the categories of time and space were radically reinterpreted, from a scientific as well as a philosophical point of view. The two-faced divinity can be transformed into a signifier of the modern human condition not only because by governing space and time he measures the movement of human existence, but also because he embodies a conception of space and time as intrinsically conjoined, that is, as relative to one another, a revolutionary idea that took by storm the realms of physics and mathematics, and of philosophy and literature, shortly after the ending of the First World War. If this seems to be a misrepresentation of the myth, all the better – the radical reuse of an ancient figure is itself representative of the use of myth by modernist writers, particularly by Montale.

To use the myth of Janus as an allegorical frame for a book on Montale's place in the modernist landscape therefore presupposes an inherent recognition of the projective nature of the mythical tale: a projection that contemporary authors were eager to explore. Whether in *The Magic Mountain*, the *Waste Land, Ulysses*, or *Ossi di seppia*, the revision and strategic redeployment of ancient myth marks modernism's own historical and philosophic claim to novelty and to a new origin story. Montale's own use of myth is initially instrumental in creating a poetic landscape of communion, of "adherence" between the lyric "I" and the reality surrounding him. His world is a place where the sudden apparitions of a Triton, of the "arciera Diana", and of other "disturbed divinities" mark the stillness of time and define a maritime Eden in which time stands still and the poetic subject strives for an identification with the natural world. Yet, soon enough, a whirlwind of

ciolirsi come uno gnomo, rendersi domestico e utile, aiutare i bambini ad attingere acqua dal pozzo. Non fu mai alcionia la Riviera ligure né panica nel senso torrenziale della parola. Fu piuttosto, nelle sue forme naturali, antropomorfa e squisitamente umana, sia pure in piccolo formato" ("The god Pan peeped in the vegetable gardens, as well; but he had to dwindle to the height of a gnome, become domestic and helpful, aiding the children to draw water forme the well. The Riviera has never been a place for Halcyon, has never inspired a D'Annunzian sense of harmony. It has been rather, in its natural forms, anthropomorphic and blatantly humane, even if in a pocket size"). For the reference to G. D'Annunzio's *Alcyone*, see *infra*.

novelty penetrates this *hortus conclusus* perched on the sea. The experience and knowledge of the outside world, epitomized by the outburst of the First World War, make clear that mythic, absolute space and time are but characteristics of an "età illusa", mere pretense of children.

From then on, Montale's use of myth aims at rewriting the original story to create a perverted analogy. Irma Brandeis is renamed Clizia on the suggestion of a verse attributed to Dante by a ground-breaking edition of Dante's *Rhymes* edited by Gianfranco Contini; but the original myth of Clizia as recounted by Ovid seems irrelevant. Similarly, the myth of Hercules's fifth labor is conveniently manipulated in "Botta e risposta I", strikingly omitting Hercules from it.[12] James Joyce rewrote the *Odyssey* expunging Ulysses from it, translating the myth in space and time to fit his own narrative agenda: Montale, even before becoming a reader of Joyce, had a clear instinct about how modern poetry should be.

2. Montale, the Modernist

> Pope Pius X knew what Modernism was: it was an attempt by certain misled Catholics to bend the doctrines of the church to the authority of modern science. He issued an encyclical to put an end to that folly. Since then, no one else has been clear about Modernism.[13]

Denis Donaghue's provocative consideration is meant to point out at the lack of clear boundaries in the definition of the literary category called "modernism". In fact, depending upon who is asked, modernism could

---

12 On myth and its re-elaboration in modernist times, see the chapter "Dalla terra desolata al paradiso artificiale", in F. Moretti, *Segni e stili del moderno*, Torino, Einaudi, 1987, pp. 195-234.

13 D. Donaghue, *Introduction*, in *The Old Moderns*, New York, Knopf, 1994, p. ix. Despite Donaghue's statement, scholars of Catholic modernism found and still find difficult to define their field of analisys, as much as their literary counterpart. According to a period catchphrase attributed to one of the most influential modernist theologians, Alfred Loisy, "il y a autant de modernismes que de modernistes": see S. Leblanc (a.k.a. H. Bremond), *Une Oeuvre Clandestine d'Henri Bremond*, ed. E. Poulat, Roma, Edizioni di Storia e di Letteratura, 1972, p. 172; see also M. Calinescu, *Five Faces of Modernity*, Durham, Duke University Press, 1987, p. 79, who notes how the statement applies to literary modernism as well. Not long after Loisy, Giorgio La Piana had issued a warning: "The future historian of Modernism will be much embarrassed by the contradictory appreciations and misjudgements which are to be found in our contemporary literature on this subject". (G. La Piana, *A Review of Italian Modernism*, «Harvard Theological Review», IX, 4, October 1916, pp. 351-375, quote from p. 351). On the history and ramifications of Catholic modernism see P. Hégy, *L'autorité dans le catholicisme contemporain: du Syllabus à Vatican II*, Paris, Éditions Beauchesne, 1975.

variably begin with the symbolist season, or with the crisis produced by Darwin's evolutionary theory. Even if the general scholarly consensus is that the term has come to describe a range of poetic, aesthetic, and theoretical positions that mark a radical rupture with tradition around the beginning of the twentieth century, the paradox that Pope Pius X's encyclical *Pascendi Domini Gregis* is the only critical document containing a clear definition of modernism may carry a kernel of truth. As Susan Stanford Friedman notes, "the term modernism slips and slides between oppositional meanings", and critics have defined it in terms of style, periodization, canonization, but "the naming of the defining characteristics of modernism are all based on a pool of tenets, people, and/or events whose selection depends upon preexisting notions of the period".[14] According to Michael Levenson, modernism goes from the last decade of the nineteenth century to the beginning of the Second World War, but the expiration date of the movement and its relationship with what followed are under debate as well, since "one critic's postmodernism is another critic's modernism".[15]

In this book, the advent of modernism is associated with the climax of the second industrial revolution, the dissemination of new technologies that effectively changed the lives of millions at the beginning of the twentieth century, the cultural shocks of the first mechanized war and of revolutionary scientific theories.[16] The following "philosophy of the crisis",

---

[14] S. Stanford Friedman, *Definitional Excursions: The Meaning of Modern / Modernity / Modernism*, «Modernism/modernity», VIII, no. 3 (September 2001), pp. 493-513, quotations from pp. 502 and 508. A similar indetermination is in the definition of Hibero-American *modernismo*: "El modernismo da tono a la época; no es un dogmatismo, no una ortodoxia, no un cuerpo de doctrina ni una escuela. Sus límites son amplios, fluidos, y dentro de ellos caben personalidades muy varias. El modernismo es, sobre todo, una actitud" ("*Modernismo* is the keynote of the times; it is not a dogma, nor an ortodoxy, nor a body of teachings, nor a school. Its boundaries are ample, fluid, and include very different personalities. *Modernismo* is, above all, an attitude"), R. Gullón, *Direcciones del modernismo*, Madrid, Gredos, 1971, pp. 18-19.

[15] A. Huyssen, *After the great Divide: Modernism, Mass Culture, and Postmodernism*. London, MacMillan, 1988, quote from p. 59. See also N. Frye, *The Modern Century*, Toronto, Oxford University Press, 1967; M. Levenson, *Introduction*, in *The Cambridge Companion to Modernism*, ed. M. Levenson, Cambridge, Cambridge University Press, 1999, pp. 1-8; and E. Wilson, *Alex's Castle: A Study in Imaginative Literature of 1870-1930*, New York and London, Scribner, 2004.

[16] Sergio Solmi, a long-time friend and interlocutor of Eugenio Montale, gauged the impact of the new scientific revolution in an article dated 1963. See S. Solmi, "Il mattino dei maghi" (1963), in *Saggi sul fantastico*, Torino, Einaudi, 1978, p. 112: "Sotto l'aggressione selvaggiamente speculativa d'uno Einstein, sotto l'analisi sperimentale degli altri grandi scienziati moderni, il mondo della fisica classica, su cui poggiava, magari inconsapevolmente – e tanto più solidamente quanto inconsapevolmente – la visione tradizionale dell'universo, è andato in pezzi" ("Under Einstein's wildly speculative aggression, under the experimental analysis of other great modern scientists, the world of classical physics, on which the traditional wiev of the universe rested, perhaps unconsciously – and more firmly in such case –, has fallen apart").

which engaged and connected many distinct European national traditions (we have only to think of Nietzsche, Bergson, James, and Michelstaedter among many others), contrasted the gnoseological practices of symbolism and realism with a new awareness of the fragmentation of the subject and of the flux inherent in human life. On this regard, modernism represents a fitting response to the cultural malaise generated by the pervasiveness of technology, and ultimately embodied in the carnage of the Great War.[17] Modernism names the cultural and aesthetic impact of these unprecedented changes and traumas, the expressive forms they took, and the theoretical reconfigurations that they engendered.

Yet, Donaghue's *boutade* also points to another less-discussed fact: that the literary movement called modernism, and the movement which aimed to reform Christian Catholic theology in accommodating traditional religious teachings with emerging scientific thought, are not ideologically separate from one another. Modernism and *modernismo* find a common origin in the philosophy of the crisis, and specifically in Henri Bergson's first books, *Essai sur les données immédiates de la conscience* (*Time and Free Will*, 1889), *Matière et mémoire* (*Matter and Memory*, 1896), and *Introduction à la métaphysique* (*Introduction to Metaphysics*, 1903). In Italy, Giuseppe Prezzolini and Adolfo Levi began diffusing Bergson's philosophy by 1904;[18] in England, T.E. Hulme began in 1909 to publish articles in *The New Age* promoting Bergson's ideas, and eventually translated *Matière et mémoire* into English. T.S. Eliot attended Bergson's lectures at the Collège de France in the winter of 1910, during his first Parisian sojourn, and later acknowledged a "temporary conversion to Bergsonism".[19] Édouard Le Roy, a leader and inspirer of Catholic modernism, was Bergson's favorite disciple and later took his seat at the Collège de France as well as at the Académie Française. When Bergson, in the pages of *L'évolution créatrice* (*Creative Evolution*, 1907), reconciled the scientific evidence of Darwinian evolutionary theory with his own notion of *élan vital*, a life force deprived of quantifiable physical characteristics and yet the basis of life itself, Le Roy interpreted the idea as a working definition for the Christian god. The consequence was that Catholic modernism was excommunicat-

---

17 A useful treatment of the subject is in M. Cacciari, *Krisis: saggio sulla crisi del pensiero negativo da Nietzsche a Wittgenstein*, Milano, Feltrinelli, 1978.

18 See G. Prezzolini, *Del linguaggio come causa di errore (H. Bergson)*, Firenze, Spinelli, 1904; A. Levi, *L'indeterminismo nella filosofia francese contemporanea. La filosofia della contingenza*, Firenze, Seeber, 1904.

19 T.S. Eliot, *A Sermon Preached in Magdalene College Chapel*, Cambridge, Cambridge University Press, p. 5.

ed within the year, and Bergson's books ended up in the *Index Librorum Prohibitorum*.

The common origin of modernism and *modernismo* thus puts Montale in the peculiar position of *trait d'union*, a point of contact between both kinds of modernism.[20] A reader of French contingentism himself (he mentions reading Lachelier, Boutroux, Bergson), Montale came early in contact with exponents of Catholic modernism and, if the Catholic faith soon ceased to interest him, his poetry demonstrates that ideas derived from Boutroux's and Bergson's books informed his philosophical background for a long time. But a common philosophical background and the belonging to the same generation are not the only reasons why Montale must be considered alongside the great figures of European modernism. Ezra Pound, T.S. Eliot, James Joyce, Valery Larbaud, and Italo Svevo were his acquaintances, correspondents, and audience; he read their work and they read his – admittedly, with various degrees of appreciation and interest in both directions. He shared with them the catastrophic experience of the World Wars and the ensuing political disappointments as well as an abiding interest in the scientific innovations of the period; as one of them, he sought to craft a new poetics that would respond to these transformations.

The themes and the characteristics evident in Montale's work, specifically in the period between the second edition of *Ossi di seppia* (Ribet, 1928) and the third book of verses, *La bufera e altro* (Mondadori, 1956) are the result of this search for a new poetics. The fragmentation of the lyric "I", the understanding of space and time as discontinuous and essentially un-measurable units, the recuperation of medieval and nineteenth century sources strongly reminiscent of that used by Pound and Eliot, the use of mythic paradigms and the willingness to make radical linguistic experiments, the attention to matters of technique, and the participation in a general poetic shift from subject to object – these are all characteristics linking Montale's poetic output to a modernist agenda. Montale shares with the main European modernist writers the poetics of *difficulty*, an ambiguous and unconventional use of the vocabulary, and an insistent idea of writing poetry in musical terms.[21]

---

20 In an analogous position was Giovanni Boine, one of the writers from the Ligurian Heritage most appreciated by Montale. See M. CANGIANO, *Tra due modernismi. La versione di Boine della* 'Morte di Dio', «Rivista di Letteratura Italiana», 3, 2015, pp. 37-52.

21 That is not to say there are only similarities: if Pound had invited Eliot to eliminate all "perhaps", all dubitative expressions, from the *Waste Land*, Montale has built some of his better received poems on the Italian equivalent of the word, "forse". See T.S. ELIOT, *The Waste Land. A Facsimile and Transcript*, ed. V. Eliot, New York, Harcourt Brace, 1971, pp. 45-77.

The task of the present book will be not so much to demonstrate that Montale *is* a modernist poet, a fact implicitly, and sometimes explicitly, accepted by recent criticism.[22] Instead *Montale, the Modernist* aims to explain *how* and *when* Montale became a modernist poet. It analyzes the trajectory of his poetry from the early symbolist verses to the fully modernist poems composed in the period 1926-27 for the second edition of *Ossi di seppia*. Beginning with Montale's early life experience, specifically his participation in World War I, the book explores how such a traumatic event changed his perspective on the world as well as influenced his ideas on the art of poetry.

Understanding Montale as a modernist poet (and, later, as an intellectual aware of the philosophical tenets of postmodernism) changes our understanding of his work. And recognizing the common traits between Montale and the authors he knew or corresponded with illuminates the European context in which his poetry evolved. The association with modernism helps the interpretation of his poetry: the fragmentation of the subject, the composition of a body of texts that welcomes and includes contradictions, the insistent use of a poetics that celebrates the multiple layering of sources and meanings, allow us to better understand the indeterminacy of the subject-agent in Montale's poems, the internal contra-

---

22 *The Cambridge Companion to European Modernism* mentions Montale only in passing and without linking him to the movement (see the chapter "Italy" in *The Cambridge Companion to European Modernism*, ed. P. Lewis, Cambridge, Cambridge University Press, pp. 75-93: 90); the same is true for *Modernism. A Guide to European Literature 1890-1930*, eds. M. Bradbury and J. McFarlane, London, Penguin Books, 1991; the volume *Italian modernism: Italian Culture Between Decadentism and Avant-Garde* does not have a section dedicated to Montale, yet he is considered there "a recognized protagonist of late modernity", in the words of R. Ceserani (see *Italy and Modernity: Peculiarities and Contradictions*, in *Italian modernism: Italian Culture Between Decadentism and Avant-Garde*, eds. L. Somigli and M. Moroni, Toronto, University of Toronto Press, 2004, p. 41). Even if they not use the word "modernism", the analyses by R. Luperini and T. De Rogatis treat of Montale's "modern classicism", linking inevitably the Italian poet to T.S. Eliot's production and practices. In fact, the connection between Montale and Eliot is a well-studied topic (see bibliography in chapter 5.4). General examinations of Italian modernism that portrait Montale as a central figure are in R. Luperini, *Il modernismo italiano esiste*, and in R. Donnarumma, *Tracciato del modernismo italiano*, opening essays of *Sul modernismo italiano*, eds. R. Luperini, M. Tortora, Napoli, Liguori, 2012, pp. 3-12 and 13-38. Apart from the two manuals mentioned at the beginning, in the English speaking world Montale's modernist awareness is generally acknowledged: S. Putnam wrote, as early as 1930, that "The dominant note in Montale is a cosmic despair. He is a sort of modern and lyric Lucretius, who has read his Einstein, his Bergson, and others" (see S. Putnam, *A Miniature Antology of Italian Poetry*, vol. II no. 4, Autumn 1930, p. 658; as quoted in H. Thomas, *Montale in English*, New York, Handsel Books, 2004, p. xvii); C.J. Brook defines Montale a "key modernist poet" in *The expression of the inexpressible*, Oxford, Clarendon, 2002, p. ix; P. McCormick in *Aspects yellowing darkly: Ethics, Intuition, and the European High Modernism*, Kraków, Jagiellonian University Press, 2010, links Eliot, Valéry and Montale in a multi-layered book that reflects on how moral intuitionism and suffering may be seen to arise in the ethical reflection of contemporary Europe as well as in the poetry of European modernism.

dictions of his poetry, and the strategic juxtaposition of his sources. The modernist technique of overcrowding the text with echoes, references and meanings reinforces the idea that it is not necessary to identify a specific source, excluding all others, for any given passage. We do not need to decide if it is more likely that Montale appropriated the makeshift verb "meriggiare" from Boine's *Frantumi* or from D'Annunzio's *Alcyone*; we should instead consider the accumulation of echoes, leaving the text free to include all possible references and all possible meanings.

Similarly, the biographical elements present in the texts do not need to exclude or contradict alternative poetic sources. For example, it is not necessary to determine if the statue of Summer mentioned in "Flussi" (OV 74) was a real statue in the garden of Montale's villa in Monterosso (it was), or instead a reminiscence of a poem from D'Annunzio; the text allows both interpretations, and possibly many more. Seen from a modernist perspective, from a perspective of accumulation and not of the singleness of meaning, the great variety of authors that have been considered as Montale's sources are not a sign of how much the European lyric tradition had weighed on him, but a sign of his freedom and compositional variety. Montale combines in a very personal style a great number of influxes and allusions, a variety of sources, of echoes from diverse poems and philosophical treatises. He demonstrates a remarkable ability in procuring, re-elaborating and transforming his sources.

On the other hand, Montale's poetic biography shows that the syncronicity between the *fin de siècle* eclipse of symbolism and the philosophical crisis that ushers in the modernist tradition is not a coincidence: the philosophical estrangement from the divine was in itself a rejection of God understood as the foundational symbol.[23] To recognize Montale's place in the European constellation of modernism, therefore, changes our understanding of modernism itself. It underscores the relationship and the philosophical proximity between Catholic and literary modernism and helps us understand literary modernism as a truly pan-European movement – one that originated and distanced itself from the extremely successful modes of symbolism after the historical shock of World War I, and which, as a movement with ramifications in many languages, was capable, exactly like the texts that compose it, of containing oxymorons and contradictions.

The book follows thematically Montale's engagements with modernist modes of literary innovation. Thus the second chapter, "In Time of War",

---

23 Interesting pages on the topic are in T. EAGLETON, *Culture and the Death of God*, New Haven and London, Yale University Press, 2014.

links Montale's biography to the historical period in which he lived, detailing the dominant scientific and philosophical ideas of the time, in order to explain the background from which his poetry originated. Reading "Non chiederci la parola..." (OV 27) as the cry of a war veteran who realizes that the certainties and hopes he held before the war have been shattered by the violence of the conflict, the chapter understands this poem as the cry of a lyric self who realizes that the experience of the war has rendered impossible the symbolist conception of a poem, which sought to represent the profound connection between the human and the natural worlds.

After considering Montale's sense of time before and after the Great war, the third chapter, "A Landscape of Many Sources," details the poet's spaces and exploits the grounds of a metaphor employed by Montale himself to recount his poetic sources. Specifically, it analyzes the shift from his early conformity with the Italian, and more specifically Ligurian, literary tradition to his later search for a different, "modern" vein of inspiration. Montale's shifting relationship to the poetic landscape is interpreted as a symptom of his emergence as a modernist writer. The poetry of the early *Ossi* seeks to "aderire alle fibre del suolo" ("adhere to the fibers of the soil") through the appropriation of the landscape of his predecessors; however, a subsequent awareness that the landscape sought and desired actually does not possess an ontological consistency, that the phenomenal world is a place where nothing *is* and everything *becomes*, frees the lyric "I" from immobility and determines his immersion in the Bergsonian "flux" and the rediscovered passage of time. An "Intermezzo" dedicated to the geographical localization of Montale's first three books of poetry follows, an exercise that reveals the increasing movement of the poetic "I" in accordance with the poet's growing European literary interests.

The subsequent chapter details in greater depth the correspondences between the poems written for the second edition of *Ossi di seppia*, and poetry of Pound and Eliot as well as their theoretical writings. "Beyond the Threshold" ends with a reading of the journey of "Arsenio," intended both as the journey within the text attempted by this alter-ego of the author, and the journey of the text that, in Mario Praz's translation, was eventually published in Eliot's «Criterion». The analysis intends to shed light on the relationship between Montale and Anglo-American modernism, contending that such a relationship was not about imitation, but rather that Montale participated in a broader shift in poetics employing his own methods and scopes. Montale was aware of the theoretical change happening in the rest of Europe, as he was aware that poetry written in Italian was running the risk of lagging behind. In the same year in which "Arsenio" appeared in the «Criterion», Montale wrote a theoretical manifesto where he spelled out the need for conceptual and formal innovation in Italian "new poetry:" "La poesia nuova ha bisogno di crearsi le proprie forme, e se le avverrà di rinascere negli stampi tradizionali imprimerà certo in essi i segni indelebili della feconda tempesta (troppo tardi in Italia!) attraversata".[24]

A sixth chapter traces a further poetic shift beyond modernism that happened after the publication of *La bufera e altro* (1956) and a long poetic sabbatical, investigating the beginning of Montale's late production, what he called the *verso* of his poetry. "Postmodern Montale" considers primarily Montale's fourth book, *Satura* (1971), and interrogates the connections between the new directions of Montale's poetry and the scientific and philosophical trends of the 1950s and 1960s. To describe Montale's late work as postmodernist in orientation is to measure the distancing of his poetics from the writing of the first three volumes: the poetic voice of *Satura* consciously explores the dialectical relationship between modern and postmodern, challenges the distinction between high and low culture, and is the result of a loss of a secure definition between subjectivity and objectivity, between self and other. The chapter includes a discussion of Julien Benda's *La trahison des clercs*, and of Cesare Vasoli's *Tra cultura e ideologia*, as important sources to explain Montale's suspension of poetic output as a symptom of the political and philosophical disillusionment experienced during the years of the reconstruction and the economic boom. Using the latter text as a guide, the chapter specifically analyzes one of the most hermeneutically complex poems of the book, "Dialogo".

The final chapter engages the short stories collected in *Farfalla di Dinard* (1956[1], 1960[2]), and specifically those set in Liguria, connecting the geographical analysis tested in chapter four with Montale's imagined autobiography in prose to better illuminate the shaping of a myth of return in the light of postmodern attention to the concepts of eco-criticism. The imagined return to the point of departure is, once more, a movement to gauge the distance travelled and to measure the distance left to go. In this, it brings the conclusions back to a consideration of the geographical connection between the extremes of the Riviera di Levante and the mythical door of Janus as conceived by Jacobus Doria.

---

24 "New poetry needs to create its form, and even if it will happen to be born in traditional schemes, it will impress them with the indelible signs of the fecund storm (too late in Italy!) crossed". E. Montale, "La lirica" (1928), AMS 1946.

Chapter II

IN TIME OF WAR

1. "The World's Time Reckoning Is an Exceedingly Complicated Combination"

The short poem "Non chiederci la parola ..." (OV 27), written in 1923, opens the section that gives its name to Montale's first book, *Ossi di seppia*. Its position as the incipit of the section has earned it plenty of attention among readers, and the poem is usually considered Montale's first manifesto of poetics.

> Non chiederci la parola che squadri da ogni lato
> l'animo nostro informe, e a lettere di fuoco
> lo dichiari e risplenda come un croco
> perduto in mezzo a un polveroso prato.
>
> Ah l'uomo che se ne va sicuro,
> agli altri ed a se stesso amico,
> e l'ombra sua non cura che la canicola
> stampa sopra uno scalcinato muro!
>
> Non domandarci la formula che mondi possa aprirti,
> sì qualche storta sillaba e secca come un ramo.
> Codesto solo oggi possiamo dirti,
> ciò che *non* siamo, ciò che *non* vogliamo.[1]

The first and the last stanza, mirroring each other by an anaphoric variation of the same negative order ("non chiederci", l. 1; "non domandarci",

---

[1] "Don't ask us for the word to square / our shapeless spirit on all sides, / and proclaim it in letters of fire, to shine / like a lost crocus in a dusty field. // Ah, the man who walks secure, / a friend to others and himself, / uncaring that high summer prints / his shadow on a peeling wall! // Don't ask us for the phrase that can open worlds, / just a few gnarled syllables, dry like a branch. / This, today, is all we can tell you: what we are *not*, what we do *not* want". trans. J. Galassi.

l. 9) address directly the reader and, a unique event in Montale's poetry, are constructed in the first person plural. The use of "noi" as subject pronoun gives the idea of a generational testament, of a group of people contrasted to the man described in the second stanza, a man confident and friendly, not perturbed by his own shadow, that is, unconcerned by his *doppelgänger* projected by the meridian sun on a squalid wall. This new generation instead gets defined solely in negative terms: by what they do *not* have, by who they are *not*, by what they do *not* want. Their soul is shapeless, their environment is as desolated as the landscape in which the "uomo [...] sicuro" walks, a wasteland described as a dusty field, where vegetation grows gnarled and dry, on par with the discourse of the generational voice. They do not possess the "word", the vocable that would make them capable of expressing and defining their own condition, nor do they possess the formula suited to open new worlds of knowledge to the reader. A word able to open worlds would be useless in such a poem, out of place like a crocus lost in a wasted, dusty land.

Montale is describing a new human condition, the condition of a generation whose identity has been shattered: we understand, by opposition, that they do fear their own shadows; we read that their certainties and their beliefs have been wiped out, and all that is left is expressible only in negative terms. In an interview dated 1968, Montale explicitely linked the themes of the poem to the trauma that his generation had suffered because of its participation in the Great War; the rejection of rhetorical formulas originates from Montale's status as war veteran, as does his refusal of a rational explanation for the atrocities he had seen.

> In quella poesia si trattava del rifiuto di una certa eloquenza, di un modo di fare poesia, *ore rotundo*. In sede, diciamo così, "filosofica" era anche il rifiuto di una spiegazione razionale, oppure fideistica, del mondo.
>
> *In che senso?*
>
> Non dimentichiamo che la mia generazione fu distrutta dalla Prima guerra mondiale. Io sono un superstite, uno di quelli che non ci hanno lasciato la pelle. La mia generazione si affacciava su un mondo in trasformazione, sentiva di non poggiare i piedi sul sicuro. Non sapeva dove sarebbe andata a finire. Sapeva soltanto ciò che non voleva. Non voleva retorica. Non voleva contraffazioni. Non voleva contrabbandi. Non voleva falsificazioni. Era il rifiuto di un'arte poetica che consideravamo superata.[2]

---

[2] E. Montale, "A vent'anni sapevo soltanto ciò che non volevo" (1968), interview by Achille Millo, AMS 1680: "That poem dealt with the refusal of a certain eloquence, of a way of writing poems, *ore rotundo*. In a, let's call it "philosophical", context, it was also the refusal of a rational, or fideistic, explanation of the world. / *In what sense?* / Let's not forget that my gen-

Despite this clear statement, "Non chiederci la parola ..." has been read as a manifesto of poetics, but not as a poem with a strong connection to the experience of the war. This is because Montale had been reticent for a long time about his experience in the trenches, and only late in his life agreed to talk about it. There is only one poem related to the military experience of the young poet in the *Ossi di seppia*, and, as we will see, it describes the battlefield as an idyllic, idealized place. In "Non chiederci la parola ..." Montale was indeed speaking for a whole generation: a generation of men shocked by a historical event of unimaginable cruelty, and shaken by the dissolution of the parameters that used to regulate civil life, from time, to space, to the principle of causality. Without those foundations reality ceased to have a logical as well as an ontological sense and had to be interpreted anew. A great conceptual distance separated this new generation from their prewar antecedents: not only they had lost faith, they had lost their identity, their position, and scope in the world; even the categories of space and time had failed them. They had to deal with an idea of space and time as discontinuous and relative concepts, while their fathers still measured their mundane existence on notions deriving from the first scientific revolution.

The scientific revolution of the seventeenth century deposited in Europe the seed of future technological discoveries, as well as some certainties, such as the idea that space and time have an absolute, independent dimension. The concepts of absolute time and absolute space, in the definitions elaborated by Newton, became the cornerstones of scientific research, the dominant interpretative model on which to base the epistemology of physical reality.[3] Even if transcendental idealism rejected the

---

eration was destroyed by World War I. I am a survivor, one of the ones who didn't lose their life. My generation looked upon a world in transformation; we felt we could not rest our feet on solid ground. My generation didn't know how it would end up. It only knew what it didn't want. It didn't want rhetoric. It didn't want counterfeits. It didn't want contraband. It didn't want falsifications. It was the refusal of a poetic art that we considered outmoded". Gianfranco Contini had understood this aspect of Montale's poetry well in advance, see G. Contini, *Montale e la Bufera*, in *Una lunga fedeltà. Scritti su Eugenio Montale*, Torino, Einaudi, 2002, p. 82: "La differenza costitutiva fra Montale e i suoi coetanei sta in ciò che questi sono in pace con la realtà (a più forte ragione col mondo immaginario se il loro è un universo fittizio), mentre Montale non ha certezza del reale". ("The fundamental difference between Montale and his contemporaries lies in the fact that they are at peace with reality [all the more so with the imaginary world if theirs is a fictional universe], while Montale is unsure of the real").

[3] See I. Newton, *The Mathematical Principles of Natural Philosophy* (1687), trans. A. Motte, New York, Daniel Adee, 1846, p. 78: "Absolute, true, and mathematical time, of itself, and from its own nature flows equably without regard for anything external, and by another time is called duration: relative, apparent, and common time, is some sensible and external (whether accurate or inequable) measure of duration by the means of motion, which is commonly

notion of absolute, objective time and space – claiming that the two are intuitions *a priori*, mere determinations inhering in the relation of material things with the formal conditions of human sensibility[4] – Newtonian physics, because of its obvious practicalities, slowly became the standard paradigm for the definition of chronology and distance in the second half of the nineteenth century. Where Newtonian physics bolstered pragmatic approaches to building a modern world, philosophical speculations on metaphysics were less impactful at the practical level. By vastly increasing people's ability to communicate and travel, as well as trade and wage war, the former gained a clear advantage in an increasingly mechanized world.

The "International Conference Held at Washington for the Purpose of Fixing a Prime Meridian and a Universal Day", held in October 1884, included scientists and politicians from twenty-five nations who, albeit not always unanimously, voted to establish the prime meridian, corresponding with the Greenwich meridian, and to institute a unit-measure of time called the universal day, which is divided in a single series from zero to twenty-four.[5] The French delegation in particular was opposed to the choice of the Greenwich meridian as the prime meridian, claiming that the prime

---

used instead of true time; such as an hour, a day, a month, a year". "Absolute space, in its own nature, without regard to anything external, remains always similar and immovable. Relative space is some movable dimension or measure of the absolute spaces; which our senses determine by its position to bodies; and which is vulgarly taken for immovable space; such is the dimension of a subterraneous, an aereal, or celestial space, determined by its position in respect to the earth. Absolute and relative space, are the same in figure and magnitude: but they do not remain always numerically the same".

[4] That is, humanity can only experience the two categories in the phenomenal world as channeled through the senses. See I. Kant, *Prolegomena to Any Future Metaphysics that Will Be Able to Come Forward as Science* (1783), trans. G. Hatfield, Cambridge, Cambridge University Press, 2005, p. 35 (4:284): "[Time and space], by the very fact that they are pure intuitions *a priori*, they prove that they are mere forms of our sensibility that must precede all empirical intuition (i.e., the perception of actual objects), and in accordance with which objects can be cognized *a priori*, though of course only as they appear to us. [...] This faculty of intuiting *a priori* does not, however, concern the matter of appearance – i.e., that which is sensation in the appearance, for that constitutes the empirical – but only the form of appearance, space and time. If anyone wishes to doubt in the slightest that the two are not determinations inhering in things in themselves but only mere determinations inhering in the relation of those things to sensibility, I would very much like to know how he can find it possible to know, *a priori* and therefore before all acquaintance with things, how their intuition must be constituted – which certainly is the case here with space and time. But this is completely comprehensible as soon as the two are taken for nothing more than formal conditions of our sensibility, and objects are taken merely for appearances; for then the form of appearance, i.e., the pure intuition, certainly can be represented from ourselves, i.e., *a priori*".

[5] See *International Conference Held at Washington for the Purpose of Fixing a Prime Meridian and a Universal Day. October, 1884. Protocols of the Proceedings* (1884). Project Gutenberg, http://www.gutenberg.org/files/17759/17759-h/17759-h.htm, accessed on June 6, 2015.

meridian should have a character of absolute neutrality; but, perhaps because France was already in charge of the preservation of the standard of space as defined by the "Convention du Mètre" held in Paris in 1875, the practicality of adopting the prime meridian already used on most nautical charts proved convincing for the majority of the experts convened.

Even if, theoretically, the global standard for measuring time had been set, in practice the world was rather slow to adapt to the new convention. The needs of railway companies, which had to coordinate their schedules across states and across continents, clashed with the *status quo* of different local times and with the parochialism of various cities and different governments. In 1891 Sir Sanford Fleming, the Canadian engineer and geographer who had represented the Canadian Confederation at the Conference of Washington, had to appeal to the House of Commons with a warning: waiting to adopt the universal day would complicate the situation later, when the population would have grown and progress would have rendered existing necessities even more urgent:

> Notwithstanding the great advance which has been made during the present century, in all the Arts and Sciences and their applications to the affairs of human life, the reckoning of time is still in a primitive condition in many countries and in an imperfect condition in every country. Difficulties have been developed since the introduction of rapid means of communication, through the twin agencies steam and electricity, which, when examined, prove that time is computed generally on principles which are untenable. The world's time reckoning is, in fact, an exceedingly complicated combination; it is productive of confusion and the confusion is apt to be increased and intensified as population increases and lines of rapid communication are multiplied.[6]

Politics played its role in Europe, but the decisive argument in favor of the adoption of the universal day was expressed by Helmuth Karl Bernhard von Moltke, the commander in chief of the Prussian Army, in a speech to the Imperial German Reichstag in 1891. Count General von Moltke was a respected *Generalfeldmarschall*; he had earned his stripes defeating the Empire of the Two Crowns in the Austro-Prussian War (which his Italian allies considered their Third War of Independence) in 1866; von Moltke focused on the logistical possibilities offered by the Prussian railways, which were capable of moving armies in markedly less time than the traditional meth-

6 Return to an Order of the House of Commons, May 15, 1891, Point 1 (c.) 1. *Memorandum on the Movement for Reckoning Time on a Scientific Basis, by which the Greatest Possible Degree of Simplicity, Accuracy, and Uniformity Will Be Obtainable in All Countries throughout the World*, Ottawa, Canada Parliament, June 4, 1891.

od of forced marches. His troops were thus able to arrive in time for battles taking place on different frontiers, canceling out the disadvantage caused by their smaller numbers. In 1870, as a commander in chief, von Moltke used the same strategy in the Franco-Prussian War, with the added advantage that he had the opportunity to plan troop movement years ahead and to build railways according to what he believed would be necessary and advantageous during the impending war. In January 1871 France was forced to sign the Armistice of Versailles; von Moltke's military success was decisive for the creation of the German Empire, uniting the German states under the leadership of Prussia. Thus, the authority with which the *Generalfeldmarschall* championed the cause of the universal day in front of the German Reichstag is understandable:

> Gentlemen, it may seem to be of slight significance that the railway traveler finds at each new railway station a new notation of time which does not accord with his watch, but all these different times become an actual difficulty of vital importance in carrying on the business of railways, especially for the services which in a military point of view must be demanded.[7]

All European powers knew a war was in sight: the nationalist movements of the second half of the nineteenth century had created new states that unbalanced the equilibrium imposed by the Restoration in 1815; colonial conquests had put the imperial powers in competition with each other, and England, Germany, France, and Italy were already at war by proxy in locales ranging from North Africa to the South Pacific; rapid technological progress made victory possible even for those contenders whose armies were smaller in size, as von Moltke had demonstrated. Between 1900 and 1914, military expenditures more than doubled in Russia, Germany, and Austria-Hungary; all other European powers followed suit; even Italy had a significant increase.[8] The increase in funding was primarily for improving equipment: tanks, planes, warships, new field guns, and other mechanical means of destruction such as mines, torpedoes, chemical weapons, and, of course, wristwatches.[9]

---

[7] Count General von Moltke, address to the Imperial German Reichstag, sitting of the 16th March 1891, trans. and reproduced in the *Memorandum on the Movement for Reckoning Time on a Scientific Basis, by which the Greatest Possible Degree of Simplicity, Accuracy, and Uniformity Will Be Obtainable in All Countries throughout the World*. Ottawa, Canada Parliament, June 4, 1891.

[8] Quantitative analysis of defense expenditures in the various nations is found in Q. Wright, *A Study of War*, Chicago, University of Chicago Press, 1965, specifically p. 670. See also D. Stevenson, *Armament and the Coming of War*, Oxford, Clarendon Press, 1996.

[9] Because of the need to precisely coordinate military actions, wristwatches during the war became part of the military equipment. See «The New York Times», July 9, 1916: "Until

In 1914 Europe came punctually to war, thanks to Newtonian physics and the scientific conception of absolute space and time.[10] Not all nations got to war on time: Italy was late. Italian tardiness was not caused by reluctance to take advantage of scientific progresses (universal time was adopted there in 1893), but because its government was undecided about which side to take. Public intellectual opinion favored a war against the Austro-Hungarian Empire, and envisioned the conflict as an extension of the Risorgimental wars for independence that would finally result in achieving complete national unification; but the Empire of the Two Crowns as well as the German Empire were, at least on paper, allies of the Italian Kingdom, by virtue of the Triple Alliance treaty signed in Vienna in 1882.

However, when the representatives of the governments of Vienna and Berlin reunited to decide what should be done in the aftermath of the assassination of the Archduke Franz Ferdinand, neither the Italian foreign ministry nor the Italian ministry of war were informed, and no Italian representative participated in the meeting. Likewise, when Austria declared war on Serbia, Italy had not been forewarned: it is possible that the Central European Allies feared that their intentions could be leaked through Italy to ambassadors of the other European powers, or more generally they did not count on the possibility that Italy would intervene as an ally, or that Austria would rather not hand over the territorial concessions promised to Italy in case of intervention.

Since the Triple Alliance provided for entrance into war only in defense of an ally that had been attacked, and it was Austria who declared war on Serbia while Germany thereafter declared war on Russia, Luxembourg, Belgium, and France, Italy was not obliged by the treaty to intervene. However, many political figures and large swaths of the population pressed for a repudiation of the Triple Alliance and a war against Austria that would complete the aspirations of the Risorgimento by conquering the "unredeemed territories", the segment of Trentino and Alto Adige (or

---

recently, the bracelet watch has been looked upon by Americans as more or less of a joke". But "the telephone and signal service, which play important parts in modern warfare, have made the wearing of watches by soldiers obligatory. The only practical way in which they can wear them is on the wrist, where the time can be ascertained readily, an impossibility with the old style pocket watch". Quoted in U. Friedman, *A Brief History of the Wristwatch: the Military Origins of Wearable Tech, a Century Before the Apple Watch*, «The Atlantic», May 27, 2015; web: http://www.theatlantic.com/international/archive/2015/05/history-wristwatch-apple-watch/391424/, accessed on June 15, 2015.

[10] I take the idea of Europe "going to war on time" from S. Kern, *The Culture of Time and Space (1880-1918)*, Cambridge, Mass., Harvard University Press, 1983. More generally, Kern's research has been instumental in the formation of the present chapter.

Süd Tirol, according to the Austrians) and of the Veneto inhabited by a largely Italian-speaking population subject to the rule of Vienna.[11] Not all Italians were interventionists; some were pacifists by conviction, others through political calculation: the Italian Socialist Party declared itself officially opposed to the war, and an editor of the Socialist daily «L'Avanti!», one Benito Mussolini, abandoned the newspaper in order to freely express his opinion in favor of the necessity of intervention, and founded one of his own, «Il Popolo d'Italia».

It is also possible that the Italian military leaders, implicitly admitting that their German and Austrian allies were correct, believed that their armed forces were unprepared for a conflict. Italian elite troops and the nation's most modern weaponry were deployed across the sea in Libya, in support of a colonial war with no end in sight. The Italian Army still confronted a severe shortage of officers, equipment, and weapons. Thus, in the wake of the crisis of July 1914, Italy declared its neutrality in August.

2. In Time of War

Italy's declared neutrality failed to prevent the rise of apprehensions and hopes in the public opinion. The family of Domingo Montale and Giuseppina Ricci, which included four sons of military age (Salvatore, Ugo, Alberto, and Eugenio) and one daughter (Marianna), followed the unfolding of events with interest. We can reconstruct their emotional condition through the letters that Marianna was writing to friends in other cities, letters that were partially published in 2006. On March 12, 1915, for example, she wrote:

> Ci sarà la guerra anche per noi? Se sì, Eugenio è già entrato nei 19 anni; la prima classe che chiamerebbero. È così delicato che non resisterebbe alla vita militare neppure in tempi normali: e in tempi normali lo scarterebbero, ma ora pigliano tutti. Mammà s'impensierisce un poco. I ragazzi non fanno che ridere e scherzare

[11] William Renzi, as well as Richard Hamilton and Holger Herwig, diverge from the mainstream interpretation, asserting that a limited circle of conservative leaders influenced the will of the public opinion. See W. Renzi, *In the Shadow of the Sword: Italy's neutrality and Entrance into the Great War, 1914-1915*, New York, Peter Lang, 1987, p. 264; R. Hamilton – H. Herwig, *Italy*, in *The Origins of WWI*, eds. R. Hamilton and H. Herwig, Cambridge, Cambridge University Press, 2003, p. 386. At the intersection of macro- and micro-history that is the object of this chapter, we must note that the Montale family, especially at the outset, supported intervention. In the correspondence kept by Marianna Montale with her friends, one observes some opposing opinions, but grassroots assemblies and rallies in favor of the war are frequently mentioned in positive light. Eugenio was the only inveterate pacifist in the family, for ethical rather than political reasons.

su questo argomento. Alberto, come quasi tutti gli universitari, è nazionalista. La Mamma sta a sentirlo e poi dice: "Era un ragazzo d'oro, ci mancava il nazionalismo a farmelo diventare guerrafondaio".[12]

Eugenio could have been drafted immediately, but he was finishing technical school and had the right to temporarily postpone his military physical, up until he received his diploma. Alberto, the third-born, was studying engineering at the University of Genoa. Perhaps he was not a warmonger, but he was an interventionist: he believed that Italy had to go to war to complete the annexation of Italophone territories still under Imperial control. So long as Italy was neutral, however, the family discussions were only discussions and the concerns were purely hypothetical. Life in the city remained unchanged: Salvatore and Ugo worked in the paint business run by their father that, thanks to the war, had increased its turnover; Alberto and Eugenio studied.

The situation changed in the spring of the following year. The conflict escalated quickly: the Ottoman Empire allied with Germany; Japan placed its naval blockade at the port of Tsingtao, a German colony in the Shangdong Peninsula on the Yellow Sea; English troops stationed in Nigeria invaded the German colony of Cameroon; South Africa occupied Namibia, another Germany colony; Indian troops fought the Turks in the battle of Bassora, in Mesopotamia; the naval forces of the various world powers clashed in both the Atlantic and the Pacific; soldiers from Australia and New Zealand reinforced the English troops engaged in the battle of Gallipoli. On April 26, 1915, when it had become clear even to the head of the German military, Helmuth von Moltke the Younger, that the plan of reproducing the Blitzkrieg strategy that had worked so well for his uncle would fail to deliver a quick victory this time around, Italy secretly signed the Treaty of London with England, Russia, and France. Italy's entrance into the war could not single-handedly change the course of the conflict; nonetheless, the Allies wanted Italy to open a third front, to the south, to further engage the land forces of Germany and Austria. Italy, in exchange for its intervention, was granted its territorial requests and a sizable loan as an advancement for the costs of war. On May 24 Italy declared war on

[12] M. Montale, in *Lettere da casa Montale (1908-1938)*, ed. Z. Zuffetti, Milano, Ancoralibri, 2006, pp. 220-221: "Will the war also reach us? If so, Eugenio has already turned 19, the first class they would call up. He is so delicate that he wouldn't be able to withstand military life, even in normal times: and in normal times they would not take him, but now they're accepting everyone. Mama is a little worried. The boys do nothing but laugh and joke when it comes to this topic. Alberto, like almost all the college students, is a nationalist. Mama listens to him and says: 'He was a golden boy; it took nationalism to turn him into a warmonger'".

Austria-Hungary. Italian troops crossed the Austrian border in Trentino and Friuli. The situation became immediately dramatic, for the troops as well as for civilians: the news that the Germans were using Zeppelins to bombard the cities of France by night forced the major cities of northern Italy, including Genoa, into blackout conditions. Marianna describes to her friends the disconcerting nightscape she sees from her window:

> Sai che anche qui la sera non si possono tenere i lumi accesi con le persiane aperte? I trams hanno le lampadine violette, velate, le lampade ad arco per le vie non sono tutte accese, hanno il cappuccio. La lanterna non funziona. Per precauzione di ogni pericolo per via aerea (...) Sono arrivati e arrivano i feriti. Qui nelle scuole di corso Firenze ce ne sono una cinquantina e parecchi sono sempre affacciati alle finestre con le braccia o con il capo fasciato...[13]

Curfew was not the only disturbing characteristic of the state of war: the conflict form the start revealed devastating and bloody. The European military hierarchies were attached to the doctrines of offensive warfare, which urged cavalry charges and bayonette assaults, and interpreted advances and retreats as signs of victory or defeat, but these traditional doctrines taught in schools of war were out of sync with the actual military reality. In a period when technological warfare was progressing, thanks to the enhanced range and precision of high caliber firearms, trench warfare instead rewarded tactics of cover and position. The consequence was hundreds of thousands sacrificed to the useless conquest of a no man's land.[14] The gravely wounded were removed from the front and shunted to various cities, and with them arrived news of the dead. At the end of October Alberto, the "warmonger", left for the Military Academy of Turin, from which he would emerge a reserve second lieutenant destined for the front line, First Sector Schio, Barrier Agno-Assa, one of the most dangerous locations on the whole front.

Eugenio, graduating from the technical institute Vittorio Emanuele in June 1915, submitted to a military examination in the recruiting center in Genoa, but was declared temporarily unfit for military service. As he was undergoing this first physical, the Italian troops launched the first in an

---

13 M. Montale, in *Lettere da casa Montale (1908-1938)*, cit., pp. 234-235 (June 13 and 14, 1915): "Did you know that even here we cannot keep our lights on with the blinds open at night? The trams have purple bulbs, shaded, the streetlamps aren't all lit, they're covered up. The lighthouse isn't operating. As a precaution against aerial dangers [...] The wounded have arrived, and are arriving. Here in the schools on Corso Firenze there are about fifty of them, and many appear in the windows with their arms or heads in bandages ..."

14 See M. Howard, *Men Against Fire: Expectations of War in 1914*, in *Military strategy and the Origins of the First World War*, ed. S. Miller, Princeton, Princeton University Press, 1985, pp. 41-57.

extended series of assaults on the Austrian trenches in the region of Trentino, around the Isonzo River. The trench warfare along the Isonzo, fought with characteristics and arms very similar to those used on the Western Front in Verdun, extended to the Alto Adige. The war against the age-old enemy was felt deeply at the level of government and among the civilian population. Government rhetoric made it seem a just and proper war, but the war's technology had also improved communications for civilians, and news traveled quickly. Thus, even Marianna could furrow her brow at the inhumanity of trench warfare: "Sai della tremenda battaglia di Verdun? I francesi non cedono e i tedeschi cocciuti si ostinano negli attacchi, senza badare all'enorme carneficina".[15] In the first year of the war the Italian army lost 39,000 soldiers, yet it greatly improved its military equipment and increased the number of forces until they reached two million men. The draft was strengthened, and while Alberto was still on the front line, two more Montale brothers were called to arms:

> Berto è proprio sulla cima del Pasubio, a 2236 metri e il 2 Luglio gli austriaci hanno bombardato per venti ore il Pasubio (...) era entusiasmato dal contegno delle nostre truppe (...) mentre i soldati nemici apparivano impauriti. Ha molto da fare lassù, è molto stanco, ma il morale è elevatissimo (...) Ugo è stato chiamato a Torino (...) Salvatore va sotto le armi domani, Genio è stato dichiarato rivedibile un'altra volta! Pensa! 76 cm. di torace![16]

Marianna wasn't sure whether to take heart from or lament the physical and psychological fragility of her younger brother Eugenio, the only one still at home. In his journal from this period, published in 1983 with the title *Quaderno Genovese*,[17] Eugenio recorded his visits made to the military recruiting center and their outcome (in February 1917 he was once again declared temporarily unfit),[18] but he made no mention of the war. Instead he jotted down impressions of clear symbolist inspiration.[19]

---

[15] M. Montale, in *Lettere da casa Montale (1908-1938)*, cit., p. 281 (March 3, 1916): "Have you heard about the awful Battle of Verdun? The French refuse to back down, and the stubborn Germans persist in their attacks, without heeding the massive bloodshed".

[16] *Ibid.*, p. 309 (July 12, 1916): "Berto is right on top of the Pasubio, at 2236 meters, and on July 2 the Austrians bombarded it for twenty hours [...] he was thrilled about the composure of our troops [...] while the enemy soldiers seemed scared. He has much to do up there, he is exhausted, but the morale is very high [...] Ugo was called to Turin [...] Salvatore is leaving tomorrow, Genio was declared temporarily unfit again! Just think! A 30-inch chest!".

[17] E. Montale, *Quaderno Genovese*, ed. Laura Barile, Milano, Mondadori, 1983. The citations from *Quaderno Genovese*, henceforth QG, come from the edition in AMS.

[18] See QG, AMS 1289.

[19] QG, AMS pp. 1289 and 1290-1291 (February 14-20, 1917): "Scogliere persichine di nubi galleggiano sul mare diafano del cielo, e sciami quadrangolari di uccelli vi si dirigono, illusi

When Ugo arrived on the Karst in May 1917, Alberto had been on the front line for nearly a year. Salvatore, too, finished officer training and arrived at the front in September 1917, just as Eugenio, at last declared fit, left for boot camp. Among all the brothers Eugenio was the one who seemed least martial to Marianna: "Se tu vedessi Genio coi capelli rasi, insaccato in un vestito vecchio, sporco e largo, con quel viso così pallido! E poi non dorme, resta intontito. Dice che gli par di essere ipnotizzato, anestetizzato".[20] Insomnia, which began to manifest at the time, would torment Montale for the rest of his life. Likewise, the sensation of being hypnotized, or anaesthetized, returned in various statements of his regarding the war and became, as we shall see, an important element of his poetics.

In spite of the insomnia and physical problems, Eugenio was anything but a coward: and we can believe him when he says he left for the war because participating had become an ethical imperative for him:

> Io non ero interventista; avrei potuto rimanere a casa perché alla prima visita ero stato fatto rivedibile. Se non fossi andato, però, mi pareva che gli amici, le donne, mi avrebbero guardato con disprezzo. Insomma bisognava farlo.[21]

Despite remaining a convinced pacifist, Eugenio went through the selection process to become a reserve officer, like Alberto and Salvatore. Marianna, who knew him well, revealed her disbelief:

> Eugenio ha passato la visita per il corso da ufficiale ed è stato fatto abile, pare. Sai la Mamma sperava in questa visita e, senza accorgermene, ci speravo anch'io [...] Eugenio ufficiale di fanteria non posso pensarlo! Così impressionabile e bimbo com'è. E poi, te l'ho mai detto? Lui non ha mai approvato questa guerra. Dice che il Vangelo dice: "Non uccidere" e tutto quello che si può dire di altro sono tutte parole. Eugenio all'assalto? Alla baionetta? È inverosimile! Questo ragazzo è capace di morire lui, ma non di ammazzare gli altri.[22]

[...]" and "*Fiume*. Le ripe che strapiombano, incassate e ferruginose, svolgono e svolgono la gran matassa verdighiacciata delle acque ..." ("Peach-blossom-tinged cliffs of clouds float upon the diaphanous sea of the sky, and quadrangular flocks of birds head towards them, deluded ..." and "*River*. Banks that jut, embedded and ferruginous, unwind and unwind the great ice-green skein of the waters").

20 M. Montale, in *Lettere da casa Montale (1908-1938)*, cit., p. 392 (September 14, 1917): "If you could see Genio with his hair shaved, swaddled in a dirty, overlarge old suit, with that pale face of his! Plus, he doesn't sleep, he's woozy all the time. He says he feels hypnotized, anaesthetized".

21 E. Montale, "Bello sì ma dopo?" (1968), report by E. Cancogni, AMS, p. 1559: "I was not an interventionist; I could have stayed home because at my first physical I was declared unfit. If I had not gone, though, it seemed to me that my friends, and women, would have looked at me disdainfully. In short, one had to go".

22 M. Montale, in *Lettere da casa Montale (1908-1938)*, cit., p. 397 (24 settembre 1917): "Eugenio passed the physical for officer training and was declared fit for battle, it seems. Mama

Eugenio entered the infantry academy in Parma, where he met, among his classmates, Sergio Solmi, with whom he would remain close his whole life, and Francesco Meriano, a poet with whom he would maintain an intense epistolary contact, especially during and in the years shortly after the war. In October 1917 the fundamental immobility of trench warfare had made it so that, having lost more than 200,000 men, the Italian army had only advanced a few miles into Austrian territory. And when the Austrian army, reinforced by German troops, attacked the Italian stronghold of Caporetto at the end of the month, the front was shifted 70 miles to the west; the progress of the Austrian army was curtailed only when the seasonal rains helped the Italian infantry transform the swollen Piave River into a natural trench. The *Regio Esercito* suffered one of the most disastrous defeats of the whole conflict, and Italians still, a century later, use the expression "it was a Caporetto" to signify a walloping defeat.

While Eugenio was in Parma for training, the Italian infantry was reorganizing to resist behind the river Piave. Troop morale was at a historical low. Ugo, home on a brief leave, admitted his despair: "Non ci torno più se si lasciano prendere quello che ci è costato tanto!"[23] Eugenio, instead, wrote a long letter to his sister from his barrack in Parma, which didn't touch on the war but rather described his interior state, his predilection for metaphysics, his deep-seated antimilitarism:

> Io sono un amico dell'invisibile e non faccio conto che di ciò che si fa sentire e non si mostra; e non credo e non posso credere a tutto quello che si tocca e si vede. Son dunque proprio un antimilitare. Anche quando scrivo non sembra che parli a mezza voce per lasciar intendere, a mezza voce, un po' di quello che non so dire neanche a me stesso?[24]

On a practical level, if the purpose of military training is to establish the soldier as an aggressor and to get him to accept and embody that identifi-

---

had her hopes up for this physical, and, without realizing it, so did I [...] Eugenio, an infantry officer, I can't imagine it! He's such a sensitive baby! Furthermore, did I ever tell you? He has never approved of this war. He says that the Bible says 'Thou shalt not kill', and anything said to the contrary is merely words. Eugenio on the attack? With a bayonet? It's so far-fetched! This boy is capable of dying himself, but not of killing others".

[23] As reported by M. Montale, in *Lettere da casa Montale (1908-1938)*, cit., p. 407 (26 ottobre 1917): "I'll never go back there if they let them take what cost us so much!".

[24] *Ibid.*, p. 409 (8 novembre 1917): "I'm a friend of the invisible, and I don't take note of anything other than that which is heard and not shown; I do not believe and cannot believe in anything that can be touched and seen. I am really *antimilitary*. Even when I write, doesn't it seem like I am speaking under my breath in order to insinuate, under my breath, a little of what I don't know how to say, even to myself?".

cation, this letter is proof that Eugenio's training was hardly efficacious.[25] The description of himself in purely negative terms, the lack of faith in the phenomenal world, the admission of ineffability of the real on the part of an I who speaks *a mezza voce* without hope of being understood, are all ideas that will reverberate in "Non chiederci la parola ...".

Montale did not stop writing poetry: on January 26, 1918 he was at work on "Elegia" (see chapter 2.4). At the end of his training he was assigned as a reserve officer in the 158th infantry regiment Liguria Brigade, and he returned to Genoa for a short leave before being transferred to his unit. Marianna's words describing the moment of their goodbyes at the train station present us with an image of a Eugenio who had reached great inner tranquility – or who, maybe, was sedated.

> Calmo, sorridente, disinvolto; tutti i parenti sono rimasti ammirati da lui; e io ti posso dire che era proprio una tranquillità la sua, non una maschera. (...) Neppure aveva quell'allegria di eccitazione che poi lascia il posto alla reazione, no; si sentiva che era "a posto", ecco, calmissimo. Anzi, più si avvicinava la partenza e più diminuiva quel fare nervoso che gli è abituale.[26]

Eugenio left for the trenches at the war's nadir: Italian army was still reorganizing and trying to recuperate troops morale after a heavy defeat. Some historians contend that Italy would have sought an armistice after the debacle of Caporetto had it not been obligated by the Treaty of London to continue the war. Others maintain that the danger of defeat reinforced domestic public opinion, augmented efforts to support the war machine, and cemented soldiers' patriotic spirits.[27] Be that as it may, Eugenio, immediately after reaching his headquarters, volunteered for the front line. At the end of the 1960s, when he finally agreed to speak about his experiences in the First World War, Eugenio recalled the episode, downplaying his act, lest someone think that he wanted to play hero:

---

25 See E.J. Leed, *No Man's Land: Combat and Identity in World War I*, Cambridge, Cambridge University Press, 1979, p. 105.

26 M. Montale, in *Lettere da casa Montale (1908-1938)*, cit., pp. 438-439 (12 aprile 1918): "Calm, smiling, carefree; all our relatives were in awe of him; and I can tell you that his was true tranquility, not a mask. [...] He didn't even have that cheerfulness stemming from excitement that soon cedes its place to revulsion, no; one could see that he was 'at peace', yes, completely calm. In fact, the closer he came to his departure, the more his nervous habits diminished".

27 Among the former P. Kennedy, *The First World War and the International Power System* in S. Miller (ed.), *Military Strategy and the Origins of the First World War*, Princeton, Princeton University Press, 1985, p. 11. Among the latter D. Stevenson, *The First World War and International Politics*, Oxford, Oxford University Press, 1988, p. 159.

Il servizio in caserma era noioso, insopportabile. Noi complementi si aspettava quasi con ansia di essere mandati al fronte. Un giorno, quando ci dissero che si chiedevano due volontari, io e un certo Cervasco ci presentammo. Non fu per patriottismo, solo per bisogno di cambiare, di andarsene. Tanto, un giorno o l'altro ci avrebbero mandato in linea lo stesso.[28]

Be it *ennui*, a sentiment of *cupio dissolvi*, or the desire to present *una bella figura*, Eugenio volunteered to command a forward post in Valmorbia that, here too we can believe him, could rapidly have become dangerous:

Il mio reparto si trovava sul fronte trentino, in Vallarsa, sotto il monte Corno. [...] In basso c'era un fiume, il Leno; la valle si chiamava Valmorbia, noi però si stava a mezza costa, fra le rocce, perché il fondo era inabitabile, vi si rovesciava un po' di tutto, rocce, sassi, fango, schegge, bombe, cadaveri, muli. [...] Sparavano? Sì, a tutte le ore anzi, cannoni, bombarde, fucili, mitragliatrici, non si sapeva mai bene perché. La cosa più rischiosa era il servizio ai piccoli posti. Lì si era vicinissimi agli austriaci, anche duecento metri.[29]

This testimony from the interview of 1968, one of the few documents we have in which Montale accepted to publicly recount his experience during World War I, describes the life in the trenches in a very different light than the idyllic terms with which the experience is narrated in the sole poem of the *Ossi* dedicated to the war: "Valmorbia, discorrevano il tuo fondo ..." (OV 41). The image of human and animal corpses precipitating in the floor of the valley portrayed here is in jarring contrast with the image of blossoming trees presented there. In the second part of the quote, Montale betrays his bewilderment about the nonsense of the combat: the accumulation of firearms in his discourse (cannons, mortars, rifles, machine guns) underscores the idea that obviously, for him, a World War is not a sufficient reason to fire a gun. He has never really understood why everybody around him used to shoot, not even fifty years later.

---

28 E. Montale, "Bello sì ma dopo?" (1968), report by E. Cancogni, AMS p. 1559: "Service in the barracks was boring, intolerable. We reserves waited, almost spasmodically, to be sent to the front. One day, when they told us they were looking for two volunteers, I and one Cervasco accepted. It wasn't for patriotism, but merely for need of a change, of a departure. In any case, one day or another they would have sent us to the line".

29 *Ibid.*: "My unit was located on the Trentino front, in Vallarsa, under Mount Corno. [...] Down below there was a river, the Leno; the valley was called Valmorbia. We, however, remained halfway up the hill, among the rocks, because the bottom was uninhabitable. Down there a little bit of everything fell in: rocks, pebbles, mud, shrapnel, bombs, corpses, mules. [...] Did they shoot? Yes, all the time in fact – cannons, mortars, rifles, machine guns – one never really knew why. The riskiest task was to serve in the small posts. There you were extremely close to the Austrians, perhaps 650 feet away".

While Eugenio was leading very confused war operations in Vallarsa, the fighting extended to the Veneto; on June 15 the Italian forces defeated the Austrians in the Battle of the Piave River. In the summer of 1918 all four Montale brothers were at the front: Salvatore was injured by a grenade explosion, but he chose to remain in a hospital on the second line; Alberto and Eugenio briefly met on the Dolomites. Salvatore and Alberto both received a distinguished service cross and were promoted. Eugenio led a platoon of forty-four in Vallarsa and, even if he made a point of never using his regulation Webley Scott 7.65mm, received an honorable distinction for having carried out a successful assault on the enemy trenches. However, the violence of the war took a toll on his nervous system: when Eugenio told his muse Irma Brandeis about his experiences on the front, his tearful reaction, noted by Irma, seemed to confirm that the trauma caused by the war was still intense in 1934:

> Quando M. mi ha detto di due dei suoi soldati condannati a morte (durante la guerra) e fucilati per furto, i suoi occhi si sono riempiti di lacrime. Un uomo saltò nel fiume mentre lo stavano bendando, e gli spararono dalla riva prima che potesse scappare. L'altro fu condotto sul luogo dell'esecuzione e subito scoppiò a piangere. "Sono il figlio di un professore di geografia!" (*Non ho mai sentito un grido così straziante ...)*. Quando M. ricordava il professore di geografia, piangeva".[30]

The war went on. In the summer of 1918, Marianna moved to the family home in Monterosso; her letters show worries for her brothers and for the losses multiplying among her relatives, acquaintances, and neighbors. When Eugenio reached her in the family's summer house for a few days of leave, Marianna once again noted how the baby of the family seemed "un po' intontito di mente" (a little dazed in the head).[31] Eugenio returned to the front almost immediately, and dating it "Monte Lopez October 1918", he wrote "Musica silenziosa".

---

30 "When M. told me about two of his soldiers condemned to death (during the war) and shot for theft, his eyes brimmed with tears. One man leapt in the river while they were blindfolding him, and they shot him from the bank before he could escape. The other was led to the execution site and immediately burst into tears. 'I'm the son of a geography professor!' (I've never heard such a heartbreaking scream ...) When M. recalled the geography professor, he was weeping". See I. Brandeis, *Una musa di Montale*, eds. J. Cook and M. Sonzogni, Balerna (CH), Edizioni Ulivo, 2008, p. 113 (entry from August 2, 1934).

31 "Monterosso – È arrivato improvvisamente Eugenio in licenza estiva. Sta bene di salute, ma è un po' intontito di mente, e questa è la cosa che più di tutto può farlo soffrire" ("Monterosso – Eugenio arrived suddenly for his summer leave. He's healthy, but a little dazed in the head, and this, more than anything else, can make him suffer"). M. Montale, in *Lettere da casa Montale (1908-1938)*, cit., p. 452 (1 settembre 1918).

In September 1918 the allied forces, reinforced by a million American soldiers, won a series of decisive battles on the French and Belgian fronts: the Argonne Offensive, the Battle of Cambrai, the Battle of the Selle. The German army began its retreat, and American, German, and Austrian diplomats started seeking an armistice. Marianna's comment in a letter to her friend Ida gives an idea of how the opinions of civilians, even far from the front, even at the end of the war, were manipulated by nationalist rhetoric:

> Aspettiamo con vivo desiderio, per quanto diffidando molto, la risposta della Germania a Wilson. Quella di Wilson ci ha soddisfatto molto. Misura, chiarezza, buon senso. Che fortuna però, la nostra, di essere dalla parte della giustizia e della lealtà! Mi pare che ora si avvicini il premio per chi ha avuto fiducia pur nei giorni di tenebre, e fiducia non solo nella vittoria, ma nel significato di questa guerra. Perché le sistemazioni territoriali avranno valore sì, ma c'è qualcosa che le sorpassa e che vale per tutta l'umanità, la vittoria di quei principi di libertà, di lealtà, di giustizia.[32]

But the October peace talks failed, and the Italian army decided to rush the attack originally planned for the following year. The situation evolved rapidly: on October 23 the Italian troops, aided by English and French reinforcements, crossed the Piave and pierced the Austrian defenses. A day later they inflicted a decisive defeat upon the imperial army in the Battle of Vittorio Veneto. On November 3 Austria signed the armistice with the allies, de facto halting the hostilities on the Italian front. The news about the cessation of the hostilities was diffused immediately, and we have a letter from Marianna detailing her emotions and the celebrations in Genoa:

> Ieri sera (...) è uscita la notizia di Trieste. E che avevano preso Matterello! Che è vicinissimo a Trento. Quindi le notizie di stamani si aspettavano! Ma non ho dormito quasi niente stanotte. Se tu sentissi, in questo momento, tutte le sirene del porto che salutano la notizia! Piangerei come una bimba.[33]

---

32 M. Montale, in *Lettere da casa Montale (1908-1938)*, cit., pp. 456-457 (October 11, 1918): "We eagerly await, though with much distrust, Germany's response to Wilson. Wilson's satisfied us enormously. Restraint, clarity, good sense. How lucky we are, though, to be on the side of justice and loyalty! It seems to me that the prize is almost here for those who kept the faith, even in dark days, and faith not only in victory, but in the significance of this war. For the territorial settlements will be valuable, yes, but there is something that surpasses them, that is valuable to all humankind: the victory of the principles of liberty, loyalty, and justice".

33 *Ibid.*, p. 460 (November 4, 1918): "Last night [...] the news came about Trieste. They had taken Matterello! Which is very close to Trento. So, this morning's news was expected! But I still hardly slept last night. If you could hear, in this moment, all the sirens from the port announcing the news! I could cry like a baby".

According to his sister's writings, a military doctor diagnosed Eugenio with nervous exhaustion just prior to the final advance, but he declined to seek treatment.[34] Instead he participated in the final battle, even if the evidence is lacking that he ever fired a shot. Five days later, he wrote to Francesco Meriano: "Sono qui a Rovereto, dove sono entrato nel glorioso 3 novembre, e non fra gli ultimi! Dopo sette aspri mesi di guerra e di sacrifizi la fortuna mi concesse di prendere parte anch'io alla riscossa finale".[35] To the other friend from the infantry school in Parma, Sergio Solmi, he sent a recently composed poem, "Suonatina di pianoforte". In the same months he also went back to "A galla".

Eugenio spent the winter as the commander of a prison camp for captured Austrian soldiers in Eremo di Lanzo, near Turin; in the spring he returned to Genoa. He was not yet demobilized, but he could consider himself at home. Instead of rejoicing in being close to home, he regretted having left Turin:

> Io ti scrivo da una lurida fureria di caserma; sono rientrato al mio deposito, e mi sento tutto pieno di tristezza per aver lasciato Torino dove ho passato [...] alcuni giorni meravigliosi.[36]

By the following Spring, Eugenio returned home. Like Septimius Smith in Virginia Woolfe's *Mrs Dalloway*, he "had gone through the whole show, friendship, European war, death, had won promotion, was still under thirty and bound to survive. He was right there. The last shells missed him. He watched them explode with indifference".[37] All the Montale brothers returned from the war, and they took back up their customary occupations: Salvatore and Ugo returned to work with their father, Alberto to the university, Eugenio to his intense program of readings. They all began to joke and to argue again, and to spend summers as a family, in Monterosso. But nothing could be as before: the war had opened the doors of Janus.

---

[34] M. Montale, in *Lettere da casa Montale (1908-1938)*, cit., p. 461. In 1941, Montale was officially discharged from the Army for "sindrome psicastenica costituzionale" ("congenital psicological weakness"). See AMS, p. xxxvii.

[35] E. Montale to F. Meriano, November 8, 1918. Quoted in "Cronologia", AMS, p. xxv: "I am here in Rovereto, where I arrived on glorious November 3, and not among the last ones! After seven harsh months of war and of sacrifices, fortune allowed me to take part in the final comeback".

[36] E. Montale to F. Meriano, 3 giugno 1919. Quoted in "Cronologia", AMS, p. xxv: "I write you from a filthy orderly room in the barracks; I've returned to my depot, and I am full of sadness at having left Turino, where I spent [...] several marvelous days".

[37] V. Woolfe, *Mrs Dalloway*, London, Urban Romantics, 2012, p. 68. See also K. DeMeester, *Trauma and Recovery in Virginia Woolfe's Mrs Dalloway*, «Modern Fiction Studies», 44, no. 3, 1998, pp. 649-673.

3. "Newton, Forgive Me":[38] or, the Fragmentation of Space and Time

At the dawn of the twentieth century the crisis in metaphysics, stemming from the second industrial revolution and already blossoming in the thought of Heidegger and Nietzsche, is doubled by a crisis in physics. Taken together, they placed in doubt not only theological and teleological beliefs but the knowledge of the very matter that constituted the phenomenal world. The revolutions of Bergson and Einstein are two sides of the same coin: one defined the tenets of contingentism asserting that intuition, and not logic, is the accurate mean to interpret the world; the other introduced the concept of discontinuity of measure in a field regulated until then by absolute parameters. Both were part of a movement of European intellectuals wanting a break from positivism, symbolism, and Newtonian physics. The war of ideas was therefore a harbinger of the real war, and the coincidence proved transformative.

The effect that the war had on modernist poets and prose writers is thoroughly argued in academic literature.[39] To frame the matter, we can say that the war put an abrupt ending to all hopes of social progress and was immediately perceived as an unprecedented trauma, frequently expressed with metaphors that compared it to the end of the world. The experience of violence at levels that occurred during the First World War deprived humanity of all certainties. After the experience of mechanical and chemical warfare, all the writers who participated in it, but also many of those who had lived it as civilians, had the clear sense that the world, as they understood it, had ended, and that nothing would ever be the

[38] A. Einstein, *Autobiographical Notes* (1949), in *Albert Einstein*, ed. P.A. Schilipp, LaSalle, IL, Open Court, 1992, v. I, p. 31. See P. Galison, *Einstein's Clocks, Poincaré's Maps*, New York and London, Norton, 2003, p. 13.

[39] See D. Brown, *The Modernist Self in Twentieth-Century English Literature. A Study in Self-Fragmentation*, Chapter 3, "Self at War", London, Macmillan, 1989; S. Hynes, *A War Imagined: The First World War and English Culture*, London, Bodley Head, 1990; T. Quirk, *Bergson and American Culture*, Chapel Hill, University of North Carolina Press, 1990, pp. 87 *et passim*; B. Bergonzi, *War Poets and Other Subjects*, Brookfield, VT, Ashgate, 1999; S. Matthews, *Modernism*, Chapter 3, "Modernist Wars and Conflicts", London, Arnold, 2004; A. Marzola, *Guerra e identità. Percorsi nella letteratura inglese del Novecento*, Roma, Carocci, 2005; P. Rae (ed.), *Modernism and Mourning*, Lewisburg, Bucknell University Press, 2007 (in it see particularly A.J. Kunka, *The Evolution of Mourning in Siegfried Sassoon's War Writing*, pp. 69-84; and M.A. Briggs, *D.H. Lawrence. Collective Cultural Reconstruction after WWI*, pp. 198-212). For a sociological understanding of the trauma created in Europe by the first World War, see R. Pound, *The Lost Generation of 1914*, New York, Coward-McCann, 1965; E.J. Leed, *No Man's Land: Combat and Identity in World War I*, Cambridge, Cambridge University Press, 1979; M. Eksteins, *Rites of Spring: The Great War and the Birth of Modern Age*, Boston, Houghton Mifflin, 1989.

same.[40] There was perhaps some disagreement about the date: for Virginia Woolf, "In or about December 1910 human nature changed";[41] according to D.H. Lawrence, "The old world ended in 1915";[42] since that year, Karl Kraus was convinced to be living "in the last days of mankind";[43] the general consensus was that as a result of the war the world had gone through an apocalypse, and humanity had gone mad:

> You may say that everyone who had taken physical part in the war was then mad. No one could have come through that shattering experience and still view life and mankind with any normal vision. (…) It had been revealed to you that beneath Ordered Life was stretched the abyss of Chaos.[44]

Ford Madox Ford perfectly expresses here the sentiment that war had given humanity a new perspective, and not a pleasant one. The combatants acquired a new set of eyes with which they could see right through the fiction of ordinary life. The intrinsic senselessness of life in the trenches stole from combatants the sense of the world's logic; time that passes, punctuated by cannon blasts, but always equal to itself in a war of endless waiting, obfuscates temporal coordinates and obliterates before and after in a dismal present: "Nulla è più squallido / di questa monotonia" (Nothing's more dismal / than this unending sameness), Ungaretti had written from a trench.[45] Studying the diaries and testimony of combatants of different nationalities, Eric J. Leed observes:

> Many noted that the roaring chaos of the barrage effected a kind of hypnotic condition that shattered any rational pattern of cause and effect, allowing, and even demanding, magical reversals. This state was often described in terms of a loss of coherence and the disappearance of any sense of temporal sequence.[46]

---

[40] See P. Fussel, *The Great War and Modern Memory*, London, Oxford University Press, 1975, p. 8.

[41] V. Woolf, *Mr. Bennett and Mrs. Brown (1924)*, in *Collected Essays*, London, Chatto & Windus, 1966, I, 320.

[42] D.H. Lawrence, *The Cambridge Edition of the Works of D.H. Lawrence: Kangaroo* (1923), Cambridge, Cambridge University Press, 2012, p. 216: "It was in 1915 the old world ended. In the winter of 1915-1916 the spirit of the old London collapsed, the city, in some way, perished, perished from being a heart of the world, and became a vortex of broken passions, lusts, hopes, fears, and horrors". A few lines later D.H. Lawrence claims, with a suggestive metaphor, that between 1916 and 1919 "the world lost its real manhood".

[43] K. Kraus, *Die letzten Tage der Menschheit* (1922), Frankfurt am Main, Suhrkamp, 1992.

[44] F. Madox Ford, *It Was the Nightingale*, London, Heinemann, 1933, pp. 40-41.

[45] G. Ungaretti, "Monotonia", in *Selected Poems*, ed. and trans. A. Frisardi, New York, Farrar, Strauss and Giroux, 2002, pp. 42-43.

[46] E.J. Leed, *No Man's Land: Combat and Identity in World War I*, Cambridge, Cambridge University Press, 1979, p. 129. See S. Kern, *The Culture of Time and Space*, p. 290.

From the narrow perspective of the trenches, even space acquires a relative meaning – the target can seem quite small to those who must center on it with precise ballistic calculations, a no man's land is enormous when it must be crossed by crawling through barbed wire, but too narrow to constitute a shelter from enemy fire. T.S. Eliot specifically addressed the issue of knowledge in the modern man in verses that embodied the idea of a fragmented text and of a text made of fragments: "Son of man, / You cannot say, or guess, for you know only / A leap of broken images [...]".[47]

As noted before, it was not only the war that had exploded the world into fragments, or that could alter diachrony. New scientific theories, formulated as the conflict raged, also authoritatively contradicted the ontological strongholds of absolute space and time that had rendered the war so brutal and deadly in the first place. Albert Einstein, a former employee of the Swiss Office for Intellectual Property in Bern, and then a physics professor at the University of Berlin, drew from a previous essay, *On the Electrodynamics of Moving Bodies* (1905), to develop a theory called the general theory of relativity, extending to gravitational fields the principle of relativity explained in the former publication. The resulting series of essais was printed between 1915 and 1917, and would come to represent a significant change in the mode of interpreting time and space both in the scientific community and in the collective imagination.[48]

The theory of special relativity, as it is known, had its origins in the need to reconcile two principles that were experimentally demonstrable but apparently incompatible: the basic principle of relativity, theorized by Galileo, and the recent discovery of the absolute value of the speed of light, hypothesized in the transformations of Lorentz and confirmed by the failure of the Michelson-Morley's experiment. Galileo argued that the laws of physics remain constant in any system that is moving at uniform speed in a straight line: imagining a boat that proceeds in a straight line and a man who walks on its bridge from stem to stern, the speed of the man with respect to the earth will be the sum of the boat's and the man's move-

[47] T.S. Eliot, *The Waste Land*, vv. 20-22, in *The Complete Poems and Plays*, 1909-1950, New York, Harcourt, 1980, p. 38.

[48] See T. Sauer, *Albert Einstein's 1916 Article on the General Theory of Relativity*, Web http://arxiv.org/abs/physics/0405066v1; accessed on 28 Aug. 2015. The metaphorical impact of Einstein's theories on Anglophone modernist literature is explained by M.H. Withworth, *Einstein's Wake*, Oxford, Oxford University Press, 2002. See also A. Friedman – C.C. Donley, *Einstein as Myth and Muse*, Cambridge, Cambridge University Press, 1989; K. Ebury, *Modernism and Cosmology*, New York, Palgrave Macmillan, 2014; as an early sample of specific case studies, S. Foster, *Relativity and the Waste Land: A Postulate*, «Texas Studies in Literature and Language», 7, n. 1 (1965), pp. 77-95.

ment; but the man on the boat will only perceive the movement relative to his own walking. Similarly, a weight falling from the mast of our (hypothetical, uniformely moving) boat will remain congruent with its own system of reference and thus will behave exactly as one falling on solid ground. Michelson-Morley's experiment, however, came to demonstrate that the speed of light remains constant, independent of its having come from a body at rest or a body in motion. How to reconcile the results of two experimentally verifiable arguments apparently in contradiction with one another? Einstein intuited that the two axioms could be reconciled only by considering space and time as measures that have no absolute value, but instead depend on the state of the system to which they refer.

It follows that the value of space and time changes when the observer passes from one system of reference to another; that is to say, in different systems, space and time assume different values. Einstein's imagination disputes the Newtonian vision of an absolute time and space and negates the very idea of simultaneity between two events that occur in different systems of reference: two events that appear simultaneous to a specific observer will not appear this way to another observer whose parameters of measurement stem from a different system. And since an absolute time identical for all observers does not exist, it follows that every measure of distance must be considered relative to a specific time, making it necessary to consider space and time intrinsically connected. They constitute a unity, a continuum in which Einstein can adequately represent the world of physical events:

> In the pre-relativity physics space and time were separate entities. Specifications of time were independent of the choice of the space of reference. [...] One spoke of points of space, as of instants of time, as if they were absolute realities. [...] Upon giving up the hypothesis of the absolute character of time, particularly that of simultaneity, the four-dimensionality of the time-space concept was immediately recognized.[49]

By demolishing the autonomy of space and time and placing them in a relative position, Einstein's calculations do not arrive at the idea of individual time elaborated by idealist philosophy, for even if space and time are not themselves absolute, their *relation* must be considered absolute: "Continuum spatii et temporis est absolutum".[50] However, this does not

---

[49] A. Einstein, *The Meaning of Relativity* (1953), London, ElecBook, 2001. ProQuest ebrary, p. 31. Web, accessed on July 16, 2015.

[50] *Ibid.*, p. 58.

prevent the arguments of the theory of relativity from going on to support, by way of a metaphor, the innovative positions of artistic and philosophical research. Einstein's notion liberated space from the restrictions of the Cartesian system, demonstrating not only that three-dimensional measurement is not the most suitable instrument for measuring the world, but also that space itself is governed by a criterion of subjectivity.[51] When the innovative force of the theory of relativity began to be understood after the end of the war, even beyond scientific circles, the ideas of non-continuous, non-synchronous time and of space independent from Euclidean geometry enormously influenced all intellectual sectors: from philosophy to pictorial art to literature.

Henri Bergson made an effort to render the idea of interior time (durée) that he had described in *Matiere et memoire* (1896; see infra) compatible with the theory of special relativity, by publishing *Durée et simultaneité* (1922).[52] Bergson employed his training in physics and mathematics to read and explain the Michelson-Morley experiment, the Lorentz equation, and the theory of relativity, before interpreting Einstein's theory as the way in which scientific thought aligns itself with humanity's belief in an individually unique, yet universal, time. Bergson's scientifically precise reconciliation of relativistic physics and philosophy, however, does not diminish the importance of the metaphorical, artistic, and literary interpretations of Einstein's theories.

Just as Leon Battista Alberti revolutionized the artistic production of the Renaissance by applying mathematical and geometrical rules to the procedure of optical deception that he called perspective, the cubist painters found a theoretical justification for their conviction that space, in reality, has four representable dimensions. Summarizing the theory of relativ-

---

[51] "The Newtonian idea of space takes for granted the congruence of different Cartesian planes, which are commensurable by linear orthogonal transformations. But the General Theory of Relativity frees the laws of the configuration of (ideal rigid) bodies from their consistency with Euclidean geometry". *Ibid.*, p. 10.

[52] H. BERGSON, *Durée et simultaneité. A propos de la théorie d'Einstein*, Paris, Alcan, 1922. On the influence of Bergson on the modernist period in general and on specific authors, see S. KUMAR, *Bergson and the Stream-of-Consciousness Novel*, London, Blackie, 1962; P. DOUGLASS, *Bergson, Eliot & American Literature*, Lexington, KY, University Press of Kentucky, 1986; T. QUIRK, *Bergson and American Culture: The Worlds of Willa Cather and Wallace Stevens*, Chapel Hill, University of North Carolina Press, 1990; B. BURWICK – P. DOUGLASS (eds.), *The Crisis in Modernism: Bergson and the Vitalist Controversy*, New York, Cambridge University Press, 1992; M.A. GILLIES, *Henri Bergson and British Modernism*, Montreal, McGill-Queen's University Press, 1996; EAD., *Bergsonism: Time Out of Mind*, in *A Concise Companion to Modernism*, Oxford, Blackwell, 2003, pp. 95-115; S. SCHWARTZ, *The Matrix of Modernism: Pound, Eliot, and early Twentieth Century Thought* (1988), Princeton, Princeton University Press, 2014.

ity as a demonstration that all temporal coordinates are relative to their specific reference systems positions it to justify the human experience of the passage of time described by Marcel in the *Recherche* and by Bloom in *Ulysses*. In short, as Katherine Ebury says in the introduction of *Modernism and Cosmology*:

> The modernist generation came of age in a period when Newtonian concepts of absolute space and absolute time were untenable (…) This might be one reason why the physics lecture Joyce depicts in *A Portrait of the Artist as a Young Man* is so chaotic and absurd.[53]

The paradigm shift in physics helped the philosophers and the poets to articulate the change; neither the physics nor the philosophical thought originated such change, but in their voicing both added force and impetus to it. This new poetic and philosophical energy underlies the strong modernist denunciation of war, and posed the challenge of defending a civilization now thought to be in ruins: "There died a myriad, / And of the best, among them, / For an old bitch gone in the teeth, / For a botched civilization", said Pound in verses later translated into Italian by Montale.[54] And W. B. Yeats, who literally counted the dead in "In Memory of Major Robert Gregory" (1918), links the ideas of final judgment and universal entropy to evoke the war as an Armageddon in the beginning of "The Second Coming" (1919):

> Turning and turning in the widening gyre
> The falcon cannot hear the falconer;
> Things fall apart; the centre cannot hold,
> Mere anarchy is loosed upon the world;
> The blood-dimmed tide is loosed, and everywhere
> The ceremony of innocence is drowned; (ll. 1-6)[55]

Many Italian authors, during and after the war, shared such sentiments, sometimes to the letter. In Italy, too, the war had had devastating consequences: 689,000 soldiers were killed, countless more were wounded and crippled; the effects of the war were devastatingly evident to the Italian population. A generation of intellectuals died in the trenches, and the force

---

[53] K. Ebury, *Modernism and Cosmology*, New York, Palgrave Macmillan, 2014, p. 2.

[54] E. Pound, *E.P. Ode pour l'élection de son sepulcre*, in *Hugh Selwyn Mauberley* (1920) ll. 1-4. See E. Pound, *New Selected Poems and Translations*, ed. R. Sieburth, New York, New Directions, 2010, p. 113. For Montale's translation (OV 739) see M. Bacigalupo, *Pound and Montale*, «Journal of Modern Literature», 23.1 (1999), p. 48.

[55] W.B. Yeats, *The Poems*, ed. D. Albright, London, Everymans Library, 1992, p. 235.

of their memories became increasingly dramatic, while their sacrifice was perceived as increasingly senseless.

Speaking on broad strokes, the Italian first-hand accounts of the First World War are characterized by remarkably homogeneous traits: the authors of the various memoirs are consistently young men of bourgeois extraction and of passionate literary education serving in the officer ranks; their recollection of the war depicts the atrocities they have seen and witnessed, but also describe the experience as a metamorphosis, as a rite of passage supported by the sentiments of solidarity felt towards the fellow soldiers and, not infrequently, towards the enemy.[56] Reserve Second Lieutenant Eugenio Montale and his comrades-in-arms Sergio Solmi and Francesco Meriano fit accordingly in such a profile.

Paradoxically, the war had united all Europeans in a single experience, and Italian writers – exactly like their Northern European counterparts – expressed their disoriented condition and their disbelief in causal rela-

---

56 Scipio Slataper, born Italian in the unredeemed Trieste region, dead at twenty-seven on Podgora in December 1915, left a book of memories that served to stoke the flames of nationalism for decades to come. See S. Slataper, *Il mio Carso* (1912), ed. Giani Stuparich, Milano, Mondadori, 1958. Carlo Emilio Gadda, whose family was friendly with the Montales, described life in the trenches, his own imprisonment at the hand of the Austrians, and his brother Enrico's death in the battlefield in his diary *Giornale di guerra e di prigionia*, published in 1965 and reviewed by Eugenio the same year for the «Corriere della Sera». See C.E. Gadda, *Giornale di guerra e di prigionia*, Firenze, Sansoni, 1965. In the review Montale draws parallels between his friend's experience and his own: "Bisogna esser stati in trincea sotto il fuoco nemico anche per un minor numero di mesi (è il mio caso personale) per rendersi conto della maniaca fedeltà delle sue osservazioni e del feroce senso di autopunizione, sorto qua e là a castigare il giovanile orgoglio di un ventitreenne studente del Politecnico che ha voluto combattere per un insieme di ragioni consce e inconsce (il suo "patriottismo") oggi incomprensibili a chi non le abbia provate, ma quarant'anni fa ben note ai giovani migliori" ("It is necessary to have been in a trench under enemy fire, even for fewer months [as is my personal experience], to appreciate the maniacal accuracy of his observations and his ferocious sense of self-punishment, rising up now and again to chastise the youthful pride of a twenty-three-year-old student at the Polytechnic who wanted to go to war for a mix of reasons both conscious and unconscious [his "patriotism"] that today are incomprehensible to those who have never experienced them but forty years ago were well known to the best young men"). Giovanni Boine, another author dear to Montale and a rabid interventist, died in 1917; his collection of poems in prose, *Frantumi*, was released posthumously a year later. Even the title makes one aware of how the book represents the world as a reality that is no longer organic or systematic, but fragmentary and lacking a logical order. See G. Rogante, *La frontiera della parola. Poesia e ricerca di senso da Pascoli a Zanzotto*, Roma, Studium, 2007, pp. 40-41: "Agli occhi di Boine la realtà si manifesta angusta e disseminata di cocci, mera successione di attimi, l'uno disconnesso del'altro, e tutti disconnessi da un qualsivoglia punto di stabilità" ("In the eyes of Boine reality manifests itself as cramped and strewn with shards, a mere succession of moments, each disconnected from the next and all disconnected from any point of stability"). On the topic, see *Le notti chiare erano tutte un'alba. Antologia dei poeti italiani nella Prima guerra mondiale*, ed. A. Cortellessa, Milano, Bruno Mondadori, 1998.

tions and ontological certainties. "The trauma of loss is *the* legacy of the war",[57] is the conventional wisdom in the texts studying Modernist authors, while literature about World War I proclaims, "the war experience was nothing if not an experience of radical discontinuity".[58] Such radical discontinuity happens with regard to the past and with one's environment, with the familiar, and with nature. This detachment is painful, as Ungaretti testifies:

Il mio supplizio
è quando
non mi credo
in armonia (ll. 32-35)[59]

After the shock caused by the First World War, the poets of the Lost Generation lost their Romantic faith in a panoramic vision of the natural world and developed a critique of the sentiment of uniformity and harmony between human and natural elements that forms the foundation of symbolism. For the poets who wrote after the First World War the landscape no longer makes sense as a place of autobiographical reconstruction. They do not have a scenery in which to orient themselves; they are left with fragments.

It is rather memory, and its re-presentation on paper, the space in which the fragments of experience long for unity: in the mentioned "I fiumi", Ungaretti reassembles an idealized version of his own dissected past, making all the rivers tied to his biography – the Serchio, the Nile, the Seine – flow into the Isonzo, the river so furiously contested between the Italians and the Austrians in which he was immersed. The fragmentation of space and time had lifted the veil and revealed that, in Montale's words, that the lyric subject discovered "il nulla alle mie spalle, il vuoto dietro / di me, con un terrore di ubriaco".[60] The only hope one had to inhabit such a world was to inhabit it by making it new.

---

57 K. Wilson, *Modernism*, London, Continuum, 2007, p. 40.

58 E.J. Leed, *No Man's Land: Combat and Identity in World War I*, Cambridge, Cambridge University Press, 1979, p. 2.

59 "My affliction / is when / I don't believe myself / in harmony". G. Ungaretti, *I fiumi*, in *Selected Poems*, ed. and trans. A. Frisardi, New York, Farrar, Strauss and Giroux, 2002, pp. 36-37.

60 E. Montale, "Forse un mattino ..." (OV 40, ll. 3-4): "nothing at my back, emptiness behind / me, and the terror of a drunkard".

4. The Antimilitarist

In reading the diary in which a twenty-one years old Montale described his days, nicknamed by the critics *Quaderno Genovese*; in scanning the letters to and from Marianna; and in considering the early poems he wrote during the experience of the war, one realizes that Montale had no intention of describing the experience of war in a direct, naturalistic fashion. The conflict is erased at first, and for the rest of Montale's life it will be recalled in ambiguous, even contradictory, terms.[61] His close friends confirm that Eugenio, back from the front, preferred to keep his experiences to himself.[62]

The *Quaderno Genovese* is almost completely devoid of references to the war. On February 1, 1917, he notes with disappointment that the porticos

---

[61] See P.G. Zunino, *E più nessuno è incolpevole: Eugenio Montale negli anni del fascismo*, in R. Bettarini, *Lettori di Montale*, Torino, Aragno, 2013, pp. 36-37: "Il primo incontro di Montale con gli orrori e i terrori del nostro tempo avvenne certamente al momento della sua partecipazione alla prima guerra mondiale. Tuttavia, sebbene quell'evento si traducesse per larga parte dell'intellettualità europea che vi fu coinvolta in una esperienza incancellabile e in un certo senso fondativa e come tale destinata a lasciare tracce importanti nelle opere di numerosi artisti, scrittori, poeti, è piuttosto singolare dover constatare come in Montale durante e dopo la guerra, e ancora nello scorrere dei successivi decenni della sua lunga vita, i riferimenti al conflitto siano assai rari ed enigmatici, alcuni addirittura contradditori" ("Montale's first encounter with the horrors and terrors of our time indubitably occurred at the moment of his participation in the First World War. However, though this event manifested itself for the majority of the European intelligentsia who were involved in it as an indelible, and in a certain sense foundational, experience and, as such, was destined to leave important traces in the works of numerous artists, writers, and poets, it must be considered quite peculiar that in Montale during and after the war, and even in the passing of the subsequent decades of his long life, references to the conflict are quite rare and enigmatic, some even contradictory"). Based on the letters sent from Montale to Francesco Meriano during and after the war, Zunino sees in Montale a sincere and fervent patriotic spirit and even, prior to the signing of the *Manifesto degli intellettuali antifascisti* in 1925, a Fascist sympathizer (see F. Meriano, *Arte e vita*, eds. G. Manghetti, C.E. Meriano, V. Scheiwiller, Milano, Scheiwiller, 1982). Without taking anything away from the poet's patriotism (See PR 597: "Il patriottismo è un'infezione dalla quale non fui sempre immune. [...] Fu un errore? Non sono ancora riuscito a pentirmene del tutto". ("Patriotism is an infection from which I was not always immune. [...] Was it a mistake? I still haven't managed to repent it entirely"), I retain the possibility that Montale feigned more enthusiasm than he actually had in his correspondence with Meriano, himself an ardent nationalist who later became a fascist "antemarcia". It is equally likely that Montale expressed more enthusiasm than he felt about his friend's poetry.

[62] "Io e Montale eravamo tornati dalla guerra, ancora così vicina e presente, però non credo che ne parlassimo mai; tanto che anche a me riuscirono forse nuovi gli accenni della sua vita al fronte che più tardi trovai nei suoi versi" ("Montale and I were back from the war, which felt so recent and present still, but I believe we never mentioned it; to the point that the details of his life at the front I later read in his verses felt new to me"). A. Barile, *La vigilia genovese di Montale*; as quoted in E. Montale, *Immagini di una vita*, ed. F. Contorbia, Milano, Mondadori, 1996, p. 69.

of the library where he studies are being used for the distribution of rations, which causes "affollamento e impossibilità di entrare" (crowding and makes it impossible to enter).[63] He considers "una gran seccaggine" ("a great nuisance") the days he is forced to spend in his father's business, standing in for the brothers who left.[64] He marks the days of his medical visits to the recruiting center, but the war is never directly mentioned. Instead, he makes note of his readings, his philosophical and literary conversations with friends, the concerts he heard, and the spectacles he saw, as if cultural activities were a way to erase the evidence of war in those days of anxiety and anticipation.

His countenance did not change after he was drafted: in the letter he wrote to Marianna from the officer training school in Parma he mentions his health, requests money to pay for the books he has acquired, and cites Rimbaud; aside from defining himself as anti-military, he does not acknowledge the war. Eugenio is not anti-military simply because he is opposed to the war, rather because for him the war is a mere contingency. He defines himself as a friend of the invisible: that which is unseen is for him more real than that which falls under phenomenal sense; for, as a good reader of Boutroux, he understands that the real, being contingent, is not necessary – since it could be different, or it could not be at all. The only non-contingent reality lies within the human soul, and it cannot be measured with the same parameters one uses to measure reality.[65] This subtraction of ontology from phenomenal reality is congruent with, and supports, the state of mind of an educated young man forced to live in circumstances he does not wish to accept, and is reflected in his poetic attempts of that period. One such attempt is "Elegia", where the realness ("il mondo") is represented as a fragile crystal ball that must be treated delicately:

> Non muoverti.
> Se ti muovi lo infrangi.
> È come una gran bolla di cristallo
> sottile
> stasera il mondo:
> è sempre più gonfia e si leva. (ll. 1-6)[66]

---

63 QG AMS 1825.

64 QG AMS 1302.

65 Émile Boutroux in *De la Contingence des Lois de la Nature* (1874), Paris, Alcan, 1902, drawing on Catholic positions, postulates the existence of a unique spiritual reality for each individual that cannot be measured with the scientific criteria of space and time. For the young Montale as reader of Boutroux, see E. Montale, "Intervista immaginaria" (1946), AMS 1479; Id., "Ho scritto un solo libro", (1975), interview by Giorgio Zampa, AMS 1720.

66 "Do not move. / If you move you shatter it. / Tonight the world / is like an enormous bubble / made of fragile crystal: / it is bloated, and it floats".

Reality is fragile and impermanent, in a word: contingent. The "you" to whom the ethical imperative of the "I" anaphorically refers, which will reappear in the texts of a mature Montale, is requested to remain immobile, that is: to avoid actions, gestures, and movements that could compromise the equilibrium of a world made of fragile crystal.

This "false reality" returns in a fundamental text in *Ossi di seppia*, "Forse un mattino andando ..." of 1923, which, as is the case here, is about the possibility of going beyond phenomenological reality, a possibility expressed in both texts with a fundamental term in Montale's lexicon, "forse", perhaps; after all, he had read that "La dottrina della contingenza può soltanto dimostrare la possibilità della libertà, non mutare la possibilità in realtà".[67] In both texts the lyric "I" vascilates between hope and fear. The hope is to stay ("noi forse resteremo", "perhaps we will endure"), and the feared element is impermanence or death, which, consistently with Montale's disposition towards the war encountered thus far, is suggested but never fully expressed. The text proceeds with another "noi forse", but the sentence is not completed: movement, utterance, the expression of emotions, all actions departing from absolute detachemnt run the risk to put an end to the world.

> Non muoverti.
> Come un'immensa bolla
> tutto gonfia, si leva.
> E tutta questa finta realtà
> scoppierà
> forse.
> Noi forse resteremo.
> Noi forse.
> Non muoverti.
> Se ti muovi lo infrangi.
>
> Piangi? (ll. 24-34)[68]

It would be natural to consider the "scoppio" (burst/outbreak) of reality here a semantic reference to the war in progress – given that in Italian

---

[67] A. Levi, *L'indeterminismo nella filosofia francese contemporanea. La filosofia della contingenza*, Firenze, Seeber, 1904, p. 40: "The theory of contingentism can only demonstrate the possibility of liberty, not change the possibility into a reality".

[68] "Do not move. / Everything bloats, and it floats / like an immense bubble. / And all this false reality / will burst / perhaps. Perhaps we will endure. / Perhaps we. / Do not move. / If you move you shatter it. // Are you crying?".

"la guerra scoppia", the war breaks out – and thus to interpret "noi forse resteremo" as the hope of surviving the deflagration of the war. But it is just as natural to think that the friend of the invisible would like to circumscribe within his crystal ball all reality, the existence of which, as he will reiterate many years later, had never been convincing to him: and therefore the explosion of the ball represents instead "la fine dell'inganno del mondo come rappresentazione" ("the end of the deception of the world as representation"),[69] the realization that the phenomenal world does not have ontological meaning and nothingness, or death, are just behind the veil of its representation.

In the poems from the front that have survived – both the war and the severe censorship of a more mature Montale – the conflict is completely ignored. So it is in "Musica silenziosa", a poem in which the symbolist *corréspondance* between music and sentiment is so evident as to give the impression, still, that poetry is a means for Montale to isolate from the reality surrounding him. We find the same in "A galla". Only a fragment, an occasional quatrain that the reserve lieutenant Montale sent to his comrade-in-arms Solmi, mentions the bombardments:

a Solmi

Desiderio di stringer vecchie mani
di rispecchiarsi in visi un tempo noti
sotto il grondare di un gelato azzurro
che la campana dello Schrapnel scuote.[70]

The metonymy "vecchie mani" (old hands), meaning "the hands of old friends", and the memory of friendship, restored in the present by desire, is opposed to the sound of the shrapnel. In the last verse the shrapnel rings (metaphorically, but not by much) a death-knell "sotto il grondare di un gelato azzurro". The "frozen azure" is the sky, described through a process of resemantizing the signifier, a technique that will become distinctive in *Ossi di seppia*. The formal elaboratedness of this quatrain recalls, in fact, "Valmorbia, discorrevano il tuo fondo ...", the only poem in *Ossi di seppia* explicitely set during the conflict. While "Montale in guerra" was written as the events unfolded, this other poem was written *après coup* on July 11, 1924. Through memory, the experience of the war is transformed into an

[69] See chapter 5.1. The quotation is from E. MONTALE, "Intervista immaginaria" (1946), AMS 1480.

[70] E. MONTALE "Montale in guerra" (1918), in *Tutte le poesie*, ed. G. Zampa, Milano, Mondadori, 1984, p. 786: "To Solmi / / Desire to shake old hands / to reflect in faces once familiar / under the gushing of a frozen azure / shaken by the Shrapnel's bell".

aesthetic experience. The bottom of the Valmorbia, in which "a little bit of everything fell in: rocks, pebbles, mud, shrapnel, bombs, corpses, mules", is here represented instead as a vernal landscape, where the breeze bears clouds of flowers. And the flowers "discorrono" the valley's basin: the transitive use of the verb is another example of resemantization. "Discorrere" means to converse, but here the verb is used as a frequentative of "scorrere", which means to "run across", and augments the literary, precious tone of the incipit.

> Valmorbia, discorrevano il tuo fondo
> fioriti nuvoli di piante agli àsoli.
> Nasceva in noi, volti dal cieco caso,
> oblio del mondo.
>
> Tacevano gli spari, nel grembo solitario
> non dava suono che il Leno roco.
> Sbocciava un razzo su lo stelo, fioco
> lacrimava nell'aria.
>
> Le notti chiare erano tutte un'alba
> e portavano volpi nella mia grotta.
> Valmorbia, un nome — e ora nella scialba
> memoria, terra dove non annotta.[71]

Right in the middle of the battle, the poem states, it is possible to feel a sense of peace (we will subsequently see how Montale returns to the idea of the forward post of Valmorbia as a place of peace), it is possible for the lyric "I" to become one with with nature, to read the warscape as a womb, actualizing a *correspondance* that would soon become inconceivable for Montale. But for now, even if humans are "volti dal cieco caso", that is, moved by a reality that has lost its sense of causality, it is still possible to construct a metaphorical bridge between a signal flare and a flower, between the flash of explosions and the dawn. This "land where the night never comes", of "permanent dawn", is so described, of course, because the moon and the signal flares transforms the night in a day, but also because, in this Edenic setting as in the other texts of *Ossi di seppia* in which

[71] "Valmorbia, flowering clouds of plants / crossed over your deeps on puffs of wind. / In us, whirled by blind chance, / oblivion of the world was born. // The shooting stopped; in the lonely womb / the only sound was the Leno's roar. / A rocket blossomed on its stem, / wept faintly in the air. // The brights nights were all a dawn / and brought foxes to my den. / Valmorbia, a name – and now in my wan memory, / land where night never comes", J. Galassi, transl.

the communion between "I" and nature comes to fruition, the passage of time is suspended: the lyric I has not yet crossed the threshold of Janus.

In the second book, *Le occasioni*, in two "Mottetti" written between 1934 and 1939 the experience of the trench is still tinged with aesthetic tones. In "Brina sui vetri" (OV 135) the "giuochi di bengala" of the tracers are again compared to fireworks, and the experience of the battlefield is tamed, equated to the beloved's sojourn in a Swiss sanatorium. But in the following motet, "Lontano, ero con te ...", one reads an unsettling attempt to explain the unexplained horrors of the war through what will happen later, as opposed to what had happened before. Since war can not bear justification or excuse, the only way to rationalize it is, paradoxically, to read in it the warning signs of something that has not happened yet. The survival of the lyric "I" happened because he was still due to encounter his angel of salvation, because the meaningful part of his life had yet to happen:

> Lontano, ero con te quando tuo padre
> entrò nell'ombra e ti lasciò il suo addio.
> Che seppi fino allora? Il logorio
> di prima mi salvò solo per questo:
>
> che t'ignoravo e non dovevo; ai colpi
> d'oggi lo so, se di laggiù s'inflette
> un'ora e mi riporta Cumerlotti
> o Anghébeni, tra scoppi di spolette
> e i lamenti e l'accorrer delle squadre. (OV 136)[72]

The subject of the poem appeared at first unintelligible to the readers. The author had to explain it in a short article published in 1950. In "Due sciacalli al guinzaglio", responding to accusations of *obscurisme* that had been raised against him, and speaking of himself in the third person under the pseudonym of Mirco, Montale recounts how, thanks to memory, imagination, and love, poetic activity seeks to give an *a posteriori* explanation of the risks run:

> Un giorno Mirco seppe che il padre di Clizia era morto, intuì quello strazio e più gli dispiacquero le tremila miglia che lo tenevano lontano, troppo lontano da

[72] "Though far away, I was with you when your father / passed into shadow and left you his farewell. / What did I know till then? The wear and tear / of *before* preserved me only for this: // that I didn't know you, and I should have. This / I know from today's barrage, when one hour of hell / forces me back in time, brings back Cumerlotti / or Anghébeni again – the mines exploding, / the moaning, and the bomb squads scambling up", trans. W. Arrowsmith.

quel lutto. E gli parve che tutte le ansie e i rischi della sua vita trascorsa convergessero verso quella Clizia ancora ignota, verso un incontro che doveva tardare, poi, tanti anni. Forse, si disse, la guerra mi ha risparmiato proprio per questo: perché senza Clizia la mia vita non avrebbe avuto alcun senso, alcuna direzione. Rivangò il suo passato, si rivide in alcuni contesi villaggi della Vallarsa, a Cumerlotti, ad Anghébeni, sotto il monte Corvo; ritrovò se stesso in mortale pericolo ma già assistito, inconsapevolmente, dalla stella di Clizia, dall'ombrellino del suo girasole. Quel giorno Mirco sedette in un caffé, e sul margine di un giornale scrisse questi versi e li buttò al vento, che li portasse a destinazione.[73]

When the war is censored, eliminated in order to realize an idyllic panorama, as in "Valmorbia ...", time stands still; on the contrary, when the misery of war acquires a meaning based in what happened afterwards, the subversion of the chronology brings with it a rupture in the logic of cause and effect. If time in the text is disjointed and incoherent, so too is space: the paradox of the poet who, though far from his beloved, is nonetheless near her ("Lontano, ero con te",) returns to but upends the thematics of the miracle of the appearance of the beloved woman, which is an integral part of the myth of Clizia. In this case it is Eugenio who appears to the muse, subverting the Newtonian laws in search of the meaning of life (his having survived at the front) and death (that of her father). At heart, Montale intuited that space and time obey to a single law: he frequently represented the voyage of memory backward in time as a katabasis, and in this case too, it is a deictic of place ("laggiù") that signifies the spatialization of memory.[74]

The war left Montale with a sense of ethical and emotional displacement that reflects the spatial and temporal displacement he felt in the trenches. Moreover, these are the years, as Clizia notes in her diary, when Montale, remembering specific events in which he participated, cannot

---

[73] E. Montale, "Due sciacalli al guinzaglio" (1950), AMS 1490-1491: "One day Mirco found out that Clizia's father had died, he felt her pain and all the more regretted the three thousand miles that kept him far, too far, from her mourning. And it seemed to him that all the anxieties and risks of his past pointed him towards that Clizia who he still had not met, towards an encounter that would happen only many years later. Perhaps, he said to himself, the war saved me for solely this reason: for if I hadn't met Clizia my life would have had no sense, no direction. He then dug up his past, he saw himself once more in these disputed villages in Vallarsa, at Cumerlotti, at Anghébeni, beneath Mount Corvo; he found himself once more in mortal danger but already assisted, without knowing it, by Clizia's star, by the tiny umbrella of her sunflower. That day Mirco sat in a café and, on the margin of a newspaper, wrote these verses, before tossing them to the wind, which bore them to their destination".

[74] The point is noted in Tiziana De Rogatis's comment to *Le occasioni*, Milano, Mondadori, 2011, p. 203. See also chapter 7.1; See "In limine" (OV 5, l. 3); "Bassa marea" (OV 162).

help but to burst into tears. Some time later, after the Second World War and the Italian economic boom, Montale eventually agreed to speak about his combat experience in interviews and in his poetry. But the tone of his recollections is then quite different from the dramatic one described by Clizia: the register is no longer dramatic, rather satirical. In a dialogue with Manlio Cancogni, for example, horror trickles in here and there in the details of the narration, but paradoxical, ridiculous, or simply affable memories get the lion's share of the attention. Montale remembers how the most perilous mission involved holding the little outposts, which were often attacked by the Austrians; nevertheless, when he himself is on duty in one of these posts, and begins to doze off instead of standing guard, he is awakened by a strange noise. This noise was not enemies drawing near, but rather the Austrians, in their own outpost, playing music on an old gramophone. He spends a paragraph describing the quality of military fare and three paragraphs describing in comic overtones the adventure of a nocturnal reconnaissance mission in which he commands the patrol but trips, falls, and needs an orderly to help him stand. The narration is particularly interesting as it captures the disorientation that continues to seep from these memories: to begin with, the orders dispatched from the Headquarters were not at all clear.

> Ricevetti un biglietto del comandante di compagnia, [...] diceva: "A mezzanotte vostra signoria dovrà scendere in basso con il suo plotone, dopodiché, volgendo a nord ovest, proseguire; indi poscia, retrocedendo a est per duecento metri e ripiegando a nord, riprendere la marcia in direzione nord-nord ovest". Non era molto chiaro. Lo feci vedere al mio sergente che rimase dubbioso.[75]

Given the premises, getting lost during the attack was inevitable:

> Quella notte per giunta pioveva, c'era nebbia e non si vedeva quasi nulla. All'ora indicata cominciammo a scendere. Incespicavo, scivolavo, cadevo e l'attendente [...] doveva sostenermi. Continuammo ad avanzare, al buio, alternando il cammino con lunghe soste, fino all'alba. [...] Dunque era arrivata l'alba. Apparvero davanti a noi degli sconosciuti con le braccia alzate, "*Bitte, Bitte*" gridavano. Avevamo fatto dei prigionieri. Li mandai indietro, noi proseguimmo ancora per poco, poi ci fermammo definitivamente. L'azione era finita. Arrivò un ufficiale

---

[75] E. MONTALE, "Bello sì ma dopo?" (1968), report by E. Cancogni, AMS, p. 1561: "I received a message from the commanding officer, [...] which recited: 'At midnight your Lordship will need to go down below with your platoon, after which, turning towards the northwest, continue; then, later, reversing toward the east for two hundred meters and drifting toward the north, resume marching north-northwest'. It wasn't very clear. I showed it to my sergeant, who shared my doubts".

che si guardò intorno, e si congratulò con me, dicendomi che gli Arditi avevano conquistato il Pozzacchio.

Continuo a far confusione, il Pozzacchio fu conquistato in giugno, del resto credo che gli austriaci lo abbiano ripreso subito dopo.[76]

At the end of the action the narrating "I" is completely disoriented: he is congratulated for the success of an attack in which he didn't consciously participate, he doesn't know where he is, and he doesn't even know the date. Not by chance in the same year, reflecting on his experience, he equated himself with Fabrizio del Dongo, the protagonist of Stendhal's *La chartreuse de Parme*, the one who wanders by chance into the Battle of Waterloo.[77] The story rambles, the narration is full of ellipses and nonsequiturs, as if it wished to express with its fragmentary rhythms the state of mind of the storyteller. Montale wishes to speak of the final advance, but he diverts, preferring to tell of the cave where he was visited by foxes, of the valley illuminated by the moon, and of the puttees on his boots.[78] Of the entrance into Rovereto, during an ongoing battle, he does not mention the corpses in the streets but the abundance of garbage.[79]

Montale recounted an engagement similar to the one described above, or perhaps the very same one, to his friend Francesco Messina, who put it in writing in a 1985 memoir and labeled it a Chaplinesque adventure to

---

[76] E. Montale, "Bello sì ma dopo?" (1968), report by E. Cancogni, AMS, p. 1562: "That night, what's more, it was raining, there was fog, and you could hardly see anything. At the appointed hour we began our descent. I tripped, I slipped, I fell, and the orderly [...] had to support me. We continued moving forward in the dark, alternating walking with long rests until dawn. [...] Then dawn had arrived. Some unknown men appeared before us, arms raised, crying out, *Bitte, bitte*. We had taken some prisoners. I sent them back, and we persisted a bit further before coming to a definitive halt. The fighting had finished. An official arrived and looked around and congratulated me, telling me that the Arditi had seized Fort Pozzacchio. / I'm mixing things up again: the Pozzacchio was seized in June; moreover, I think the Austrians took it back immediately afterwards".

[77] E. Montale, *Genova nei ricordi di un esule* (1968), SM 2875: "Ero un pessimo ufficiale di fanteria, una specie di Fabrizio del Dongo immerso in fatti e cose più grandi di me" ("I was a terrible officer, a sort of Fabrizio del Dongo, a character immersed in events too big for him").

[78] E. Montale, "Bello sì ma dopo?" (1968), report by E. Cancogni, AMS pp. 1561-1562: "Ho ancora divagato, ma le fasce erano proprio un tormento, specie in quell'occasione, e anche un disonore, perché, essendo all'offensiva, avremmo dovuto far bella figura, e io invece ..." ("I digress again, but the puttees were truly a torment, especially on that occasion, and also a disgrace because, being on the offensive, we should have cut a good figure, and I instead ...").

[79] *Ibid.*, p. 1562: "Non credo di aver mai visto un caos come quello. Porte sfondate, mucchi di spazzatura dappertutto. [...] Soprattutto colpiva quell'abbondanza di spazzatura. Non capisco da dove l'avessero tirata fuori" ("I don't believe I had ever seen such chaos. Doors smashed in, piles of garbage everywhere. [...] I was struck, above all, by that abundant garbage. I couldn't fathom from where they had extracted it").

underscore its parodic nature, although he could also have considered it an extract from *The Good Soldier Švejk*:

Eravamo in una trincea, in mezzo al fango, a un centinaio di metri dal nemico. Arrivò l'ordine di conquistare la postazione avanzata. Erano le quattro del mattino, con atmosfera fittamente brumosa. Sottotenente di complemento, io comandavo un plotone. Balzammo fuori e subito alla bruma si aggiunse il polverone causato dallo scoppio delle granate. Là, là, là, indicavo ai miei soldati con il frustino, ma quelli sembravano incerti. (La pistola d'ordinanza non l'ho mai usata). Sembrava il finimondo. Anch'io vagavo nel polverone. Tutt'a un tratto io scivolai nella trincea nemica che era già stata evacuata. Mi diedi un gran da fare a chiamare i miei soldati: qui, qui, qui! E così occupammo la posizione. Il comando, informato della felice operazione, mi elogiò per eroico comportamento.[80]

In this case, too, the directions are incomplete, the night is dark and foggy, the subject and his platoon once more, "volti dal cieco caso", lose their way and conclude the operation happily… by accident. The fog obscures the tragedy of war, transforms it into another war in which firearms are left unused, in which enemy bombs produce semiotic confusion and cooperate in creating a sense of loss equally shared by the narrator and his comrades. It was the end of the world, and no-one knew where they were: in the general mayhem the adverbs of place "here" and "there" had lost their meaning. If we consider the image of getting lost in the trenches on a metaphorical, other than on a literal, level, we can appreciate how the result of the conflict was to destroy spatial and temporal cohordinates in the participants, and by extention in the civilization they used to represent.[81]

---

[80] The episode is found in E. Montale, *Lettere e poesie a Bianca e Francesco Messina*, Milano, Scheiwiller, 1995, p. 222: "We were in a trench, stuck in the mud, about a hundred meters from the enemy. The order arrived to seize the forward post. It was four in the morning, the atmosphere dense with haze. As a reserve second lieutenant, I commanded a platoon. We jumped out, and immediately added to the fog was the cloud of dust caused by grenade explosions. There, there, there, I showed my soldiers with the switch, but they seemed uncertain. (The regulation pistol I never used). It felt like the end of the world. I was lost in the dust cloud too. All of a sudden I fell into the enemy trench that had already been evacuated. I shouted to call my soldiers: here, here, here! And so we occupied the post. The commander, informed of the propitious operation, commended me on my heroic conduct". Montale makes it clear he never used his regulation pistol again in "L'onore", from *Quaderno di quattro anni* (OV 529, ll. 7-13): "un giorno / senza sparare un colpo / della mia Webley Scott 7,65 / senza uccidere senza possedere neanche un'ombra dell'arte militare / avevo fatto fronte ai pochi stracci / dell'oste avversa" "one day / without shooting a single bullet / from my Webley Scott 7,65 / without killing without possessing even an ounce of the art of war / I faced a few rags / from the enemy's army".

[81] E.J. Leed, *No Man's Land: Combat and Identity in World War I*, Cambridge, Cambridge University Press, 1979, p. 123: "The actualities of combat on the surface of the trench system

The enemy soldiers are as lost as Lieutenant Montale is (perhaps even more); the true antagonists of the story are not the known enemy, but the military hierarchies who never show up and only make themselves heard *ex machina* through orders, incomprehensible directives, and commendations from above. The enemy soldiers are instead friends waiting to happen, people with whom one can talk, in spite of the linguistic difference, thanks to the fraternizing bonds of culture. An incident that had a profound impact on Montale, who would recount it in verses and in interviews more than fifty years after the facts, has as a protagonist an Austrian soldier who surrendered to his platoon and, when searched, was revealed to carry poetry books instead of ammunition. "Fu nel 1918, proprio sul finire. Ero in Vallarsa. Incontrai questo austriaco con le mani alzate in segno di resa. Mi disse qualche parola indecifrabile. Nelle tasche teneva dei libri di poesia invece di munizioni".[82] The idea of intelligence with the enemy acquires here a most literal meaning. An intelligent enemy contrasts with the senseless stupidity of the war, while the humanities reconstruct an episode of civilization and understanding, as poetry annuls the language barrier.

After the war, when he ended up commander of the prison camp of Eremo di Lanzo, the Austrian prisoners are once more represented as good men with whom he could get along, friends with whom to enjoy an evening at the opera.

> Fui assegnato a un campo di prigionieri austriaci a Lanzo Torinese. Ero tenente, l'ufficiale più alto in grado, comandavo io. I miei prigionieri erano dei bravissimi giovani. Andavamo molto d'accordo, io parlavo un poco il tedesco, loro un po' l'italiano. Qualcuno di loro mi scrisse dopo la guerra. La sera andavamo a Torino,

---

produced a profound disorientation in most of those who inhabited it. [...] The feeling of being lost in the trenches – while often a literal experience – is also a metaphor for the effects of trench warfare upon the sensory perceptions of combatants".

[82] E. MONTALE, "Non ama essere nella storia per qualche verso ..." (1977), interview by Giulio Nascimbeni, AMS 1728: "It was 1918, practically at the end of the war. I was in Vallarsa. I met this Austrian with his arms raised to signal his surrender. He said some indecipherable word to me. In his pockets he kept books of poetry instead of ammunition". The episode is recounted in verse in the poem "L'eroismo" (1975), which appears in *Quaderno di quattro anni*. Interestingly, in the poem the Austrian snipers "ticchettano" [tick], like clocks that mark the time of life and death: "Ma dove ho combattuto io che non amo / il gregge degli inani e dei fuggiaschi? / Qualche cosa ricordo. Un prigioniero *mio* /che aveva in tasca un Rilke e fummo amici / per pochi istanti; e inutili fatiche / e tonfi di bombarde e il fastidioso ticchettio dei cecchini", "And where did I fight, I who do not like / the herd of the inane nor of the absconder? / I remember something: a prisoner *of mine* / with Rilke in his pocket and we were friends / for an instant; and pointless labors / thuds of mortars and the nagging tick of the snipers" (OV 535, ll. 8-14). The idea of literature spurring fraternization among those who should be enemies returns in the context of the Second World War, in the short story "La poesia non esiste" (1946), PR 179.

all'opera. Sì, a volte me ne portavo con me uno o due, fra quelli che avevano passione per la musica e il bel canto.[83]

This expression of *camaraderie*, more common in the authors who described the First World War than one could suspect,[84] can also be explained in relation to the trauma caused by the war. In the words of Eric J. Leed, "In a war in which all combatants were victims of material, in which an industrial technology was the 'true' aggressor, identification with the enemy and its dominant motive – survival – was logical, even necessary".[85] Because the trauma is present, and it lingers; in fact, it is rendered all the more evident by the attempt at displacement. An episode involving an execution by firing squad is recounted at the end of the cited 1968 interview with a state of mind opposite the one witnessed by Clizia:

> Andammo avanti, sulla strada di Trento. In un paese, non saprei più dirne il nome, assistetti alla fucilazione di un nostro soldato, colpevole di saccheggio, credo che avesse rubato un orologio. Alla scarica vidi chiaramente una cosa bianca che saltava in aria, il cervello, mentre il corpo s'afflosciava giù. No, non mi fece un grande effetto. Ma cosa poteva fare effetto in tali circostanze? Era come un sogno. Un grande sogno in cui tutto poteva accadere. Io avanzavo come un sonnambulo. Subito dopo ci dissero che avevamo vinto la guerra. Anche quella notizia non mi procurò una grande emozione; certo ero soddisfatto d'essere ancora vivo, però non provai nulla di ciò che si potrebbe immaginare. Pensavo che fra poco avrebbe ripreso quell'odiosa vita di caserma, già ricordavo la Valmorbia come un luogo dove si potevano trovare dei momenti di pace, idillici.[86]

---

[83] E. Montale, "Bello sì ma dopo?" (1968), report by E. Cancogni, AMS p. 1564: "I was assigned to a camp of Austrian prisoners at Lanzo Torinese. I was a lieutenant, the high-ranking official, I was in command. My prisoners were good young men. We got along quite well, I spoke a little German, they a little Italian. Some of them wrote to me after the war. At night we would go to Turin, to the opera. Yes, sometimes I brought one or two of them with me, the ones who were passionate about music and the bel canto".

[84] See A. Lafon, *La camaraderie au front*, Paris, Armand Colin, 2014.

[85] E.J. Leed, *No Man's Land: Combat and Identity in World War I*, Cambridge, Cambridge University Press, 1979, p. 107.

[86] E. Montale, "Bello sì ma dopo?" (1968), report by E. Cancogni, AMS, p. 1562-1563: "We pressed on, on the road to Trento. In a town I would no longer be able to name, I assisted in the execution by firing squad of one of our soldiers, guilty of looting – I believe he had stolen a watch. When they opened fire, I clearly saw a white thing leaping into the air, the brain, while the body sagged down. No, it didn't have a big effect on me. But what could affect us under those circumstances? It was like a dream. A grand dream in which anything could happen. I moved on like a sleepwalker. Immediately afterward they told us that we had won the war. Even that news didn't much move me; sure, I was happy to be alive still, but I didn't feel anything like what one would imagine. I thought that soon enough the odious barracks life would resume, and already I remembered the Valmorbia as a place where one could find idyllic moments of peace".

In a context in which the awareness of time, highlighted in the detail of the stolen watch, inevitably leads to death, Eugenio's sleepwalking, alienation, and the dullness noted by Marianna are instrumental in surviving the horror and violence, while they reinforce the paradoxical idea of a theater of war in which one could find peace. They are a way to deny to oneself the experience of horror and to deny to others that you were a victim of it. Apathy and lack of emotions are common symptoms shown by soldiers suffering from post-traumatic stress disorder, but the military apparatus was not ready to consider them a psychological consequence of the involvement in war-related events. The symptoms of shell shock were regarded as a sign of cowardice or, worse, as insubordination. Fear and disorientation were experienced by the combatants as a misconduct of which to be ashamed, a betrayal of the patriotic cause and even of one's brothers-in-arms: in short, as a weakness to be repudiated.[87] Only a physical event producing a material wound was worthy of consideration; in fact, soldiers wounded in an act of war were routinely promoted or decorated, as it happened to Eugenio's brother Salvatore. The medical system was not ready to recognize psychological damage; which is why Eugenio after being diagnosed with a nervous breakdown in October 1918 did not leave the battlefield: either because he wasn't allowed or, but there's really no difference, because he choose not to.

The trauma continued to exist despite the shame. The shame prevented Montale from narrating the horrors he had witnessed in *Ossi di seppia* and for a long time afterwards; yet even if the horror of war is not rendered explicitly in *Ossi di seppia*, still it influenced Montale's writing. The generational manifesto "Non chiederci la parola ...", as we have seen, is a poem occasioned by the war, and it could not have been written had Montale not been a veteran. It expresses the trauma of a cohort that has lost its synderesis on the battlefield. Nothing is left to them, their poiesis exists solely in negative terms. They are contrasted by the undivided man of the second stanza, the one not shattered by self-awareness, the one who is carefree because he still thinks he's placing his feet on solid ground. The verses describing him are arranged in a single sentence in the middle of the poem: his mere presence splits the discourse of the "noi". The quatrain dedicated to him is unrelated to the logical thread of discourse, but it adds elements

[87] The medical term *shell shock* was actually coined in 1915 by the British psychiatrist Charles Myers to classify the pathology of traumatized combatants; see R. Holmes, *Firing Lane*, Jonathan Cape, 1985, p. 256 *et passim*. See also E.J. Leed, *No Man's Land: Combat and Identity in World War I*, Cambridge, Cambridge University Press, 1979, pp. 166 et *passim*; A. Marzola, *Guerra e identità. Percorsi nella letteratura inglese del Novecento*, Roma, Carocci, 2005, p. 127.

to our understanding of the text through accumulation; just as Cubism disassembled perspectival perception with the aim of being able to reassemble the forms of space in complete freedom, so Montale disarticulates the structure of discourse so as to comprehend the functional disposition of the materials and fragments that constitute it.

In Montale's words, the poem aims to represent the refusal of a rational explanation of the world. If the war has no explanation, and the war is the world in which Montale's generation moves, the conclusion of the syllogism is that the world itself has no explanation. The logic running the world is not causal but casual, since the world is regulated by contingency, and the young men and women facing existence in this desolated landscape have many points in common with the Generation of 1914. Those who do not indulge in rhetoric, do not allow conterfeits, contraband, or falsification are also well described by the words of Robert Caserio when he says that "the creators of modernist works are negative demystifiers: they unmask absolutism, rationalism, idealism – and all illusions".[88] As an existential proclamation, not as a declaration of poetics, "Non chiederci la parola ..." will later become the manifesto of the anti-fascist underground movement.

That said, the poem is also a manifesto of poetics. Commenting on this text in 1968, Montale explains that the experience of war made him feel the need to surpass the rhetoric of the old poetry, and the new generation he describes does not possess the definitive word, the formula capable of revealing hidden secrets, the power of symbolic imagination. The language of the new poerty is no longer capable of transcending the real, of revealing the ineffable connections between things. That's for the better, since symbolist stylistic elements are not any more suited to representing a changed reality in which humans can no longer imagine themselves as part of a natural whole, in which the logic of cause and effect is upturned, in which science is proving that to a disorienting space corresponds a fragmented time. Ultimately, "Non chiederci la parola..." represents a generation of modern poets declaring the impossibility of putting further trust in symbolic language: since the symbol claims to capture the universal in the particular, it does not have any currency in modernist poetics, where there are no universals to be captured, rather countless particulars irreconcilable in a meaningful whole.

---

[88] R. Caserio, *The Novel in England, 1900-1950*, New York, Twayne, 1999, p. 82. See also G. Bertone, *Letteratura e paesaggio*, Lecce, Manni, 2001, p. 106.

Chapter III

A LANDSCAPE OF MANY SOURCES

1. "One of the Most Picturesque Regions of Italy"

For a traveler leafing through the 1899 Baedecker guide to Northern Italy, the Ligurian landscape emerges in sinuous, poetic lines:

> The Riviera, the narrow sea-border of Liguria, divided by Genoa into an eastern (*Riviera di levante*) and a larger western half (*Riviera di ponente*), which belongs to France from Ventimiglia westwards, is one of the most picturesque regions of Italy. It affords a delightful variety of landscapes, bold and lofty promontories alternating with wooded hills, and richly cultivated plains near the coast. At places the road passes precipitous, and frowning cliffs are washed by the surf of the Mediterranean, while the summits are crowned with the venerable ruins of towers erected in bygone ages for protection against pirates.[1]

At the turn of the twentieth century, tourists from Britain, Germany, Russia, and other Northern European countries flocked to the Italian Riviera, drawn by the beauty of the landscape and the salubrity of the climate. The railway connected major European cities to this liminal province with its long, curving strip of seashore, and the newly accessible towns and villages became a potent draw. And yet, as Baedecker's evocation of the Ligurian picturesque suggests, the region's attractions were already literary commonplaces in indigenous and foreign literature alike. Paul Valéry's *La nuit de Gênes* captured the transformative qualities of the capital city of the region; interestingly, his "syndrome de Gênes" points out the necessary mediation of a Ligurian locale in the conception of a literary work.[2] A locale that, one generation later, Valery Larbaud loved as well. Nietzsche began writing *The Gay Science* by the light of a bonfire on the Riviera di Levante.

---

1 K. Baedeker, *Baedecker's Northern Italy*, Leipsic, Baedeker, 1899, p. 82.

2 See M. Onfray, *Le désir d'être un volcan. Journal hédoniste*, Paris, Grasset 1996, p. 320 *et passim*; see also M. Quaini, *L'ombra del paesaggio: Orizzonti di un'utopia conviviale*, Reggio Emilia, Diabasis, 2006, p. 53.

Sigmund Freud and Gottfried Benn had been enthralled by the landscape's rugged beauty.[3] The so-called Poets' Gulf, a few miles east of the Cinque Terre, was painted by J.M.W. Turner during the first half of the nineteenth century and attracted Byron, Shelley, D.H. Lawrence, and George Sand to its shores. Alongside such international attention, and distinct from it, the region's towns and hamlets also cultivated their own bards who celebrated the pleasures and struggles of these marginal, sleepy cliff-side locales.

Indeed, the attributes that made Liguria attractive to tourists – its liminal, provincial, otherness, its rugged sceneries – were also the source of its inhabitants' angst; the proverbial harshness of the landscape was a state of mind for its inhabitants as well as a physical environment.[4] The region's famed remoteness and austerity were well-worn tropes, immortalized first by an unusually rich generation of writers at the turn of the twentieth century: Ceccardo Roccatagliata Ceccardi, Mario Novaro and his brother Angiolo Silvio, Giovanni Boine, Camillo Sbarbaro, and others who would later be identified as the Linea Ligure (Ligurian Heritage) by their readers and commentators.

The visions of Liguria immortalized in the writing of the Linea Ligure tended towards an ossified, isolated portrait of the region, but at the beginning of the twentieth century Liguria was as deeply interconnected with the rest of Italy and Europe as its inhabitants could be: while Ceccardi was born into a family of modest financial means and never left the region, Mario Novaro had an advanced degree in philosophy from the University of Berlin, and Giovanni Boine studied in Milan and in Paris. Liguria experienced modern technological development: the electrification of the streets and the mechanization of the port of Genoa; the creation of spaces destined to receive the audiences of the *cinematografo*; the development of a coastal railroad, which connected Genoa and Turin both to Paris and to small towns that had previously only been accessible by sea; and the diffusion of literacy and the press. These technological advancements made even these small centers aware of contemporary cultural and commercial trends.

Growing up in the years of touristic discovery, the young Eugenio Montale would have experienced both the delights of a Ligurian vacation and the cultural constraints of the provinces: his childhood was spent between winters in the family's house in Genoa and summers at the Casa

[3] For an analysis of the influence of the Ligurian landscape on German modernism, see M. Kolb, *Nietzsche, Freud, Benn, and the Azure Spell of Liguria*, Toronto, University of Toronto Press, 2013.

[4] For a discussion of the cultural insulation of Genoa in the first part of the twentieth century, see G. Marcenaro, *Eugenio Montale*, Milano, Bruno Mondadori, 1999.

delle due palme, the yellow house flanked by two palms in Monterosso, the western-most village of the Cinque Terre. Marked indelibly by these places, Montale would grow to consider his own Liguria a kind of private, deeply personal landscape, so much so that years later, after World War II, he could not tolerate the signs of change.

In a short poem in prose written in Florence in 1943, and published in *La bufera e altro* (1956), Montale reflects on this primal link between landscape and selfhood: "È curioso pensare che ognuno di noi ha un paese come questo, e sia pur diversissimo, che dovrà restare il *suo* paesaggio, immutabile; è curioso che l'ordine fisico sia così lento a entrare in noi e poi così impossibile a scancellarsi".[5] Montale's conviction that individuals are defined by the places they experience and come to know intimately, specifically during childhood, finds particular expression in *Ossi di seppia (Cuttlefish Bones*, 1925), which celebrates the construction of a poetic self powerfully defined by its encounter with the landscape of Genoa and the Cinque Terre. In the following collections, *Le occasioni* (*The Occasions,* 1939) and *La bufera e altro (The Storm and Other Things*, 1956), the Ligurian landscape still features occasionally – but no longer as the sole character. It is reimagined from different perspectives and linked to the themes of time and memory.

However, the seemingly personal, unique connection between space and self that Montale celebrates is something of an illusion, for writing about Liguria in the early twentieth century was already an entry into a distinct literary tradition with its own *topoi* and commonplaces. Montale, who did not receive a formal literary education, was an avid reader of local literary journals, and through these journals he came into contact early on with the writing of the so-called Ligurian Heritage.[6] He was personally acquainted with some of the writers: though he never managed to meet Boine, and avoided Ceccardo Roccatagliata Ceccardi, fearing his cane,[7] his friendship with Camillo Sbarbaro and Adriano Grande became meaning-

---

[5] "It is curious to realize that each of us has a landscape equivalent to this one, even if it may be completely different, which will remain *his own* landscape, immutable; it is curious to think that the physical aspect of things is so slow to percolate in us, but eventually becomes impossible to expunge". "Dov'era il tennis ..." ("Where Once Was the Tennis Court ..."), in *La bufera*, OV 215.

[6] The journals most central to Montale's literary formation were «La Riviera Ligure», directed by Mario Novaro, and the Florentine «La Voce», directed by Giuseppe Prezzolini and Giuseppe De Robertis.

[7] In a 1967 article, Montale remembered his fear of the cane with which Ceccardi used to stroll. See "Ricordo di Sbarbaro", SM 2866: "mi ero tenuto lontano: forse temevo la *cravache* dell'autore del *Viandante*" ("I stayed away from him: perhaps I feared the *cravache* of the author of *Viandante*).

ful on both a personal and literary level. Recognizing Montale's indebtedness to his literary predecessors alerts us to the poet's initial conformity with the literary tradition, and also highlights his gradual separation from it – a movement that we witness in later editions of the *Ossi di seppia* and in the later collections. Though the young Montale drew deeply on familiar representations of the Ligurian landscape to construct the early *Ossi*, he would later abandon these commonplaces to craft a new literary voice.

It is not possible, however, to discern a sudden break, an immediate change of direction, in his descriptions of the Ligurian landscape, nor of the phenomenal world in general. The manuscript Montale sent to his friend and correspondent Francesco Messina in July 1923, for example, includes three *ossi brevi*: of these, "Portami il girasole" still reflects a belief in a symbolic reading of phenomenal matter, while "Non chiederci la parola" and, more to the point, "Forse un mattino", with its intuition of a reality existing beneath the illusory screen of sensible appearances derived from a recent reading of Schopenhauer, point to a fracture between the world and the poetic self. Likewise, in the poems composed in 1924, we find a symbolic representation of the real (as in "Spesso il male di vivere…", OV 33) overlap with a potent yearning to break through "la rete / che ci stringe" ("The net / that tightens around us", OV 5 ll. 15-16).

It is only from the poems written in 1926 onward that we discern a complete disconnection between Montale's poetry and the representation of its landscape, as well as a disconnection between Montale's poetry and the Ligurian heritage. If Montale's landscape regenerates and reactivates the elements of a literary tradition and engages its literary predecessors in the poems written before 1924, the later verses, from the suite "Mediterraneo" to the poems added to the second edition of the *Ossi di seppia* ("Delta", "I morti", "Incontro"), reveal a fracture between the modern self and his environment. In the later verses, the representation of the Ligurian landscape itself changes, as does its function: the poetic self can no longer find refuge in the landscape, in the comforting consonance between man and nature. He becomes detached from the familiarity of place – both actual locales and literary *topoi* – and seeks to explore. His quest for a new poetic language and mode will shape the development of Montale as a modernist poet.

2. Places, Commonplaces, and Displacements

When Montale began to build his poetic style in the years around 1916, the myth of the Ligurian landscape and of its proverbial harshness was a literary subject in its own right. Many writers had attempted to capture its beauty in both poetry and prose, from Petrarch's description of the eastern part of Liguria seen from the sea in the *Itinerarium,* and in the unfinished Latin epic *Africa,* to Foscolo's celebrated odes, written during the author's Genoese sojourn and located in Sestri Ponente. In the ode to his acquaintance Luigia Pallavicini, a young woman from one of Genoa's Dogal families whose celebrated beauty was threatened by an equestrian accident ("A Luigia Pallavicini caduta da cavallo" ["To Luigia Pallavicini on the occasion of her falling from a horse"]), we find a conjunction between literary and literal terminology: the coast of Genoa is, to use Foscolo's words, a "petrosa riva",[8] a definition that in the Italian poetic tradition has expressed an asperity, a roughness of the poetic language since Dante's series of sonnets entitled *Rime petrose.* We read there, for instance:

> Suonan gli antri marini
> allo incalzato scalpito
> della zampa, che caccia
> polve e sassi in sua traccia.[9]

The "marine caverns" are located in a high, rhetorically ample style, and appear with a similar description in the twin ode "All'amica risanata" ("To my dear friend restored to health"), where the syntagm acts as the first element of a simile derived from classical sources ("Qual dagli antri marini / l'astro più caro a Venere ...").[10] Even Foscolo's classicizing style must bend from its elevated diction to accommodate the stony characteristics of the Ligurian landscape. Foscolo, who certainly did not grudge adjectives, acknowledged that the Ligurian landscape was little suited to eloquent effusions; later poets would seek a similar correspondence between the harsh and unyielding characteristics of the landscape and their own expressive tone.

For those who came to be defined as the poets of the Linea Ligure, the landscape, at the beginning of the twentieth century, became an emblem of existence: arid, coarse, burned by the sun, and constrained by the sea, which marked the immovable limit of the values external to the self. Ceccardi, Boine, and Novaro would all influence Montale's approach to poetry, as well as his vocabulary. In the much-cited "Intenzioni (Intervista immaginaria)" ("Intentions [Imaginary Interview]") of 1946, Montale himself records the influence of "alcuni poeti liguri" ("some Ligurian poets") on his work: "Dov'essi

---

8 "A Luigia Pallavicini caduta da cavallo", l. 77: "a stony shore".

9 "A Luigia Pallavicini caduta da cavallo", ll. 56-60: "The marine caverns resonate / from the hurried bustling / of the hoof, which kicks / brittle and stones in its proceeding".

10 "All'amica risanata, ll. 1-2: "As from the marine caverns / the star dearest to Venus ...".

meglio aderivano alle fibre del nostro suolo rappresentano senza dubbio un insegnamento per me" ("In the places where they did adhere to the fibers of our soil, they clearly represented a learning opportunity for me").[11] The nature of the Cinque Terre is reproduced realistically following the teachings of "adherence" derived from the expressivity of the Ligurian poets.

The Ligurian poets thus represent not only a point of arrival for the aspirations of the young Montale, but also a hinge between the inheritance of the past and the poet's own desire for expression.[12] In addition, Montale draws heavily on the great symbolist poet of the generation before him, Gabriele D'Annunzio. D'Annunzio had established a precedent with his descriptions of Versillia in *Alcyone,* against which Montale could not but measure himself.[13]

To explore Montale's landscapes in *Ossi di seppia* therefore is not only to map the places of which he writes, but also to excavate the literary topoi upon which his work is built: to realize that the landscape in the book is not only formed by the overlapping of geological strata but is a literary palimpsest as well. To do so, we must investigate the most important literary sources of his landscapes. Montale's experience of the Ligurian heritage and of the great symbolist poets of the previous generation illustrates how the poet inserted himself into, borrowed from, and transformed existing patterns of description and terminology. The intertextual resonance reveals how actual and literary landscapes combined in the early years of poetic self-definition: to craft a landscape, for Montale, was effectively to craft a poetic self. Later, having left the familiar places for Florence and Milan, Montale would measure his distance from these predecessors, marking his difference in style and subject matter through a distancing in the representation of his environment.[14]

Despite Montale's subsequent claims to a universalizing lyric voice,[15] his *oeuvre*, especially at its inception, needs to be read in a perspective that is

---

11 The influence of the poets of the Ligurian heritage over the young Montale is not limited to modes of landscape description; it is nonetheless revealing how Montale, remembering Ceccardi, Boine, Novaro, and Sbarbaro, meant to underscore precisely this aspect of their work, and how influential it was on his own.

12 On the subject of the influence of the Ligurian heritage, see R. Mosena, *Le affinità di Montale. Letteratura ligure del Novecento*, Roma, Studium, 2006.

13 See C. Garboli, *D'Annunzio e la scoperta della Versilia*, in *D'Annunzio e la scoperta della Versilia*, ed. A.M. Andreoli, Firenze, Maschietto e Musolino, 1999, p. 17 *et passim*.

14 See S. Verdino, *L'ultimo paesaggio di Montale*, «Nuova corrente», 58 (2011), pp. 27-44.

15 In 1927, in a postcard to his friend Piero Gadda Conti, Montale described the Ligurian landscape as "universalissimo", a mock superlative that underscores how he understood such landscape as a versatile metaphor. See P. Gadda Conti, *Montale nelle Cinque Terre (1926-1928)*, «Letteratura», XX (1966), 79-81, p. 278.

also regional, rooted in the particularities of Liguria.[16] The young Eugenio spent his winters in Genoa and his summer vacations in Monterosso; his first infatuations took place in Genoa and in Monterosso, with Paola Nicoli and Anna degli Uberti respectively, both characters who, under different *senhals*, will inform his verses. He studied in Genoa, first at a Barnabite primary school, then in a technical school, then at the school of the old Maestro Sivori, where he studied voice performance hoping to become a professional opera singer. In Monterosso, he reunited with his extended family, enjoyed long periods of vacation, fell prey to the stillness of the meridian heat, and wrote his first poems. The Riviera di Levante was his only geographical horizon until 1917, when he left for military school and, as we have seen, for the trenches of the First World War. Returning to Genoa after the war, he experienced the Fascist rise to power before definitively leaving the city in 1927 on a life journey that would only sporadically take him back (see chapter 7.1).

The first discernible shift in Montale's poetics – one that traces his passage toward modernism – becomes clear in a comparative reading of the first two editions of *Ossi di seppia*. In the *primi Ossi* (the first edition of *Cuttlefish Bones*, Gobetti 1925), Montale remains embedded in the Ligurian landscape as a literary palimpsest, while from the poems added to the *secondi Ossi* (the second, augmented edition of the book, Ribet 1928) onwards, he progressively frees himself from the bonds of the regional tradition. Over the course of his poetic career, we see Montale establish a firmer poetic voice that no longer requires the scaffolding of previous writers: by the time of *Satura* (1971), Montale openly parodies his early sources. But this separation of the poetic self from its predecessors is characterized by a separation from the Ligurian landscape itself, as though the physical places of youth cannot be disentangled from their poetic figurations.

In the two following sections I will outline Montale's poetic debts to the Ligurian heritage, as well as to Gabriele D'Annunzio. Revisiting the historiographical tradition concerning Montale's sources, I describe how Montale's evocation of the Ligurian landscape drew on but also strongly diverged from his antecedents. If landscape is considered an instrument for shaping a poetic voice and a vehicle for inserting oneself in a poetic tradition, unpacking the sources of Montale's early poetry becomes an exercise in reconstructing not only the foundational tropes in his landscape, but also the poetic persona he sought to craft for himself.

---

[16] See F. Croce, *La storia della poesia di Eugenio Montale*, Genova, Costa & Nolan, 2005, p. 8 *et passim*.

2.1. *The Ligurian Heritage*

Ligurian themes present in Montale's "Meriggiare pallido e assorto" – the walls, the enclosed gardens, the afternoon heat – expand familiar tropes in the region's existing literature. The harsh territory of Liguria is already present in the *Sonetti e poemi* of Ceccardi, with its "magri ulivi" ("lean olives") and "case rose dal salso" ("houses consumed by salt").[17] In the short collection of poetry *Murmuri ed echi* (*Murmurs and Echoes,* 1912) by Mario Novaro, a poet from Diano Marina of great sensibility and modest circulation, the apprentice poet found a village "ròso dalla salsedine" ("consumed by saltiness") in which "il tardo fiore dell'agave" ("the late flower of the agave") blooms, over the "muri a secco di pietra forte / che reggono l'arida terra in Liguria" ("the dry walls of hard stone / which support the arid earth in Liguria").[18]

Montale will engage earlier poets not only in a contest over the landscape's particular character, but also in the expressive tone to which the landscape corresponds. The concept of the limit, for instance, so important for the poetry of the young Montale, is a geographic element before it is a literary one, shared among the verses of more than one author.[19] We see this in Boine's volume of lyrical prose, *Frantumi,* precisely in "Limite", as well as in Novaro's "Proda d'erba", which begins:

> Stretta proda d'erba
> pende sul mare
> con scabri ulivi
> frondadargento.[20]

Liguria itself is a region of confines: its liminality is an essential characteristic for anyone who attempts a description. The recollection of Genoa as the city of Janus is useful, once more, to understand Montale's landscape as a threshold.

---

17 See A. Nozzoli, *Montale e l'ombra di Ceccardo*, in *La Liguria di Montale*, eds. F. Contorbia and L. Surdich, Savona, Sabatelli 1996, pp. 123-135.

18 All the aforementioned examples belong to "Fioretti", in the section of *Murmuri ed echi* entitled *Tondo d'erba*. See M. Novaro, *Murmuri ed echi*, ed. G. Cassinelli, Milano, All'insegna del pesce d'oro, 1994, pp. 95-108.

19 See R. West, *Eugenio Montale: Poet on the Edge*, Cambridge, Mass., Harvard University Press, 1981.

20 M. Novaro, *Murmuri ed echi*, ed. G. Cassinelli, Milano, All'insegna del pesce d'oro, 1994, p. 39, ll. 1-4: "Narrow shore of grass / hangs over the sea / with scabrous olive trees / silverbranched".

Reading Boine's *feuilletton, Il peccato* – published serially in «La Riviera Ligure» from 1914 to 1916 – Montale found the "muretto di cocci puntuti a difesa" ("the wall defended by pointed shards"), which in the last stanza of "Meriggiare pallido e assorto" becomes emblematic of the inaccessibility of the real. The very verb in the infinitive tense, which opens the poem, ("meriggiare", in the unusual sense of "to spend the afternoon") was possibly inspired by a passage from *Frantumi*, where we read: "È così bello a volte meriggiare, all'ombra di un carrubo in faccia al mare!" ("It is so pleasant to spend some afternoons in the shade of a carob tree, in front of the sea!").[21] Other borrowings from Boine are similarly used: the "barbaglio enorme" ("enormous glare") which appears in *Ossi brevi* to "invischia[re] / gli occhi" ("capture the eyes"); and a landscape that is "un frinire di cicale per tutto, barbaglio accecante bianchiccio, case nette, sfacciate senz'ombra" ("a chirping of cicadas everywhere, a blinding white glare, clean houses, uncovered without shade").[22] The ascent in Boine's writings is "sassosa, incassata fra i muri sgretolati bianchi di cinta" ("stony, enclosed between crumbling white walls"); his is a world of "orti e giardini con su svettanti le cime dei mandorli e dei limoni lucide-verdi" ("vegetable plots and gardens below the soaring peaks of almonds and bright-green lemons") and "un bruciare vasto di sete" ("a vast burning of thirst"). Montale draws on these images for many of the keywords in his own poetic lexicon. The young poet is conscious of the fact that his verse, so closely linked to the geographical locale, inevitably bears resemblance to the work of his fellows. Corresponding with Angelo Barile, first he notices a consonance between Barile's "Primasera" and his own "Clivo"; later on he realizes that "Forse è una sola affinità di materia. Non siamo nati negli stessi paesi? (più o meno). E non si può uscire dal generico se non correndo il rischio di assomigliare, talvolta, ad altri. L'importante è di essere, abbastanza spesso, sé stessi".[23]

Despite Montale's later change of heart regarding Boine's poetry (whom he labels a "poeta a metà", ["only half a poet"] in 1946),[24] it is clear

---

21 G. Ioli, *Frantumi e rottami: note su Boine e Montale*, in *La Liguria di Montale*, eds. F. Contorbia and L. Surdich, Savona, Sabatelli, 1996, pp. 147-158.

22 G. Boine, *Il peccato, Plausi e Botte, Frantumi, Altri scritti*, ed. D. Puccini, Milano, Garzanti, 1983; all quotations are from chapter 1. See also E. Giachery, *Luoghi, sopralluoghi e poesia di Montale*, in *La Liguria di Montale*, eds. F. Contorbia and L. Surdich, Savona, Sabatelli, 1996, pp. 43-50.

23 E. Montale, *Giorni di libeccio, Lettere ad Angelo Barile (1920-1957)*, eds. D. Astengo, G. Costa, Milano, Archinto, 2002 (April 15, 1932): "Perhaps it is merely an affinity of matter. Aren't we born in the same land? (more or less). And one could not overcome the generic without running the risk of resembling, at times, other poets. The important thing is to be, often enough, oneself".

24 Writing to Francesco Meriano in 1919, Montale defended Boine's poems and prose poems against the negative judgment of his friend: "Seguo anche la tua collaborazione all'*Ardita*

that he pondered over the collection *Frammenti* by the poet from Porto Maurizio: the specific lexical borrowings remain witness to it, as well as the sincere expression of grief that the young Montale recorded in his journal when he received the news of Boine's death in 1917.[25] Boine's "strapiomba" ("overhanging"), for example, reappears in a poem of 1922, "Non rifugiarti nell'ombra" (OV 29), in which we find the "falchetto che strapiomba / fulmineo della calura" ("hawk that overhangs / the explosion of heat").[26] The presence of a "mare pulsante" ("pulsating sea") that rolls and engulfs is found not only (and obviously) in all of "Mediterraneo" but also in *Fine dell'infanzia* (OV 65), where another verb used by Boine, "ingolfarsi", ("to engulf oneself") appears as an *apax* in Montale's poetry. Montale receives from Boine the peculiar evocation of place and Ligurian ambience, which he then extends into a new, multifaceted poetic meditation.

But it is in the verses of Sbarbaro that we find with greater insistence the themes that later converge in the *Ossi*. Montale was fond of Sbarbaro (a section of *Cuttlefish Bones* is dedicated to him, as well as a very insightful, albeit double-edged, literary portrait) and studied his work at great length. While reviewing Sbarbaro's *Trucioli* in 1920, Montale wrote, "Il centro dell'ispirazione qui è l'amore del resto, dello 'scarto', la poesia degli uomini falliti e delle cose irrimediabilmente oscure e mancate: bolle di sapone, *épaves*, trascurabili apparenze, arsi paesaggi, strade fuori mano" ("the center of his inspiration here is love of the remnant, of the scrap, the poetry of fallen men and of irreparable things, obscure and forgotten: bubbles of soap, wrecks, insignificant appearances, burnt landscapes, paths off the beaten

---

e molto spesso sono d'accordo teco [...] Tuttavia in qualche affermazione non mi trovo con te: che il povero Boine non avesse animo di poeta mi pare non possa dirsi da chi ha letto bene *Plausi e botte*. Pensa al carattere di quella mirabile prosa e pensa agli ultimi poemetti di *La Riviera Ligure*". ("I am also following your contributions to *Ardita*, and I frequently agree with you [...] However, when it comes to certain claims I don't stand with you: that poor Boine lacks the soul of a poet, it seems to me, cannot be said by anyone who has read well *Plausi e botte*. Think of the character of that exquisite prose. Think of the final short poems in *La Riviera Ligure*"). See F. Meriano, *Arte e vita*, eds. G. Manghetti, C.E. Meriano, V. Scheiwiller, Milano, Scheiwiller 1982, p. 151. For the later judgment, see "Intenzioni (intervista immaginaria)" (1946), AMS 1477.

25 Under the date May 21, 1917 Montale wrote this entry in his personal journal: "È morto Giovanni Boine!!! Questa notizia mi ha fatto male. Per l'avanguardia (parlo della parte seria di essa) il danno è incalcolabile. [...] Mi dispiacerà sempre non averlo conosciuto: la *Riviera Ligure* ne resta come diminuita", ("Giovanni Boine has died! Such painful news. For the avant-garde movement (I mean the respectable part of it) the damage is immense. [...] I will always be sorry of not having had the possibility to meet him: *Riviera Ligure* seems now diminished in importance"). See QG, AMS 1325.

26 See G. Ioli, *Frantumi e rottami: note su Boine e Montale*, in *La Liguria di Montale*, eds. F. Contorbia and L. Surdich, Savona, Sabatelli, 1996, p. 153.

track"].[27] He intuited that Sbarbaro first loved "le strade che riescono agli erbosi / fossi",[28] and "la vita che scoppia dall'arsura" ("the roads that lead to grassy / ditches" and "life that explodes with burning heat").[29] Montale's analysis of Sbarbaro's key themes reveals his own intellectual predisposition and his self-conscious identification with the most representative poems of the Ligurian heritage. The signs of burning and aridity (*arsura, aridità*), emblems of an existential condition first identified in Sbarbaro's poetry, are present in all of the *Ossi brevi*,[30] like the sign of the wall, so typical of Ligurian reality, yet particularly adaptable for fruitful symbolism.

The connection with Sbarbaro's poetry goes beyond simple lexical borrowings. The "lastrici sonori della notte" ("the resonating pavements, at night") in "Esco dalla lussuria" ("Exiting Lust") are replicated in Montale's "vie lastricate di mattoni" ("streets paved with stones"),[31] while several other locutions from Sbarbaro find precise echoes in the *Ossi*. Sbarbaro's figures – the seaweed, the petrels, the parasitic wilt, the narrow streets enclosed between the houses and the walls of the gardens – find kinship in Montale's verse; yet the lexical level is not the only one in which Montale has something to learn from his older associate. Sbarbaro translates Baudelaire's antihero not only from French into Italian but also from Paris to Genoa: it is Sbarbaro's transposition that gives this familiar nineteenth-century figure a modernist dimension, replete with a sense of alienation, uncertainty, and a forced discordance with the natural world. In his citations of Sbarbaro, Montale, himself an attentive reader of Baudelaire, exposes a triangulation among the successive personifications of the figure of the *flaneur*.

Montale's thematic return to Sbarbaro in the *stanza* that concludes "Meriggiare pallido e assorto" demands particular comment alongside the opening *terzina* of *Primizie*:

> Vo nella notte solo
> per vicoli deserti
> lungo squallide mura.[32]

---

27 See E. Montale, "Camillo Sbarbaro" (1920), SM 3.

28 "I limoni" (OV 9, ll. 4-5).

29 "La farandola dei fanciulli sul greto…" (OV 43, l. 2).

30 See e.g. "Gloria del disteso mezzogiorno", OV 37, ll.9-10: "L'arsura in giro, un martin pescatore / volteggia s'una reliquia di vita", ("Drought all around, a kingfisher / hovers on a relic of life").

31 See C. Sbarbaro, "Esco dalla lussuria", in *Pianissimo* (1914), C. Sbarbaro, *L'opera in versi e in prosa*, eds. G. Lagorio and V. Scheiwiller, Milano, Garzanti, 2016, p. 25, l. 3. E. Montale, "Lettera levantina", now in *Poesie Disperse* (OV 773).

32 C. Sbarbaro, "Vo nella notte solo", in *Pianissimo* (1914), *L'opera in versi e in prosa*, eds.

Both poetic personae walk alongside a wall that cannot be crossed: the echo suggests not only that the wall (*muro*) and its variants (*muretto, muraglia*) are a fundamental presence in the Ligurian landscape, but also that the act of walking alongside the wall represents a metaphor for life and its existential labor. Thus in stanza 19 of "Vo nella notte solo" we encounter a *flanêur* who, after a short-winded vitality, is distinguished by abjectness and fear.

> E mi butto da lato e rasento
> di nuovo le mura, se il piede nel lastrico inciampa
> o nella pausa del vento
> un fanale divampa
> trasalendo di sciocca paura.[33]

This lyric "I", who shares in the lifestyle of Baudelaire's protagonists, winces at the flickering of a gas lamp and is consumed by an existential terror, can be read as one of the missing links between Montale's modernist poetry and its symbolist predecessor. For Sbarbaro's translation of the *poête maudit* to Genoa gives Montale a model for finding his own poetic persona. Thus, Montale, who writes of his lyric self as wandering "zitto / tra gli uomini che non si voltano, col mio segreto" ("silent / among men who never turn back, with my secret"),[34] is the repository of an undisclosed knowledge that "non vede la gente nell'affollato corso" ("the people of the crowded streets do not see").[35] Similarly, in the poem "Talor, mentre cammino per le strade", which transforms Genoa into a city quite similar to the Paris of the *Fleurs du mal* and which is an antecedent for Montale's "Forse un mattino ...", Sbarbaro passes "tra gli uomini che non comprende, tra la vita che gli sopravanza e gli sfugge", as Montale says ("among men who he does not understand, among the life that surpasses him and shirks him").[36]

In the years between 1922 and 1925, however, the fundamental theme of the *Ossi* is no longer the landscape *per se* but rather the necessity of finding a means of transcending that landscape, of breaking free of its materiality. Montale will cease his search for emblems in the world around him in order to look for a miracle, understood as the moment when the human

G. Lagorio and V. Scheiwiller, Milano, Garzanti, 2016, p. 13, ll. 1-3: "I walk alone in the night / through deserted alleyways / along squalid walls".

33 *Ibid.*, p. 15: "And I will jump to the side and graze / the wall once again, wincing with silly fear / if the foot on the pavement stumbles / or in the windbreak a light flares".

34 "Forse un mattino..." (OV 40, ll. 7-8).

35 "So l'ora in cui la faccia più impassibile ..." (OV 36, l. 4).

36 E. Montale, "Camillo Sbarbaro" (1920), SM, p. 5.

is permitted to escape sense experience and discover the truth of things. In this shift, "[dal] fisico al metafisico" ("from the physical to the metaphysical"),[37] Montale's strategic allusions to his poetic predecessors will diminish. Landscape remains a key theme in Montalian poetry, but comes to be perceived from an angle so personal that it suddenly overcomes all possible predecessors. This change in style did not go unnoticed by contemporary readers, but it wasn't necessarily interpreted as a welcome transition. Pietro Pancrazi for example, the very critic who coined the longstanding formula of a Montale "fisico" opposed to the subsequent Montale "metafisico", perceived the change in style, but did not understand the underlying necessity of "making it new." [38]

2.2. *Traversing D'Annunzio*

Apart from his engagements with Sbarbaro and the Linea Ligure, a cursory reading of *Ossi di seppia* also brings to light moments in which Montale adopts a tone inspired by D'Annunzio, arguably the most influential Italian poet of the period. "I limoni", for instance, a text that in its intention refers more to Sbarbaro or Pascoli than to D'Annunzio, begins with "Ascolta" ("listen"), as does the first line of *Pioggia nel pineto* (then modified, in the second version, with a demure atonic particle, "Ascoltami"), and closes with other elevated ("alti") verses with respect to the poem's tone ("e in petto ci scrosciano / le loro canzoni / le trombe d'oro della solarità").[39] Some lines of *Riviere,* with their "sparir carne / per spicciare sorgente ebbra di sole, / dal sole divorata",[40] manifest an intention that, to judge by the tone, veers towards D'Annunzio in inspiration rather than to the cited Sbarbaro: we recognize a similar intention in the concluding quatrain of *osso breve* "Portami il girasole...":

> Portami tu la pianta che conduce
> dove sorgono bionde trasparenze
> e vapora la vita quale essenza;
> portami il girasole impazzito di luce.[41]

---

[37] See P. Pancrazi, *Eugenio Montale poeta fisico e metafisico* (1934), in *Scrittori d'oggi*, Serie III, Bari, Laterza 1946, pp. 248-256.

[38] See *ibid.*, p. 255.

[39] "I limoni" (OV 10, ll. 47-49): "and trumpets of gold pour forth / epiphanies of Light!", trans. W. Arrowsmith.

[40] "Riviere" (OV 101, ll. 32-34): "to dissolve as flesh / and flow back, a spring drunk on sunlight, / devoured by sunlight...", trans. W. Arrowsmith.

[41] "Portami il girasole..." (OV 32, ll. 9-12): "Bring me the flower that lead us out / where

The symbolist overtones, the exquisite words, the need to explore the secret consonances between man and nature permeate several verses of this period, including the section *Mediterraneo*.[42]

Indeed, Montale begins *Ossi di seppia* with the ambition of creating a Ligurian counterpart to D'Annunzio's *Alcyone*; he is stimulated by the idea that the marine landscape of the Cinque Terre has not yet found its poet. He takes some of the material that helps him shape this project from D'Annunzio – principally, numerous words that refer to landscape, all of them rare or archaic, all belonging to an elevated poetic diction. Montale refers to D'Annunzio when he needs to heighten the lexical structure, to substitute a common term with one more refined, or of classical derivation. Thus, the vegetable garden of "In limine" – when it requires a keyword to express its function as a privileged place in which the wind "rimena l'ondata della vita", and where one can evade a constricting reality – becomes "un pomario" ("an orchard"), a word with noble antecedents.

In his preface to the *Canti Barocchi* by Lucio Piccolo, Montale explicitly identifies D'Annunzio as an archetype for contemporary Italian poetry, using terms that suggest the basis of his own engagement with the older poet:

> D'Annunzio nella recente tradizione italiana è un poco come Hugo nella sua posteriorità francese, da Baudelaire in giù: è presente in tutti perché ha sperimentato o sfiorato tutte le possibilità linguistiche e prosodiche del nostro tempo. In questo senso non aver appreso nulla da lui sarebbe un pessimo segno.[43]

Montale limits D'Annunzio's influence to aspects of formal invention, arguing that he had performed an irreproducible function in Italy, "perché ha sperimentato o sfiorato tutte le possibilità linguistiche del nostro tempo" ("because he experimented and touched upon all the linguistic and prosodic possibilities of our time"). Previously, D'Annunzio had appeared as a negative comparison in a discussion of Guido Gozzano's poetics:

> Colto, intrinsecamente colto se anche di non eccezionali letture, ottimo conoscitore dei suoi limiti, naturalmente dannunziano, ancor più naturalmente di-

---

blond transparencies rise / and life evaporates as essence. / Bring me the sunflower crazed with light", trans. W. Arrowsmith.

42 See e.g. "Antico, sono ubriacato dalla voce" (OV 52); "Ho sostato talvolta nelle grotte" (OV 54); "Noi non sappiamo quale sortiremo" (OV 56).

43 E. Montale, preface to L. Piccolo, *Canti barocchi e altre liriche* (1956), SM 1905-1911: "In the recent Italian critical tradition, D'Annunzio is treated a little like Hugo is by subsequent French writers, from Baudelaire onward: his influence is present everywhere because he experimented and touched upon all the linguistic and prosodic possibilities of our time. In this sense, not to have learned anything from him would be a terrible sign".

sgustato dal dannunzianesimo, (Gozzano) fu il primo dei poeti del Novecento che riuscisse (com'era necessario e come probabilmente lo fu anche dopo di lui) ad *attraversare D'Annunzio* per approdare a un territorio suo, così come, su scala maggiore, Baudelaire aveva attraversato Hugo per gettare le basi di una nuova poesia.[44]

To reverse the direction of Montale's criticism, to turn it back towards the poet himself rather than toward his subject, implies that a poet speaks to other poets in order to underline that which matters to him. This explains Montale's own sentiments toward D'Annunzio: he was conscious of how much reading D'Annunzio affected his own poetry. The parenthetical insertion in the quoted passage on Gozzano suggests that Montale had anticipated, if not actually suggested, the connections between his work and the poetry composed by the *Vate*. Indeed, the number of references to D'Annunzio reveals a young reader who, attracted by the lexical majesty of the famous poet, tried to imitate him even as he simultaneously engaged in a competition for supremacy.

Yet in the later poems of the *Ossi brevi* we can see a detachment from D'Annunzio's poetics. The Symbolist experience of "panismo" – the abolition of the distance between the I and its object, so called because the word παν refers both to the Greek god of wild nature and poetry, and the word that indicates "everything" – tends in D'Annunzio to coincide with the task of writing poetry. In Montale, however, the two experiences eventually diverge. The separation between nature and the moment of authenticity allows us to understand Montale's subsequent poetics as the "necessità di sguardo disincantato alla realtà frammentaria e disintegrata" ("necessity of a disenchanted gaze on a fragmentary and disintegrated reality") that demands "il rifiuto preliminare dell'immersione acritica nella natura come rifugio, o come giustificazione dell'atonia" ("a preliminary refusal of an acritical immersion in nature as a refuge, or as a justification of weakness").[45] This fundamental change in poetics, which can be traced through the texts written between 1922 and 1924, concerns the passage from a conception of the self as at one with the natural world, to a negative idea of a landscape understood as a net that imprisons the poetic voice.

---

44 E. Montale, "Gozzano, dopo trent'anni" (1951), SM 1279: "Learned, intrinsically learned, even if not by exceptional reading, an excellent connoisseur of his own shortcomings, naturally a D'Annunzian, but even more naturally disgusted by D'Annunzianism, [Gozzano] was the first among the poets of the twentieth century to succeed (as was necessary then, and as was probably so even after him) in moving beyond D'Annunzio to land in his own territory, as, on a larger scale, Baudelaire had passed Hugo to establish the basis of a new poetry".

45 See P.V. Mengaldo, *Da D'Annunzio a Montale*, in *La tradizione del Novecento*, Torino, Bollati Boringhieri, 1996, p. 90.

3. Mixed Metaphors

The Ligurian heritage and D'Annunzio were not the only poets who influenced the young Montale. His early appreciation for French symbolism emerges in the poems written around World War I and is a recurring element in peritextual comments. The testimony of F.R. Leavis recounts that Montale still could, at an advanced age, recite from memory Paul Valéry's "Le cimetière marin", one of the texts that most heavily influenced *Ossi di seppia*.[46] His indebtedness to transalpine poetry is already plainly spelled out in the pages of *Quaderno Genovese*, where he has written down readings of Baudelaire, Rimbaud, Huysmans, Villiers de l'Isle d'Adam, and Rémy de Gourmont.[47] When he reads the *Poèmes Barbares* by Leconte de Lisle, whose Parnassianism made him suspicious, the young poet questioned himself: "La sua poetica è disprezzabile ma la sua arte è unica veramente; un poeta, direi quasi suo malgrado".[48] However, he continues, the future of poetry will not result from such Parnassian verses: "Ma l'avvenire non è per questa via: occorre penetrare le più nascoste voci della natura; e non fotografare!" [49] To grasp nature's most clandestine voices, to enter into harmony with them, one must imitate the protagonist in the *Accordi* series, published by Montale in the journal *Primo Tempo* in 1922 (see chapter 3.5).

---

46 See F.R. Leavis, "Xenia" in E. Montale, *New Poems*, New York, New Direction Books, 1976, p. xxiv: "What makes (Montale's poetry so peculiarly) congenial I can begin to suggest by recalling the occasion when, a couple of years ago, I had the honour, at Milan, to meet Montale. How it was that someone present came to quote 'Le cimetière marin' I can't now remember, but Montale and I found ourselves reciting, in relays, Valéry's poem".

47 Certainly before the war Montale aspired to become a symbolist poet: see the aptly entitled "Canto simbolico", QG AMS 1293; see also QG AMS 1294: "Arthur Rimbaud è del resto, mi son convinto, un poeta straordinario, un colosso" ("Furthermore, Arthur Rimbaud is, I am convinced, an extraordinary poet, a colossus"); in QG AMS 1296, commenting on a book of criticism by Giovanni Papini, Montale invents an irregular superlative to express the extent of his debt to the French poets: "Papini: *La Paga del Sabato*. Sciocchezze, ma buonissimo il capitolo: *Ciò che dobbiamo alla Francia*. Le dobbiamo tutto infatti! Io poi … tuttissimo …" ("Papini: *La Paga del Sabato*. Nonsense, but with a terrific chapter: *Ciò che dobbiamo alla Francia*. In fact, we owe everything to France! And speaking for myself … more than everything …") Eugenio's passion is so marked that Marianna even writes of it to her friends: " … subisce l'influenza dei francesi, molto, Rimbaud, Baudelaire e altri. Già ci ha una passione tale per questi!" ("… he is under the influence of the French, deeply, Rimbaud, Baudelaire, and others. Indeed, he has such a passion for them!") See M. Montale, *Lettere da casa Montale (1908-1938)*, cit., p. 372.

48 E. Montale, QG AMS 1303: "His poetics are despicable, but his art is truly unique; a poet, I'd call him, almost in spite of himself".

49 E. Montale, QG AMS 1304: "However, the future lies not on this path: we need to grasp nature's deepest voices, and not to take pictures!"

The Romantic origins of symbolism are clear to Montale, but this awareness does not prevent him from highlighting the innovative traits of the movement – the musicality of the verse, the centrality of the lyric "I", the unconventionality of its themes.[50] Among the critics, he esteems the Duhamel of *Les poètes et la poésie,* for he conceives of poetry as:

escavazione, sondaggio, penetrazione (creazioni di nuovi rapporti, accostamenti, immagini, analogie). Per lui (ed ha ragione) l'immagine è una *conoscenza* del mondo, che vale quanto quella scientifica, ed ha un carattere grande e quasi religioso. [...] Adora Rimbaud, Baudelaire, Mallarmé etc. che ritiene per grandissimi. Secondo lui il Simbolismo significa non solo una grande scuola letteraria, ma *l'avvento di un nuovo modo di pensare.*[51]

In the second decade of the twentieth century Montale sees in symbolist poetry the advent of a new way of thinking: symbolism is an aesthetic ideal and a hermeneutical instrument as respectable as scientific research. In the same period, T.S. Eliot was also reading Baudelaire in order to assemble the elements of a new poetics. For instance, "the possibility of juxaposition of the matter-of-fact and the fantastic,"[52] whose influence would be revealed in the writing of *The Waste Land.* Eliot and Montale are not alone in drawing from the symbolist experience instructions for composing poetry with attributes of modernity: Sbarbaro, as noted before, but also Dino Campana, whose verses Montale will get to know only after his move to Florence, model their lyric personae on the *promeneur solitaire* of Baudelaire. Sbarbaro walks the *promeneur* towards modernity by crafting a

---

[50] E. Montale, *ibid.*: "Il simbolismo non è che il romanticismo che prende coscienza *artisticamente* di sé. Il romanticismo ebbe ed avrà sempre più una coscienza spirituale di sé stesso; occorre ora che coscientemente si esterni su un'arte individualistica e spregiudicata; col simbolismo si è cominciato. Il romanticismo è insomma una corrente, una rivoluzione *psichica* la cui oggettivazione *cosciente* e *artistica* avviene col Simbolismo. Il primo è dunque un movimento *spirituale*; il secondo un movimento *artistico* figlio del primo". ("Symbolism is just romanticism that is aware of itself *artistically*. Romanticism had and will forever have a spiritual awareness of itself; now we need to give voice consciously to an individualistic, impartial art; with symbolism this process has begun. Romanticism is, in short, a current, a *psychic* revolution whose *conscious, artistic* objectification occurs with Symbolism. Thus, the former is a *spiritual* movement, the latter an *artistic* movement born from the former").

[51] E. Montale, QG AMS 1326: "*excavation, probing, penetration* (creations of new relationships, combinations, images, analogies). For him (and he's right) the image is an *awareness* of the world with a grand, almost religious quality, an awareness worth as much as the scientific one. [...] He adores Rimbaud, Baudelaire, Mallarmé, etc., all of whom he considers tremendous. According to him, Symbolism signifies not only a great literary school but also *the advent of a new way of thinking*". See G. Duhamel, *Les poètes et la poésie*, Paris, Mercure de France, 1912.

[52] See chapter 5.4.

poetic "I" who refuses to conform to the role of the oracle, by creating a character excluded both from human society and from nature; Sbarbaro's lyric "I" represents what Lukács will call the reification of the individual, the commodification of humanity caused by the capitalism that arose from the industrial revolution.[53]

Boine's *Il peccato*, published in 1914, can also be considered a modernist novel: and so it seemed, in fact, to Italo Svevo, who made a parallel between the novelist from Porto Maurizio and his friend Joyce.[54] The plot tells of a provincial young man, tellingly called only by the author's own initial, who falls in love with Maria, a novice in a convent, having heard her sing in church. The ethical and existential doubts of the protagonist are worked out on the page in a dilation of interior time, while the figure of the narrator remains concealed under the direct representation of the thoughts and impressions of the character. Boine's use of a stream of consciousness, similar to the one with which the European modernists were currently experimenting, was unprecedented in Italy, if one excludes the first two novels Svevo had published in semi-clandestine editions.

Montale's modernism takes some cues from these texts: both Boine and Sbarbaro demonstrate how the Ligurian geography can be emblematic of the experience of separation and detachment from the surrounding environment that characterizes the more mature texts of *Ossi di seppia*. By following these examples and by describing his landscape in written form, Montale initially intended to fashion an image of himself as a poet in a territory that already had many sources. The commonplaces in the description of such a landscape, the very terminology he appropriates, are instrumental in constructing the image of an author among authors.

It is symptomatic, therefore, that during the Second World War, Montale, in the middle of a sabbatical from poetry that would later motivate the need for a radical change in his method of writing verses, describes his

---

[53] Sbarbaro's modernism sparks from the self-awareness of the lyric "I", from the recognition of his own discontinuity, his own fissures, his being separated from the phenomenal reality. It would be reductive to read all of Sbarbaro's poems from a Marxist perspective, but there are certainly elements to note in particular texts, *e.g.* the commodification of the body of the prostitute and the subsequent reification of the subject in "Esco dalla lussuria". See C. Sbarbaro, "Esco dalla lussuria", in *Pianissimo* (1914), C. Sbarbaro, *L'opera in versi e in prosa*, eds. G. Lagorio and V. Scheiwiller, Milano, Garzanti, 2016, pp. 25-26.

[54] I. Svevo, letter to E. Montale from Charlton, July 5, 1926: "Ho letto *Il peccato* di Boine. M'ha interessato enormemente. [...] La sua introspezione precorre quella del Joyce. È un'altra cosa ma talvolta ne eguaglia la potenza lirica" ("I read Boine's *Il peccato*. It interested me enormously. [...] His introspection anticipates Joyce's. It's another thing altogether, but at times he matches his lyric potency"). In I. Svevo – E. Montale, *Carteggio*, ed. G. Zampa, Milano, Mondadori 1976, p. 24.

own juvenile production by juxtaposing two different metaphors: one vegetal metaphor, which underscores the fact that the *Ossi* belong to a specific poetic *terroir*, and another metaphor of movement, as if his traversal of a biographically and literarily familiar landscape had required him to set forth on a poetic path that would inevitably bring him to other places.

> Le mie poesie sono funghi nati spontaneamente in un bosco [...] Il bosco ... non era vergine; era stato concimato da molte esperienze e letture. [...] Dovevo inserirmi in una tradizione viva, cioé passare da una porta che era l'unica (in quel momento) per me accessibile.[55]

The poetic tradition of the Ligurian landscape is a gateway for Montale, just as Liguria itself, in so much as it is a place dedicated to Janus, is a gateway between different worlds. The opening of the temple doors, which according to the mythological traditions signals the beginning of a conflict, also suggests a change of status, representing the gateway between adolescence and adulthood. It indicates that one has reached poetic and intellectual maturity. It marks the beginning of a new time to be consumed in a new space.

Montale in his later age tends to minimize the influences received from preexisting traditions, expressing reservations about the work of Sbarbaro, calling Boine "a half-poet", going so far as to claim he forgot D'Annunzio:[56] but the echoes of the Ligurian writers and of D'Annunzio will reverberate at length in the poetic practice of Montale. We could interpret Montale's declarations of unfamiliarity as a further confirmation of his arrival at a modernist poiesis:

> Modernists do not discard their predecessors – no matter how vociferously they claim to do so, careful study reveals ongoing interaction with the precursor

---

[55] E. Montale, "Dovevo inserirmi in una tradizione viva" (1955), AMS 1539: "My poems are mushrooms born spontaneously in a wood. [...] The wood ... was not untouched; it had been fertilized by many experiences and readings. [...] I had to insert myself into a living tradition, to pass through a door that was the only one (in that moment) accessible to me".

[56] See E. Montale, "Intervista immaginaria" (1946), AMS 1477: "Ammirai la fedeltà e l'arte di Sbarbaro, ma Boine era poeta a metà e Ceccardo, che lo era per intero, non si rese mai conto dei propri mezzi" ("I admired the fidelity and the art of Sbarbaro, but Boine was a half-poet and Ceccardo, who was a whole one, never realized his own means"). In a 1971 review of a book of criticism about D'Annunzio for the «Corriere della Sera», Montale asserts to have "almost forgotten" D'Annunzio's work: "Se invece questo libro cadesse tra le mani di chi abbia poca o punta dimestichezza con le altre opere del poeta o le avesse, com'è il mio caso, quasi dimenticate, allora forse l'impressione sarebbe diversa" ("If instead this book had fallen into the hands of one who had little to no familiarity with the poet's other works or who had, as I did, almost forgotten them, then perhaps the impression would be different"). See E. Montale, "Variazione 31", PR 608.

they are actively denying – rather they unite aspects of each of the theories in their own approaches toward literature.[57]

The *Ossi di seppia* are, therefore, an account of the experience of passing through a tradition, of passing from one geographical location to another, from one time to another, from one mode of poetry – tied to experiences and Romantic theories – to another one that would be new, syncretic, modern. We see in the *Ossi* the passage from a desired symbolic identification of the "I" with nature to the realization that such an identification is no longer possible – the very natural process of growing up, of entering adulthood, comes to signify the inachievability of the desire.

In the young Montale, the poet of "Meriggiare", of *Accordi*, of "Riviere" and "Quasi una fantasia", the sentiment of uniformity and harmony with the natural element is deliberately sought after; but "Fine dell'infanzia" and the suite *Mediterraneo* recount the experience of his passage through the tradition. Eventually, the texts added to the second edition of the book emphasize a modern lyric "I", self-consciously out of place and contradictory, but inexorably marching toward the new tradition of modernity. The immobile motion of "Arsenio" brings this heteronymous representation of Montale's lyric "I" all the way to England, to be published in T.S. Eliot's «*Criterion*».

4. Infinite Noon

One of the central motifs of Montale's early poetry, which goes hand in hand with the desire for communion with nature, is the experience of a suspension of time, an "eternal instant" that signals the occurrence of cosmic contact, or in his words, nirvana. The apathy of the summer day is certainly a real experience that Montale lived during his vacations in Monterosso, as we read in a letter to Francesco Meriano written in the late summer of 1919:

> Questi pomeriggi in Riviera sono magici ma terribili col loro nirvana disgregante: sole sole sole e un mare immenso che bolle. Si diventa una forza qualunque del cosmo; qualche cosa come a leggere i libri di Lafcadio Hearn.[58]

---

[57] See M.A. Gillies, *Henri Bergson and British Modernism*, Montreal, McGill-Queen's University Press, 1996, p. 41.

[58] E. Montale, in F. Meriano, *Arte e vita*, cit., p. 152: "These afternoons in the Riviera are magical but terrible with their destructive nirvana: sun sun sun and an immense sea that boils. One becomes some kind of cosmic force; something similar to reading the books of Lafcadio Hearn".

The idea of natural instruments, sun and sea, that operate to dissolve the lyric "I" into "some kind of cosmic force" is often depicted in the verses of this period. The earliest poem to be included in the eponymous section of *Ossi di seppia*, "Meriggiare pallido e assorto", is a masterpiece of technical craft begun by Montale as early as 1916, with its final stanza revised in 1922.[59] While not the first of his poems to appear in print, it is a convenient starting point for an analysis of the interaction between poetic and natural sources in the early *Ossi*: "Meriggiare" provides a model that shows how Montale uses and revises the vocabulary and technical instruments (rhyme, assonance, onomatopoeia) of the Italian tradition at the beginning of his poetic career, as well as his approach to the peculiar landscape in which *Ossi di seppia* is located.[60]

The poem describes the experience of spending a lonely, muggy afternoon in the Cinque Terre, and introduces many of the elements that constitute Montale's landscapes:

> Meriggiare pallido e assorto
> presso un rovente muro d'orto,
> ascoltare tra i pruni e gli sterpi
> schiocchi di merli, frusci di serpi.
>
> Nelle crepe del suolo o su la veccia
> spiar le file di rosse formiche
> ch'ora si rompono ed ora s'intrecciano
> a sommo di minuscole biche.
>
> Osservare tra frondi il palpitare
> lontano di scaglie di mare
> mentre si levano tremuli scricchi
> di cicale dai calvi picchi.
>
> E andando nel sole che abbaglia
> sentire con triste meraviglia
> com'è tutta la vita e il suo travaglio
> in questo seguitare una muraglia
> che ha in cima cocci aguzzi di bottiglia.[61]

---

59 See OV 870.

60 See E. Pasquini, *La memoria culturale nella poesia di Eugenio Montale*, Modena, Mucchi, 1991, pp. 20-22; see also P.V. Mengaldo, *La tradizione del Novecento*, Torino, Bollati Boringhieri, 1996, p. 54.

61 OV 28: "To laze at noon, pale and thoughtful, / by a blazing garden wall; to listen, / in brambles and brake, to blackbirds / scolding, the snake's rustle. // To gaze at the cracked

The stone wall ("muro", l. 2, and then "muraglia", l. 16) built by local masons without any cement, so typical of the region's countryside, performs two different tasks: it encloses private property (the "orto", or vegetable garden, l. 2) and, by working as a containment wall, levels the steep ground, making it fertile and cultivable. The poem's setting, during the hours of meridian heat – a motif present in the Mediterranean tradition from classical antiquity – represents a time of day propitious for poetry: it is an instant in which time, miraculously, seems to stand still (ll. 1-2 and l. 13).[62]

Other characteristic details abound: the discreet presence of emblematic animals heard ("merli", "serpi", l. 4, "cicale", l. 12) and seen ("formiche", l. 6); the eye observing the sea from an elevated point of view; the "triste meraviglia" (l. 14) perceived in the act of walking beside the wall, which is here a prohibitive and exclusionary figure crowned by shards of glass ("cocci di bottiglia", l. 17). Such verses, at first glance, seem filled with elements taken from the phenomenal landscape, as if the landscape itself functioned as inspiration and yielded to its representation.

In a note roughly contemporary to the first draft of the poem included in the *Quaderno Genovese* we read a definition of what he calls "impressionistic poetry:"

> *Linee di una poesia impressionistica* – Fusione completa, inscindibile, di psicologia e *paesismo* (non-io, insomma), come nella vita ci avviene sempre. La natura dev'essere poi trasformata, sezionata, capovolta magari; colta cioè negli elementi soli che operano sulla sensibilità poetica, all'atto della pura intuizione. È l'occhio freddo che abbraccia e fotografa tutto; il momento fantastico-lirico sceglie fra la realtà, trasforma e assimila. Poesia insomma che colga della nostra vita il *momento*, considerato nella esistenza nostra come sola realtà semplice irredutibile e inconvertibile. Non-io visto a traverso lo specchio prismatico dell'io. Poesia doppia, matrimonio della fantasia con la materia (?) esterna. Il ritmo assecondi la cre-

---

earth, the leaves / of vetch, to spy the red ants filing past, / breaking, then twining, massing / at the tips of the tiny sheaves. // To peer through leaves at the sea, / scale on scale, pulsing in the distance, / while the cicada's quivering cry shrills from naked peaks. // And then, walking out, dazed with light, / to sense with sad wonder / how all of life and its hard travail / is in this trudging along a wall spiked / with jagged shards of broken bottles", trans. W. Arrowsmith.

62 For an inclusive approach to the theme of the meridian hour, see F. Giusti, *Il meriggio e la poesia. L'ora meridiana nella poesia italiana della prima metà del Novecento*, «Otto/Novecento», Anno XXIX, n. 2, maggio/agosto 2005, pp. 161-169. A detailed analysis of D'Annunzio's "Meriggio" as a pre-text for Montale's "Meriggiare pallido e assorto ..." is in C. Ott, *Torso-Göttin Sprache. Eugenio Montales Poetik im Medium seiner Lyrik*, Heidelberg, Universitätsverlag Winter, 2003, pp. 67-82.

azione *nervosamente*: non trascurare il suono di una lettera. Le parole dipingano e suggeriscano: diano l'idea. La musica dia il sentimento.[63]

Here, "impressionistic poetry" derives from the fusion, or the "marriage", between external reality (photographed by the "eye") and the psychology of the 'I.' The signifiers, following symbolistic dictates, must capture the idea, while the sound of the words themselves must reproduce the sentiment. The word "*nervosamente*", italicized in the original, returns to the sonorous dissonances of Débussy's music, which Montale knew and appreciated; we note how the tone of Montale's prose never questions the possibility of knowing the world and gathering it into language in its "realtà semplice irredutibile e inconvertibile". To build an impressionistic text it is sufficient, finally, to refer to external materiality ("la materia esterna") and the prismatic mirror of the self ("specchio prismatico dell'io"). Yet, symbolistic overtones notwithstanding, the intuition of the young poet looks further ahead. The passage implies that Montale was conscious of how the representation of nature in poetry was not a mimetic operation, but the result of a process. The eye, as though it were a scientific instrument, photographs an external object, but it is the psychology of the individual mind (that "specchio prismatico dell'io") that transforms, dissects, and converts this material into a work of art.

Only two years earlier, Georg Simmel had published his seminal essay, *Die Philosophie der Landschaft,* in the German review, «Die Güldenkammer», though Montale probably did not know it, since he did not know German, and the journal itself had a limited circulation. In it, Simmel re-conceived the nexus between self and space, theorizing a separation between nature, "the infinite interconnectedness of objects, the uninterrupted creation and destruction of forms, the flowing unity of an event that finds expression in the continuity of temporal and spatial existence" [64] – i.e., the phenomenal

[63] E. MONTALE, QG AMS 1298: "*Outlines of impressionistic poetry*: Complete, inextricable fusion of psychology and *paesismo* (the non-self, in short), as often occurs in life. Nature must then be transformed, dissected, possibly even upturned; cultivated, that is, only in those elements that operate on the poetic sensibility, in the act of pure intuition. It is a dispassionate eye that embraces and photographs all; it chooses the fantastic-lyrical moment from reality, transforms and assimilates. Poetry, in sum, that gathers from our life the *moment*, considered the only simple, irreducible, inconvertible reality in our existence. The non-self seen through the prismatic mirror of the self. Double poetry, the marriage of the imagination with external materiality (?). Rhythm should accompany creation *nervously*: do not neglect the sound of a letter. Words should paint and suggest: they should give an idea. Music should give the sentiment". On the consonance between such approach and the post-symbolist poetry of the Group de l'Abbaye, see the notes by Laura Barile in the original edition of the book, p. 128 and pp. 162-163.

[64] G. SIMMEL, *Die Philosophie der Landschaft*, «Die Güldenkammer», vol. 3 issue 2, 1913;

world – and landscape, understood as a construction of the individual gaze. Landscape refers both to the aesthetic process of creation as well as its final product, the work of art, since the two mutually constitute one another: "Nature, which in its deep being and meaning knows nothing of individuality, is transfigured into an individuated 'landscape' by the human gaze that divides things up and forms the separated parts into specific unities".[65] The concepts expressed by the German philosopher and the Italian poet-to-be are intriguingly similar. Both writers believe that the human gaze creates the work of art by transfiguring nature into an individual landscape, and they both emphasize the unity or wholeness of nature as phenomenal matter: "To talk of 'a piece of nature' is in fact a self-contradiction. Nature is not composed of pieces – it is the unity of a whole. The instant anything is parceled out from this wholeness, it is no longer nature pure and simple since this whole can be 'nature' only within that unbounded unity, only as a wave within that total flux".[66] According to Simmel, the activity of the human gaze transforms nature into a landscape, which is also the process of creating the work of art and consequently becomes the work of art itself; the eye embraces the totality of the real and, according to Montale, transforms it, dissects it, assimilates it, to create poetry.

"Meriggiare" unfolds just such a process. The poem follows an observing eye through numerous verbs linked to sight, but it does not have an 'I', that is, a poetic subject: all the verbs that should syntactically refer to a subject ("meriggiare" in its meaning of "to spend the meridian hours", l. 1, "ascoltare", l. 3, "spiare", l. 6, "osservare", l. 9, "andando", l. 13, "seguitare", l. 13) are in the infinitive mood or, in one occurrence, in the gerund. Infinitive and gerund, in English as well as in Italian, are modes that do not have, and do not need, a subject: the "I" is erased, annulled into the landscape and made one with it. The use of the infinitive and the consequent suppression of the first person pronoun, which creates an annihilation of the self within the landscape, a veritable vanishing act that reverberates in different parts of the *Ossi*, could then signal a yearning desire for a communion with nature.

Yet, nature is not the only source for this poem, which shares strong ties with the Italian poetic tradition in terms of its form and vocabulary. Its use of the infinitive recalls Giacomo Leopardi's most famous *idillio*, aptly

---

English translation by J. Bleicher, *The Philosophy of Landscape*, «Theory, Culture & Society», vol. 24 (7-8) 2007, pp. 20-29. The quote is from p. 21.

65 *Ibid.*, p. 22.

66 *Ibid.*, p. 21.

entitled "L'infinito", which describes a subject whose gaze over the sea is partially impeded by a hedge. It is only because of such impediment that the mind is capable of gazing over "unending spaces and superhuman silences" and, through the power of imagination, seems almost to reach this realm before the subject is shipwrecked, at the very end, in a sea that is both an actual sea and the sea of memory. The concluding hendecasyllable, probably the most famous in all Italian poetry, has as its subject a verb in the infinite tense: "E naufragar m'è dolce in questo mare" ("To shipwreck in this sea is sweet to me"). Montale consciously imitates and surpasses Leopardi's strategic play on a tradition of poetic formalism: while "L'infinito" extends the sonnet with an extra line, underscoring Leopardi's intention of *not* writing a sonnet, Montale writes a seventeen-line poem (formally, a *sonetto caudato* with an extra line) in variable meter. There are certainly differences: in Leopardi's poem the limit points towards infinity, but in Montale's the infinite returns to the limit, to the insurmountable wall. Yet there are also similarities: landscape, here as there, is an instrument for shaping a poetic voice, a vehicle for inserting oneself into a poetic tradition. For Leopardi, lyric poetry presupposed an identity of subject and object; the young Montale, in a passage shortly after the one just mentioned, describes the function of the author, assuming a communion of the poet, the work of art, and the reader:

> Comunione coll'opera d'arte è comunione coll'artista creatore; sdoppiamento; a volte fusione completa con lui; annullamento dunque della propria personalità. / / È la gioia di non essere più; la gioia anzi di essere un altro! [67]

This fantasy of fusion and communion, in which poet and reader are one, demands the erasure of one subjectivity into another, and it is a similar co-mingling of poet into landscape that Montale envisions.

Leopardi is not the only reference to a poetic tradition: further analysis reveals concealed literary sources converging in this formally formidable text. The opening verb in the infinitive tense, "meriggiare", is a poetic neologism that had been used by three of the poets that Montale was reading at the time: Giovanni Boine, Giovanni Pascoli, and Gabriele D'Annunzio, and can also be found in one of the most famous operas by Giuseppe Verdi, *L'Otello*.[68] Similarly, the verb "palpitare", usually reserved to describe

---

[67] E. MONTALE, QG AMS 1291: "Communion with the work of art is communion with the artist-creator; doubling; at times complete fusion with him; erasure, therefore, of one's own personality. / / It is the joy of no longer existing; the joy, rather, of existing as another!"

[68] G. BOINE, *Il peccato, Plausi e Botte, Frantumi, Altri scritti*, ed. D. Puccini, ed., Milano, Garzanti, 1983, p. 298: "È così bello a volte meriggiare, all'ombra di un carrubo in faccia al mare!"

the rhythmic pulse of the heart, had already been used by D'Annunzio to define the movement of the sea. "Cocci di bottiglia", the shards of glass that conclude the text, are mentioned both in *La signorina Felicita* by Guido Gozzano and in *I sobborghi* by Govoni.[69] There are different plausible derivations, echoes, borrowings; one aspect of Montale's modernity, even at this early stage, is that his linguistic borrowings add different, accumulating layers of meaning, in which one source does not exclude another. Such a consideration of Montale's literary antecedents modifies our understanding of the poem's aesthetic process. What had appeared to be a seamless, unmediated marriage between "the photographic eye" looking at the natural world, and the "prismatic mirror of the I", is now also revealed to be a re-presentation of the literary tradition. Literary and naturalistic landscapes coalesce.

In this integration of literary representation and history, "Meriggiare" is often taken as an example of Montale's poetics. But considering the dates of composition of the poem's different parts reveals a difference, signaling a distinct transition, an early and a later poetic trajectory. The text is therefore also exemplary of Montale's transformation into a modernist poet. Revised in 1922, the last stanza of "Meriggiare" has a different tone from the previous ones and introduces a new intellectual direction, disrupting the synergy between the natural world and the poetic self. It begins with a gerund which, contrary to the infinitive, is a mood indicating a progression in time. While time in the infinitive is, by definition, infinite, the gerund puts the accent on the duration of the action it indicates, underscoring the experience of temporality. Furthermore, while the previous stanzas are solely describing the space, or, to use Simmel's words, transfiguring nature into an individuated landscape by virtue of the human gaze, the last stanza introduces a metaphor in the third line that explodes the closed form of the quatrain by inserting a dissonance with the off-rhyme *travaglio.* The third line divides the voice from the landscape, breaking the unity of self and nature. The metaphor, introduced by "com'è", locates human life at odds with the natural world and builds on the theme of rupture presented by the blinding sun that erases the lingering gaze of the previous stanzas.

("It is so beautiful at times to laze in the afternoon, in the shadow of a carob tree, in frot of the sea!"). Arrigo Boito, *Otello*, act II, scene I: "È suo costume / girsene a meriggiar tra quelle fronde / con la consorte mia". Gabriele D'Annunzio uses it twice. See G. Ioli, *Frantumi e rottami: note su Boine e Montale*, in *La liguria di Montale*, Savona, Sabatelli 1996, pp. 147-58; P.V. Mengaldo, *La tradizione del Novecento. Da D'Annunzio a Montale*, Torino, Bollati Boringhieri, 1996, pp. 15-115; E. Montale, *Ossi di seppia*, ed. T. Arvigo, Roma, Carocci, 2001, p. 87.

69 See L. Blasucci, *Gli oggetti di Montale*, Bologna, il Mulino, 2002, p. 58.

This inability to see the physical world leads to an apprehension of the *triste meraviglia*, the sad awareness of the disconnection between the human condition and the phenomenal world. The new direction signaled by the revision of the fourth stanza points to a profound shift in Montale's poetics: the poetic persona no longer yearns for communion with the landscape but is instead painfully aware of his separation from it. The wall, whose glass shards are a savage reminder of the fate awaiting those who trespass its boundary, excludes him. The difference between the three quatrains and the last stanza, despite the apparent similarity of form, exemplifies the poetic chasm between the ur-Montale and the modernist author of *Ossi di seppia*.

Looking back at his own literary development after WWII, Montale identifies "Meriggiare" as an important node in the relationship between poetry and landscape:

> Nel '16 avevo già composto il primo frammento *tout entier à sa proie attaché:* Meriggiare pallido e assorto (che modificai più tardi nella strofa finale). La preda era, s'intende, il mio paesaggio.[70]

Montale draws from Racine to highlight poetry's charged pursuit of landscape as its ostensible object. In *Phèdre* the eponymous heroine uses the phrase "Toute entière ..." to describe Venus's vendetta: of course such language describes her own internal agony. In echoing the imagery of predator and prey to describe the evolution of the poetics of *Ossi di seppia* Montale hints at his own quest for a poetic identity, which in turn is defined by its quest for a representation of landscape. In the gap between the first three stanzas and the fourth one, we glimpse the shift from a young and accomplished, but fundamentally derivative, poetic mode, to a philosophically grounded, innovative approach to poetic representation.

5. From a "vena torbida" to a "venatura più limpida": Retracing a poetic transformation

The significance of Montale's revision of "Meriggiare" in 1922 brings us back to the significance of chronology in reading this work. The po-

[70] E. Montale, "Intenzioni (Intervista immaginaria)" SM 1478: "In 1916, I had already composed the first fragment completely attached to its prey: "To laze at noon, pale and thoughtful", which I would modify later in the final stanza". By "its prey", I meant, obviously, my landscape".

ems in *Ossi di seppia* are inconspicuously out of chronological order: "In limine", written in 1924, opens the collection, while "Riviere", written in 1920, closes it. Montale himself noted that, "La poesia più antica del libro – "Meriggiare ecc." – è del 1916; la più recente – "Arsenio" – del 1927. La disposizione delle liriche è approssimativamente cronologica solo in qualche gruppo; ma i vari gruppi devono intendersi paralleli".[71] Such comments, which seek to erase any diachronic difference between the poems, added to the confusion created by the false declarations that Montale liked to disseminate in order to confound his readers when he deemed them too curious.[72] This has led to a neglect of the significant variance between early and late poems, as readers have followed Montale's lead in emphasizing thematic grouping over poetic evolution over time. To be sure, such a compelling refusal of a linear historical narration can be seen as a feature of Montale's approach to a modernist poiesis: while the early suite *Accordi* expressed the feelings and the transformations of its female protagonist in a progressive narration, all sections in the *Ossi* reject linear ideas of time and narration.[73] In any case, it is clear that Montale organized the contents of *Ossi di seppia* not according to a chronological and systematic order, but through the coagulation of themes and opportune juxtapositions. The collection is structured like a symphony, in thematic clusters, and was intended to be read as such: there is an introduction, the establishment of a theme, repetition and variation of a theme, then the introduction of different themes, the fusion of different themes, and a final culmination.

---

[71] E. Montale, note to the third edition of the *Ossi di seppia*, Lanciano, Carabba, 1931: "The oldest poem in the book – *Meriggiare* etc – is from 1916; the most recent – *Arsenio* – is from 1927. The disposition of the lyrics is approximately chronological only in some groups; but the various groups are intended to be parallel to each other".

[72] For example, apropos of the poem that concludes *Ossi di seppia*, "Riviere" (OV 99), Montale declared to Rosanna Bettarini: "Quanto agli *Ossi*, "Riviere" è senza dubbio tra le ultime. Doveva essere la *summa* o il congedo di tutto il resto. Data 1924", ("About the *Ossi*, "Riviere" is certainly among the last ones. It was intended as the *summa*, or envoy, for the whole book. Date: 1924"). Letter from E. Montale to R. Bettarini dated Feb. 1, 1980, in R. Bettarini, *Scritti montaliani*, Firenze, Le Lettere, 2009, p.180. We know instead, from documents and other declarations, that it was written in March, 1920 (see OV 892). Similarly, in a letter to Claire Huffmann dated April 21, 1978, Montale declared that "Quasi tutti i 'Mottetti' sono del '20": while the documents and the biographical events recounted in the texts confirm that the series has been written after 1930 (C. Huffmann, *Montale, Eliot and the Poetic Object*, in Ead., *Montale and the Occasions of Poetry*, Princeton, Princeton University Press, 1983, p. 81 note 17; see also OV 903-916).

[73] See J. Logenback, *Modernist Poetics of History*, Princeton, Princeton University Press, 1987. For a problematization of the Modernist notions of time, history and myth see also P. Sica, *Modernist Forms of Rejuvenation: Eugenio Montale and T.S. Eliot*, Firenze, Olschki, 2003, pp. 4 *et passim*, and the bibliography there presented.

However, to understand the evolution of Montale's thought diachronically, to trace the emergence of a new poetic voice within the book, we need to reconstruct the chronology of the poems in the *Ossi*.

While Montale's comments direct the reader to think of the 1925 *Ossi* in terms of its groupings, the distribution of the texts in the various sections of the first edition makes for some rather dissonant associations that are better understood by recreating the chronological order in which the poems were written. For example, "I limoni", a poem written in 1922 that contains a first intimation of contingentist philosophy (the "anello che non tiene"), opens the section *Movimenti,* but is immediately followed by "Corno inglese", a poem from 1916, the only one accepted from the early suite *Accordi,* clearly inspired by an earlier phase of thought. Similarly, "Fine dell'infanzia", written in early 1924, precedes the triptych "L'agave sullo scoglio", which dates from 1922 and can also be ascribed to an earlier poetics. The 1928 edition of the book further complicates the situation: the sub-section *Altri versi,* written in 1926, is interpolated between *Versi a Camillo Sbarbaro* (late-1923 to early-1924) and the subsection *Sarcofaghi* (second half of 1923). In the third edition (Carabba 1931), the same subsection *Altri versi* is moved to become the conclusion of the section *Movimenti* with the clear intention of creating a thematic connection (or a reprise, to use a musical term) between this section and the subsequent one entitled *Ossi di seppia.* But the two poems that constitute *Altri versi,* wedged between "Sarcofaghi" and "Non chiederci la parola ..." effect a further temporal jump.

One final example of such chronological and poetic dissonance is worth considering: the brief cycle inspired by Paola Nicoli, including "Crisalide", "Marezzo" and "Casa sul mare", written in the summer of 1924, is inserted in the section *Meriggi e ombre* between "Arsenio" and "I morti", poems that were written in summer 1927 and 1926 respectively, and that spring from a different source.[74] While the transformation of Montale's poetics has been observed in the differences between the first and the second edition of *Ossi di seppia,* as Montale added new poems, attention to the diacronical strata of the poems included in the first edition already signals a change.

Thus, after "Meriggiare", which contains traces of Montale's shifting poetics within its textual strata, we should consider the *Accordi,* a series of seven poems that represent the earliest published work of the young Mon-

[74] Luperini's emphasis on "Arsenio" as an indispensable preamble to the poems that follow, because it introduces a landscape where renunciation and the ethical decision derive from the responsibility and choice of the subject, is only possible because "Arsenio" represents the culmination of a process of poetic transformation that is already evident in the poems from 1924. See R. Luperini, *Montale e l'allegoria moderna*, Napoli, Liguori, 2012, p. 21.

tale, appearing in the second issue of *Primo Tempo* (in June 1922) together with "Riviere". In the 1925 edition of *Ossi di seppia,* Montale includes only one of these very early poems ("Corno inglese") while choosing "Riviere" to be the final poem of the volume; the other texts ("Violini", "Violoncelli", "Contrabbasso", "Flauti-Fagotto", "Oboe", "Ottoni") would remain forgotten until their "rediscovery" by Giacinto Spagnoletti, who would publish them in October 1960 in *Espresso-mese.*[75] When asked about the chronology of the poems, Montale refused to reveal a precise date; but in doing so, he reveals an important detail about the poem that concludes the *Ossi:*

> [...] con assoluta precisione non saprei dare una data a quelle poesie [di *Accordi*]: sono certamente posteriori al primo vero e proprio *Osso* ("Meriggiare", del '16), ma assai anteriori a "Riviere" (marzo 1920), poesia riassuntiva dei miei Juvenilia, da me inserita negli *Ossi,* sebbene vi stia a disagio (è una sintesi scritta prima dell'analisi!).[76]

Montale locates the *Accordi* between the poetic moments framed by the first draft of "Meriggiare" and "Riviere", but is also conscious that the latter poem stands uncomfortably as the concluding poem of the 1925 *Ossi.* Written in 1920 as a synthesis of the "Ossi brevi", "Riviere" sits awkwardly as the conclusion of the book published in 1925. Here, Montale reveals a self-conscious change in poetics, which takes place after "Riviere" (understood as an emblem of his juvenilia) but before the publication of the book, that is, between 1920 and 1925, a period of great interest for modern Italian literature in general.[77] To return to the *Accordi* and examine Montale's decision to include only "Corno inglese" with "Riviere" in the first *Ossi* sheds light on the nature of this change.

The title *Accordi* refers to music (meaning "chords"), and also implies texts in "agreement", in "accordance" with the natural element. The subtitle, *Sensi e fantasmi di una adolescente*, specifies that the lyric "I" does not correspond to the I of the writer, but partakes of the tradition of dramat-

---

[75] See OV 864 *et passim.*

[76] E. Montale, letter to Giacinto Spagnoletti. Related by G. Spagnoletti, *Preistoria di Montale*, in *Omaggio a Montale*, Milano, Mondadori, 1966, p. 121: "I would not be able to date these poems [of "Accordi"] with absolute precision: they certainly postdate the first true and proper *Osso* (*Meriggiare*, 1916), but are somewhat earlier than *Riviere* (March 1920), a poem that sums up my Juvenalia and that I inserted into *Ossi*, even if it is uncomfortable there (it is a synthesis written before an analysis!)".

[77] See R. Ceserani, *Italy and Modernity: Peculiarities and Contradictions*, in *Italian Modernism: Italian Culture between Decadentism and Avant-Garde*, eds. M. Moroni and L. Somigli, Toronto, University of Toronto Press, 2014, pp. 35-62: 51 *et passim.*

ic monologue derived from Browning and coincidentally explored in the same span of years by both Eliot and Pound. The series begins with *Violini*, in which an unnamed Adolescent using a vocabulary heavily influenced by Pascoli ("strade erbite", "balestrucci") laments the excessive variety of choices that her youth offers: "Gioventù troppe strade / distendi innanzi alle pupille / mie smarrite", ("Youth, too many roads / you display in front of my / hesitant eyes"). We are told that she is awaiting a miracle:

Sono qui nell'attesa di un prodigio
e le mani mi chiudo nelle mani.
Forse è in questa incertezza,
mattino che trabocchi
dal cielo,
la più vera ricchezza e tu ne innimbi
tutto che tocchi! [78]

This scene of expectation with the promise of a "prodigio" will be repeated many times in Montale's poetry, most famously during Arsenio's descent. But here, unlike in later poems, the expectation is fulfilled. As soon as she has finished praying ("le mani mi chiudo nelle mani"), she realizes that true richness is to be found in her youth and in its potential. The link between a state of mind and the elements of the natural world is highlighted by the rhymes (incertezza : ricchezza, trabocchi : tocchi). When the prodigy occurs, it is an "accordo", a consonance with nature:

Occhi corolle s'aprono
in me – chissà? – o nel suolo:
tutto vaneggia e nella luce nuova
volere non so più né disvolere.[79]

These lines conjoin eyes and flowers, the "I" and the soil, as the new light of dawn paradoxically confuses the will of the subject. The expected miracle consists in such state of perfect communion with the natural world:

Solo
m'è dato nel miracolo del giorno,
o cuore fatto muto,

[78] OV 765, ll. 10-16: "I'm here waiting for a prodigy / and the hands I fold in my hands. / Perhaps it is in this uncertainty, / oh morning overflowing / from the sky, / the real richness and you overcloud / everything you touch!".

[79] *Ibid.*, ll. 17-20: "Eyes petals open / in me – who knows? – or on the ground: / everything wanders and in the new light / I'm no longer able / to want or want not".

scordare gioie o crucci,
ed offrirti alla vita
tra un mulinare arguto
di balestrucci! [80]

Dawn itself is miraculous; in this instant, the protagonist is in perfect harmony with the world. Like the protagonists of D'Annunzio's "La pioggia nel pineto", she becomes one with the natural elements surrounding her.

A similar move occurs in the second poem of the series, entitled *Violoncelli*, where the instruments enact an explicit prosopopoeia: music itself (the music of Débussy as well as the music of the words in the text) addresses the unnamed adolescent on behalf of Love, convincing her to transcend her earthly form and attain the perfect status of cosmic harmony:

La tua forma
più vera non capisce ormai nei limiti
della carne: t'è forza di confonderti
con altre vite e riplasmarti tutta
in un ritmo di gioia; la tua scorza
non t'appartiene più. Sarai
rifatta dall'oblio, distrutta dal ricordo,
creatura d'un attimo. E saprai
i paradisi ambigui dove manca
ogni esistenza: seguici nel Centro
delle parvenze: (ti rivuole il Niente!) [81]

The chiasm – "rifatta dall'oblio, distrutta dal ricordo" (l. 19) – is highlighted by the metrics of the *verso martelliano* that slows down the rhythm in this hendecasyllabic poem (and which reverberates with l. 3, a *martelliano sdrucciolo,* l. 5, as well as l. 10). In this verse, nouns and verbs seem interchanged: we might expect that it is oblivion ("oblio") that destroys, while remembrance ("ricordo") remakes, rather than the opposite. But here, at the "Centro / delle parvenze", we find a nothingness ("il Niente") that is everything, an ambiguous paradise where the erasure of the real con-

---

[80] *Ibid.*, ll. 21-27: "Only in the miracle of the day, / heart made mute / I can forget good fortune and sorrows, / and I can offer you to life / in a dawning pointed with swallows!".

[81] OV 766, ll. 13-23: "Your truest form / is not contained by the limits / of the flesh: you are forced to confuse / with other lives and remould / in a joyful rhytm; your former shell / does not belong to you anymore. You will be / redone by oblivion, consumed by remembrance, / creature of a moment. And you will know / the ambiguous paradises where every existence / is lacking: follow us to the Center / of resemblances: (you are desired by Nothingness!)".

strains the "I" to abandon her mortal body in order to merge with other lives and to be reshaped.

And once more a miracle occurs, a moment in which time is suspended; this is the occasion when mere appearances dissolve and the confusion of vision and the numbing of the senses is followed by the con-fusion – the merging – with nature itself, as we see in "Oboe", the fifth poem in the series:

> Ci son ore rare
> che ogni apparenza dintorno vacilla s'umilia scompare,
> come le stinte
> quinte
> d'un boccascena, ad atto finito, tra il parapiglia.
>
> I sensi sono intorpiditi,
> il minuto si piace di sé;
> e nasce nei nostri occhi un po' stupiti
> un sorriso senza perché.[82]

"Oboe" explicitly captures the moment of simple, irreducible, and inconvertible existence. These are the "ore rare" in which appearances vacillate, are humiliated (in the etymological sense of "disappearing into the ground"), and vanish. The metaphor that compares the landscape to a theater looks ahead to a similar image in "Forse un mattino ..." (written in July 1923). However, while the early poem confidently asserts the actuality of getting beyond appearances, the later one begins with "Maybe ..." and shrouds in doubt the accomplishment of the miracle. And if the vanishing of appearances is welcomed here by a smile, the emptiness of the world is approached there with terror: "Vedrò [...] / il nulla alle mie spalle, il vuoto dietro / di me, con un terrore di ubriaco".

This intellectual gap between the early and the late poems, which registers the difference between a late symbolist approach and a later descent into modernist alienation, is already evident within the series *Accordi*. Looking back in 1925, Montale would choose only "Corno inglese" out of the seven poems to be included in *Ossi di seppia*, for its proximity to the emotions of a later poem like "Forse un mattino ...". In a letter addressed to Giacinto Spagnoletti after the "rediscovery" of the series, Montale commented on the reason why only one specific text could be recovered:

---

82 OV 770: "There are infrequent hours / when all apparences around vacillate humble disappear, / like the faded / side scenes / of a proscenium, after the end of the act, in the confusion. // The senses are numb, / the moment likes itself; / and a smile without a reason / is born in our marveled eyes".

Il *Corno inglese* era l'unica della serie che potesse staccarsi dal ciclo: del quale mi dispiaceva, e tuttora mi dispiace, il senso generale e anche l'ingenua pretesa di imitare gli strumenti musicali (a parte quel po' di amido che vi si avverte qua e là). Devo dunque concludere che nel mio giovanile château d'eaux (così definì Lorenzo Montano la mia poesia) accanto a una vena più torbida, o addirittura *dentro* quella vena, si facesse strada assai per tempo la venatura più magra, ma più limpida degli *Ossi*.[83]

What separates "Corno inglese" from the other poems, according to Montale, is its disconnection from the "senso generale" – that is, the representation of an immersion in a broad cosmic harmony. He locates the source of a new inspiration in this early poem, using a metaphor derived from the landscape: the image of a murky spring that hides a purer strain within ("accanto a una vena più torbida, o addirittura *dentro* quella vena, si f[a] strada ... la venatura più magra, ma più limpida degli *ossi*"). This metaphor describes the significance of "Corno inglese" for the *Ossi* as a whole, as it is the only text of the series that does not chronicle a successful process of assimilation with the surrounding space, but rather an unsatisfied desire for it. The dense texture of sonorous consonants reveals a stronger technique than that of the excluded texts, but this is not why it finds its place in the *Ossi*. The Ligurian landscape that subtends these lines, and the presence of several keywords that will recur in the *Ossi* – the wind that sweeps ("spazza"), the "mare che scaglia a scaglia livido, / muta colore", the "tromba / di schiume intorte" – absent in the other *Accordi*, brings this poem closer to the texts written subsequently and grants it citizenship in the collection.

In *Corno inglese,* the miracle is awaited, but contrarily to the other poems, we do not know if it will take place:

Il vento che stasera suona attento
– ricorda un forte scotere di lame –
gli strumenti dei fitti alberi e spazza
l'orizzonte di rame
dove strisce di luce si protendono
come aquiloni al cielo che rimbomba
(Nuvole in viaggio, chiari

[83] E. MONTALE, letter to Giacinto Spagnoletti, see G. SPAGNOLETTI, *Preistoria di Montale*, cit., pp. 121-122: "*Corno inglese* was the only one in the series which could have been separated from the cycle: of which I did not like, and even now do not like, the general sense and the ingenuous pretence of imitating musical instruments (and a certain rigidity surfacing here and there). I should therefore conclude that in my youthful *chateau d'eaux* (this is how Lorenzo Montano defined my poems), near a murkier vein, or indeed, *inside* that vein, there developed an early pathway to the leaner, more limpid vein of the *Ossi*".

reami di lassù! D'alti Eldoradi
malchiuse porte!)
e il mare che scaglia a scaglia,
livido, muta colore
lancia a terra una tromba
di schiume intorte;
il vento che nasce e muore
nell'ora che lenta s'annera
suonasse te pure stasera
scordato strumento,
cuore.[84]

The long and convoluted period, stretched by a relative clause and a parenthesis to the point that the subject ("il tempo") needs to be reiterated with an anaphoric effect, is based on an octative verb ("suonasse"), whose mood looks ahead to the conditional "Forse" that opens "Forse un mattino ...". But in that later poem the miracle is a glimpse through the veil of the phenomenal world to discover that reality is, finally, nothing. Here, the desired miracle involves the heart vibrating in one with nature to produce a melody that would be, ultimately, the poem itself. But the heart, the same heart that in *Violini* fell silent at the miracle of the day, is now defined as "scordato" ("forgotten"). The double meaning of the participle refers both to a forgetting and to disharmony – it is a dissonance in clear contrast with the title of the series, and one that will look forward to Montale's disjunctive modernist allegories in the volumes to come.[85]

[84] OV 11: "The intent wind that plays tonight / – a wild clangor of blades come to mind – / the instruments of the thick trees and sweeps / the copper horizon / where streaks of light are trailing, / kites in the sky that roars / (Clouds traveling, bright / kingdoms up above, / ajar entries of High Eldorados!) / and the livid sea / which, scale by scale, / turns color, hurls / a horn of of contorted spume ashore; / the wind that's born and dies / in the hour that slowly goes dark – / if only it could play you too, tonight / discordant instrument, / heart". Trans. modified from J. Galassi.

[85] See R. Luperini, *Montale e l'allegoria moderna*, cit., p. 11: "non è certo un caso che "Corno inglese", l'unico degli *Accordi* a essere inserito nel primo libro, nasca proprio dall'impossibilità dell'accordo e anzi dalla constatazione dolorosa di una dissonanza fra il cuore – "scordato strumento" – e la natura", ("It is certainly no accident that "English Horn", the only one of the *Accordi* to be included in the first book, is born precisely from the impossibility of accords and indeed from the painful realization of a dissonance between the heart – "untuned instrument" – and nature").

Chapter IV: Intermezzo

PLACING THE POETRY

Proviamo a considerare la poesia di Montale da una certa distanza, come un paesaggio visto da lontano.[1]

The preceding chapters have examined – and later chapters will continue to examine – the topic of place and landscape in Montale's poetry, both literally and figuratively. This intermezzo is instead intended to engage with the *location* of the poetry in the landscape, considering the places in the poems through their geographical coordinates but also as a symptoms of experiences, exposures, memories, intellectual and emotional elements.

In assigning a geographical location to the poems, I have taken into account: the toponymy in the text, when expressly indicated – e.g., Valmorbia in "Valmorbia, discorrevano il tuo fondo..." (OV 41), and Portovenere in the epigraph of "Là fuoriesce il tritone..." (OV 35); the presence of particular landmarks related to Montale's biography – e.g., the "Vasca" of the eponymous poem (OV 71) is an artificial pond in the garden of the Villa delle due palme; "Flussi"(OV 74) mentions the statue of Summer that adorned the same garden; the presence in a text of particular *topoi* linked to a specific locale – e.g., the reference to the peculiar trajectories of the railroad tracks around the Cinque Terre locates "Egloga" (OV 72) in that specific geography; and the "adherence" of particular locales to Montale's biography – e.g., if Paola Nicoli is the addressee of "In limine", and the poem has been composed in her house in Albaro, as Paolo De Caro contends, then the vegetable garden there described must be located in Genoa; instead, the short cycle dedicated to the same Paola Nicoli in 1924, including "Crisalide", "Marezzo", "Casa sul mare", is dense with terms and themes connected with Monterosso, even if "la Peruviana" was not part of

[1] R. Luperini, *Montale e il canone poetico del Novecento italiano*, in *Montale e il canone poetico del Novecento*, eds. M.A. Grignani, R. Luperini, Roma, Laterza, 1998, p. 361: "Let's aim to consider Montale's poetry from a certain distance, like a landscape seen from afar".

the group of friends and acquaintances spending the summer in the Casa delle due palme).[2]

The experiment, however, is not meant to confine the single poems: in part because some verses do not allow a geographical localization, or refer to multiple locales (e.g., "Quasi una fantasia", OV 18, begins in the familiar context of the city of Genoa and ends in an imagined space), and in part because an exclusive localization would reduce the multiple interpretations that every poetic text, and specifically Montale's, could yield. The significance of the maps belies in the geographical variation verifiable in the first three books, not in the positioning of each given poem.

If we proceed to place Montale's poetry with a view from above, the geographical differences between *Gli ossi di seppia*, *Le occasioni*, and *La bufera e altro* seem evident enough; the *Ossi* (Fig. 1) all take place along the coastal line between Genoa and La Spezia, which is also the path of the railway, reproducing a journey that for Montale linked the duties of the city to the pleasures of the seaside vacation, and therefore is often mentioned in the poems, prose, and letters.[3] The map indicates the Riviera di Levante as a veritable door of Janus, a liminal place partaking at the same time of land and sea, of the "età illusa" and the disillusion of adulthood, and a threshold to be crossed to begin the journey of life.[4] The sole exception in the first book is "Valmorbia, discorrevano il tuo fondo …" which, as we know, is set in the trenches of Trentino.

The places in *Le occasioni*, in contrast (Fig. 2), are much more diverse. The volume makes mention of Liguria and Tuscany, but also refers to other Italian and French locales, as well as to settings in Switzerland, Germany, Austria, and England.

The geographical area expands further still in the pages of *La bufera e altro* (Fig. 3), a volume in which the section *Flashes e dediche* alone extends from Scotland to the Middle East.

---

[2] See P. De Caro, *Invenzioni di ricordi; vite in poesia di tre ispiratrici montaliane*, Foggia, Centro Grafico Francescano, 2007, pp. 145 *et passim*.

[3] See *e.g.* "Egloga" (OV 72) in *Ossi*; "Accellerato" (OV 130) and "Al primo chiaro" (OV 147) in *Occasioni*; "Le Cinque Terre" (1946), the prose at the beginning of *Fuori di casa* (PR 233-237); and the letter to Irma Brandeis dated Sept. 7, 1938, in *Lettere a Clizia*, eds. R. Bettarini, G. Manghetti, F. Zabagli, Milano, Mondadori, 2006, p. 137.

[4] See I. Calvino, "Liguria" (1973), in *Saggi 1945-1985*, ed. M. Barenghi, Milano, Mondadori, 1995, p. 2376: "La forma in cui le nostre abitudini mentali ci rappresentano la Liguria non è d'una superficie ma d'una linea, o meglio d'una strada, che segue approssimativamente l'arco della sua costa, da Ponente a Levante" ("The shape in which our mental habit represents Liguria does not correspond to a surface, rather to a line, or better a road, that approximately follows the arc of the coast, from West to East").

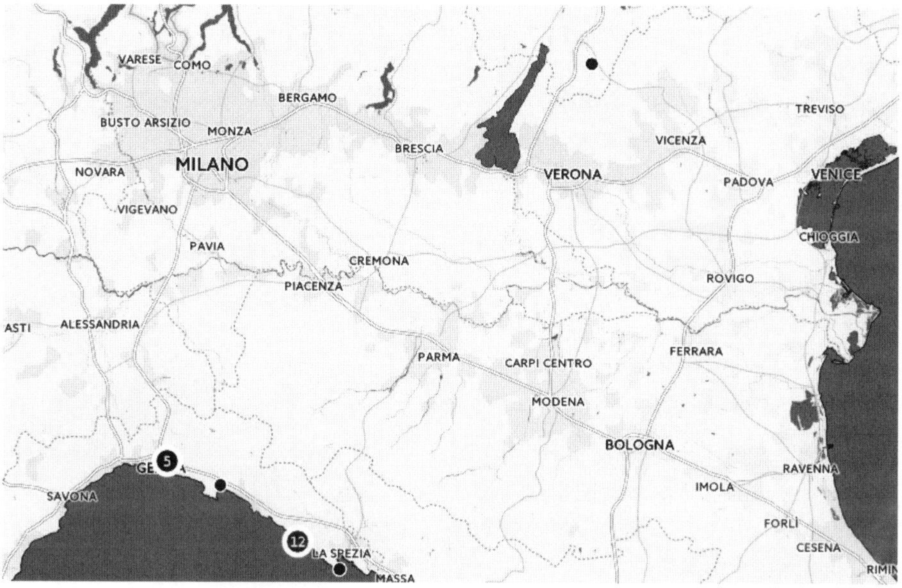

1

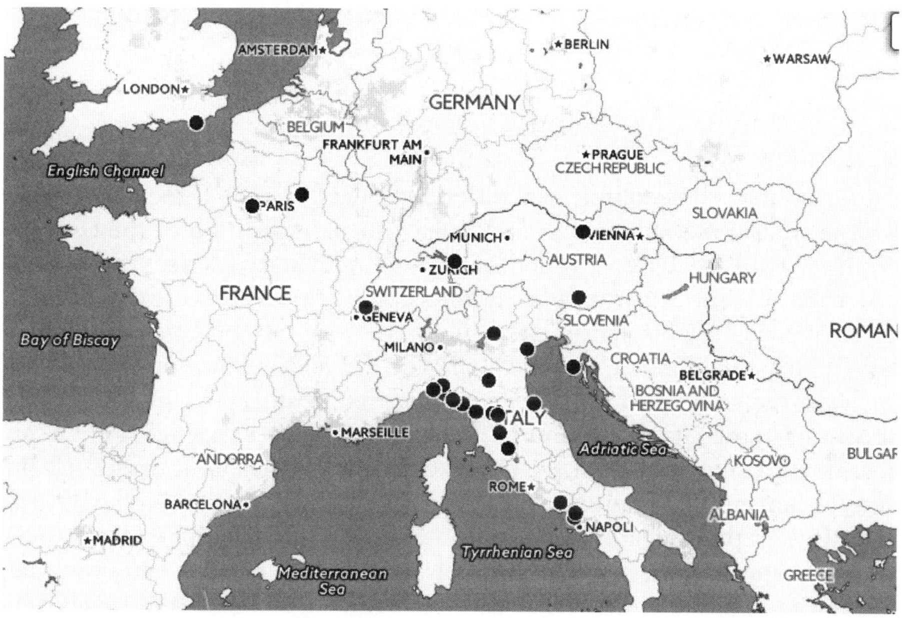

2

Fig. 1. *Ossi di seppia*. Five poems are located in Genoa and twelve in Monterosso. Fig. 2. *Le occasioni*.

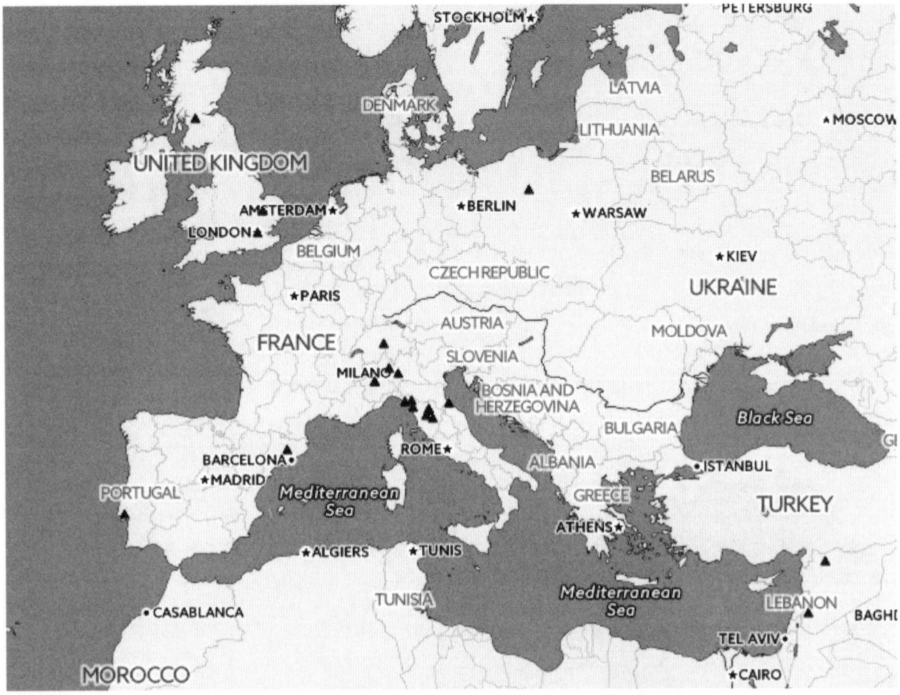

Fig. 3. *La bufera e altro.*

Of course, the geographical differences between the three books have a biographical component. At the time of the composition of the *Ossi* the young Montale had not traveled much beyond his experiences in the war, apart from some trips with his family, and a trip to Rome that had dire consequences for his sentimental life.[5] The Montale of *Le occasioni* had left Liguria for Florence, first to work for the editor Bemporad and then to direct the Gabinetto Vieusseux, one of the most important cultural institutions in the city and a landmark for the expats of the Anglo-American world. He also toured Europe, to the extent the Fascist authorities would allow. Many poems from *La bufera e altro* were instead written after World War II and reproduce locales that Montale had visited primarily for professional reasons. Observing the three maps in a sequence, we can note that the center of the circumference remains fixed in the Genoa-Florence-Milan triangle, but the radius extends until it reaches, to the west, Finisterre,

[5] See "Una visita" (OV 706) and "Postilla a una visita" (OV 707) in *Quaderno di quattro anni.*

nomen omen the extreme point of continental Europe, and, to the east, Aleppo and Palmyra.

Seen from above, the three books seem to suggest a sequence of centrifugal motion that departs from the Riviera di Levante's ideal threshold and moves away from the place in which time remains immobile, gaining more and more ground in the subsequent books. The first map is congruent to the critical tenet of the *Ossi* as a book about landscape, geography, poetics of a place, localization of the subject in the landscape, and localization of the poetry in its tradition.[6] However, the later maps confirm that, after "Fine dell'infanzia" (OV 65), Liguria had transformed from a privileged space that catalyzes the conditions for the symbolist *correspondence*, to a place to be left behind.[7]

After leaving the mythical space where time, too, is an immobile, infinite noon, *Le occasioni* is a volume of movement: a movement in space, as the map attests, relative to a movement in time. The very concept of an "occasion" – the instant in which one may begin to comprehend the essence of the real, in which the redeeming angel could appear, in which a keepsake could recover the event that was or that could be – involves a coincidence of space and time with an event in the phenomenal world. Memory exercises a control over time, as we know, but also over space, because it mediates spatial differences, as Michiel de Certau notes.[8]

---

[6] See T. Arvigo, *Guida alla lettura di Montale. Ossi di seppia*, Roma, Carocci, 2001, p. 18, for whom the *Ossi* reproduce "uno spazio liminare, un 'inter-spazio' di indecisione e sofferenza fissato tra monti e mare, sul «limbo di terra», «su lo scoglio», «in limine». In questo senso gli *Ossi* sono, al contrario delle raccolte successive che si configurano talvolta anche come *carnet de voyage*, poesia della più assoluta stanzialità, nella quale prende corpo con più forte contrasto l'idea dell'erranza esistenziale" ("a liminal space, an 'inter-space' of indecision and distress, fixed between mountains and sea, in a "leap of land", "on the cliff", "in limine". In this sense the *Ossi* contain, in contrast with the following books that sometimes take shape as *carnet de voyage*, poetry of the most absolute stability, in which, clearly in contrast, the idea of existential wandering is materialized").

[7] See F. Croce, *La primavera hitleriana e altri saggi su Montale*, Genova, Marietti, 1997, p. 177: "Il paesaggio ligure, il paesaggio dei ricordi d'infanzia e di giovinezza, che fa costantemente da fondale al primo libro di versi montaliano, non è insomma – come si aspetterebbe – un luogo caro dove rifugiarsi, non è il "porto sereno di saggezza" di cui si favoleggia in *Riviere*. In alcuni dei più memorabili componimenti di *Ossi* 1925 è (proprio all'esatto opposto) il luogo da cui evadere" ("The Ligurian landscape, the landscape of childhood memories and of youth, which constantly forms the backdrop of Montale's first book of poetry, is not, in short – as we might expect – a beloved place of refuge, it is not the fabled 'serene gateway of wisdom' in *Riviere*. In some of the more memorable components of the 1925 *Ossi* it is [exactly in opposition] a place from which to escape").

[8] See M. de Certau, *L'invention du quotidien. Vol. I, L'art de faire*, Paris, Union Générale d'Éditions, 1980, p. 161 : "La mémoire médiatise des transformations spatiales. Sur le mode du 'moment opportun' (kairos), elle produit une rupture instauratrice. Son étrangeté rend

Le occasioni incorporates an implicit paradox: on the one hand, the texts emphasize Bergson's concept of the irreducibility of *flux*, or personal time, into scientific forms of measurement; on the other hand, the occasion *in* the text and *of* the text, by definition fleeting and impalpable, does not disappear nor cease to be only thanks to the power that the text has to make it durable on the space of the page. Such a paradox is hardly unique to Montale's poetry, of course: it is, rather, a process common to many texts by authors of the period who based their post-Newtonian understanding of the world on the philosophy of Bergson. Steven Connnor is not speaking directly of Montale here, but his argument perfectly describes Montale's poetics:

> Even those writers (and there were many) who followed Henri Bergson's counsel that time should be rendered as pure and fluid process rather than artificially frozen into instants, even those modernist writers found themselves condemned to spatialize or suspend time in attempting to be true to it. Virginia Woolf's 'moment of vision' and Joyce's 'epiphanies' are both instances of the distillation of time into spatial significance, time yielding its meaning by being suspended.[9]

The *Occasioni* celebrate the permanence of the memorial act, and represent the past in the space of the written texts; in its turn, the event engraved with the poem acquires a permanence into time thanks to the space of the page.[10] The text makes the past present, but not all of the past has the possibility of being re-presented. Only the "occasional", fragmented episode can force memory to rescue it from the passage of time, from the precipitous flux of temporality, with a mechanism similar to Proust's *intermittences du coeur*.[11] In Proust, involuntary memory is triggered by a repetition of an identical sensation in the past and present that allows for a bridge

---

possible une transgression de la loi du lieu" ("Memory mediatizes spatial transformations. It produces a fecund rupture on the mode of the "opportune instant" [kairos]. Its strangeness makes possible a transgression of the law of the place").

9 S. Connor, *Postmodernist Culture: An Introduction to Theories of the Contemporary*, Oxford, Basil Blackwell, 1989, pp. 117-118.

10 For a modernist take of the age-old idea that art salvages memory from temporality, see G. Deleuze, *Proust and Signs*, London, The Athlone Press, 2000, specifically pp. 15-25 and pp. 52-65.

11 In the previously cited postcard sent from Montale to Piero Gadda Conti and published by the latter in *Letteratura*, Montale takes his distance from this French expression, labeling it "un gergo proustiano che io non uso" ("Proustian jargon that I don't use"), p. 279. On the similarities between Proust's and Montale's memory see M. Santini, *La farfalla di Dinard e la memoria montaliana*, La Spezia, Agorà, 1999, p. 21 *et passim*.

between the two. Montale's "occasions" follow exactly the same rationale, but they only desire, rather than make possible, the connection between two emotions and two moments in time.[12] One can read many poems from *Le occasioni* from this perspective: many of the "Mottetti", many of the major texts from the fourth part, "La casa dei doganieri" (OV 161), "Bassa marea" (OV 162), "Stanze" (OV 163), "Sotto la pioggia" (OV 165), "Punta del Mesco" (OV 166), "Costa San Giorgio" (OV 167), "Notizie dall'Amiata" (OV 181). Only in rare cases, as in "Ti libero la fronte dai ghiaccioli" (OV 144), the occasion actually takes place and the numinous presence of the beloved is described as real. This is not to suggest that the naturalistic texts completely disappear from the books that follow the *Ossi*: for example, "L'estate" (OV 169), in *Occasioni*, is still tied to a "physical" style. Montale is aware of this fact: explaining the poem to Irma Brandeis, he writes:

> L'Estate mi pare molto sulla linea delle mie vecchie cose, ma con maggiore approfondimento stilistico. La tecnica vi è meno evidente perché è accresciuta e le parole sono più fluide, meno intarsiate e incastonate di una volta. È una poesia che, pur essendo assolutamente 1935 (non avrebbe potuto essere scritta nel 1933) potrebbe essere *capita* (non ammirata) da un Leopardi, se potesse leggerla. È l'assorbimento, e insieme la liquidazione, della *tradizione*. Dopo di che dovrebbe venire uno che ri-inventasse tutto ex-novo: Lingua, sintassi, metrica.[13]

Let's ignore the consonance with Pound's "Make it new" since, in 1935, after the two had seen each other frequently but then lost touch because of their diverging political opinions, this might not be a voluntary reference

---

[12] See E. Montale, *Lettere a Clizia*, cit., p. 26 (October 31, 1933), for help in framing the "occasion" on the biographical level as the representation of an impossible desire: "Veramente questa corrispondenza transoceanica è una cosa molto buffa e obbliga a fare i conti con situazioni che non esistono più e con altre che si ignorano. A volte mi pare così ridicolo che si viva in due parti lontane della palla terrestre, con in mezzo quel piccolo lago del mare; mi pare che con uno sforzo di volontà potrei *materializzarti* qui, almeno nei momenti di maggiore necessità. Ma sono illusioni" ("This transoceanic correspondence is quite odd and demands that one come to terms with situations that no longer exist and with others that go ignored. At times it seems ridiculous to me that we live in two distant parts of the globe, with that little lake of a sea in the middle; it seems to me that by the force of my will I could *materialize you* here, at least in my moments of greatest need. But these are illusions").

[13] "L'estate" seems to me to be quite in line with my old things, but with a great deal more stylistic depth. The technique there is less obvious because it has grown, and the words are more fluid, less embellished and encrusted than they once were. It is a poem that, though absolutely a product of 1935 (it could not have been written in 1933), could have been *understood* (not admired) by a Leopardi, if he could have read it. It is simultaneously the absorption and the liquidation of *tradition*. Afterwards someone should come to reinvent everything *ex novo*: language, syntax, meter"). Letter to Irma Brandeis dated September 7, 1935, in E. Montale, *Lettere a Clizia*, cit., p. 172.

to Pound's dictamina. However, it is necessary to consider how Montale reveals a full awareness of the clear-cut division between tradition (Leopardi, Romanticism, a lyric "I" immersed in the landscape) and the innovations that he adopts. If, to quote Foucault, the twentieth century sees "an important dividing line between those who believe that they can still locate today's discontinuities in the historical-transcendental tradition of the nineteenth century, and those who try to free themselves once and for all from that tradition",[14] Montale is part of the latter group, and we witness his attempt to release his poetic activity from the constraints of tradition.

A similar point to the one made regarding the *Occasioni* could also be made regarding the texts of *La bufera e altro*, with the caveat that the new book, whose provisional title was not coincidentally *Romanzo (Novel)*, joins an outline of narrative structure to a recovery of linear time and the chronological disposition of the poems.[15] The Ligurian localization continues to appear, but it is now relegated explicitly to memory ("L'arca" OV 200, "A mia madre" OV 203), when it is not directly the suggestion of texts written many years prior: "Due nel crepuscolo" (OV 213), for instance, is very reminiscent of "Incontro" (OV 96), a poem added to the second edition of the *Ossi*. Like "Incontro", it is dedicated to the figure of a woman who died by water, inspired by Anna degli Uberti, and though it appeared in a 1956 book, it had been written thirty years before.[16] It is, therefore, the text of a Montale who had not yet moved to Florence that opens *Intermezzo*, a section of *La bufera* that consists of three texts, all dedicated to recovering memories of the Cinque Terre.[17] In it the prose-poem "Dov'era il tennis..." (OV 215) particularly ties the Ligurian landscape to memory: the title evokes the experience of remembering a past landscape that no longer exists; the quest to recover such a place requires a journey through time as well as space.

It is significant that the section regarding the memory of Liguria immediately precedes "Flashes e dediche", which is frequently interpreted as Montale's *Reisebilder*.[18] *Farfalla di Dinard*, the collection of short stories

---

[14] M. Foucault, *What is an author?* in *The Foucault Reader*, ed. P. Rabinow, New York, Random House, 1984, p. 105.

[15] There are some important exceptions: see R. Luperini, *Montale e l'allegoria moderna*, cit., p. 31.

[16] See R. Bettarini, *Scritti montaliani*, Firenze, Le Lettere, 2009, p. 144; see also OV 937.

[17] In the chapbook *Finisterre* (Lugano 1943) the section is titled *In Liguria*: see OV 937.

[18] See M. Forti, *Eugenio Montale. La poesia, la prosa di fantasia e d'invenzione*, Milano, Mursia, 1974, pp. 253-254: "Il fedele collezionista di luoghi montaliani potrà, infine, aggiungere alla già lunga teoria di luoghi deputati Siena e San Gusmè, Reading e Londra, le luci di Mayfair, Ely

published in the same year as *Le occasioni*, and *Fuori di casa*, a 1969 collection of travelogues that Montale produced while working as a reporter for the «Corriere della Sera», also begin with memories of the Ligurian setting before creating a distance and venturing all over Italy and Europe. It is as if the initial time and place were the same for all of his books, in prose and in poetry, as if the biographical point of departure could not but coincide with the artistic one. Ultimately, reconsidering the pattern of conjunction of particular spaces and times throughout Montale's work allows to give a sense to his writings as a whole, as per Luperini's suggestion.

---

e Glasgow, Edimburgo e Damasco, i geli dell'antilibano e la pioggia d'Armor; le rive del Llobregat, Sesto Calende, Aleppo e Palmira. Altri luoghi, probabilmente anche più determinanti per il suo sviluppo di fondo, ha offerto la poesia montaliana; ma non si potrà dimenticare quanto il viaggio, in sé, sia stato determinante di questa sezione della *Bufera*, e come, frequentemente, esso sia riuscito a costituire una vera e propria metafora della stessa vita che resta, infine, il tema di fondo di questo e degli altri (passati e futuri) libri di Montale" ("The faithful collector of Montalian places will be able to add to the long string of elected places: Siena and San Gusmè, Reading and London, the lights of Mayfair, Ely, and Glasgow, Edinburgh and Damascus, the icy cold of the Anti-Lebanon Mountains and the rains of Armor; the banks of the Llobregat, Sesto Calende, Aleppo, and Palmyra. Other places, probably even more significant to his development, are present in Montale's poetry; but one ought not to forget how significant is the voyage itself in this section of *Bufera*, and how, frequently, it successfully constituted a true and proper metaphor of the same life that remains, finally, the fundamental theme of this and other [past and future] books by Montale").

Chapter V

BEYOND THE THRESHOLD

1. Make It Difficult

We can only say that it appears likely that poets in our civilization, as it exists at present, must be *difficult*.[1]

In the same span of years during which Montale's poetry passed over the threshold, his life, most notably his intellectual life, also underwent a sudden acceleration. Even before the 1920s Eugenio had been an avid reader, both of literature and philosophy: his sister Marianna recalls that between 1916 and 1917 he read *On the Freedom of the Will* and *The Philosophy of the University* by Schopenhauer, in addition to *Matter and Memory* by Bergson. He certainly read more later, especially when Marianna began – unusually for a young Genoese woman from a good family – to take philosophy courses with the intent to earn a bachelor's degree.[2] Some documentation remains of what Montale read beyond the evidence that can be found in his poems and theoretical writings. Marianna notes that her brother, prior to World War I, was interested in Kantian idealism and opposed to skepticism.[3] Upon his return, however, the accumulation of his readings rendered his positions more volatile, as Montale himself wrote

---

1 T.S. Eliot, *The Metaphisical Poets* (1921), in *The Sacred Woods and Major Early Essays*, Mineola, N.Y., Dover Publications, 1998, p. 128.

2 On the figure of Marianna as a philosophy student, see Laura Barile in E. Montale, *Quaderno Genovese*, ed. L. Barile, Milano, Mondadori, 1983, pp. 180 *et passim*.

3 See M. Montale, *Lettere da casa Montale (1908-1938)*, cit., p. 323 and p. 346: "Ora lui ha cambiato idea circa l'essenza della materia. È sulla strada dell'idealismo assoluto. Le cose esistono solo in quanto si pensano [...]" ("Now he has changed his mind about the essence of matter. He is on the road to absolute idealism. Things exist only in so much as they are thought of [...]"); "Giorni fa accennava allo scetticismo, ma con che tono! [...] E aggiungeva che quando uno dice che non c'è niente di assoluto, su per giù ha perso il ben dell'intelletto" (Days ago he touched on skepticism, but with such a tone! [...] And he added that when someone says that nothing is absolute, that person has more or less lost his gift of reason").

to his brother-in-arms Francesco Meriano: "Io sono in *crisi*: non c'è giorno che non impari qualche cosa di nuovo e che non abbia a modificare qualche vecchia idea; e non so ancora dove mi porteranno i miei viaggi mentali".[4]

We know that in 1920 he read *La teoria dello spirito come atto puro (The Theory of Mind as Pure Act)* by Giovanni Gentile, and then investigated Benedetto Croce's idealism.[5] The "Intervista immaginaria" of 1949 reconstructs in a nutshell his philosophical path during these years:

> Direttamente io conosco pochi testi dell'esistenzialismo, ma lessi molti anni fa qualche scrittore come Sestov, un kierkegaardiano molto vicino alle posizioni di questa filosofia. Dopo l'altra guerra, nel '19, mi dette molta soddisfazione l'immanentismo assoluto del Gentile, per quanto mal decifrassi l'imbrogliatissima teoria dell'atto puro. Più tardi preferii il grande positivismo idealistico del Croce; ma forse negli anni in cui composi gli *Ossi di seppia* agì in me la filosofia dei contingentisti francesi, del Boutroux soprattutto, che conobbi meglio del Bergson. Il miracolo era per me evidente come la necessità.[6]

The influence of Benedetto Croce's ideas continued beyond Montale's interest in contingentism, on the political plane as well as on the philosophical one: Montale was one of the few Italian intellectuals to sign the "Manifesto degli intellettuali antifascisti" proposed by Croce in 1925 in response to the "Manifesto degli intellettuali fascisti" circulated by Gentile. A letter to Enzo Ferrieri testifies that Montale was still reading Croce's *Poesia e non poesia (Poetry and Non-Poetry)* in October 1927.[7] The development of Montale's philosophical theories from idealism to a Kierkegaardian brand of existentialism to contingentism would have repercussions in his poetry.

---

[4] E. Montale, letter to F. Meriano dated April 6, 1920, in F. Meriano, *Arte e vita*, cit., p. 157: "I am in crisis: not a day goes by that I don't learn something new and have to modify some old idea; and I no longer know where my mental voyages will bring me".

[5] See E. Montale, *Giorni di libeccio. Lettere ad Angelo Barile (1920-1957)*, eds. D. Astengo, G. Costa, Milano, Archinto, 2002, p. 41; and A. Barile, "La vigilia genovese di Montale", as quoted in E. Montale, *Immagini di una vita*, Milano, Mondadori 1996, p. 69.

[6] E. Montale, "Intenzioni (Intervista immaginaria)" (1946), AMS 1479: "I know few existentialist texts directly, but many years ago I read writers like Sestov, a Kierkegaardian very close to the positions of this philosophy. After the other war, in '19, I found much satisfaction in Gentile's immanentism, as far as I could badly decipher his incredibly tangled theory of the pure act. Later I preferred the great idealistic positivism of Croce; but perhaps in the years in which I wrote the *Ossi di seppia* the philosophy of the French contingentists acted in me, especially that of Boutroux, whom I knew better than Bergson. The miracle was for me as evident as necessity".

[7] M.A. Grignani, *La costanza della ragione. Soggetto, oggetto e testualità nella poesia italiana del Novecento*, Novara, Interlinea, 2002, p. 33.

After the hiatus necessitated by his military duties, Montale began to write again. "Riviere" is from 1920; the following year he drafted "Debole sistro al vento", and in 1922, the year in which his first poems were published, his "murky vein" overflowed.[8] He wrote "I limoni", "Debole sistro al vento", "Non rifugiarti nell'ombra", "Egloga", "L'agave su lo scoglio", and he finished "Meriggiare pallido e assorto", all texts in which elements of the landscape are used to illuminate the emotions of the "I". The triptych "L'agave su lo scoglio", for example, utilizes the Ligurian winds to signify the phenomenology of the subject's disquiet and distress. Sirocco, Tramontana, and Maestrale are selected as emblems of many states of mind: perplexity, anguish for the hostile fury of the world, perturbation, and hope in the moment of the natural elements' pacification. In "I limoni", for the first time, a metaphysical longing appears. Yet the incipit is of clear symbolist provenance, and the names of Pascoli and D'Annunzio are usually mentioned to provide a genealogy for the Virgilian topos of the *Humilesque myricae*.[9] The second stanza repeats the theme of time's suspension and describes a consecrated place, a pocket-sized, metropolitan Eden in which one can enjoy the experience of perfect calm,[10] and some hendecasyllables can leave a Parnassian aftertaste.[11] And yet, despite the symbolist imprint of the poem, in it the idea of the miracle, of the unforeseen, extraordinary, contingent event, breaks through.

As in the *Accordi*, in "I limoni" the idea of the miracle is tied to a communion with the natural world, and to an apparition of the divine; but the terminology of the third stanza is unusually precise, and the transcendental longing is transformed into an unexpected cognitive moment that permits the intuition to grasp the essence of reality beyond appearances:

> Vedi, in questi silenzi in cui le cose
> s'abbandonano e sembrano vicine
> a tradire il loro ultimo segreto,
> talora ci si aspetta
> di scoprire uno sbaglio di Natura,
> il punto morto del mondo, l'anello che non tiene,

---

[8] The reference comes from the definition of his early poetry that Montale sent to G. Spagnoletti, see chapter 3.5.

[9] VIRG. *Ecl.* IV, 2.

[10] See OV 9, ll. 18-21: "Qui delle divertite passioni / per miracolo tace la guerra, / qui tocca anche a noi poveri la nostra parte di ricchezza / ed è l'odore dei limoni" ("Here, by some miracle, the war / of conflicted passions is stilled, / here even we the poor share the riches of the world – / the smell of lemon tree").

[11] E.g., "e piove in petto una dolcezza inquieta" (l. 17).

il filo da disbrogliare che finalmente ci metta
nel mezzo di una verità.
Lo sguardo fruga d'intorno,
la mente indaga accorda disunisce
nel profumo che dilaga
quando il giorno più languisce.
Sono i silenzi in cui si vede
in ogni ombra umana che si allontana
qualche disturbata Divinità.[12]

The stanza seems to be divided in half. In the first part we read of Nature's mistake, the standstill, the ring that does not hold, the thread to untangle – all elements of an optative metaphysical consciousness, metaphors of human intuition capable, with the help of art, of lifting the veil of the conventions that usually impede us from reaching true consciousness. The second part instead – with its dichotomy between the glance that searches all around and the mind that probes, reconciles, separates – seems to turn back to an idea of textual construction similar to that expressed in the *Quaderno Genovese*, where the eye had the task of rendering permanent sensible appearances, and the poetic "I" had the task of choosing, assimilating, and transforming the elements observed by the eye. Verses in which the "I" seems to yearn for a numinous knowledge are followed by verses in which the mechanism creating the landscape through the union of imagination with external material is confirmed, as had occurred in "Meriggiare pallido e assorto". It is a contradictory sign, but an important one: this "flaw in Nature" is a first occasion of the "attesa del miracolo" ("wait for the miracle") that will be repeated frequently in the texts from 1923-1924: "Forse un mattino", "Crisalide", and "Fine dell'infanzia".

In 1923, in fact, aside from poems of clear symbolist inspiration, like "Portami il girasole", and texts in which the sentiment of homogeneity and harmony with the external world is still represented as at least temporarily feasible, like "Là fuoriesce il Tritone" and "Gloria del disteso mezzogiorno", Montale also writes verses that, breaking with previous inspiration, demonstrate the application of his philosophical readings. "Non chiederci la parola" and "Forse un mattino andando ...", written in or before July

---

12 OV 9, ll. 22-36: "See, in these silences when things / let themselves go and seem almost / to reveal their final secret, / we sometimes expect / to discover a flaw in Nature, / the world's dead point, the link that doesn't hold, / the thread that, disentangled, might at least lead us / to the center of a truth. / The eye rummages, / the mind pokes about, unifies, disjoins / in the fragrance that grows / as the day closes, languishing. / These are the silences where we see / in each departing human shade / some disturbed Divinity", trans. W. Arrowsmith.

1923, are the first texts in which one can observe the intention to "torcere il collo alla nostra vecchia lingua aulica" ("wring the neck of our old courtly language"), and the wish to bring an end to "l'inganno del mondo come rappresentazione" ("the deception of the world as representation").[13] The citation from Schopenhauer is not accidental: in 1923 Montale was actually reading the texts of German existentialism, of Nietzsche, and above all he was expanding his knowledge of the contingentism of the French school, following in the footsteps of Marianna's academic studies. Many years later, with typical understatement, Montale would attempt to minimize the influence that these authors had had on him: "Mia sorella studiava filosofia. Qualcosa di più del nome di Boutroux e di Bergson mi sarà passato tra le mani. Ma aggiungerei Lachelier. Poco tuttavia".[14] The three generations of spiritualist thought mentioned – highlighting the dichotomy between body and mind, reaffirming the importance of the spiritual life, and the independence of the free will – resonate with the anti-positivist thought of Giuseppe Rensi, a neo-idealist thinker who had been transformed by his participation in World War I, as Montale recalls, into a "filosofo scettico che possedeva una notevole sensibilità per la musica e per la poesia".[15] He was a professor of moral philosophy at the University of Genoa and Marianna's teacher. She introduced her brother to at least a pair of his volumes: *La scepsi estetica* and *Interiora rerum*.[16] The spiritualist theories also resonated with the positions of Marianna's spiritual adviser, Father Giuseppe Trinchero, a Barnabite priest of modernist tendencies who, according to Marianna, piqued the interest of her younger brother. Another Barnabite, Father Giovanni Semeria, was one of Eugenio's teachers in high school and a family friend of the Montales, whom he sometimes visited in Monterosso during the summer to explain the tenets and the desiderata of Catholic modernism.[17]

---

13 E. Montale, "Intenzioni (Intervista immaginaria)" (1946), AMS 1480. See *infra*.

14 E. Montale, "Ho scritto un solo libro" (1975), interview by G. Zampa, AMS 1720: "My sister was studying philosophy. Something more than the name of Boutroux and Bergson would have passed through my hands. But I would add Lachelier. Little, though".

15 E. Montale, "L'arte spettacolare" (1952), AMS 105: "A skeptic philosopher who possessed a striking sensibility for music and poetry".

16 G. Rensi, *La scepsi estetica*, Bologna, Zanichelli, 1920; Id., *Interiora rerum*, Milano, Unitas, 1924. For an interpretation of the figure of Giuseppe Rensi in the philosophical formation and in the poetry of Montale, see A. Comparini, *Iride: l'Alcesti di Montale*, Borgomanero (No), Ladolfi, 2014; and C. Scarpati, *Scepsi e ascesi all'epoca degli* Ossi, in *Sulla cultura di Montale*, Milano, Vita e Pensiero, 1997, pp. 7-32.

17 See D. Astengo, *Introduzione* in E. Montale, *Giorni di libeccio. Lettere ad Angelo Barile (1920-1957)*, eds. D. Astengo, G. Costa, Milano, Archinto, 2002, p. 13: "Padre Semeria, insegnante di Eugenio all'Istituto Vittorino da Feltre, qualche volta faceva visita a Monterosso. Il

In fact, literary modernism and Catholic modernism have a common genealogy in contingentism, and specifically in the thought of Bergson in its early stages. Édouard Le Roy, one of the leaders of Catholic modernism, had studied with Bergson and had summarized the latter's positions in a 1913 book, *A New Philosophy: Henri Bergson*:[18] the result was that the works of Bergson were placed on the Index of the Catholic Church.[19] This did not stop the diffusion of his ideas, not even in Catholic, provincial Genoa, which was, according to Eugenio's recollections, "piena di modernisti" ("full of modernists").[20] Even if Montale was not able to attend Bergson's lectures, as Eliot and Ungaretti had done in Paris in the winter of 1910-1911, he certainly read Bergson's books: and the Bergsonian inspiration that had informed Eliot's "Rhapsody on a Windy Night" is also a cornerstone, as we shall see, of the *osso breve* "Forse un mattino".

The general opinion of scholars of English and American modernism, however, is that one should not be too quick to associate the literary movement solely with Bergsonism.[21] This holds true also for Montale, not so

---

modernismo era di moda a Genova, e sulla terrazza della villa, il barnabita parlava di Tyrrell e Le Roy, Loisy e Bonaiuti" ("Father Semeria, a professor of Eugenio at the Instituto Vittorino da Feltre, sometimes visited Monterosso. Modernism was fashionable in Genoa, and on the terrace of the villa the Barnabite priest talked about Tyrrell and Le Roy, Loisy and Bonaiuti"). See also the poem "L'odore dell'eresia" in *Diario del '71 e del '72* (OV 464), and M. Montale, *Lettere da casa Montale (1908-1938)*, cit., p. 357. An exhaustive essay on Eugenio Montale's ties to Catholic modernism can be found in F. Contorbia, *Montale, Genova, il modernismo*, in Id., *Montale, Genova, il modernismo e altri saggi montaliani*, Bologna, Pendragon, 1999, pp. 13-52.

18 É. Le Roy, *A New Philosophy: Henri Bergson* (1913), Web: Project Gutenberg http://www.gutenberg.org/files/1347/1347-h/1347-h.htm accessed 14 August 2015.

19 An unsigned article published in New York's «The Independent», commenting extremely critically upon the Congregation's decision regarding the Index of Prohibited Books, offers a bit of context and underscores the importance that French contingentist philosophy held for the Catholic modernist movement: in *The Banning of Bergson*, «The Independent», July 20, 1914, pp. 85-86, we read: "The works of Henri Bergson have followed the works of Maurice Maeterlink to the purgatory of the Index Librorum Proibitorum and *Creative Evolution* and *The Blue Bird* are now together upon the list of books which no good Catholic may own or read without the express permission of his spiritual adviser. [...] The Congregation never gives reasons for its decisions – a wise precaution – but it is assumed that the principal objection to Bergson, besides the general one of meddling with sacred subjects, is that his philosophy savors too much of the heresy of divine immanence. Bergson's philosophy was seized upon with immense enthusiasm by young Catholics in France because it seemed to afford them a way by which they could reconcile their loyalty to the Church with the acceptance of modern science. His most devoted disciple is a Catholic, Édouard Le Roy, whose recent book on the ethical import of Bergsonism has received the emphatic endorsement of Bergson himself. The whole Modernist movement was in fact based upon a trend of which Bergson has become the chief exponent".

20 E. Montale, "Ho scritto un solo libro" (1975), AMS 1720.

21 T. Quirk, *Bergson and American Culture: The Worlds of Willa Cather and Wallace Stevens*, Chapel Hill, University of North Carolina Press, 1990, p. 14: "Bergsonism had become the prin-

much because we should give credit to his minimizing comments, but because an analysis of the texts reveals that the Genoese poet was also receptive to the ideas of the other philosophers he mentioned.[22] Furthermore, Montale did not aspire to the construction of a coherent philosophical system that would give structure to various texts. On the contrary, he behaved with his philosophical sources as he did with his literary ones: he blended a variety of sources and influences into an intellectual patchwork without forcing them into a rigid system. The art of collage is, at base, a purely modernist process, and Montale was a great amalgamator who appropriated concepts, ideas, and images without worrying about their coherence. This can at times lead to evident contradictions, such as, in the "Intervista immaginaria" already cited, the use and negation, at little distance from each other, of the Schopenhauerian formula of the "world as representation".[23]

Philosophical readings, contradictory or not, were not alone in broadening Montale's cultural horizons. In 1924, Roberto (Bobi) Bazlen, a young Triestine, moved to Genoa to take a job in the local offices of the Atlantic Refining Company; shortly after arriving in the city, Bazlen met Montale. Their similarities, most notably their ages, aspirations, and reluctant employment in the chemical industry, enabled the young men to immediately become great friends. And though Bazlen's Genoese employment lasted only a few months, their friendship would last a lifetime. Writing a moving "Ricordo di B. B." in 1963, Montale does not hide the important role his friend played in his own cultural formation.

---

cipal catalyst for the transformation of sensibility and the appropriation of a new reality, but it was not alone in performing its radical revisions on the way one was to understand the world". See also S. Schwartz, *The Matrix of Modernism: Pound, Eliot, and early Twentieth Century Thought* (1988), Princeton, Princeton University Press, 2014, p. 31: "It would be a mistake, however, to identify Modernism too closely with Bergson's theory of art or attribute too much to his influence. Other philosophers of this period also stress the opposition between abstraction and experience, and in some cases their influence on particular poets is greater than Bergson's. T.S. Eliot owes far more to Bradley's formulation of this distinction than to Bergson's. [...] Hence, we should not consider Bergson in isolation from other philosophers; rather we should view him as one participant in a development that includes other philosophers as well".

22 There are several studies on the philosophical readings done by Montale in the period of the composition of *Ossi di seppia*: apart from those already mentioned, a selected list should include A. Pipa, *L'influence de Boutroux et de Bergson sur Montale*, «Revue des Études Italiennes», 22 (1976), pp. 193-204; P. Bigongiari, *Montale tra Boutroux e M.lle de Scudéry*, «Il Bimestre», n. 6, gennaio-febbraio 1970, pp. 11-20; M. Forti, *Eugenio Montale*, Milano, Mursia, 1983, specifically p. 68; R. Lampugnani, *Immanenza e trascendenza di Montale: l'esempio di Bergson*, «Spunti e ricerche», 6, n. 1 (1990), pp. 57-75; E. Bonora, *Conversando con Montale*, Milano, Rizzoli, 1983, pp. 75-76; E. Rosada, *Il contingentismo di Montale*, «Studi novecenteschi» X, 1983, pp. 5-56; E. Boretti, *Montale e Bergson*, ««Le lingue del mondo», 50, n. 2 (1985), pp. 103-116; G. Bardazzi, *Schopenhauer tra Montale e Sbarbaro*, «Studi novecenteschi», 15 (1988), pp. 63-107.

23 E. Montale, "Intenzioni (Intervista immaginaria)" (1949), AMS 1480 and 1482.

Quando venne a trovarmi, nell'inverno del '23-'24, mandatomi non so da chi, egli fu per me una finestra spalancata su un mondo nuovo. Ci vedevamo ogni giorno in un caffè sotterraneo presso il Teatro Carlo Felice di Genova. Mi parlò di Svevo, facendomi poi pervenire i tre romanzi dall'autore stesso; mi fece conoscere molte pagine di Kafka, di Musil (il teatro) e di Altenberg. Conoscevo già la poesia di Saba, ma Bobi mi rivelò anche Giotti, Bolaffio, e più tardi, Carmelich.[24]

It was actually Bazlen who jokingly suggested an analogy between Eusebius (the name that Schumann had chosen to describe the passive side of his own personality) and Eugenio, inaugurating the long series of heteronyms through which Montale, *à la Pessoa*, would be fond of defining himself, in poetic texts as well as in his correspondence and conversations with friends. The reference to Schumann is not coincidental: Bazlen, who came from a cultural zone of strong German influence, and who already possessed a solid cultural formation and an acute critical spirit, introduced Eugenio to literature in German and to his preferred Triestine authors. One of these, Umberto Saba, would, on Bazlen's invitation, participate in the subscription that rendered possible the publication of the Gobetti edition of the *Ossi*.[25] Despite their formally maintained cordial rapport, Saba and Montale never became close companions. Another encounter induced by Bazlen would instead reveal itself to be quite important for the young poet: an encounter first with the work and then with the person of Italo Svevo, *nom de plume* of Ettore Schmitz, who Bobi considered the only Italian novelist worthy of being called "modern".[26]

Bazlen requested copies of *Una vita* and *Senilità* directly from Svevo to send to Montale; the novels had limited circulation at the time, and had received a tepid welcome upon their publication. In fact, *Senilità*, which had

---

24 E. MONTALE, "Ricordo di Roberto Bazlen" (1965), SM II 2728 ("When he called on me in the winter of '23-'24, sent to me I know not by whom, he was, for me, an open window into a new world. We would get together every day in an underground café near Genoa's Carlo Felice Theatre. He told me about Svevo, then he made me acquire the same author's three novels; he presented me with many pages of Kafka, of Musil [the theater], and of Altenberg. I already knew the poetry of Saba, but Bobi revealed to me also Giotti, Bolaffio, and later, Carmelich"). See also "Lettera a Bobi", in *Diario del '71 e del '72*, OV 454; "La madre di Bobi", in *Poesie disperse*, OV 786.

25 R. BAZLEN, *Scritti*, ed. R. Calasso, Milano, Adelphi, 1984, p. 358.

26 "Mi ho fatto dare, da Italo Svevo, i suoi due primi libri: *dimmi se devo mandarteli a Monterosso, o pure a Genova.* Il secondo libro: 'Senilità', è un vero capolavoro, e l'unico romanzo moderno che abbia l'Italia (pubblicato nel 1898!). Stile tremendo!" ("I made Italo Svevo give me his first two books: *tell me if I should send them to you in Monterosso, or rather in Genoa.* The second book, *Senilità* [*Senility*] is a true masterpiece, and the only modern novel that Italy has (published in 1898!). Tremendous style!") R. BAZLEN, *Scritti*, ed. R. Calasso, Milano, Adelphi, 1984, p. 359.

previously been published in installments in the Triestine newspaper «L'Indipendente», received a more severe reaction than the first book.[27] Svevo, discouraged by the silence that emerged around his books, abandoned his literary activity and decided to concentrate on his day job in the Veneziani firm, which belonged to his wife's family and which often sent him to London to manage the interests of the English branch. His travels required him to become fluent in English, and in 1907 Svevo hired James Joyce as a tutor from the Berlitz School in Trieste. The young novelist and the aging industrialist each appreciated the labors of the other: when the Irish writer was forced to move to Paris in 1914 by the war, he recommended Svevo's first two books to his French translator, Valery Larbaud. Larbaud appreciated Joyce's recommendation, and after the war edited an issue of the journal *Le Navire d'Argent*, half of which he dedicated to the Triestine author. Svevo, for his part, reassured by Joyce's interest in his work, resumed writing after the war's end. He published his third novel, *La coscienza di Zeno*, through the editor Cappelli of Bologna in 1923, a year after the publication of *Ulysses*. In *Ulysses*, according to the assertions of Svevo's daughter, the character Leopold Bloom has much in common with Joyce's Triestine pupil.[28]

Thanks to Bazlen's friendship, Montale participated in this network of international modernism. He received Svevo's novels, and in 1925 he was probably the only Italian outside of Trieste to have read all three; in return, he read them many times, and wrote three articles about them, which were published between 1925 and 1926.[29] A coincidental encounter in front of La Scala in the winter of 1926 reinforced the friendship between the two men, who had already begun to correspond.[30] Montale received from Svevo the address of Larbaud, and sent the translator an article about him that Montale recently published in *Baretti*, along with a copy of the first edition of *Ossi di seppia*.[31] Larbaud responded, initiating an intellectual relationship of long duration and great importance for the formation of

---

27 I. SVEVO, *Una vita*, Trieste, Ettore Vram, 1892; I. SVEVO, *Senilità*, Trieste, Ettore Vram, 1898. On the relationship between Montale and Svevo, see M. FORTI, *Svevo Romanziere*, Milano, All'Insegna del Pesce d'Oro, 1966, pp. 149-163. Montale reviewed Forti's book in the «Corriere della Sera», January 8, 1967, SM 2842-2843.

28 See N. LAGIOIA, *Svevo, Joyce: storia di un'amicizia* (2012), «Minima&Moralia»: web http://www.minimaetmoralia.it/wp/svevo-joyce-storia-di-unamicizia/ (retrieved on September 9, 2015). See also S. PRICE, *James Joyce and Italo Svevo, The Story of a Friendship*, London, Somerville Press, 2016.

29 *Omaggio a Italo Svevo*, «L'Esame», 1925, SM 72; *Presentazione di Italo Svevo*, «Il Quindicinale», 1926, SM 94; *Profili: Italo Svevo*, «L'Italia che scrive», 1926, SM 108.

30 The encounter is described in E. MONTALE, "Poesia e società" (1946), SM 661-664.

31 E. MONTALE, "Valery Larbaud" (1925), SM 31-36.

Montale's cultural horizons.[32] Later Montale had Larbaud give him the address of Joyce, to whom he also wrote, sending a copy of his review of *Gens de Dublin*, the French version of *Dubliners* prefaced by Larbaud, which he had read the previous summer.[33] Joyce responded by sending a copy of *Dedalus* and they held a brief correspondence.[34]

The relations between Montale and Anglo-American modernism intensified in 1924, when Ezra Pound moved from Paris to Rapallo, a town on the Ligurian coast halfway between Genoa and Monterosso. The fame of the American expatriate exerted a powerful attraction on Montale, who confirmed to have met Pound shortly after his arrival in Rapallo. Remembering him at a distance of many years, by which time Pound had been extradited to the United States and confined in a mental institution, Montale maintains a certain admiration for the peculiarity of his character:

> Quando lo conobbi, intorno al '25, Pound era un bell'uomo, aitante, il mento adorno da un pizzo *poil de carotte*. Giocatore di tennis, musicista appassionato che salvò dalla distruzione non so quante musiche inedite di Vivaldi [...].[35] In quel tempo Pound aveva già una storia, Eliot lo aveva salutato "miglior fabbro", Yeats e Joyce gli erano amicissimi, il gruppo degli 'esuli' (Hemingway ed altri) lo considerava un maestro. Erudito, ma di una erudizione che sapeva di digesto, di corso accelerato, fluido ma non corretto parlatore della nostra lingua, aveva allestito una discussa edizione delle poesie di Cavalcanti e collaborava a riviste italiane con note spesso illuminanti. Le sue poesie erano allora raccolte nel volume *Personae* ch'egli mi dedicò stampandovi a ceralacca il cammeo del suo anello, inciso da Gaudier Brzeska.[36]

---

32 Montale's letters to Larbaud can be read in E. MONTALE, *Caro Maestro e Amico. Carteggio con Valery Larbaud (1926-1937)*, ed. M. Sonzogni, Milano, Archinto, 2003.

33 E. MONTALE, "*Dubliners* di James Joyce" (1926), SM 148.

34 On the rapport between Montale and Joyce, see F. CONTORBIA, *Montale, Genova, il modernismo, e altri saggi montaliani*, cit., pp. 53-72.

35 Pound's intervention on the manuscripts by Vivaldi preserved in the National Library of Turin, which did not properly constitute a "salvage from distruction", is reconstructed in F.M. SARDELLI, *L'affare Vivaldi*, Palermo, Sellerio, 2015.

36 "When I met him, around '25, Pound was a handsome man, well-built, chin adorned with a goatee *poil de carotte*. Tennis player, passionate musician who saved from destruction I know not how much unpublished music by Vivaldi [...]. At that time Pound already had a history, Eliot had hailed him as "the better craftsman", Yeats and Joyce were close friends of his, the group of "exiles" (Hemingway and others) considered him a master. Erudite, but of an erudition that smacked of the digest, of an accelerated course, a fluid but incorrect speaker of our language, he had prepared a much-discussed edition of the poems of Cavalcanti and he collaborated with Italian journals with often illuminating notes. His poems were then gathered in the volume *Personae*, which he dedicated to me, stamping it in sealing-wax with the cameo of his ring, which was engraved by Gaudier Brzeska". E. MONTALE, "Se i biglietti da mille fossero quelli di Ezra Pound" (1955), SM 1883-1888; see also E. MONTALE, "Ezra Pound" (1958), SM 2134. For the reference to the dedication sealed with Pound's ring, which Montale recalls often,

Montale read the poems contained in the volume that Pound had dedicated to him, and they left a strong impression on him. Surely Pound also received a copy of *Ossi di seppia*, but we have no evidence that he ever read it. It is possible that Montale came to know the work of Eliot through Pound: in the words of Massimo Bacigalupo, "Montale's encounter with Pound, and through Pound with Eliot's *Waste Land*, surely played a role in his modernist shift".[37]

A 1927 letter from Montale to Svevo confirms an exchange of reading recommendations between the American and the Italian poet, and it reveals that the peculiar literary beliefs of Pound had a disorienting effect on his young colleague:

> Io parlavo giorni fa con un poeta americano molto amico di Joyce ed Eliot, il poeta Ezra Pound al quale Ella deve farmi il favore di mandare *Senilità* che ammira attraverso il *sentito dire* dei cenacoli; e questo Pound che passa per un genio (Eliot gli ha dedicato un poema) mi dice corna del mondo anglosassone e un mondo di bene del nostro mondo. Anche Bobi è ammiratore di Pound. Chi si orizzonta più?[38]

Montale visited Pound several times in Rapallo, and then, when he moved to Florence, Pound visited him on various occasions. The two poets exchanged books, kindnesses, and literary recommendations for some years, until their relationship chilled. It was Pound's support of the fascist regime, and not his egocentrism, that created the distance; as Montale recalls, "I nostri rapporti non dico che si siano del tutto raffreddati, ma entrarono in una fase di letargo perché Pound aveva delle opinioni politiche non diciamo diverse dalle mie, ma diametralmente opposte".[39]

In 1926, the government of the Fascist Party was swiftly transforming itself into a regime; Montale, who had come out as antifascist by signing

---

see "Fronde d'alloro in un manicomio" (1949), SM I, 793; "Biografie al microfono", interview by Giansiro Ferrata (1961), AMS 1611; and "L'alluvione ha sommerso...", OV 310.

37 M. Bacigalupo, *Pound and Montale*, «Journal of Modern Literature», 23.1 (1999), p. 53.

38 E. Montale, letter from Florence dated Aug. 27, 1927, in I. Svevo – E. Montale, *Carteggio*, ed. G. Zampa, Milano, Mondadori, 1976, p. 63: "A few days ago I spoke with an American poet who is good friends with Joyce and Eliot, to whom you must do me the favor of sending *Senilità*, which he already admires, thanks to the hearsay of the cenacles; and this Pound who passes for a genius (Eliot dedicated a poem to him) spoke poorly to me of the Anglo-Saxon world and had a world of good to say about our world. Even Bobi is an admirer of Pound. Who can get one's bearings anymore?".

39 E. Montale, "Biografie al microfono", interview by Giansiro Ferrata (1961), AMS 1611: "Our relations, I won't say that they totally chilled, but they entered into a lethargic phase because Pound had certain political opinions that were, let's not call them different from mine, but rather diametrically opposed to mine".

the "Manifesto" of Benedetto Croce the year before, began to find Genoa a less-than-welcoming place: he dreamed of leaving, asked his friends for tips on finding work in Trieste or Milan, and began to despair of the mental, social, and political health of his fellow-citizens, as he wrote to his comrade-in-arms Sergio Solmi:

> Qui poi sono un *outcast* in tutti i sensi, un pezzo fuor dall'ingranaggio. La stretta fascista qui è diventata forte, e chi non è dei loro non può vivere. Nelle due giornate del duce sono successi deliri incredibili. I giornalisti esteri erano sbalorditi.[40]

At long last, Montale was offered a position in the Florentine editor Bemporad's glorious publishing house of scholastic texts. He experienced the distance from Genoa as a liberation; the theme of escape from the phenomenal world, so present in the texts of the first edition of the *Ossi*, is not present in the handful of poems written to appear in the second edition: poems in which the need for a miracle remains, but the desired occasion is no longer linked to a substantial immobility of the lyric "I". The subject's immobility returns, at the most, in oxymoronic formulas that indicate how the voyage of the "I" is meant to be understood as more metaphysical than real: the "immoto / andare", the "ben noto delirio / d'immobilità" of "Arsenio".

That said, the move did not free Montale from insomnia, his permanent torment; his work for Bemporad was unsatisfying and modestly rewarded. Montale wrote to Sergio Solmi: "Non ho un soldo e da mesi non leggo un libro. Non parliamo della musa. Credo di essere completamente secco".[41] The initial economic privation caused by the move to Florence was compensated by other characteristics of the city. At the end of the 1920s, Florence occupied an eccentric position in the Italian ideological map; the presence of many foreign scholars and students, primarily Englishmen, Germans, and Americans, contributed to making the city a cultural center buzzing with lively exchanges of ideas. In Florence intellectuals could move with a certain degree of freedom; journals and correspondences that were not necessarily approved by the regime circulated

---

40 E. Montale, letter to Sergio Solmi dated June 2, 1926, in G. ZAMPA, *Introduzione*, SM LVI-LVII: "Here, moreover, I am an outcast in every sense, a piece out of joint. The fascist hold here has become strong, and whoever is not one of them cannot live. In the two days of [the visit of] the *Duce*, there have been incredible ravings. The foreign journalists were stunned".

41 E. Montale, letter to Sergio Solmi dated February 29, 1927, in G. ZAMPA, *Introduzione*, cit., SM LVI-LVII: "I don't have a cent, and I haven't read a book in months. Let's not speak of the muse. I believe I am completely dried up".

throughout the city, and it was common to find newspapers and journals from abroad. After the "October incidents", the Florentine *squadristi* were restrained in their violent actions by the Fascist Party, which hired many of them in its hierarchy and confined or imprisoned others.[42]

Eugenio's concern for his own muse was unjustified: after a brief hiatus, Montale wrote his first poem in Florence, "Arsenio", the chronologically final poem of the *Ossi*, a text that represents both literally and metaphorically the voyage of his poetry and of the "I", and a text that, according to the criticism, represents a turning point in Montale's approach to composing poetry. However, the freedoms afforded by Florence only lasted for a limited period of time: when Hitler visited the city in 1938, Florence was firmly under fascist control.[43] Despite being under facist control, the writers and artists who gathered in Piazza Vittorio at the Le Giubbe Rosse café were only watched, and not threatened or worse, by the squads that gathered in the Caffè Concerto Paszkowski across the way.

The journal *Solaria* was born at the tables of Le Giubbe Rosse a few months before Montale's arrival in the city; Alfredo Carocci, the young director, had inaugurated the first issue with a commemoration of Piero Gobetti, a journalist and editor, and the first publisher of *Ossi di seppia*, who had been long persecuted by fascists, and who died in Paris in February 1926. Montale immediately felt at ease with his friends at *Solaria* and regularly participated in the column "Zibaldone", where he reviewed new Italian and international literature. In fact, to counteract the asphyxiating domestic political situation, the journal took to translating and suggesting to its reader translations of the great masters of European modernism: Proust, Gide, and Valéry; Kafka, Joyce, and Eliot; and later the American Beats and the French *nouveau roman*. As for Italian literary production, next to the flourishing generation of contemporary poets (Ungaretti, Luzi, Montale himself), *Solaria* put forth the Triestine writers of the border, Saba and Svevo, who, being of Jewish descent, were hardly agreeable to the regime. The editors and collaborators of *Solaria* rendered the pro-European sentiment that had guided Montale's cultural formation in his Genoese

---

42 See A. Lyttleton, *The Seizure of Power: Fascism in Italy 1919-1929*, London and New York, Routledge 2004, p. 277 *et passim*; W.L. Adamson, *Avant-Garde Florence: From Modernism to Fascism*, Cambridge, Mass., Harvard University Press, 1993, pp. 227 *et passim*; M. Millan, *The Institutionalization of* Squadrismo: *Disciplining paramilitary Violence in the Italian Fascist Dictatorship*, «Contemporary European History» 22/4, November 2013, pp. 551-573; R. Ben-Ghiat, *Mapping Squadrist Violence*, «Contemporary European History» 22/4, November 2013, pp. 579-583.

43 R. Mancini, *Liturgie totalitarie. Apparati e feste per la visita di Hitler e Mussolini a Firenze (1938)*, Firenze, Le Cariti, 2010.

years into an instrument of defense against the incipient autarchy and the darkening of Italian political and cultural life. For if it is true that "verso il 1927 i giovani che si riunirono alle *Giubbe Rosse* per dar vita alla piccola *Solaria* non erano liberi" ("around 1927 the young men who gathered at the *Giubbe Rosse* to bring life to the little *Solaria* were not free"), it is also true that the editorial staff of the journal was composed of "un gruppo che opponeva un no o un 'ni' a tutti i si che erano impartiti dall'alto" ("a group that opposed a no, or an opposition of some kind, to all the yeses that were bestowed from on high").[44]

At the tables of Le Giubbe Rosse Montale also met Mario Praz, a Roman literary critic and lector of Italian literature at the University of Liverpool.[45] The two were united by their interest in modernist English literature and became close friends; they cultivated their friendship by exchanging poems in makeshift English, attempting parodies of Pound's and Eliot's poems.[46] Praz, who was already collaborating at *Criterion*, finally gave the Genoese poet what Svevo, Larbaud, Pound, and Orlo Williams could not or would not give him: access to T.S. Eliot. He gave Montale access to Eliot's texts, which Montale allegedly still did not know,[47] and access to the *Criterion* in an authorial capacity. He also translated Montale's most recent poem, only just published in *Solaria*, and sent it to Eliot, who, after many months of waiting, published it in the June 1928 edition with the original Italian facing it.[48]

Praz was a scholar of Romantic poetry and had especially appreciated the "connexion between nature and soul"[49] in the *Ossi*. However, this did

44 E. Montale, "Piccolo Baedecker 1954 della Firenze che scrive" (1954), SM 1637.

45 E. Montale, "Ho scritto un solo libro" (1975), Interview By G. Zampa, AMS 1724.

46 M. Praz, *The House of Life*, London, Methuen, 1964, p. 211.

47 According to Montale, but his declarations ought to be taken with a grain of salt: "Prima di allora [that is, prior to Praz lending him Eliot's *Ariel Poems*] non avevo letto di Eliot che una o due delle sue liriche giovanili, del periodo che fu chiamato laforguiano: 'Portrait of a Lady', 'The Love Song of Alfred Prufrock', tradotte in francese". ("Prior to that point I had not read Eliot, except for one or two of his youthful lyrics, from that period referred to as Laforguian: 'Portrait of a Lady', 'The Love Song of J. Alfred Prufrock', translated into French.] E. Montale, "Eliot e noi" (1947), SM 714; see *infra*.

48 E. Montale, "Arsenio", trans. M. Praz, in *Criterion*, VII (June 1928), pp. 54-57. For the history of English translations of Montale, see A. Francini, *Cronaca di una lunga fedeltà: il caso dei poeti statunitensi. Introduzione a Montale tradotto dai poeti*, «Semicerchio», 1997, pp. 11 *et passim*.

49 Praz concluded his column about Italian poetry for the *London Mercury* in January, 1928 with these sentences: "Eugenio Montale's [*Cuttle-fish Bones*], first published in 1925 and now going through a second edition, fully deserves the name of poetry. Montale's verse has all the elusive magic of the Ligurian sea-coast, the infinite movement of those arid promontories mashed by the surge of the charging sea. The Ligurian landscape is constantly suggested in these poems; the connexion between nature and soul could not be more intimate". M. Praz, as quoted in H. Thomas, *Montale in English*, New York, Handsel Books, 2004, p. xvii.

not prevent him from perceiving certain consonances between Eliot and Montale, "similar flowers to blossom at the same time in distant and apparently unrelated branches".[50] For Praz the two poets are so in tune that the contact between them is instinctive, automatic: it is only natural that the American should appreciate "Arsenio" translated into English, just as it is only natural that Montale should wish to "appropriate" Eliot, translating his verses into Italian:

> When in 1928 I submitted to Eliot my translation of Montale's "Arsenio" he must have recognized in the poem the accent of a kindred inspiration. And when about the same time I lent to Montale in Florence "A Song for Simeon" and "La Figlia the Piange" in the *Ariel Poems*, the Italian poet was so much impressed that he felt the desire to make the two poems his own by translating them.[51]

Initially, Montale was happy about the translation of "Arsenio" and the prospect of publication in a journal that he considered the apex of international modern poetry. He wrote enthusiastically to his correspondents about the reception of the translation of "Arsenio".[52] He also bragged about it to Valery Larbaud:

> Je vous unis une petite pièce à moi dans la version de Mario Praz qui paraîtra en Février 1928 dans *The Monthly Criterion* avec l'original vis-à-vis. Mais je tiens que vous lisiez aujourd'hui même ce tour de force de traduction littérale et veritablement... littéraire. C'est une réussite peu ordinaire.[53]

---

[50] M. Praz, *Montale and Eliot*, in *T.S. Eliot. A Symposium*, eds. R. March and Tambimuttu, Chicago, Henry Regnery Company, 1949, p. 244. In the following paragraph, Praz abandoned the metaphor to clarify the analogy between the two poets: "In our century, in the period between the two wars, two poets have arisen in the Anglo-Saxon world and in Italy, whose outlooks show remarkable affinities which can only partially be accounted for through the same cultural influences. *The Waste Land* and *Ossi di seppia* conjure up the same vision of a barren, disconsolate world, of a desperate aridity searching every cranny of the rocks for a drop of water". In Praz's opinion, Montale and Eliot even resembled each other physically, as well as in demeanor: "For a long time the figures of the two poets were associated in my mind: I saw a family likeness in their outward appearance of sallow, prematurely aged men, slow, unemphatic in their manners, seemingly incapable of strenuous physical effort, reserved and concentrated in an inner vision, unworldly, like priests of an unhallowed religion" (p. 246).

[51] M. Praz, *Montale and Eliot*, in *T.S. Eliot. A Symposium*, eds. R. March and Tambimuttu, Chicago, Henry Regnery Company, 1949, p. 246. Praz's recollection of the poems he lent to Montale is imprecise, see *infra*.

[52] E. Montale, *Lettere a Nino Frank*, in *Almanacco dello Specchio*, Milano, Mondadori, 1986, p. 29: "[Arsenio in traduzione] è piaciuto tantissimo a T.S. Eliot, a Ezra Pound e ad altri formidabili intenditori" ("Arsenio in translation was well liked by T.S. Eliot, by Ezra Pound, and other formidable experts"); see also p. 44.

[53] E. Montale, *Caro Maestro e amico. Carteggio con Valéry Larbaud (1926-1937)*, ed. M. Sonzogni, Milano, Archinto, 2003, p. 91: "I enclose one of my poems, in the translation by Mario

When Praz lent him the little booklet of *Ariel Poems*, Montale set about translating "A Song for Simeon", published in *Solaria* in December 1929; he also presumably translated "La figlia che piange" – which was published only in 1933 in the Genoese journal «Circoli» – and the first two stanzas of the first part of *Ash Wednesday* (see OV 1161). The translation of "Animula" can also be dated to between 1928 and 1933, though it was only published in 1947 as a coda to Montale's article "Eliot e noi" ("Eliot and us") in the monographic issue of «L'immagine» that was released for the occasion of Eliot's visit to Rome.[54] If we can believe Luciano Rebay, in this period of time Montale would also have translated Eliot's "Hollow Men", "Preludes", and "Morning at the Window".[55] The conditional tense is required here because Montale provided imprecise, if not deliberately false, information on that front. Even in the aforementioned article "Eliot e noi", in fact, Montale affirms to have translated "A Song for Simeon" and "La figlia che piange", drawing from the edition of the *Ariel Poems* that had been loaned to him by Mario Praz:

> Quelle poesie m'erano state prestate da Mario Praz, nella loro edizione (credo la prima) degli *Ariel Poems*, una serie di volumetti di sole quattro pagine, contenenti una breve lirica e una illustrazione di tipo postcubista. Prima di allora non avevo letto di Eliot che una o due delle sue liriche giovanili, del periodo che fu chiamato laforguiano: "Portrait of a Lady", "The Love Song of Prufrock", tradotte in francese.[56]

Praz; it will be published in February 1928 in the *Monthly Criterion*, with the original on the facing page. But I would like you to read immediately this tour de force of a literal, and… literary, translation. The result is quite extraordinary".

54 E. Montale, "Eliot e noi" (1947), SM 713-719.

55 L. Rebay, "Un cestello di Montale: le gambe di Dora Marcus e una lettera di Roberto Bazlen", in *La poesia di Eugenio Montale*, eds. E. Campailla and C.F. Goffis, Firenze: Le Monnier, 1984, p. 108; Rebay claims to have received the manuscripts of the three translations from Montale. See also T. De Rogatis, *Montale e il classicismo moderno*, Pisa-Roma, Istituti Editoriali e Poligrafici Internazionali, 2002, pp. 109 *et passim*, specifically note 55. Montale evokes the conclusion of *The Hollow Men* ("This is how the world ends / not with a bang but a whimper", T.S. Eliot, *The Complete Poems and Plays*, p. 59) in verse 9 of "Niente di grave", in *Satura*, OV 341.

56 E. Montale, "Eliot e noi", SM 713-714: "Those poems were loaned to me by Mario Praz, in their edition (I believe the first) of the *Ariel Poems*, a series of small volumes of only four pages, each containing a brief lyric and a post-Cubist illustration. Prior to that point I had not read Eliot, except for one or two of his youthful lyrics, from that period referred to as Laforguian: 'Portrait of a Lady', 'The Love Song of J. Alfred Prufrock', translated into French". In the "Note" that prefaced the translations published in «Circoli», III, n.6 (December 1933), pp. 50-57, Montale correctly observed that the *Ariel Poems* are composed of "Journey of the Magi", "A Song for Simeon", "Marina", "Animula", and "Triumphal March". The fact that in «Circoli» the translations of "La figlia che piange" and "Canto di Simeone" appear one next to the other may be the origin of Montale's *lapsus memoriae*.

According to this assertion, in 1928 Montale knew seven of Eliot's poems: the five contained in *Ariel Poems*, and the first two poems of *Prufrock* in the French translation. What Montale, who as usual was trusting in his memory as he wrote,[57] could not remember in 1947 was that "La figlia che piange", indeed translated by him, was not part of the *Ariel Poems* – it is the poem that closes the *Prufrock* collection. And therefore he should not even have known it, given that he claims to have known only the first two texts of *Prufrock*, and not even in the original language. Certain textual coincidences, on which we shall expand later, confirm that in 1927 Montale knew both *Prufrock* and *The Hollow Men*; and it is also very likely that thanks to his association with Pound, he would have known *The Waste Land*, too, which Eliot had dedicated "al miglior fabbro", a fact that Montale knew, as revealed in his aforementioned letter to Svevo, dated 1927. And yet, still in the same article, Montale asserts that he came to know *The Waste Land* only after having read the *Ariel Poems*, which is to say after having met Praz, which is to say in 1928, according to the recollection of Praz mentioned above. In this recollection Praz, just like Montale, errs in placing "La figlia che piange" in the *Ariel Poems*, an error probably caused by the fact that while he was participating in the symposium in honor of Eliot being awarded the Nobel Prize, he had Montale's article in front of him and trusted his friend's memory without checking the texts.

Thus, to summarize: in 1927-28 Montale knew more of Eliot's poems than what he would claim in 1947 to have known at that time. It would be easy to interpret his behavior as a case of anxiety of influence: since Montale's name was frequently juxtaposed with Eliot's in the specialist press not only in Italy, but also abroad. For example, in June 1934 «The Times Literary Supplement» ran a long article on modern Italian poetry, in which Montale was singled out as the poet who had made the greatest impression among the poets of his generation, and who was said to have the closest affinities to Eliot.[58] There would be nothing strange in observing that Montale had been influenced by "the most influential man of letters of the twentieth century";[59] and besides, an anxiety of influence and a desire to see one's own innovative talent recognized are not incompatible sentiments. In fact, in this way one could doubly argue for Montale's

---

[57] In fact, Montale agreed to write "una testimonianza" for "gli amici dell'«Immagine»" ("friends from «Immagine»") and not "uno studio approfondito che un'insufficiente documentazione mi renderebbe difficile" ("an exhaustive study, which insufficient documentation would render difficult for me"), *ibid.*

[58] H. Thomas, *Montale in English*, New York, Handsel Books, 2004, p. xvii.

[59] H. Kenner, *The Invisible Poet: T.S. Eliot*, London, Methuen, 1979, p. 9.

convergence with the modernist movement: through Eliot's influence on him, and his effort to hide this influence, the Italian poet did nothing more than follow one of the commandments prescribed by Pound in 1913: "Be influenced by as many great artists as you can, but have the decency either to acknowledge the debt outright, or to try to conceal it".[60]

It would be reductive to consider Montale's modernism as born solely out of his reading of Eliot or Pound: their poiesis may have offered him examples of how modernist poetics could take form, yet Montale is right in a more fundamental sense when he disavows the connection with Eliot, when he says that "Gli *Ossi* scritti prima del '25, *Arsenio* scritto nel '27, la conoscenza (precoce) di Pound e quella (tardiva) di Hopkins mi avrebbero portato nell'attuale posizione anche se Eliot fosse stato assai diverso o non fosse stato".[61] In a common background, including influences from the French symbolists and contingentist theories, in a common interest in the scientific discoveries of their time, in a common reaction to the atrocities of mechanized war and to the fears for the future of Europe, we find more solid ground for comparison and a better understanding of what it meant to be a European modernist.

2. Mediterranean Studies

While discussing "Meriggiare pallido e assorto…", I have pointed out that the changes in the poetry of the *Primi Ossi* are observable, *in nuce*, in the difference between the three stanzas of "Meriggiare" written in the infinitive in 1916 and the final one, written or modified in 1922, which contains a gerund, thereby introducing the concept of the temporality of human existence and, at the same time, of the suffering that is indivisible from it. Analogously the *Primi Ossi*, considered as a whole, can be interpreted as as the description of a disruption and a displacement concerning both subject and object of the poetic discourse. Such trajectory, from expressing the momentary happiness of enchantment to the moment of disillusionment of adulthood, is not immediately intelligible in the book,

---

[60] E. Pound, "A Few Don'ts by an Imagiste" (1913), in *Literary Essays of Ezra Pound*, ed. T.S. Eliot, London, Faber, 1960, p. 5.

[61] E. Montale, letter to Piero Bignogiari dated July 19, 1949. See P. Bigongiari, *Dal «correlativo oggettivo» al «correlativo soggettivo»*, in *Montale e il canone poetico del Novecento*, eds. M.A. Grignani and R. Luperini, Bari, Laterza, 1998, p. 424: "The *Ossi* written before 1925, *Arsenio* written in 1927, my (precocious) acquaintance with Pound and my (belated) one with Hopkins – these would have brought me to my present position even if Eliot had been quite different or had not existed at all".

because the poems are positioned according to thematic structures, and are placed programmatically in a fragmentary and dissonant manner, instead of being organized in a diachronic succession. It would be impossible then to propose a clear-cut division, a precise moment in which the young Montale realized that the desired union between the individual and nature was no longer possible, and as a consequence, that symbolist tropes were no longer capable of representing the modern human condition.

There is no clear-cut division, no way to pinpoint the precise moment of the change, because the two veins, Montale tells us, are parallel: they flow one beside the other, perhaps even one inside the other. In some poems dated 1923 and 1924 the city of Genoa and the nature of the Cinque Terre are still reproduced realistically, following the teachings of "adesione" ("adhesion") derived from the Ligurian poets. We recall the *Intervista immaginaria*, in which Montale wrote: "Conobbi presto (non di persona, se si eccettua Sbarbaro) alcuni poeti liguri: Ceccardo e Boine, fra gli altri. Dov'essi aderivano alle fibre del nostro suolo rappresentarono senza dubbio un insegnamento per me".[62] The poets of the Ligurian heritage *adhere* to the fibers of the soil; however, when Montale uses the verb "aderire" in the *Intervista immaginaria* to describe himself, a few pages after the passage cited, he includes it with a very different concept:

> Volevo che la mia parola fosse più aderente di quella degli altri poeti che avevo conosciuto. Più aderente a che? Mi pareva di vivere sotto una campana di vetro, eppure sentivo di essere vicino a qualcosa di essenziale. Un velo sottile, un filo appena mi separava dal *quid* definitivo. L'espressione assoluta sarebbe stata la rottura di quel velo, di quel filo: una esplosione, la fine dell'inganno del mondo come rappresentazione.[63]

He starts by declaring his quest for "adherence", and yet he stops abruptly, to ask to himself and to his readers: but adherent to what? The logic of the thought quickly switches direction: adherent to an explosion, to the end of the deceit of the phenomenal world. Is this contradictory?

---

62 E. Montale, "Intenzioni (Intervista immaginaria)" (1946), AMS 1477: "I knew soon (not in person, with the exception of Sbarbaro) some Ligurian poets: Ceccardo and Boine, among others. Where they adhered to the fibers of our land, they represented without doubt a learning for me".

63 E. Montale, "Intenzioni (Intervista immaginaria)" (1946), AMS 1480: "I wanted my words to adhere more closely to those of other poets who I had known. Adhere more closely to what? I seemed to be living under a bell of glass and yet I felt I was close to something essential. A subtle veil, a thread, barely separated me from the definitive *quid*. The absolute expression would have been the rupture of that veil, of that thread: an explosion, the end of the deception of the world as a representation".

Absolutely. Some would consider such contradiction as the unmistakable sign of a great work of modern literature:

> The modern physicist continues to live in the Newtonian world of the layman while knowing its limited, almost illusory, character. Or in other words, the common sense table continues to exist but only within a human scale of reference. Several of the greatest works of modern literature are characterized by such a double awareness. They use realist representation, indeed they often use it consummately, yet with an x-ray awareness of its constructed, or purely human, character.[64]

As pointed out, the texts are contradictory too: the letter Montale sent to Francesco Messina in 1923 included "Portami il girasole...", a text in which the flower of the first verse still has a strong symbolic connotation (in so much as it is an antidote to the "terreno bruciato dal salino" of l. 2 and it guides one toward the place where "vapora la vita quale essenza", l. 11), where "svanire / è dunque la venture della venture" (ll. 7-8), and where the annulment of the I in the landscape is still desirable and achievable. But the same manuscript also contains "Non chiederci la parola", in which a different flower, the crocus – resplendent "in mezzo a un polveroso prato" (l. 4): a symbol, like the sunflower, of the omniponent word that expresses itself, not coincidentally, in "lettere di fuoco" (v. 2) – is contradicted in its role as a symbol and declared impossible. The poet, having survived the war, can no longer utter a spell, a formula to reach and communicate a full awareness of the reality that surrounds him. The abilty to communicate the reality is possible, perhaps, for the undivided man about whom he speaks in the second stanza, for the man unshattered by self-consciousness: it is certainly not possible for "noi", for us, for the survivors, who are by this point only able to express ourselves through negations.[65]

That's why "Riviere", a text in which the I wishes to disappear, closes the book, even though the author later denounced the incongruity of the placement.[66] In texts that followed, "Non rifugiarti nell'ombra" (1922, OV

---

64 M. Bell, *The Metaphysics of Modernism*, in M. Levenson (ed.), *The Cambridge Companion to Modernism*, Cambridge, Cambridge University Press, 1999, p. 12.

65 This reading of the variations occurring in the book is meant to be parallel to Romano Luperini's, who analyzes the presence of musical elements in "Accordi", "Ministrels", "Caffè a Rapallo", and "Arsenio", to conclude that Montale's abandonment of a "consonance" ("accordo", literally) with his musical references is symptomatic of the abandonment of the symbolic modes. "Congedo dalla musica e congedo dal simbolismo – da una poesia di sensazioni impressionistiche – vanno di pari passo". ("Abandonment of music and abandonment of symbolism – of a poetry made of impressionistic sensations – move in step". See R. Luperini, *Montale e l'allegoria moderna*, cit., p. 96.

66 E. Montale, "Intenzioni (Intervista immaginaria)" (1946), AMS 1480.

29), "Gloria del disteso mezzogiorno" (1923, OV 37), "Debole sistro al vento" (1921-3, OV 44), "Egloga" (September 1923, OV 72), the connection between noontime light and paralysis, between suspended time and the immobility of the lyric I, is made even more explicit. Liguria is the mythical place where it is possible to witness manifestations of the divine: as is the case in "Là fuoriesce il Tritone" (1923, OV 35), a rarely analyzed but significant text in the *Ossi brevi*. In "Là fuoriesce il Tritone" we can witness the suspension of time; it is a poem in which the present and past coincide:

Portovenere

Là fuoriesce il Tritone
dai flutti che lambiscono
le soglie d'un cristiano
tempio, ed ogni ora prossima
è antica. Ogni dubbiezza
si conduce per mano
come una fanciulletta amica.

Là non è chi si guardi
o stia di sé in ascolto.
Quivi sei alle origini
e decidere è stolto:
ripartirai più tardi
per assumere un volto.[67]

As indicated by the inscription, this short *Osso* is set in Portovenere, a small village of fishermen slightly east of the Cinque Terre. At the far end of the wharf, where it is supposed the temple of Venus that gave the town its name was once located, a church dedicated to San Pietro was built; this historical commingling of pagan and Christian elements is reflected in the text, resulting in the image of the pagan god Triton emerging from the sea near the church, which is named, however, with a Latinism: "tempio" ("temple"). It is as if paganism and Christianity interpenetrate, as if the place's eternal present elides the diachrony between one faith and another, transporting the promontory into a timeless place. Time is suspended, and even spatial measurement is voided, and the I can pass from "là" to "quivi" without moving. In this privileged place self-awareness is unnecessary

67 "There Triton surges / from waves that lap / the sills of a Christian / temple, and every future hour / is ancient. All hesitation / is taken by the hand / like a friendly little girl. // There no one regards himself / or heeds his own words. / Here you are at the origin, / to decide is a foolish act: / you'll leave later / to assume a face".

("Là non è chi guardi / o stia di sè in ascolto"); it is unnecessary to possess an individual identity or to make choices. This text is an example of how the suspension of space and time in the *Ossi* between 1922 and 1923 is not viewed negatively: rather, the Ligurian landscape is represented as a seaside Eden where the meridian heat could suffocate reality in a divine stillness. However, beginning in 1924 the lyric I wishes to escape from this Eden, from this *hortus conclusus*, as we see in "In limine" (OV 3), which indeed takes place in a garden/reliquary and which was, originally, tellingly titled "La libertà".[68]

It would be simple enough to trace this need for escape back to biographical elements: Eugenio wants to leave Genoa, a city in which he will not be able to lead a satisfying intellectual life.[69] However, he also wishes to lacerate the veil that hides the deception of the world as representation, to leave behind the limitations imposed by an outmoded lyric language. The third of the group of poems sent to Francesco Messina, "Forse un mattino andando in un'aria di vetro", is enlightening:

> Forse un mattino andando in un'aria di vetro,
> arida, rivolgendomi, vedrò compiersi il miracolo:
> il nulla alle mie spalle, il vuoto dietro
> di me, con un terrore di ubriaco.
>
> Poi come s'uno schermo, s'accamperanno di gitto
> alberi case colli per l'inganno consueto.
> Ma sarà troppo tardi: ed io me n'andrò zitto
> tra gli uomini che non si voltano, col mio segreto.[70]

The "I" we read here is different from the I inhabiting and performing the earlier poems of *Ossi di seppia;* first, he fantasizes of acquiring a knowledge that makes him different from the rest of humanity ("I'll quietly go

---

68 See OV 861.

69 On January 30, 1926 he wrote to Sergio Solmi (AMS XXVIII): "Vivessi mill'anni qui, non romperò mai quella scorza di camarille, di mafie ecc. che è infrangibile ed impermeabile: almeno per me. [...] Se dovessi vivere ancora sei mesi nelle condizioni di questi due anni, son certo che impazzirei. Ma non lascerò passare sei mesi" ("Here [in Genoa] – even in a thousand years I would not be able to break the coterie of mafia, etc. that is infrangible and impermeable: at least for me. [...] If I have to continue living for another six months in the conditions of these past two years, I am certain I will go mad. But I will not allow six months to pass".

70 See OV 40: "Maybe one morning, walking in air / of dry glass, I'll turn and see the miracle occur- / nothingness at my shoulders, the void / behind me- with a drunkard's terror. // Then, as on a screen, the usual illusion: / hills houses trees will suddenly reassemble, / but too late, and I'll quietly go my way, / with my secret, among men who don't look back", trans. W. Arrowsmith.

my way, with my secret, among men who don't look back"), a concept mirrored in the twin poem *Non chiederci la parola*, where an "us" defying any positive definition is proudly opposed to "l'uomo che se ne va sicuro, / agli altri ed a se stesso amico, / e l'ombra sua non cura che la canicola / stampa sopra uno scalcinato muro!" (ll. 5-8). Such rupture in the bond of human fraternity is motivated and accompanied by a severance between the individual and his landscape: in a poem dominated by the semantic field of vision (even the "miracolo" is, etymologically, something that must be seen) the "I", looking back in a propitious instant, is able to see the lie in the ontological world surrounding him. What "must be seen", the miracle, is nothing, "nulla". That nothing is the real surrounding, while the landscape (that is, the landscape described in the previous poems, containing "trees houses hills") is merely the "usual illusion". The whole landscape ceases to exist, no longer the place of autobiographical representation, while the truth can only be glimpsed at in an instantaneous and impermanent illumination.[71]

Here the desire to shatter the "deception of the world as representation" proves most evident; we have the true manifestation of a miracle in verses that show the effects of reading Schopenhauer and Bergson.[72] The miracle is vastly different from the one desired in the youthful suite "Accor-

---

[71] See the letter written to Paola Nicoli on August 24, 1924 in E. Montale, *Autografi di Montale, Fondo dell'Università di Pavia*, eds. M. Corti and M.A. Grignani, Torino: Einaudi 1976, p. 27: "È un po' difficile che io riesca a lavorare per ora; il mio genere è tutta *un'attesa del miracolo*, e di miracoli in questi tempi senza religione se ne vedono pochini. Finito il libro – e finito può quasi dirsi – o sposterò la visuale, mutando genere, o silentium. Non ho nessuna voglia di vivisezionarmi di più" ("It is difficult for me to work, at the moment: my genre is based on waiting for a miracle, and one does not sees many miracles in out times without religion. When I will be done with the book – and the book is almost done – either I move my perspective, with a new genre, or *silence*. I do not desire to vivisect myself any further").

[72] See A. Schopenhauer, *The World as Will and Idea*, trans. R.B. Haldane and J. Kemp, London, Kegan Paul, Trench, Trübner & Co., 1909, pp. 499-500: "Such a man, who, after many bitter struggles with his own nature, has finally conquered entirely, continues to exist only as a pure, knowing being, the undimmed mirror of the world. Nothing can trouble him more, nothing can move him, for he has cut all the thousand cords of will which hold us bound to the world, and, as desire, fear, envy, anger, drag us hither and thither in constant pain. He now looks back smiling and at rest on the delusions of this world, which once were able to move and agonise his spirit also, but which now stand before him as utterly indifferent to him, as the chess-men when the game is ended, or as, in the morning, the cast-off masquerading dress which worried and disquieted us in a night in Carnival. Life and its forms now pass before him as a fleeting illusion, as a light morning dream before half-waking eyes, the real world already shining through it so that it can no longer deceive; and like this morning dream, they finally vanish altogether without any violent transition". In Schopenhauer, unlike in "Forse un mattino...", the recognition of the phenomenal world's lack of onthological reality generates a smile and a sense of indifference in the discerning spirit.

di"; here the revelation does not lead to divinity, extrinsic or immanent, but to the discovery of nothing, of the void that rests behind the cinema screen of ontology. This knowledge is still tied to vision, as in the theoretical postulates of the *Quaderno Genovese*, but vision does not reveal knowledge of the intimate secrets of things. On the contrary, it reveals only knowledge in negative, which engenders terror. Referring back to what has been said in previous chapters, it seems clear that the lyric "I" does not aspire to the experience of ontological totality: such an experience becomes impossible, because there is no longer a reality to get to know. What also seems clear here is the subjective character of the experience of time and space: the "I" pays witness to an unveiling of reality that is not granted to those around him, those who "non si voltano" ("do not turn"); his time and space are not analogous to those of other men. The knowledge of the deception of the real is not an accomplishment from a gnosiological point of view; rather, the knowledge results in dread, as it unveils a secret that isolates and renders speechless any who possess it. The "I" is therefore left with no choice but to proceed on his path: the gerund "andando" reproduces the existential experience that concludes "Meriggiare pallido e assorto".

The landscape, which in the early poems is captured in its profound but mysterious harmony with humankind, is represented later as alien and hostile, fragmented and uncertain, even nonexistent. A few months after having written "Non chiederci la parola..." and "Forse un mattino...", Montale was personally acquainted with Pound, as well as, one supposes, with Pound's work. It is as if Montale had adapted to his own lyric condition the opening quatrain of Pound's *Hugh Selwyn Mauberley*:

> For three years, out of key with his time,
> He strove to resuscitate the dead art
> Of poetry; to maintain "the sublime"
> In the old sense. Wrong from the start – (l. 1-4)[73]

He realized that to resuscitate the "dead art of poetry", to "maintain 'the sublime'", was "wrong from the start" and "out of key with his time". The "I" could no longer find in the landscape a refuge and a mirror, nor a comforting consonance between man and nature. The subject became detached from the familiarity of place – both actual locales and literary scenery – to seek a new poetic language and mode. The encounter with Pound, and the kinship Montale felt with Pound's poetic diktats, undoubtedly

[73] E. Pound, *E.P. ode pour l'élection de son sépulchre*, ed. Richard Sieburt, Ezra Pound, New Selected Poems and Translations, New York, New Direction Books, 2010, p. 111.

exercised a strong influence on Montale: to quote Massimo Bacigalupo again, "Montale was well aware of Pound as a poet of stature. And there is a distinct change from *Ossi di seppia* to *Le occasioni* in the direction of obscurity, fragmentation, and collage, use of foreign quotations".[74] However, even before meeting Pound, Montale had perceived that one era had come to an end, and another was beginning.

The suite "Mediterraneo", a single composition divided into nine stanzas of irregular measure, and the long poem that follows it, entitled "Fine dell'infanzia", have to be read together. They represent the bildungsroman of the young poet, who relates with the Mediterranean Sea, which is a father, a master of poetry, a natural element, or a mythical element. At the outset of the series, as one sees in "A vortice s'abbatte..." (OV 51) and even more in "Antico, sono ubriacato...", (OV 52), the "I" and the sea reflect each other and complement each other, and are each part of the other:

> Antico, sono ubriacato dalla voce
> ch'esce dalle tue bocche quando si schiudono
> come Verdi campane e si ributtano
> indietro e si disciolgono.
> La casa delle mie estati lontane
> t'era accanto, lo sai,
> là nel paese dove il sole cuoce
> e annuvolano l'aria le zanzare.
> Come allora oggi in tua presenza impietro,
> mare, ma non più degno
> mi credo del solenne ammonimento
> del tuo respiro. Tu m'hai detto primo
> che il piccino fermento
> del mio cuore non era che un momento
> del tuo; che mi era in fondo
> la tua legge rischiosa: esser vasto e diverso
> e insieme fisso:
> e svuotarmi così d'ogni lordura
> come fai tu che sbatti sulle sponde
> tra sugheri alghe asterie
> le inutili macerie del tuo abisso.[75]

---

[74] M. Bacigalupo, *Pound and Montale*, «Journal of Modern Literature», 23.1 (1999), p. 53.

[75] OV 52: "O Ancient, I am drunk on the voice / that breaks from your mouths when they unfold / like green bells, then collapse, / dissolving. / The house of my distant summers / stood, as you know, next to you, / there in the land of the searing sun / where mosquitoes are dense as clouds. / Petrified by your presence then and now, / sea, I deem myself no longer worthy of the solemn admonition / of your breath. You taught me that / the minuscule ferment / of my heart was merely a moment / of yours; that your venturesome principle /

The sea has a voice: it speaks through its mouths, it breathes, and it has a heart; in opposition, the lyric "I" has a seabed and transforms into stone. While the sea is personified (starting with the evocation: "antico"), the "I" is reified, because the two are one. The Mediterranean is the "paese incorrotto" ("unspoiled land") that welcomes the "I" in need of a fatherland. And yet, in the suite's central poem, the moment of separation arrives; it is the time when the tempo of the chords is disrupted:

> Giunge a volte, repente,
> un'ora che il tuo cuore disumano
> ci spaura e dal nostro si divide.
> Dalla mia la tua musica sconcorda,
> allora, ed è nemico ogni tuo moto.[76]

The "I" wishes to maintain a consonance with the natural elements, but such a connection is simply impossible. A human cannot be "fuori dal tempo" ("outside of time") because the desire to know steers him toward the moment, the Bergsonian flux, and it resists the other desire, the desire to let oneself loose in the reconstitutive power of the sea itself and to reach the place in which all contradictions are resolved.

> Avrei voluto sentirmi scabro ed essenziale
> siccome i ciottoli che tu volvi,
> mangiati dalla salsedine;
> scheggia fuori dal tempo, testimone
> di una volontà fredda che non passa.
> Altro fui: uomo intento che riguarda
> in sé, in altrui, il bollore
> della vita fugace – uomo che tarda
> all'atto, che nessuno, poi, distrugge.
> Volli cercare il male
> che tarla il mondo, la piccola stortura
> d'una leva che arresta
> l'ordegno universale; e tutti vidi
> gli eventi del minuto
> come pronti a disgiungersi in un crollo.[77]

---

is deeply engrained in me: to be vast and various, / and unchanging at the same time, / to cleanse myself of every filth / imitating you who leave on the shores / cork seaweed starfish / the useless wreckage of your abyss".

[76] OV 55, ll. 1-4: "Suddenly, at times, there comes / a moment when your inhuman heart, / estranged from ours, terrifies. / Then your music clashes with mine, / your every movement is hostile", trans. W. Arrowsmith.

[77] OV 57, ll. 1-15: "I would have liked to feel rough, elemental / as the pebbles you tumble

As was the case with "Forse un mattino...", the "I" who finds "il male / che tarla il mondo", the "piccola stortura / [...] che arresta / l'ordegno universale", does not enjoy a privileged or esoteric experience; the knowledge of reality is a knowledge of impermanence, of transience, and it leads to dissolution, the shared destiny of all mortal beings. Thus, the conclusion of the suite, "Bene lo so: bruciare, / questo, non altro, è il mio significato" (OV 59, ll. 22-23), is in evident contrast with the Symbolist tenet of corresponding with nature: no longer vanishing, becoming one with everything, but burning, wasting away – with no other ambition or other purport.

Analogously, the poem "Fine dell'infanzia" (OV 65), at once the consummation and the explanation of "Mediterraneo", initially tells of a space and time in which one could live in communion with nature; it describes an Eden in which one could give names to things. The place is a house on the sea, quite similar to the Casa delle due palme in Monterosso; the time is the time of infancy, in which "Ogni attimo bruciava / negl'istanti futuri senza tracce" (ll. 55-56), a description that closely recalls both the concept of personal time theorized by Bergson, the *flux*, and the lines "ogni ora prossima / è antica" in "Là fuoriesce il Tritone..." As in that poem, the "I" has no need to separate itself from the natural element, no need to possess self-awareness. There are no rules to separate "l'anima" from the "consenso esterno" in the mythical infancy described in "Fine dell'infanzia":

> Norma non v'era,
> solco fisso, confronto,
> a sceverare gioia da tristezza.
> Ma riaddotti dai viottoli
> alla casa sul mare, al chiuso asilo
> della nostra stupita fanciullezza,
> rapido rispondeva
> a ogni moto dell'anima un consenso
> esterno, si vestivano di nomi
> le cose, il nostro mondo aveva un centro.[78]

---

about, / pocked by salt, a timeless shard, witness / to a cold, persistent will. I was / anything but: a man intent / on observing, in himself and others, the furor / of fleeting life; a man who defers / doing, which therefore can never be undone. / I chose to look for the evil / gnawing at the world, the little warp / in the lever that locks / the universal gears; and I saw / all the events of the instant / as though poised to collapse and crumble", trans. W. Arrowsmith.

[78] OV 65, ll. 59-68: "There were no rules, / no measure, no sure way / of dividing joy from sadness. / But when those country paths brought us home / to the house by the sea, to the cozy shelter / of our wide-eyed childhood, / a consensus beyond us / instantly responded / to every stirring of the soul, / things were clothed with names, / our world was centered". W. Arrowsmith, transl.

In that mythical time nature did not have to be read or interpreted. It simply *was*:

> Eravamo nell'età verginale
> in cui le nubi non sono cifre o sigle
> ma belle sorelle che si guardano viaggiare.[79]

The description of the mythical time of infancy concludes with a verse more elucidatory in its simplicity than the others: "Eravamo nell'età illusa" (l. 79). The "età illusa" is not simply the age of illusions: etymologically it is the age of games ("ludi"), which is to say childhood. "Il – ludere" is the intensifier of the Latin verb "ludere", "to play a game": "illudere" is what children do when pretending, when simulating a reality that does not exist.

The contrast with the second part of the poem, which addresses, in fact, the *end* of the mythical time of infancy, is underscored by the passage from the imperfect tense, which in Italian emphasizes repetition and the duration of an action, to the preterite, which indicates a definite (and finite) time.[80] The precipitous passage of time leads to the moment of the deception's unveiling, to the end of the age of illusions:

> Un'alba dové sorgere che un rigo
> di luce su la soglia
> forbita ci annunziava come un'acqua;
> e noi certo corremmo
> ad aprire la porta
> stridula sulla ghiaia del giardino.
> L'inganno ci fu palese.
> Pesanti nubi sul torbato mare
> che ci bolliva in faccia, tosto apparvero.
> Era in aria l'attesa
> di un procelloso evento.[81]

The act of opening the door is a metaphysical gesture comparable to the discovery of the "anello che non tiene". Reality itself becomes adver-

---

[79] *Ibid.* ll. 69-71: "We were in that virginal age / when clouds are neither ciphers or symbols / but beautiful sisters, and you watched them go by", trans. W. Arrowsmith.

[80] *Ibid.* l. 80: "Volarono anni corti come giorni", ("Years as short as days flew by").

[81] *Ibid.* ll. 84-94: "A dawn suddenly came, heralded / by a sunburst on the shining / lintel. It broke like a great wave. / And we of course ran to open / the door that cracked on the gravel / leading to the garden. / The illusion stood revealed. / Suddenly over the wild water seething / at our feet, thick cloudpack appeared. / Expectation of a storm / filled the air", trans. W. Arrowsmith.

sarial through this gesture. The landscape thus becomes a problem: it is no longer the traditional background against which the poet exhibits his own particular sentiments, but an object of investigation within which the poet discovers the rupture of the youthful idyll and the enmity of the world. The crisis of this fabled harmony is also the crisis of symbolist *correspondences*.

When speaking of a poet who will use the metaphor of the *bufera* (tempest) to describe the Second World War, it does not seem a stretch to hypothesize that the "procelloso evento" in line 94 is also a reference to war: the terrible war that shattered the notions of the individual, of time and space, that was both the cause and the effect of the world's passage to the modern age. The First World War was a moment of rupture and of ideological transition, capable of hastening the disappearance of the old order. The world of Montale, which had been immobile, began to move.

3. "The Interpretative Key Never Fits Twice into the Montalean Door"

Even before coming to know Pound and reading Eliot's work, Montale had theorized and put into practice a poetry with characteristics that we recognize as modernist: he aimed to build a body of texts that programmatically deny the reader the possibility of complete comprehension; [82] in such texts, the literal meaning cannot be negotiated at first glance because it resonates with multiple metaphors and significations. The text does not

[82] Since 1915 Montale believed that the poetic work of art must be a keynote able to resonate in a hundred different echoes. See E. Montale, QG AMS 1316-1317: "La visione di un bel quadro rappresentante un paesaggio (e fors'anche del paesaggio stesso) ci lascia un po' freddi; mentre certi effetti pittorici ottenuti per mezzo della semplice parola in poesia ci dànno un fremito di soddisfazione. Perché ciò? Nel primo caso l'opera ha tutto in sé e non richiede la nostra collaborazione: noi rimaniamo di fronte all'opera, passivi e inerti. Nel secondo caso invece, le parole del poeta rappresentano di per sé stesse ben poco; occorre che noi concorriamo con l'artista, mediante uno sforzo personale più o meno grande, a creare in noi le sue visioni e le sue sensazioni. [...] L'opera d'arte dev'essere quindi un tasto che deve, toccato, centuplicarsi in noi con reti di risonanze e di echi [...] Non importa poi se una stessa poesia, sarà talvolta intesa da venti persone, p.es., in venti modi diversi" ("Viewing a fine landscape painting [and perhaps even the landscape itself] leaves us a bit cold, while certain pictorial effects obtained by means of a simple word in a poem give us a thrill of satisfaction. Why is this so? In the first instance, the work contains everything in itself and has no need of our collaboration: we remain before the work, passive and inert. In the second instance, instead, the poet's words represent in themselves next to nothing; we must work with the artist, through more or less extensive personal exertion, to create in ourselves his visions and his sensations. [...] The work of art must therefore be a key that should, when touched, centuple itself in us with networks of resonances and echoes. [...] It does not matter, then, if a single poem should occasionally be interpreted by twenty people, for instance, in twenty different ways"). See also QG AMS 1329.

demand that it be understood, but rather it aims to create an impasse, a moment of suspension of indecision in the reader that cannot be rationally explained. In this logic, it is revelatory to consider the variations of meaning of the metaphorical elements of the *Ossi di seppia*. The metaphor used in one text, whether a natural element, a real object, or an imagined one, will not necessarily bear the same signification in a different text: in other words, borrowing from Arrowsmith, "the interpretative key never fits twice running into the Montalean door".[83] For example, the metaphor of the "ramo", the branch of a tree, in "I limoni" and in "Quasi una fantasia" represents the possibility of communication between nature and the individual: it indicates the legibility and the intelligibility of the phenomenal world. Conversely, in "Non chiederci la parola…" the same metaphor is associated with the negation of the communicative process.[84] Vessels and boats are equally unstable metaphors: in "Fuscello teso da muro" the "trealberi" is the embodiment of a numinous event, while in "Crisalide" instead it is an instrument of salvation ("barca di salvezza", l. 54). The two vessels must be of similar metaphysical origin, though, since in both cases they proceed without leaving a trace in the sea.[85] The vegetalization of humanity can be represented both positively and negatively: in "La farandola dei fanciulli…" the "cespo umano" of the children grows in communion with natural elements, and in "Crisalide" the "cespo" that "riverdica" (l. 90) describes the attractiveness of the desired woman; conversely in "Arsenio" and "Incontro", the vegetalization of the lyric "I", of his alter ego, and of the female protagonist of the unsuccessful encounter, indicates a human life that has not realized its full potential.[86] The most complex and multi-

[83] See W. Arrowsmith's notes in E. Montale, *Cuttlefish Bones*, trans. W. Arrowsmith, New York, London, Norton & Co., 1993, p. 198.

[84] See "I limoni" OV 9, ll. 13-14: "più chiaro si ascolta il susurro / dei rami amici nell'aria che quasi non si muove", ("More clearly now you hear the whisper / of genial branches in that air barely astir"); "Quasi una fantasia" OV 18, ll. 19-21, "Lieto leggerò i neri / segni dei rami sul bianco / come un essenziale alfabeto", ("Elated, I'll read the black / signs of branches on the white, / like an alphabet of being". W. Arrowsmith, transl.); "Non chiederci la parola…" OV 27, ll. 9-10, "Non domandarci la formula che mondi possa aprirti, / sì qualche storta sillaba e secca come un ramo", ("Do not ask us the word that can open a world / but only a few syllables, twisted and dry as a branch").

[85] See "Fuscello teso dal muro…" OV 24, ll. 25-27: "Chi è in alto e s'affaccia s'avvede / che brilla la tolda e il timone / nell'acqua non scava una traccia" ("Who's looking from above realizes / that the deck glows and the rudder / leaves no trace in the water"); and "Crisalide" OV 85, l. 68: "Nell'onda e nell'azzurro non è scia" ("It doesn't leave a trace / in the wave nor in the sky"). They were probably built by the same shipwright who built Cato's vessel, from *Purg.* II, 1-54.

[86] "La farandola dei fanciulli…" (OV 43, ll. 3-4) "Cresceva tra rare canne e uno sterpeto / il cespo umano nell'aria pura" ("Among a scattering of reeds and brush / the human plant

faried metaphorical element of the book is ultimately the Mediterranean Sea which is "vasto e diverso e insieme fisso";[87] it references many different elements, even in opposition or contradiction with each other, but it always remains itself. The Mediterranean can be the place where life begins, or the resting place of the dead; it is called a father, and it can be a maternal figure; a master of the poetic arts, or the delirious counterpoint to the "I". The coherence of metaphorical significance is not a concern for the author of *Ossi di seppia*.

The young Montale shared with the Anglo-American modernists a post-Symbolist cultural formation (developed in the shadow of the modern classics of French literature and philosophy), as well as an awareness of the shift in the historical conditions of the Continent. Montale's poetry, like that of Pound and Eliot, is rich with literary citations and allusions that not only serve to contrast the author with his own literary antecedents but also to create a state of semantic saturation in which links and references lead the reader into the labyrinthine path of the text. This *modus operandi* of charging the verse with the utmost possible degree of meaning is made possible by the awareness that poetic language becomes meaningful only in relation to other languages, and from these other languages it wishes to, and must, differentiate itself; Montale knows well that "Il linguaggio di un poeta è un linguaggio storicizzato, un rapporto. Vale in quanto si oppone o si differenzia da altri linguaggi".[88] Montale's ambiguous, unconventional use of vocabulary derives precisely from this awareness, through a procedure that predates the *Ossi*, and that will continue in the poems of his later books: the process of the re-semanticization, or re-etymologization, of the lemmas employed in the text.

A select few nouns, verbs, and adjectives lose their common meaning in order to assume different ones, available to the reader only through a reflection upon the word's etymology and context. In contrast with the use adopted a decade later by the Florentine poetic trend known as Hermeticism, to which Montale has improperly been likened, and which calls for the substitution of one lemma (quite often a preposition) in place of anoth-

---

leafed in the pure air", trans. W. Arrowsmith); Arsenio in OV 81, ll. 46-47, is instead a "giunco [...] che le radici / con sè trascina" ("a reed dragging its roots"); in "Incontro" (OV 96, ll. 25-26 and 17-18) the mass of people who surround the narrating "I" are "sargassi umani" ("human seaweed"), not endowed with a life of their own: "vite no: vegetazioni / dell'altro mare che sovrasta il flutto" ("not lives, but vegetations / of the other sea that stands above the flux").

[87] See OV 52, ll. 16-17.

[88] "A poet's language is historicized, is a relationship. It matters in as much as it opposes or differentiates itself from other languages".

er to disorient the reader, Montale's process of re-etymologization entails a meaning that is precise, but different from the most common meaning. We find an early occurrence of this practice in "I violini", where "tutto vaneggia" (l. 19). According to the dictionary, "vaneggiare" is translated as "to rave", "to wander in one's mind"; Montale ascribes it instead an unexpected meaning linked to its etymology: "to become empty", "to vanish". In a following *accordo* entitled "Violoncelli", the verb "capire" ("to understand") is again used in an etymological sense: "la tua forma / più vera non capisce ormai nei limiti / della carne" (ll. 13-15) ("your truest / form is no longer contained by the limits / of the flesh"), a shift of meaning reflected in English by the verb "to comprehend", which means both "to understand" and "to include". Immediately after, the verses "T'è forza di confonderti / con altre vite" do not mean "You must confound yourself / with other lives", but rather "Your merging with (con-fondere) other lives is inevitable".

From the *Accordi*, the procedure seeps through into the *Ossi*, where it becomes a most evident constituent of Montale's poetry. The poem dedicated to his experience in the trenches begins with: "Valmorbia, discorrevano il tuo fondo / fioriti nuvoli di piante agli àsoli" (OV 41, ll.1-2). "Discorrere" means "to engage in conversation", but here the wildflowers whirled in the wind are not amicably conversing, an interpretation that the transitive use of the verb disallows; rather, they "dis-corrono", dart away in the breeze. In "I limoni", the lyric "I" appreciates "le strade che riescono agli erbosi / fossi" (OV 9, ll. 4-5): even if in common parlance the verb "riuscire" means "to succeed", "to be able to", here the paths of which he is fond "ri-escono", i.e., "lead infallibly" to the grassy ditches. A few lines later, the syntagm "divertite passioni" (l. 18) does not imply that the poetic I is enjoying himself, but rather that his passions are diverted, a meaning logical in English but not at all intuitive in Italian. In the incipit of "Quasi una fantasia", the expression "Raggiorna, lo presento" (OV 18, l. 1) derives not from the commonly used verb "presentare" but from a makeshift "presentire" modeled from an existing noun, "presentimento", and it signifies "I have a pre-sentiment of the day": a purport mirrored in "Il canneto rispunta ..." ("Assente, come manchi in questa plaga / che ti presente e senza te consuma", OV 39, ll. 9-10). Even the description of childhood as the "età illusa" that has already been noted is the result of this process, which does not stop with the publication of *Ossi di seppia*, as the use of the verb "ripartire" in "Xenia I, 3" demonstrates.

Montale does not owe this process to his perusal of modernist authors; likewise, the construction of a lyric "I" as an anti-hero – an alienated subject ill at ease with traditional institutions, characterized by a fragmented identity, living in a contradictory world – may well have been suggested to Montale by Sbarbaro's *Trucioli* and Boine's *Il peccato*, without requiring models like Hugh Selwyn Mauberley or the lyric "I" of *Waste Land*. However, this is not to say that Joyce, Eliot, and Pound taught Montale nothing: rather, thematic and lexical coincidences demonstrate that the texts written for the second edition of the *Ossi* benefited from his direct acquaintance with Pound and from the attention that Montale was reserving for English modernism.

We know that Montale read *Dubliners* in the French translation prefaced by Valery Larbaud in August 1926 in Monterosso: [89] he wrote a review of the book for *La Fiera Letteraria*, in which he says he appreciated the story "The Dead", though he restricts himself to a brief account of it, as he does with all the others, too: "Ne 'I morti', che è il racconto più lungo e convincente del libro, un uomo di mezza età, marito felice da vari anni, scopre all'improvviso di non avere avuto mai alcuna importanza nella vita della propria fedele sposa".[90] The central idea of the story, that the dead remain among the living and interact with them, evidently stuck with the poet: still in Monterosso, between August 14 and 16, he composed "Incontro", "Delta", and "I morti", a short cycle dedicated to a young Roman woman, Anna Degli Uberti, dubbed Annetta, Arletta, Capinera in other texts. Anna was in the habit of spending her summers in Monterosso with her family, a paying guest in the house next to the Casa delle due palme. Eugenio, having returned from the war, began to consider her a fixed component of his "estati lontane", his "distant" summers. But after the summer of 1924, the Degli Uberti family decided to spend its vacations on the Adriatic Coast. Montale never saw her again; he imagined her dead, even if she were not, and he continued to number her among the muses of his poetry till the end. In fact, he wanted a poem inspired by her, "Ah!" (OV 708), to be placed last in the last book of poems he published, *Altri versi*.

If it is true that the Romantic commonplace of the dead young beloved was certainly known to Montale through the mediation of Leopardi, and if it is true that several textual references link the figure of Annetta to that of Leopardi's Silvia, it is also true that here the same subject presents some substantial differences from the Romantic treatment of the *topos*.[91]

---

[89] J. Joyce, *Gens de Dublin*, Paris, Plon, 1926. See P. De Caro, *Invenzioni di ricordi. Vite in poesia di tre ispiratrici montaliane*, Foggia, Centro Grafico Francescano, 2002, p. 64 *et passim*; see also T. Arvigo, *Guida alla lettura di Montale. Ossi di seppia*, Roma, Carocci, 2001, p. 213.

[90] "In 'The Dead', which is the longest and most convincing story in the book, a middle-aged man, happily married for several years, suddenly discovers that he never counted for anything in the life of his faithful spouse". E. Montale, "*Dubliners* di James Joyce" (1926), SM 146.

[91] On the Leopardian genealogy of the figure of Annetta, see G. Lonardi, *Il fiore dell'addio. Leonora, Manrico e altri fantasmi del melodramma nella poesia di Montale*, Bologna, il Mulino, 2003, p. 250 *et passim*, and P. De Caro, *Invenzioni di ricordi. Vite in poesia di tre ispiratrici monta-*

In the poems from the summer of 1926, the subject of a death that is not really death connects to and reflects the life / non-life of the lyric I, already present since the texts of 1924; the dead, separated from the world of the living, continue to interact with them, and the possible feeble encounters of the I with these phantasms are announced by signs, premonitions, revelations. The dead are drawn to the world of the living by their own memories. From the living they are "divisi appena" ("barely separated"); indeed, they brush against the living.

Così
forse anche ai morti è tolto ogni riposo
nelle zolle: una forza indi li tragge
spietata più del vivere, ed attorno,
larve rimorse dai ricordi umani,
li volge fino a queste spiagge, fiati
senza materia o voce
traditi dalla tenebra; ed i mozzi
loro voli ci sfiorano pur ora
da noi divisi appena e nel crivello
del mare si sommergono... (OV 93, ll. 28-37)[92]

Without excluding a connection between Annetta and Silvia, the influence of the modernist poets seems evident in the triptych of summer 1926: so much so that, to the subject of the dead / not-dead, who leave the sea-sepulchre because they are attracted by the hell on earth, we may add the idea that the world of the living is the true hell, and life is nothing more than a path of expiation and penitence. The idea of the sea-sepulchre also appears in "Mr. Apollinax", the ninth poem of Eliot's *Prufrock*: "Where worried bodies of drowned men drift down in the green silence, / Dropping from fingers of surf".[93] And since we have reasons to believe that Montale had effectively read the whole *Prufrock*, it is worthwhile to note that in the verse that follows the one just cited, Mr. Apollinax's head is presented "with seaweed in its hair" (l. 14): a harbinger of the vegetalization of the Genoese

---

liane, Foggia, Centro Grafico Francescano, 2002, pp. 44 *et passim*. Piero Cataldi and Floriana d'Amely also propose as intertext the "Dialogo di Federico Ruysh e delle sue mummie" from the *Operette morali* for the subject of "I morti". See E. Montale, *Ossi di seppia*, eds. P. Cataldi and F. d'Amely, Milano, Mondadori, 2002, p. 235.

92 "So too perhaps / even the dead in the ground may be denied / all repose: a force more pitiless / than life pulls them thence, from all around / driving them toward this coast – ghosts / tortured by human memories, breaths / without voice or substance, betrayed / by darkness; and even now their thwarted flights, / so close to us still, brush by, / then drift down in the sea / that sifts them...", trans. W. Arrowsmith.

93 T.S. Eliot, *The Complete Poems and Plays, 1909-1950*, cit., p. 18, ll. 11-12.

bourgeoisie in the "sargassi / umani fluttuanti" that we find in the second poem of the triptych dedicated to Anna degli Uberti, "Incontro".

In "Incontro" the beloved is depicted as already dead: she is, in fact, "submerged", ("sommersa", l. 46).[94] Eugenio imagines encountering her, or encountering her ghost, while walking "sulla strada / che urta il vento forano":

> Si va sulla carraia di rappresa
> mota senza uno scarto,
> simili ad incappati da corteo,
> sotto la volta infranta ch'è discesa
> quasi a specchio delle vetrine,
> in un'aura che avvolge i nostri passi
> fitti e uguaglia i sargassi
> umani fluttuanti alle cortine
> dei bambù mormoranti. (OV 96, ll. 19-27)[95]

The Sunday stroll of the Genoese bourgeoisie is described in an echo from Dante, a link that plunges these citizens devoted to their postprandial custom into the circle of the hypocrites:[96] furthermore, a low, leaden sky gives the impression that the city is submerged and that its inhabitants have been transformed into sea-tangle, as specified by the verses that precede the lines just cited: "vite no: vegetazioni / dell'altro mare che sovrasta il flutto" (ll. 17-18). Once more we can see thematic convergences, not just with Joyce's "The Dead" but also with the use that Eliot makes of the *Divine Comedy* in verses 63-64 of *The Waste Land*. Eliot describes the London crowd by citing in his own way *Inf.* III, 55-57, and *Inf.* IV, 25-27 (as he himself indicates in the footnotes):

> Unreal City,
> Under the brown fog of a winter dawn,
> A crowd flowed over London Bridge, so many,

94 The first draft of *Incontro* had "Arletta" in place of "sommersa", providing a name and a personality for the woman who, Montale imagines, appears to him thanks to a "miracolo": the *adnominatio* Arletta/Annetta initially tied this poem to the one dedicated to Arsenio/Eugenio. See OV 890.

95 "We move around a rutted road, caked / mud, grooved, undeviating, / like a hooded cortège crawling / nder a weary sky lowering now / almost to street level, in air / so dense it tangles our steps, / and this human seaweed writhes / and sways in the breeze like curtains / of whispering bamboo", trans. W. Arrowsmith.

96 "And they were dressed in cloaks with cowls so low / they fell before their eyes, of that same cut / that's used to make the clothes for Cluny's monks. / Outside, these cloaks were gilded and they dazzled; / but inside they were all of lead, so heavy / that Frederick's capes were straw compared to them". *Inf.* XXIII, 61-66, trans. A. Mandelbaum.

I had not thought death had undone so many.
Sighs, short and infrequent, were exhaled,
And each man fixed his eyes before his feet.[97]

The coincidence is too coincidental to be a coincidence. The false living beings, men reified into seaweed, inhabit a city with infernal traits like the one experienced by the inhabitants of Eliot's "Unreal City", which is a city similar to both the chthonic city that we will discover in "Arsenio", and the city described at large in Montale's second book, *Le Occasioni*.

As we know, Montale will later deny having read *The Waste Land* in 1926, and he certainly knew, independently of Eliot, the verses of Baudelaire from the "Tableaux Parisiens" that inspired the first section of the *Waste Land*, which Eliot dutifully cites in his own "Notes on The Waste Land": "Fourmillante cité, cité pleine des rêves, / Où le spectre en plein jour rapprocha le passant".[98] Baudelaire's poetry is an unavoidable precedent for both Eliot and Montale, being the first to connect the images of death, woman, and city in *Les Fleurs du Mal*, as Walter Benjamin observed:

> What is unique in Baudelaire's poetry is that the images of women and death are permeated by a third, that of Paris. The Paris of his poems is a submerged city, more submarine than subterranean. The chthonic elements of the city – its topographical formation, the old deserted bed of the Seine – doubtless left their impression on his work.[99]

Montale's verse is filled with allusions to Baudelaire's poetic output, even beyond the *Ossi*. Sometimes these intertextual links are very dense, such as those between "Quasi una fantasia" and "Rêve parisien", and sometimes they are made explicit, as in the case of "Il balcone" and "Le balcon" or "Corrispondenze" and "Correspondances". In this specific circumstance we can conjecture that Montale returned to the verses of his beloved Baudelaire at the suggestion of Eliot, a precious model of how to translate the waste land that is the bed of the Seine into the Genoese river Bisagno, "sterile / d'acque, vivo di pietre e di calcine" ("devoid / of water, alive with stones and limewash").[100] It is a triangulation moderated by the common

---

97 T.S. Eliot, *The Waste Land*, in *The Complete Poems and Plays, 1909-1950*, cit., p. 39, ll. 60-65.

98 C. Baudelaire, *Les Fleurs du Mal*, "Le Sept Vieillards" vv. 1-2. See Also T.S. Eliot, *The Complete Poems and Plays, 1909-1950*, cit., p. 51.

99 W. Benjamin, *Paris, Capital of the Nineteenth Century*, in *Reflections*, ed. and trans. P. Demetz, New York, Schocken Books, 1986, p. 157.

100 "Incontro", OV 96, ll. 10-11.

understanding that, if for Baudelaire hell on earth was a metaphorical image, then for the poets who wrote after the First World War, hell on earth was instead a horribly real concept.[101]

Montale's *lapsus memoriae* makes one suspect that he had read *Prufrock* prior to 1928, and there are other textual references to consider between Eliot's first books and the poems composed for the second edition of the *Ossi*. The concluding tercet of "The Love Song of J. Alfred Prufrock", for example, resonates with the final part of "Incontro", in which the encounter with the vegetal woman predicts and anticipates the moment of the death of the lyric "I".[102] Likewise, the concluding couplet of the first of the "Préludes" juxtaposes two elements recurring in "Arsenio": "A lonely cab-horse steams and stamps. / And then the lighting of the lamps". The first verse recalls the "spiazzi / deserti, ove i cavalli incappucciati / annusano la terra" (ll. 2-4), the second the "globi accesi, dondolanti a riva" (ll. 36), namely the lanterns that illuminate the seafront. Tiziana De Rogatis also indicates a possible intersection with "The Hollow Men", given that line 12, in which the Hollow Men are presented as "Paralyzed force, gesture without motion", could serve as a reference for the"immoto andare", the "troppo noto / delirio d'immobilità" that characterizes the figure of Arsenio.[103] The same Arsenio, in fact, lends himself to being interpreted as one of these "Hollow Men" living in a hollow land, a lifeless puppet that cannot shake off its sloth in order to seize the opportunity to transform itself, as if a new Pinocchio, into a real man.

4. Arsenio's Journey

A glance at the voyage of "Arsenio" – intended both as the trans-lation from Italian to English completed by the text through the intervention of Praz, and as the journey completed within the text by the eponymous character – may help us to better understand the complex relationship that

---

[101] In a talk given at the Italian Institute of London in 1950, Eliot clarified that the intention of his allusions to Dante in *The Waste Land* was "to present to the mind of the reader a parallel, by means of contrast, between the *Inferno* and *Purgatorio*, which Dante visited and a hallucinated scene after an air-raid". T.S. Eliot, "What Dante Means to Me" (1950), in *To Criticize the Critic and Other Writing*, Lincoln and London, University of Nebraska Press, 1991, p. 128.

[102] "We have lingered in the chambers of the sea / By sea-girls wreathed with seaweed red and brown / Till human voices wake us and we drown". T.S. Eliot, *The Complete Poems and Plays, 1909-1950*, cit., p. 7.

[103] OV 81, ll. 22-23. See T. De Rogatis, *Montale e il classicismo moderno*, Pisa-Roma, Istituti Editoriali e Poligrafici Internazionali, 2002, p. 110.

exists between the poetry of Montale and the poetry of Anglo-American high modernism. In particular, it may help to orient our thoughts in the *vexata quaestio* that has agonized Montale's readers since the 1930s, namely, determining the actual extent of the influence exerted by the works of T.S. Eliot upon the imagination of the Genoese poet.[104] "Arsenio" deserves a pivotal place in a discussion of Montale's modernism, since it is routinely considered to be "la prima prova montaliana pienamente convergente con la tecnica eliotiana del correlativo oggettivo" ("the first of Montale's attempts that fully converges with Eliot's technique of the objective correlative"), and because it represents the historical point of contact, both poetic and biographical, between the Anglo-American Nobel Prize winner and the Italian one.[105]

The character of Arsenio is both Montale's alter ego and his lyric anti-hero, a character who demonstrates a clear break from the previous

---

[104] While establishing a link between Montale and European modernism has not been a primary interest of readers and critics, the specific connection between Montale and T.S. Eliot has been analyzed from many points of view. A selected bibliography on the subject includes: M. Praz, *Montale and Eliot*, in *T.S. Eliot. A Symposium*, eds. R. March and Tambimuttu, Chicago, Henry Regnery Company, 1949, pp. 244-248; S. Pannella, *E. Montale e T.S. Eliot*, «Galleria», IV, nn. 5-6, (December 1954), pp. 244-256; P. Gathercolle, *Two Kindred Spirits: Eugenio Montale and T.S. Eliot*, «Italica», XXXIII, 3, 1955, pp. 170-179; L. Caretti, *Un caso di affinità: Eugenio Montale*, in *T.S. Eliot in Italia*, Bari, Adriatica Editrice, 1968, pp. 49-80; C. Huffman, *T.S. Eliot, Eugenio Montale and the Vagaries of Influence*, «Comparative Literature» 27 (1975), pp. 193-207 (and Ead., *Montale, Eliot and the Poetic Object*, «Italian Quarterly», XXI, no. 81, Summer 1980, pp. 63-82); R. Meoli Toulmin, *Shakespeare e Eliot nelle versioni di Montale*, «Belfagor» n. 26, 1981, pp. 453-471; G. Talbot, *Montale's Mestiere Vile. The Elective Translations from English of the 1930s and 1940s*, Dublin, Irish Academy Press, 1995; L. Barile, *Adorate mie larve. Montale e la poesia anglosassone*, Bologna, il Mulino, 1990; P. Bigongiari, *Dal «correlativo oggettivo» al «correlativo soggettivo»*, in *Montale e il canone poetico del Novecento*, cit., pp. 424-428; M.A. Grignani, *Montale, Solmi, Praz e la cultura europea: dalla Francia all'Inghilterra*, *ibid.*, pp. 165-188; G. Singh, *Il rinnovamento poetico di Montale, Pound ed Eliot*, in *Il secolo di Montale: Genova 1896-1996*, ed. Fondazione Mario Novaro, Bologna, il Mulino, 1998, pp. 229-248; S. Mancini, *Montale ed Eliot attraverso La Bufera e i Four Quartets: tempo, trascendenza e storia*, «Quaderni del '900», II, 2002, pp. 71-88; T. De Rogatis, *Montale e il classicismo moderno*, Pisa-Roma, Istituti Editoriali e Poligrafici Internazionali, 2002 (and Ead., *Mappe del tempo: Eugenio Montale e T.S. Eliot*, Ospedaletto, Pisa, Pacini, 2012); P. Sica, *Modernist Forms of Rejuvenation: Montale and T.S. Eliot*, cit.; M. Sonzogni, *Debiti e doni della tradizione poetica: Montale tra T.S. Eliot e Samuel Beckett. Appunti su Montale traduttore e tradotto*, «The Italianist», 25 (2005), pp. 173-207.

[105] See P. Cataldi – F. d'Amely, in *Eugenio Montale: Ossi di seppia*, Milano, Mondadori p. 203. Sources consulted treating specifically "Arsenio" include: E. Vittorini, *Arsenio*, «Circoli», 6, 1931, pp. 79-101; A. Seroni, *Ragioni critiche*, Firenze, Vallecchi, 1944, pp. 95-110; S. Ramat, *Il libro come «opera»: la strada di Arsenio*, «Italianistica», n. 11 (1973), pp. 268-304; C.F. Goffis, *Lettura di "Arsenio"*, in *Letture montaliane*, Genova, Bozzi, 1977, pp. 69-84; E. Giachery, *La metamorfosi dell'orto*, Roma, Bonacci, 1985, pp. 48-76; A. Marchese, *Amico dell'invisibile*, Torino, SEI, 1996, pp. 190-192; T. Arvigo, *Guida alla lettura di Montale. Ossi di seppia*, Roma, Carocci, 2001; G. Guglielmi, *Montale, Arsenio e la linea allegorico-dantesca*, in *Montale e il canone poetico del Novecento*, cit., pp. 369-381.

style, opening the possibility for a poetry written in the third person, following Eliot's recommendation to construct an "objective" text. Some thematic resemblances analyzed in the previous section may suggest that Eliot's *Prufrock* was a direct influence. However, the poem as it appeared in the *Criterion* makes one suspect that the translator intended to render it more modernist than it actually was, or at least to render it more similar to the poetry of Eliot. An examination of the first stanza offers sufficient evidence – first in the original:

> I turbini sollevano la polvere
> sui tetti, a mulinelli, e sugli spiazzi
> deserti, ove i cavalli incappucciati
> annusano la terra, fermi innanzi
> ai vetri luccicanti degli alberghi.
> Sul corso, in faccia al mare, tu discendi
> in questo giorno
> or piovorno ora acceso, in cui par scatti
> a sconvolgerne l'ore
> uguali, strette in trama, un ritornello
> di castagnette.

and then in translation:

> Dust, dust is blown about the roofs, in eddies;
> It eddies on the roofs and on the places
> Deserted, where are seen the hooded horses
> Sniffing the ground, motionless
> In front of the glistening lattices of the hotels.
> Along the promenade, facing the sea, you slide,
> Upon this afternoon of sun and rain,
> Whose even, close-knit, hours
> Are shattered, so it seems, now and again
> By a happy refrain
> Of castanets.

The repetition in the first verse of the original is purely metrical: three proparoxytones unbalance the opening hypermetrical hendecasyllable towards the enjambement with the verse that follows, and the trope of enjambement recurs multiple times, in the first stanza as well as in the following ones, as the distinctive trait of the poem. This is a remarkable fact in a poem that strives to express the "immoto andare" of its main character: the tripping of the verses reproduces the difficult, impeded movement of Arsenio. Yet, at least in the first stanza, Praz chooses not to emphasize the fits and starts of the text, and the distinctive trope of the translation becomes one of anaphora and repetition. As Andrea Gareffi has noted in his analysis of the translation,

> Tre parole sdrucciole l'una dopo l'altra nel medesimo verso meritavano tre ripetizioni articolate. Tre ripetizioni che non solo non erano nell'originale, ma che Montale non ammette quando è lui a tradurre in italiano. [...] Le tre ripetute ripetizioni colpiscono subito *Arsenio*: l'incipit, «Dust, dust»; la frase mediana, «about the roofs / on the roofs», dove la ripetizione contiene una variazione; e la clausola del primo verso, ripresa all'inizio del secondo «in eddies / it eddies», dove la ripetizione è complicata per di più quale ripetizione di omofoni con valore grammaticale differente, essendo la parola in questione una volta nome, la seconda volta verbo di terza persona.[106]

It is hardly necessary to state that anaphora and repetition are typical tropes of Eliot's early poetry. We might suspect, therefore, that Praz had in mind a specific reader for this particular translation, and tried to render Montale's poetry as familiar as possible for that single reader.

There is another detail to consider – a minuscule detail, certainly, but one that stands out in this otherwise extremely accurate and, as Montale noted, faithfully literal translation: "Arsenio" takes place during the day, at noon in fact, as line 35 specifies, and the text plays with the opposition between the light of the sun and the darkness caused by the storm, which transforms the protagonist's stroll into a Dantesque katabasis. In the context of the poetry of the *Ossi*, the meridian setting is an important detail because the chthonic experience of Arsenio during the meridian hour is in plain opposition to the motif of corresponding with nature that occurred during the "gloria del disteso mezzogiorno" ("glory of the extended midday"). The infernal city where Arsenio descends is no longer the city described in 1922, where "da un malchiuso portone / tra gli alberi di una corte / ci si mostrano i gialli dei limoni" ("through a gate ajar / among the trees in a courtyard / we see the yellows of the lemon trees," W. Arrowsmith, transl.); it is rather a place where an alienated subject must bal-

---

106 "Three proparoxytones, one after the next in the same verse, called for a mirroring of the accents in three distinct words. Three repetitions that not only were not in the original, but that Montale also does not permit when he himself is translating into Italian. [...] The three repeated repetitions affect "Arsenio" immediately: the incipit, 'Dust, dust'; the central phrase 'about the roofs / on the roofs', wherein the repetition contains a variation; and the clause in the first verse that is picked up again in the second, 'in eddies / it eddies', where the repetition is even more complicated, as it is a repetition of homophones with different grammatical significances, for the word in question is, first, a noun and, second, a third person verb". A. Gareffi, *I ritmi della mente di Montale*, «Sincronie», VII, 13, 2003, pp. 93-94. See also C. Ubaldi, *Arsenio e la profezia del forse*, «Sincronie» X, 20, 2006, p. 234.

ance and interpret confusing signs that belong to an ever-changing landscape: the sounds of the castanets, shingles, and violins; the sight of the horizon overhung by a waterspout; the sight of a lonely, icy multitude of dead, at a time when the day is night and the summer is winter. These are all elements of the delirious immobility of Eugenio/Arsenio, in a city where air and sea, light and dusk, life and death are inextricably intermingled. The translation instead takes place in an *afternoon* (l. 7), an afternoon so dark as to almost be night. Yes, it is a detail: but it is striking that this change draws the figure of Arsenio nearer to that of Prufrock, whose love song began as such: "Let us go then, you and I, / when the evening is spread out against the sky" (ll. 1-2). Praz's Arsenio, like Prufrock, begins his journey in a cityscape at dusk.

As we have seen, Praz believed that there were many consonances between Montale and Eliot; he felt that they resembled each other physically and in terms of demeanor, that they were flowers blossomed on different branches of the same tree. It seems that this conviction seeps into his translation of "Arsenio", which he prepared for Eliot to read and which he proposed to *Criterion*. In the same way, it was Praz who launched, during an official occasion, the idea that Montale made use of Eliot's objective correlative: he declared it during the conference on Eliot that followed the conferring of his Nobel Prize. According to the *Festschrift*, Praz declared:

> It is remarkable that Montale [...] should have developed a formula very close to the correlative objective through his reading of Eliot's verse. For in the thirties Montale, growing fully aware of Eliot's power, without loss of originality enriched his own technique with devices strongly reminiscent of Eliot.[107]

Doubtless, Praz believed he was doing his friend a great favor by placing his name beside that of a recent winner of the most coveted literary prize in the world. This critical starting point, which has a basis of truth, in time has been transformed, however, into a simplification and a cliché. Oriented by Praz's declarations, the criticism has long flattened Montale's poetics of the object into Eliot's theory of the objective correlative, and Montale has regularly been described as "the Italian T.S. Eliot",[108] to the point that today the authors of the "Objective Correlative" article on Wikipedia consider Montale's poetics completely assimilated to those of

[107] M. Praz, *Montale and Eliot*, in *T.S. Eliot. A Symposium*, eds. R. March and Tambimuttu, Chicago, Henry Regnery Company, 1949, p. 246.

[108] The formula eventually crystallized in R. Poggioli, *Essays in European Literature*, Cambridge, Harvard University Press, 1965, p. 214.

Eliot, stating in an aside: "The 'occasion' of E. Montale is a further form of correlative".[109]

Montale himself certainly reinforced the possibility of a parallel, mentioning Eliot frequently in his own theoretical writings.[110] In these writings, it seems that he highlights the aspects of Eliot's work that best accord with his own, and that he attempts – as he had done while writing on Gozzano and as Saba had accused him of doing – to explain the poetry of the other poet by explaining his own, or perhaps vice versa. Montale would employ the same parameters to describe himself and Eliot: for example, in the "Intervista immaginaria" he had declared that an intention of the *Ossi* was to build a new poetic language, citing the first line of Verlaine's "L'art poétique", "Prends l'éloquence et tords-lui son cou!" Of himself Montale says: "All'eloquenza della nostra vecchia lingua aulica volevo torcere il collo, magari a rischio di una controeloquenza".[111] Two years later, he uses the same quote to celebrate the style of Eliot: "Il precetto di Verlaine (ma di origine baudelairiana anch'esso) 'prends l'éloquence et lui tords le cou' tocca con Eliot il suo maggior compimento espressivo".[112] Still in the "Intervista immaginaria", Montale describes the poetry of *Le occasioni* as "un frutto che dovesse contenere i suoi motivi senza rivelarli, o meglio senza spiattellarli".[113] Reading beyond the tangle of metaphors that often dovetails Montale's writing, one can recognize the resemblance between a poetry that "contiene i suoi motivi senza rivelarli", and one that "sprigiona il sentimento senza dichiararlo" ("releases sentiment without announcing it") as Eliot's is.[114]

---

109 https://en.wikipedia.org/wiki/Objective_correlative, accessed on 24 June 2015.

110 It is possible that Eliot is the single modern poet to whom Montale dedicated the greatest number of commentaries. The articles are: "Omaggio a T.S. Eliot" (1933), SM 495-496; "Eliot e noi" (1947), SM 713-719; "Buon viaggio, Mr. Eliot" (1947), SM 719-722; "Il poeta T.S. Eliot premio Nobel 1948" (1948), SM 764-766; "Troppo scuro troppo chiaro" (1950), SM 954-959; "Invito a T.S. Eliot" (1950), SM 983-992; "Assassinio nella cattedrale" (1958), SM 2125-2129; "Ricordo di T.S. Eliot" (1965), SM 2691-2695; "Un'aria di casa" (1962), SM 2994-2995.

111 E. Montale, "Intenzioni (Intervista Immaginaria)" (1946), AMS 1480: "I wanted to wring the neck of the eloquence of our surpassed courtly language, perhaps at the risk of a counter-eloquence".

112 E. Montale, "Il poeta T.S. Eliot premio Nobel 1948" (1948), SM 765: "Verlaine's precept (which also has origins in Baudelaire) 'prends l'éloquence et lui tords le cou' reaches with Eliot its greatest expressive achievement".

113 E. Montale, "Intenzioni (Intervista Immaginaria)" (1946), AMS 1480: "a fruit that must contain its motives without revealing them, or better still, without squashing them".

114 See E. Montale, "Invito a T.S. Eliot" (1950), SM 988. The fact that Montale, while speaking of Eliot, seems to speak of himself is mirrored by the fact that Eliot too, in the same period, seems to speak of Montale when he speaks of himself: as when he says he had learned

Montale recognizes in Eliot an initial Symbolist inspiration; he considers him a poet-musician, a title he also bestowed upon himself in various interviews and critical writings. The connection to the famous article of his youth on Gozzano becomes even stronger because Montale recycles the vocabulary used on that occasion: Eliot, like Gozzano, makes "cozzare l'aulico col prosastico" ("an elevated tone clash with the prosaic"):

> In lui la parola prosastica convive accanto a quella aulica, il tono diventa lirico per accensione interiore, non già perché ubbidisca alle leggi di un metronomo. Eliot giunge spesso al canto dal recitativo, al tono alto dal tono più parlato che possa darsi. È soprattutto (diciamo la parola) un poeta-musicista.[115]

Montale's evaluation of Eliot confirmed his adherence to Eliot's style among readers. It is unsurprising, therefore, that toward the end of the 1940s Montale intensified his efforts to minimize his early interest in (and consequently his debt to) Eliot's poetry and the theoretical writings. Before the protest of independence in the already-cited letter to Bigongiari (see 5.1), Montale had declared his non-involvement with the theory of the objective correlative, even if only parenthetically, in the "Intervista immaginaria":

> Ammesso che in arte esista una bilancia tra il di fuori e il di dentro, tra l'occasione e l'opera-oggetto bisognava esprimere l'oggetto e tacere l'occasione-spinta. Un modo nuovo, non parnassiano, di immergere il lettore *in medias res*, un totale assorbimento delle intenzioni nei risultati oggettivi. Anche qui, fui mosso dall'istinto non da una teoria (quella eliotiana del "correlativo oggettivo" non credo esistesse ancora, nel '28, quando il mio "Arsenio" fu pubblicato nel «Criterion»).[116]

---

from Baudelaire the possibility of juxtaposing the matter-of-fact and the fantastic: "I think that from Baudelaire I learned first, a precedent for the poetical possibilities, never developed by any poet writing in my own language, of the more sordid aspects of the modern metropolis, of the possibility of fusion between the sordidly realistic and the phantasmagoric, the possibility of the juxtaposition of the matter-of-fact and the fantastic". See T.S. ELIOT, "What Dante Means to Me" (1950), in *To Criticize the Critic and Other writings*, cit., p. 126.

115 E. MONTALE, "Invito a T.S. Eliot" (1950), SM 990: "In his work prosaic words cohabitate with courtly ones; the tone becomes lyrical through interior ignition, not because he is obeying the laws of a metronome. Eliot frequently arrives at song from the recitative, at a high tone from the most spoken tone possible. He is, above all, (let's say the word) a poet-musician".

116 E. MONTALE, "Intenzioni (Intervista immaginaria)" (1946), AMS 1481-1482: "Admitting that in art there may exist a balance between the external and the internal, between the occasion and the object of the work it was necessary to express the object, and hide the occasion-impulse. A new way, not Parnassian, to plunge the reader *in medias res*, a total absorption of the intentions into the objective results. Even here, I was moved by instinct, not by a theory (I don't think Eliot's theory of the 'objective correlative' existed yet, in 1928, when my 'Arsenio' was published in «Criterion»)".

In reality Eliot had written "Hamlet" in 1919, and documents reveal that Montale, from at least 1931, knew quite well what the objective correlative was.[117] In the preface to the resubmission of the translations of Eliot in «Circoli», dated 1933, Montale displays familiarity both with Eliot's poetic production up to that point and with his theoretical writings, as he mentions both *The Sacred Wood* and the *Selected Essays*.[118] Beginning in the 1950s, contradicting the declarations of respect published previously, Montale shows marked reservations towards the recent production of the Anglo-American poet. Only a few months prior he had described Eliot as a poet-musician, but in 1951 he writes instead that in Eliot music and thought are often not harmonious:

> T.S. Eliot ha un tono da grande poeta ma in lui musica e pensiero stentano spesso a mettersi d'accordo. La *Terra desolata* mi pare unita solo esteriormente, cucita con lo spago. Le sue prime liriche, alcuni degli *Ariel Poems* e varie scene del *Cocktail Party* sono probabilmente le sue punte più alte. Eliot ha un bel parlarci di classicismo: per vincere egli ha bisogno di farci sentire l'odore del cloroformio.[119]

From then on, every time that he broaches the subject, Montale underscores the independence of his own objective poetics from the theory of the objective correlative:

> Qualcuno mi mosse il rimprovero di avere adottato [nelle *Occasioni*] il metodo eliotiano del "correlativo obiettivo": che è di fornire un oggetto (la poesia) in cui il motivo sia incluso in forma di suggerimento, non però spiegato o commentato in termini psicologici. La verità è che io avevo tradotto nel '29 tre brevi poesie di

---

117 He declared as much in "Della poesia d'oggi": "Il poeta non deve soltanto effondere il proprio sentimento, ma deve altresì lavorare una sua materia verbale, 'fino a un certo segno', dare della propria intuizione quello che Eliot chiama un 'correlativo obiettivo'. Solo quando è giunta a questo stadio la poesia esiste, e lascia un'eco, un'ossessione di sè" ("The poet must not only give expression to his own sentiment, but must also cultivate a verbal substance of his own, 'fino a un certo segno' ['up to a certain point'], must give of his own intuition what Eliot calls an objective correlative. Only when it has reached this stage does poetry exist, and leave an echo, an obsession, of itself"). See E. Montale, "Della poesia d'oggi" (1931), interview by L. Gigli, AMS 1530.

118 E. Montale, "Omaggio a T.S. Eliot" (1933), SM 495-496.

119 "Eliot has the tone of a great poet, but in him music and thought find it difficult to come to an agreement. The *Waste Land* seems to me united only outwardly, sewn together with thread. His first lyrics, some of the *Ariel Poems*, and various scenes of *Cocktail Party* are probably his highest peaks. Eliot has a lovely way of speaking to us of classicism: to succeed he must make us smell the odor of chloroform". E. Montale, "Il cammino della nuova poesia" (1951), SM 1155. One notes that Eliot's "highest peaks" remain those translated by Montale at the end of the 1920s; about Montale's predilection for *Cocktail Party* see also "Due destini", in *Quaderno di quattro anni* (OV 515), where the sacrifice of Clizia and that of Celia in *Cocktail Party* are compared.

> Eliot, ma nient'altro conoscevo di quel poeta; mentre parecchie mie pagine degli anni precedenti già mi imponevano quella strada.[120]

In 1972, in an article that is concerned with both Eliot and Pound, he reaffirms the difference between himself and them, distinguishing what he approves in their work from what he does not care for, insistently declaring that the mechanism of the objective correlative "has always been known":

> Il fatto che io abbia tradotto tre *Ariel Poems* di Eliot fin dal loro apparire mi ha procurato una reputazione di eliotista che non mi compete. Molto di Eliot non conosco: e di quel che conosco non tutto trova eco in me. [...] E che dire del famoso correlativo obiettivo? Che un'emozione poetica trovi la sua corrispondenza in un oggetto che non è la sua espressione ma, direi, la sua incarnazione, questo si è sempre saputo.[121]

Given Montale's noted reluctance to reveal sources and debts in his own poetic production, these distance-taking measures have failed to convince critics of the originality of Montale's poetics of the object. The persistent denial of Eliot's influence on his poetry, in combination with the conspicuous presence of the latter in his theoretical writings, has led readers to see an *excusatio non petita* – an approach similar, moreover, to the one Montale had taken toward Paul Valéry.[122] Only recently have more critically nuanced positions emerged, like that of Tiziana De Rogatis, who mediates the influence of Eliot with the influence of Valéry and Alain; that of Paola Sica, who, without wishing to establish directions of influence or hierarchies, analyzes the works of both poets in order to find the themes

---

120 "Someone reproached me for having adopted [in the *Occasioni*] Eliot's method of the 'objective correlative': which is to provide an object (the poem) in which the motive is included in the form of a suggestion, which is neither explained, however, nor commented upon in psychological terms. The truth, though, is that I had translated in 1929 three brief poems of Eliot's, but I knew nothing else of the poet, while several pages of mine from years prior were already imposing that path on me". E. Montale, "Poesie di Eugenio Montale" (1960), AMS 1495.

121 "The fact that I had translated three of Eliot's *Ariel Poems* has, since their appearance, given me a reputation as an Eliotist that I do not deserve. Much of Eliot I do not know: and of what I do know not everything finds an echo in me. [...] And what to say of the famous objective correlative? That a poetic emotion should find its correspondence in an object that is not its expression but, I would say, its incarnation, is something that has always been known.] E. Montale, "Un'aria di casa" (1972), SM 2994.

122 Tiziana De Rogatis has shown that Valéry's influence on Montale can be detected in poems as early as "Meriggiare" and "Maestrale", while Montale resisted a connection between his poetry and Valéry's since 1925. T. De Rogatis, *Montale e il classicismo moderno*, p. 46 *et passim*, and R. Luperini, *Montale o l'identità negata*, p. 44 *et passim*. See also Montale's September 26, 1925 letter to Solmi in "Cronologia", SM LVI.

they have in common; and that of Piero Bigongiari, who distinguishes the objective correlative of one from the subjective correlative of the other.[123]

In fact, even having ascertained the existence of real textual correspondences between the Eliot of *Prufrock* and *Hollow Men* and the poems written between 1927 and 1928 for the second edition of the *Ossi*, even having established that Montale was not forthright about the poems of Eliot's he knew and which of them he had translated, there are further considerations that may suggest Montale was not far from the truth when he said that he would have arrived at the same results "anche se Eliot fosse stato molto diverso o non fosse stato" ("even if Eliot had been very different or had not been at all"). It would be convenient to dismiss the case of the poetic genealogies from Baudelaire and Dante as a direct influence of Eliot on Montale, but it would not be completely correct to do so. Dismissing these genealogies would overlook the fact that Montale, in recognizing in Baudelaire the precedent for the poetical possibility of representing the more sordid aspects of the modern metropolis, could refer to his own reading of *Les Fleurs du mal*, as well as the mediation of Sbarbaro's verses. The juxtaposition of the matter-of-fact and the fantastic in the *Ossi* date back at least to 1922-1924, when Montale had not yet met Pound and had read quite little of Eliot. Likewise, considering the presence in Montale's verses of Dantean references as simply the result of Eliot's example would, on the one hand, not acknowledge the fact that echoes from the *Rime petrose* and from the *Divine Comedy* appear in the *Ossi* in a time frame that precedes the encounter with Pound, and on the other, would not acknowledge the interest and admiration that Montale felt for the Dante criticism of Irma Brandeis and Gianfranco Contini, scholars Montale befriended in the early stages of his Florentine residence. This is to say that essentializing the modernist poetics of Montale around the formulas and examples of Eliot is, above all, to make the mistake of excluding all the Italian poet's other possible influences and experiences.

The critical fortune that has smiled upon Eliot's formula of the objective correlative must not make one forget that "finding a set of objects, a situation, a chain of events which shall be the formula of that *particular* emotion" [124] is not a new process; in fact, Eliot (and Pound before him)

---

123 T. De Rogatis, *Montale e il classicismo moderno*, cit., p. 22 *et passim*, particularly pp. 95-123; P. Sica, *Modernist Forms of Rejuvenation: Montale and T.S. Eliot*, cit.; P. Bigongiari, *Dal «correlativo oggettivo» al «correlativo soggettivo»*, in *Montale e il canone poetico del Novecento*, cit., pp. 424-428.

124 T.S. Eliot, *Hamlet and His Problems* (originally "Hamlet", 1919), in *The Sacred Wood and Major Early Essays*, Mineola, New York, Dover Publications, 1998, p. 58.

found the theoretical justification for it by analyzing the *Divine Comedy*.[125] If it is difficult to pinpoint the theoretical differences between Eliot's "objective correlative" and Montale's "occasione", it is equally complicated to find the differences between these two and Pound's "Image" and Joyce's "epiphany".[126] A few peculiarities nothwithstanding, all of these poetic procedures find a common genealogy in Bergson's idea that specific images generate an "emotional equivalent" in the spectator or reader: "In seeing these images pass before our eyes we in our turn experience the feeling which was, so to speak, their emotional equivalent".[127] This phenomenon occurs due to what Bergson calls "intuition", or rather "the kind of intellectual sympathy by which one places oneself within an object in order to coincide with what is unique in it and consequently inexpressible".[128] Even if Bergson's "intuition" is by definition inexpressible, the mechanism that triggers it finds an equivalent in poetry, where "many diverse images, borrowed from very diverse orders of things, may, by the convergence of their action, direct consciousness to the precise point where there is a certain intuition to be seized".[129]

Through the mediation of T.E. Hulme, who translated *An Introduction to Metaphysics* into English, Bergson's definition of the capacity of human intuition reaches Pound, who renamed it "Image" (with a capital "I").[130] For Pound the 'Image' is not a visual description, as it was in the writings of Bergson and Hulme, but rather the effect such visual description imprints on the "I". As it is explained in the fragmented manifesto that appeared in *Poetry* in March 1913:

> An 'Image' is that which presents an intellectual and emotional complex in an instant of time. It is the presentation of such a "complex" instantaneously which gives that sense of sudden liberation; that sense of freedom from time limits and

---

125 See T.S. Eliot, "Dante" (1920), *ibid.*, pp. 93-100; and Id., "What Dante Means to Me" (1950), in *To Criticize the Critic and Other Writings*, Lincoln and London, University of Nebraska Press, 1965, pp. 125-135.

126 See F.O. Matthiessen, *The Achievement of T.S. Eliot*, Oxford, Oxford University Press, 1959, p. 61. See T. De Rogatis, *Montale e il classicismo moderno*, p. 103, note 27.

127 H. Bergson, *Time and Free Will: An Essay on the Immediate Data of consciousness*, trans. F.L. Pogson, New York, Harper and Row, 1910, p. 15.

128 H. Bergson, *An Introduction to Metaphysics*, trans. T.E. Hulme, London, Macmillan, 1913, p. 6.

129 *Ibid.*, p. 14.

130 On the correspondence between Pound's and Hulme's prescription for modern poetry, see R. Beasley, *Theorists of Modernist Poetry: T.S. Eliot, T.E. Hulme, Ezra Pound*, London and New York, Routledge, 2007, pp. 38 *et passim*.

space limits; that sense of sudden growth, which we experience in the presence of the greatest works of art.[131]

We find many concepts that resonate with the theory and practice of Montale's poetry in Pound's "A Retrospective" and "A Few Do and Don'ts by an Imagiste"; it is not difficult to link Pound's recommendations to produce sparingly and to limit the exposition to the essential to Montale's own precepts:

> Un poeta non deve rovinarsi la voce solfeggiando troppo, non deve perdere quelle qualità di timbro che dopo non ritroverebbe più. Non bisogna scrivere una serie di poesie là dove una sola esaurisce una situazione psicologica determinata, un'occasione.[132]

The parallel between art and music found in Pound's "A Retrospect", and corroborated in "A Few Do and Don'ts…", beyond finding correspondence in Montale's own thought, leads back to the relationship between Montale and Eliot: for if Pound had recommended to the young imagiste "to compose on the sequence of the musical phrase, not in sequence of a metronome",[133] we read that Montale, in praising Eliot, had said that "in lui […] il tono diventa lirico per accensione interiore, non già perché ubbidisca alle leggi di un metronomo".[134] To those who claimed after Praz that Montale "enriched his own technique with devices strongly reminiscent of Eliot", one could respond that the "objective" processes of Eliot and Montale resemble each other because both keep sight of the precepts of Pound, and because both find a common denominator in the philosophy of Bergson.

One could also recur to a *reductio ad absurdum* and argue that the objective process that Montale will call "occasione" was influenced by Joyce's concept of "epiphany":

> By an epiphany he [Stephen Hero] meant a sudden spiritual manifestation, whether in the vulgarity of speech or of a gesture or in a memorable phase of the

---

131 E. Pound, "A Few Don'ts by an Imagiste" (1913), in *Literary Essays of Ezra Pound*, ed. T.S. Eliot, London, Faber, 1960, p. 5.

132 "A poet must not ruin his voice by solmizating too much; he must not lose those tonal qualities that he would never regain afterwards. It is unnecessary to write a series of poems when a single one exhausts a particular psychological situation, an occasion". E. Montale, "Intenzioni (Intervista immaginaria)" (1946), AMS 1478.

133 E. Pound, "A Retrospect", in *Literary Essays of Ezra Pound*, ed. T.S. Eliot, London, Faber, 1960, p. 3.

134 E. Montale, "Invito a T.S. Eliot" (1950), SM 990: "In his work […] the tone becomes lyrical through interior ignition, not because he is obeying the laws of a metronome".

mind itself. He believed it was for the man of letters to record these epiphanies with extreme care, seeing that they themselves are the most delicate and evanescent of moments.[135]

If we give the noun "vulgarity" the meaning that Montale would have given it – the etymological meaning of "spoken language", "prosaic tone" – then Stephen Hero's epiphany describes the occasion, as it appears in "Mottetti", in "Punta del Mesco", and in "Costa S. Giorgio". The *reductio ad absurdum* exists in the fact that the similarities between epiphany and occasione are indeed evident, but Joyce expunged this passage from the rewritten version of *Stephen Hero*. In *Portrait of the Artist as a Young Man*, the definition does not appear, and thus it is not likely that Montale could have read it.

Rather than considering Montale's poetics of the object as a derivation of Eliot's formula, it would be more appropriate to think that Montale participated, with his own methods and aims, in that general shift from subject to object that, beginning with Bergson, had a more or less evident influence upon all modernists of the subsequent generation.[136]

---

135 J. Joyce, *Stephen Hero* (1906), New York, New Directions, 1963, p. 211.

136 See S. Schwartz, *The Matrix of Modernism: Pound, Eliot, and early Twentieth Century Thought* (1988), Princeton, Princeton University Press, 2014, p. 54: "Pound identifies concrete experience with objects of perception, and argues that the poet should express his individual feelings by presenting exactly what he sees. Eliot also demands fidelity to the object; he contrasts the Romantic poet, who expresses his inner life by creating a vague and dreamlike atmosphere, to the Classical poet, who transmutes his emotions into their 'objective correlative'. Although today we may object to this distinction between Romantic and Classic, we will later see that together with Hulme and Pound Eliot is participating in a shift from subject to object that marks one of the differences between nineteenth- and twentieth-century thought".

Chapter VI

POSTMODERN MONTALE

1. Is Montale a Narcissist?

In the 1960s Montale's proverbially reserved attitude, at a time when the public opinion was heavily polarized, made his political stance less intelligible than it would now appear at a hindsight. For instance, an official from the police headquarters in Milan, responding to a request from the Ministry of Internal Affairs, compiled a profile of Montale enlisting him in the infamous *Categoria Z*, the one reserved for dangerous subversives. Apparently, in the mind of the police, neither Montale's post-war political commitment nor his current articles and interviews could neutralize his participation, nine years prior, to the steering committee of a Casa della Cultura in Milan, or his presence at an encounter between Russian and Italian poets. For the Direzione Generale di Pubblica Sicurezza, Montale was a left-wing radical:

> ... Nel 1951, fu membro del Consiglio Direttivo della Casa della Cultura, con sede in questa via Borgogna n. 3 – alla quale aderiscono intellettuali milanesi di sinistra.
>
> Partecipò al secondo incontro fra i poeti italiani e russi, tenutosi a Mosca, nella primavera del 1958. [...]
>
> Serba regolare condotta in genere. Non risulta iscritto a partiti politici ma si dimostra orientato verso ideologie di sinistra.[1]

---

[1] Note from the Questura di Milano, April 11, 1960. To the Ministero dell'Interno, Divisione Affari Riservati. In: Archivio Centrale dello Stato, Ministero dell'Interno, Direzione Generale di Pubblica Sicurezza, Divisione Affari Riservati; Categorie Permanenti: Categoria Z (Anarchici, Socialisti, Comunisti), Envelope 390. "In 1951, he was a member of the Board of Directors of the Casa della Cultura, located in via Borgogna 3, – to which leftist Milanese intellectuals adhere. He participated in the second meeting between Italian and Russian poets, held in Moscow, in the Spring of 1958. [...] He maintains regular conduct generally. He is not affiliated to any political party but he is oriented towards a leftist ideology".

In contrast to this far-fetched representation of Montale's political position, the opposite understanding of Montale as a bourgeois narcissist proposed by Pier Paolo Pasolini has at least some merit.

"Montale è o non è un narcisista?" ("Is or isn't Montale a narcissist"?) asks Pasolini at the beginning of his review of *Satura*, Montale's fourth volume of poems published in 1971.[2] Filled with images of a privileged, socially successful existence, and marked by a self-reflexive meditation on the author's vocation as a poet, *Satura* seems to present its creator as a self-involved widower unconcerned by the social and political struggles of Italy in the aftermath of the protests of 1968. Pasolini reads *Satura* as Montale's embrace of a poetics that deliberately shunned any quest for social justice or political engagement, and consequently a betrayal of the anti-fascist political ideals he upheld during the Second World War. His accusation of "qualunquismo" (political indifference) and nihilism cast a long shadow over the interpretation of *Satura* and on Montale's entire late production, making it difficult to see connections between the engagement of Montale's celebrated early works and the disjunctive, ahistorical, and yet still theoretically dense turn of the final volumes.

But did Montale abandon the ethical stance of the first three books? Does he become a successful poet and journalist, who chronicles his travels and life experiences with increasing narcissism, or can we see in the new poetics of *Satura* and subsequent volumes a turn towards a philosophical and poetic stance that reflects on the social conditions of the postwar period? When in his review Pasolini identifies a new voice in Montale's poetry, and labels the elements that seem to mark it as symptoms of a despicable bourgeois poetics, he rejects at once *Satura's* preoccupation with the failure of the political promises signaled by the end of the war in 1945, and what we might now call a postmodern emphasis on the end of history.

La bufera registered the trauma of the war on the individual psyche, but Montale's contemporary reflections make clear how his concern was not about the war *per se*. War was merely "l'altra emergenza", the other emergency, not the actual, immediate one, since the conflict was within humanity at large, and could not be eradicated from man's soul: "Sulla terra il vero e il falso sono sempre da rifare, sono sempre in questione, giorno per giorno, senza scampo. [...] Non dobbiamo attendere a braccia incrociate la fine di questa battaglia, non dobbiamo illuderci di esserne usciti fuori. [...]

---

[2] P.P. Pasolini, "Satura" (1971), in *Scritti sulla letteratura e sull'arte*, Milano, Mondadori, 1999, p. 2560.

La battaglia ha da continuare in noi",[3] he writes at the dawn of liberation in 1944, referring to the particular war being waged in the mountains of Northern Italy between the resistance and Fascist troops bolstered by German support as well as to a cosmic struggle. And yet, as early as 1947 Montale's engagement with politics turned into a sour disillusion, the result of his disappointing involvement with the Partito d'Azione and of his distrust of both the capitalist and the socialist systems. After the publication of *La bufera*, he took a long sabbatical from poetry.

Montale's suspension of poetic output was a symptom of the personal disillusionment that followed during the years of the reconstruction and the economic boom. There are, of course, precedents of poets deciding to take a several year sabbatical from their verses, especially among poets admired by Montale, such as Valéry and Eliot. The pauses between the publication of Montale's first three books also make his postwar silence and eventual shift in focus unsurprising, as they signal a writing process that required long gestational periods that often coincided with profound stylistic changes from one collection to the next. And yet Montale, since his early poetic efforts, had never spent such a long period without actually writing verses. This poetic hiatus, which spans from the two *Conclusioni provvisorie* ("Piccolo testamento" and "Il sogno del prigioniero", written respectively in 1953 and 1954) ending *La bufera*, to the composition of "Botta e risposta I" in 1961, suggests a long reflection about the place of poetry in a new social and political landscape marked by the collapse of philosophical systems and by mass consumerism, and a need to rethink modernist convictions in the postwar years. *Satura* is the product of that rethinking, a response to new intellectual and social realities; it marks a new phase of Montale's work and the emergence of a strong postmodernist voice in Italian poetry.[4]

---

3 "On earth the true and the false always have to be redone, are always in question, day after day, without a reprieve. [...] We must not await, with arms crossed, the end of this battle, we must not delude ourselves that we have emerged from it. [...] The battle must continue in us". E. MONTALE, "Voci alte e fioche" (1944), AMS 74 and 76. The same concept returns in "Il sogno del prigioniero", the poem concluding *La bufera e altro*: "La purga dura da sempre, senza un perché" (l. 11) ("The purge persists from time immemorial, without a reason why"). "Altra emergenza" refers to l. 32 of "Ballata scritta in una clinica" (OV 209).

4 Frederic Jameson's *Baudelaire as Modernist and Postmodernist*, in C. HOŠEK – P. PARKER (eds.), *Lyric Poetry Beyond New Criticism*, Ithaca, Cornell University Press, 1985 pp. 247-263, has been useful in framing the theoretical approach of this chapter. In my understanding of *Satura* as a postmodernist book I have utilized, at times verbatim, ideas that Montale used in his review of William Carlos Williams's work. I was convinced of Williams's relevance in the formation of a postmodernist conscience by J. LOWNEY, *The American Avant-Garde Tradition. Williams Carlos Williams, Postmodern Poetry, and the Politics of Cultural Memory*, Lewisburg (PA),

To describe Montale's late work as postmodernist in orientation is to measure the self-conscious distancing of his poetics from the writing of the first three volumes. The new poetic voice of *Satura* deliberately explores the dialectic relationship between modern and postmodern, engaging many now familiar antinomies: metaphysics / irony, metaphor / paradox, narrative / antinarrative, the distinction between high and low culture, and the loss of a secure definition between subjectivity and objectivity, between self and other.[5] The common postmodernist annulments – the end of ideology, the end of history, the end of authorial presence – all play a role in the composition of *Satura*. An attentive reading of the poems, as well as an exploration of the philosophical sources behind them, reveals how Montale was utterly conscious of the cultural turn he was living: he shared the neo-humanistic enthusiasm of Garin, but was also cognizant of the post-Hegelian disillusionment impregnating the work of Garin's pupil, Cesare Vasoli. In the two decades that followed the end of World War II he was not only the cultural emissary of the «Corriere della Sera» at the European Parlament in Strasbourg, which kept him abreast of the latest political theories and practices, but also covered the Rencontres Philosophiques Internationales in Geneva (where he was a delegate in 1948), and the Venetian conventions of the Società Europea di Cultura, where he may or may not have heard Henri Lefebvre expound the theory regarding the distinction between physical and social space that would later animate his most famous book, *La production de l'espace*. Certainly, many of the poems in *Satura* make us think that Montale was aware of the understanding of space as a practiced place and of its ramifications.[6]

His dissatisfaction with the philosophical and scientific systems that sustained his thought in the past impels the verses to express a veritable legitimation crisis of the present times, questioning value, progression, and authority. Among the values canvassed by the poems are identity ("in me i

---

Bucknell University Press, 1997. For two distinct perspectives on Montale's postmodernism see F. Giusti, *Nove indizi di postmodernismo in Satura*, «Contemporanea, Rivista di studi sulla letteratura e la comunicazione», 7, 2009, pp. 49-69, and M. Borio, *Satura. Da Montale alla lirica contemporanea*, Pisa-Roma, Serra, 2013, pp. 49-71. A limited analysis of the postmodern aspects of Montale's late prose works is in R. West, *Montale profeta del postmoderno*, in *Montale e il canone poetico del novecento*, cit., pp. 202-210.

[5] For a critique of the binary opposition modernism/postmodernism, and on postmodernist redefinition of the modernist period, see S. Schwartz, *The Postmodernity of Modernism*, in *The Future of Modernism*, ed. Hugh Witemeyer, Ann Arbor, University of Michigan Press, 1997, pp. 9-32; and I. Hassan, *The Dismemberment of Orpheus: Towards a Postmodern Literature* (1973), New York, Oxford University Press, 1982, pp. 264 *et passim*.

[6] H. Lefebvre, *The Production of Space* (1958), Oxford, Blackwell, 1974.

tanti sono uno anche se appaiono / moltiplicati dagli specchi", "Il tu" (OV 273); "Non sono mai stato certo d'essere al mondo", Xenia II, 7, OV 303), the ontology of the real (Xenia I, 14: "Tu sola sapevi che il moto / non è diverso dalla stasi, / che il vuoto è il pieno e il sereno / è la più diffusa delle nubi"), hierarchies, history, poetry, language, and the very possibility of communication. As history loses its teleological capability, so do the texts: their disposition in the book no longer attempts to convey a narrative progression, and the poems are deliberately giving the impression of chance arrangement. As a result, the novelistic aspects of Montale's former structures leave room for a clearly diaristic composition.

This abandonment of the structured, literary form of the "canzoniere" in favor of the rhizomatic structure of the chronicle, interconnected at both the phonic and the thematic level, is the result of a specific intellectual agenda.[7] Montale seeks to describe the new organization of the book as casual, effortless.

> I miei primi tre volumi avevano finito per comporsi, anche se non proprio deliberatamente, secondo lo schema del canzoniere. Uno schema che esclude un certo numero di contenuti. In questi ultimi quattro anni invece ho scritto poesie come venivano, senza sapere se le avrei pubblicate, senza collocarle in nessuna casella, senza chiedermi se e fino a che punto erano una continuazione delle altre o se andavano per una nuova strada.[8]

The canzoniere has very precise components and limitations that are no longer respected in this new book, according to its author. However, his reference to the myth of absolute inspiration, to poems that "come" by themselves, is rendered more realistic when a sympathetic interviewer like Raffaello Baldini compels Montale to return to this argument and reveal his philosophical frame:

> La storia, come necessaria tendenza a un fine, secondo me è un'illusione coltivata dalla filosofia post-hegeliana: storicismo e marxismo. Sono filosofie di ciò che accade. Si prostrano davanti al fatto compiuto, magari lo divinizzano. La storia che coincide con l'essere, necessariamente, la storia che è tutto, mi pare non dia all'uomo nessun senso di responsabilità e lo lasci completamente disarmato.

---

7 See S. Agosti, *Il testo poetico. Teoria e pratiche d'analisi*, Milano, Rizzoli, 1972, pp. 193-207, and E. Montale, "*Satura* di Eugenio Montale" (1971), interview by Maria Corti, AMS 1699-1700.

8 "My first three volumes ended up being composed, though not really deliberately, according to the framework of the canzoniere. A framework that excludes certain subject matters. In these last four years, instead, I wrote poems as they came, without knowing if I would publish them, without placing them in boxes, without asking myself if, and up to what point, they were a continuation of the others or if they followed a new path". E. Montale, "La poesia e il resto" (1971), interview by Raffaello Baldini, AMS 1707-1708.

Insomma, l'equazione: tutto ciò che è reale è razionale, non si regge, io credo, su basi serie. Direi anzi, e lo dicono altri migliori di me, che non si possono nemmeno scrivere storie. Si possono fare cronache, registrare fatti, date, avvenimenti.[9]

The demise not only of the absolute characters of space and time, but of a general teleological view of history, prompts the abandonment of the canzoniere form: a form very much involved with calendar and diacronicity, as the 366 poems of the original *Canzoniere* can attest.

The inclusion of prosaic vocabulary and minor, slight, paltry subjects drawn from daily life (see "In vetrina", OV 317; "Intercettazione telefonica", OV 323) next to poems that, on the contrary, presuppose a complex philosophical underpinning or that address more canonical subjects ("La storia", OV 315; "Dialogo", OV 327) is not merely a result of writing poems "come venivano", but a consequence of the understanding that the collapse of history disrupts the possibility of crafting a narrative. What is left, pragmatically, is the possibility of writing a chronicle, of keeping a diary, of jotting down impressions connecting scattered incidents. This is what *Satura* does, and the books that follow, as it can be understood by their titles (*Diario del '71 e del '72*; *Quaderno di quattro anni*), are cast in the same mold.

Within the single poems of this new period, similarly, we will look in vain for the development of a narrative thread, characteristic of the most eulogized poems of *La bufera*: "L'orto", "Proda di Versilia", "La primavera hitleriana". Rather, the poems frequently return upon themselves, syntactically constructed upon anaphora or zeugmas. Montale is directed towards a poetry rejecting narrative closure, without the purpose of representing the world or the authority of its author.

Satura demonstrates a new way to compose with everyday words, arrayed in nursery rhymes or lodged in blocks of text. It spreads its themes throughout the full length of the book and gives pride of place to the *petit riens* of quotidian life. It goes without saying that the volume contains no notions of traditional verse, except perhaps in the form of flotsam and jet-

---

9 E. MONTALE, "La poesia e il resto" (1971), interview by Raffaello Baldini, AMS 1712: "History, as a necessary tendency toward an end, is in my opinion an illusion cultivated by post-Hegelian philosophy: historicism and Marxism. They are philosophies of that which happens. They prostrate themselves before the completed act, perhaps they divine it. The history that coincides with existence, necessarily, the history that is everything, seems to me not to give to humankind any sense of responsibility, leaving it completely unarmed. In sum, the equation: all that is real is rational, it does not stand, I believe, on serious foundations. Rather, I would say, and others better than me say it too, that one cannot even write stories. One can only make chronicles, record facts, dates, events".

sam, nearly always dissolving into a new harmonic context. It transforms lullabies and *boutades* into verses that approach traditional metric forms with the science of empty spaces and suspensions, with the help of optics, of enjambments, and of deliberate assonances that link one strophe to the next. One could say that nothing exists in these verses beyond the miracle of a word that simultaneously materializes and annihilates the minor occurrences of a life by now uniform, without problems and hopes, but not without a lofty, stringent acceptance of our enigmatic earthly adventure. The Nobel Prize committee's explanation of their selection of Montale refers to the verses of *Satura* when it declares: "his distinctive poetry, with great artistic sensitivity, has interpreted human values under the sign of an outlook on life with no illusions".[10]

2. A Mirror Against the Molochs

Established in 1943, the Comitato di Liberazione Nazionale ("National Liberation Committee", or CLN), was an umbrella organization composed of representatives of the partisan fighters from various political orientations. After the armistice in 1945, and with the validation of the Allied forces, the CLN assumed responsibility for conveying the embattled nation into the postwar period by facilitating elections and referenda. At the end of the war, its Tuscan section nominated Eugenio Montale to its Arts and Culture Committee.

Montale's credentials as an artist and as anti-fascist were immaculate. In 1925 he had signed Benedetto Croce's "Manifesto degli intellettuali antifascisti", and in 1938 he had been fired from his position at the Gabinetto Viesseux because he did not belong to the Fascist party. His second book of poetry, *Le occasioni*, was the book of choice for partisan fighters of every political orientation who left home to undertake guerrilla warfare in the mountains.[11] His figure, as artist and intellectual, was representative of

---

[10] The Nobel Prize in Literature, 1975. Nobelprize.org. Nobel Media AB 2014, Web. 14 Jul 2015, http://www.nobelprize.org/nobel_prizes/literature/laureates/1975.

[11] Over the years, a consistent bibliography has accumulated on the subject of Montale as inspiration for partisan fighters during World War II. Among the major contributions are M. Forti, *La poesia di Eugenio Montale: la poesia, la prosa di fantasia e d'invenzione*, Milano, Mursia, 1973, p. 22; G. Pampaloni, "Con *Le occasioni* dentro lo zaino", in *La poesia di Eugenio Montale: Atti del Convegno Internazionale tenuto a Genova dal 25 al 28 novembre 1982*, eds. S. Campailla and C.F. Goffis, Firenze, Le Monnier 1984, pp. 263-269; V. Faggi, *Montale a Brescia*, Brescia, La Quadra, 1993. I. Calvino, *Autobiografia politica giovanile*, in *Saggi 1945-1985*, ed. M. Barenghi, Milano, Mondadori, 1995, tome II, p. 2743. Giorgio Strehler interviewed by Giulio Nascimbeni, *Monta-*

that part of Italy that never compromised with Fascism. The chapbook *Finisterre*, whose anti-tyrannical stance was clear from the invocation of Agrippa d'Aubigné in its epigraph, was published clandestinely in Switzerland in 1943 thanks to the good offices of Gianfranco Contini; it was later republished in a second, augmented edition by the printer Barbera in Florence soon after the liberation of the city.

After the liberation of Florence by the Allied Forces, Montale plunged into a frenzy of political and cultural activity: he enrolled in the Partito d'Azione ("Action Party", or Pd'A), a political party of liberal inspiration that pushed for the transformation of Italy into a republic and that attracted many anti-fascist intellectuals and thinkers who did not identify with communist or socialist ideals, nor with the pro-Catholic agenda of De Gasperi's party, the Democrazia Cristiana. He directed the daily «L'Italia libera», a wing of the Pd'A, and together with Alessandro Bonsanti, Arturo Loria, and Luigi Scaravelli, founded the biweekly magazine «Il Mondo». At the same time he collaborated with «Il Corriere del Popolo», the daily edited by the Tuscan section of the CLN, and in 1946 he began a collaboration with the «Corriere d'Informazione», the postwar incarnation of the most famous Italian daily, the Milanese «Corriere della Sera», which had heavily compromised itself, like most of the Italian press, under the Fascist regime.

In the immediate aftermath of the war Montale was emphatically engaged in the process of reconstruction. He wrote articles and short stories exhorting Italian intellectuals to dismiss their habit of "legare il cane dove vuole il padrone" ("tying the dog where the master desires"),[12] underlining how the Italian "*intelligencia*" [sic] had been a primary force in the opposition to fascism, and how only an agreement between intellectuals and the proletariat would be a suitable bulwark against the dangers of future absolutism: "Venivano dal popolo Gobetti e Rosselli, cioé le figure più italianamente ispirate della lunga vigilia antifascista? [...] In questo popolo, che da solo non saprebbe guidarsi, e in pochi uomini degni di condurlo è riposta ogni speranza per il domani".[13] Such an allegiance between *intellettuali* and *popolo*, as well as between Italians of the North and of the South, should "afferrare il momento propizio per non permettere alle forze responsabili

le nello zaino di Strehler, «Corriere della Sera», February 10, 1996, p. 25; and É.Ó. CEALLACHÁIN, *Eugenio Montale: The Poetry of the Later Years*, Oxford, Legenda, 2001, p. 6.

12 E. MONTALE, "Augurio" (September 19-20, 1944), in AMS p. 65.

13 E. MONTALE, "L'Italia rinunzia?" (1945), AMS 41: "Did they come from the masses, Gobetti and Rosselli – those most inspired in the Italian fashion, of the long antifascist vigil? [...] In these masses, who alone would not know how to steer themselves, and in the few men worthy of conducting them is placed every hope for tomorrow".

del fascismo di ricostituirsi",[14] since the danger of fascist supporters returning to power was real and tangible.[15]

Despite the intensity of Montale's political activism, his effective participation in the foundational phase of the newly democratic nation was short-lived. The Pd'A was soon revealed to be a fragile political creation, not able to achieve the communion of intentions between intellectuals and the populace imagined by the poet. In the national elections of June 1946 the party won less than 2 percent of the vote across the nation, and it dissolved soon after because of internal dissidence.[16] A few years later, in an interview, Montale seemed almost embarrassed to narrate his brief political experience:

> Iscritto per qualche tempo al Partito d'Azione, ne ero uscito disgustato, ben consapevole che tutte quelle chiacchiere sarebbero finite in nulla. Io avevo sperato (ingenuamente) che dopo la caduta del fascismo gli italiani si sarebbero riuniti attorno a un programma minimo fronteggiando [...] fascisti e clericali. La forza del Partito comunista lo impedì con l'aiuto dei clericali, che avevano assoluto bisogno di un comunismo forte, ma non fortissimo, per render del tutto impossibile qualsiasi soluzione democratica.[17]

In fact, the parties that emerge as victors in the 1946 elections are the communists, the socialists, and the Christian democrats, foreshadowing a division in Italian politics that would continue until the end of the Cold War.

---

14 E. Montale, "L'Italia rinunzia?" (1945), AMS 39: "seize the propitious moment and not permit the forces responsible for fascism to regroup".

15 In the short story "I galleggianti", published on October 30, 1944 in «La Gazzetta del Popolo», Montale denounced the return of fascist hierarchs in the newly liberated Florence to the political arena: there are those who, speaking English well, bustle to do the honors in the house towards the allied friends; there are those who never abandoned their own positions in the university and continue to maintain them by suddenly changing their ideological colors; and the nameless protagonist, a figure for the author, mentions the episode of a Fascist purge that closely resembles the dismissal of Montale himself from the Gabinetto Vieusseux. See PR, pp. 742-743.

16 The Partito d'Azione had obtained little success even in the administrative elections of March 1946. Montale's state of mind with regard to these elections is well-expressed in the short story "L'asino di Buridano", published in «Il Mondo» in March of the same year (see PR, pp. 669-673). The atmosphere after the war, the enthusiasm of young journalists who began to work during the reconstruction, and the rise and fall of the Action Party are recounted in C. Levi, *The Watch*, New York, Farrar, Straus & Young, 1951.

17 E. Montale, "Dialogo con Montale sulla poesia" (1960), AMS 1602: "Enrolled for some time in the Action Party, I emerged from it disgusted, fully aware that all their chatter would end in nothing. I had hoped (naively) that after the fall of fascism Italians would rally around a common-core program, confronting [...] fascists and clericalists. The power of the Communist Party obstructed it with the help of the clericalists, who absolutely needed a strong communism, but not too strong, in order to render utterly impossible any democratic solution". See also E. Montale, "Il sangue d'Europa" (1965), SM II 2742-2744.

By 1947, Montale's initially optimistic engagement transformed into disillusion, as the change of tone in his prose attests. The short story "Quasi una fantasia" recalls the events that led to his dismissal from the Gabinetto Vieusseux in a melancholic, almost resigned tone.[18] Similarly, the anti-fascist protagonist of the novella *Casa sul Magra*, Adolfo, whose biography partially recalls Montale's own, is dispossessed of his lover, his house, and his provisions by a formerly Fascist childhood acquaintance who has remade himself in the postwar years.[19] The disillusionment registered in these stories might well stand for Montale's own experience of the compromised circumstances of the period. Alessandro Bonsanti, one of the intellectuals with whom Montale had founded the liberation journal «Il Mondo», had also been the card-carrying fascist chosen by the Podestà to replace him at the Gabinetto Vieusseux.[20] In 1948 Montale, recently hired at the «Corriere della Sera», met Indro Montanelli, a journalist who had supported the Fascist regime (and after the war argued that his support was in reality a critique). In 1945 Montale had written a scathing review of Montanelli's novel *Qui non riposano*, a book that sought to level the ethical field between fascists and partisans. In Montale's eyes, Montanelli had benefited professionally from the benevolence of the regime: now, three years after that book review, he had to share an office with Montanelli as a colleague.[21]

But it was not only the manifest recycling of Fascist intellectuals and functionaries in the political and social life of the Italian republic that made Montale despair. It was also the fact that the various parties, for better or worse derived from the partisan factions of the war years, soon manifested their interest in taking advantage of political and economic power in the reconstruction, instead of promoting the common interest and the just governance of the country. Their pursuit of power caused Montale, a staunch republican, to become disillusioned by the government of the newly proclaimed republic. His disappointment is evident in a reading of

[18] Later reprinted in the volume *Farfalla di Dinard* under the title "Il colpevole", PR 167-172. See also S. Betocchi, *Gli anni di Montale al Vieusseux di Firenze*, «Italica» 71, n. 3 (Autumn 1994), pp. 331-324.

[19] E. Montale, "Casa sul Magra" (1947), PR 711-715.

[20] Bonsanti's nomination in 1934 followed a period of receivership in which the Gabinetto Vieusseux was directed by two functionaries from the City Council, Filippo Cristini and Rodolfo Ciullini (see E. Montale, *Caro Maestro e Amico. Carteggio con Valery Larbaud*, ed. M. Sonzogni, Milano, Archinto, 2003, p. 100, n. 4). Bonsanti described his troubled relationship with the regime in the autobiographical novel *La nuova stazione di Firenze*, Milano, Mondadori, 1965.

[21] E. Montale, "Una tragedia italiana" (1945), AMS 43-48, review of I. Montanelli, *Qui non riposano*, Milano, Tarantola, 1945.

the articles and the short stories penned in 1947, such as "Aut Aut", where in the country of Livonia, an imaginary European country recently made into a republic by national referendum,

> era al Governo, anzi allo sgoverno, da alcuni anni un variopinto accozzo di uomini di provenienza e di partiti diversi, i quali neutralizzandosi a vicenda, anziché collaborare, stavano portando il Paese alla rovina.[22]

Montale was worried by the ideological discord that resulted from the division of Europe by the Allied forces. After a brief period of enthusiasm he distanced himself from political activity over concerns about the pitfalls of prevailing ideologies; communism, he felt, did not provide citizens enough liberty, and capitalism was too likely to usher in the commodification of human beings.

With his exit from politics came the role of a *personnaliste convaincu*, as he explains during a lecture (9 September 1947) at the Rencontres Internationales in Geneva. The oration offers a glimpse into Montale's ideological position in the late 1940s. On the one hand, he notes the social and political changes brought about by the technological progress of contemporary society, and he fears them, worrying about a decline of humanistic culture in the civilization of the masses.[23] On the other hand, he is certain that socialist ideology, as a system deprived, by definition, of any transcendental possibility, cannot represent a solution to the ethical needs of modern society that, precisely because it is entirely imminent, needs a synderesis.[24]

---

22 E. Montale, "Aut aut" (1947), PR 728: "It was in the Government, or rather the misgovernment, for some years a colorful jumble of men of different provenances and different parties who were mutually neutralizing each other rather than collaborating, that they were bringing the Country to its ruin".

23 E. Montale, "Je suis un personnaliste convaincu" (1948), SM 726 : "Le progrès technique, c'est-à-dire, selon la plus grand partie d'entre nous, le développement de la civilization mécanique et industrielle, peut-il changer la société sans détruire la personnalité, sans nuire à l'homme en tant qu'homme qui se reconnaît un sens psycologique individuel, une destinée morale tout à fait singulière et irremplaçable?" ("Will technical progress, i.e., according to the common opinion, the development of a mechanical and industrial civilization, be able to transform society without destroying the personality, without marring the man who recognizes himself as a psycological individuality, as an individual with a moral destiny entirely unique and irreplaceable?"). For an analysis of Montale's worries about the mechanization of Western civilization in the postwar period, expressed clearly in his articles about England, see É.Ó. Ceallacháin, *Eugenio Montale: The Poetry of the Later Years*, cit., p. 11.

24 E. Montale, "Je suis un personnaliste convaincu" (1948), SM 727-728 : "On nous assure que, quand l'exploitation des travailleurs par le monde du capital ne sera plus possible ni concevable, le terrain sera aussi balayé pour les épreuves d'un nouvel homme moral. [...] Mais le socialisme en soi – en tant que mouvement humain qui a des buts purement humains à accomplir – le socialisme en soi, peut-il suffire à l'homme qui se soucie de sa propre destinée?" ("We

The crisis between capitalist and socialist systems compels intellectuals to take a position, but such a position is not necessarily on either side: the clerk must instead be a "problematizer", a critical mirror of the changes in society. Montale's recommendations for the demeanor of "the clerk" were possibly suggested by a book, *La Trahison des Clercs*, by Julien Benda, an author whom he knew and for whom he would elsewhere bestow measured praise. In Benda's book, the traitorous clerk is the intellectual who is imprisoned by national, political, class, or racial interests, and abdicates his essential task, which is the disinterested quest for the truth.[25] Like Montale's poetry, which was meant to denounce a visceral disagreement with the ontological world, had instead been largely interpreted as a response and a protest to a particular historic time and a particular political situation, Benda's work, which condemned how early twentieth-century European intellectuals had allowed political interests to contaminate their intellectual vocation, had been seen as targeting contemporary Fascist governments. All intellectuals, believers and nonbelievers, should become "critical mirrors" of both Molochs, the one embodying the capitalist and the other representing the socialist system:

> Quel doit être donc le devoir des hommes de bonne volonté? Quelle doit être l'attitude des clercs, des hommes de culture, des hommes de foi, devant la crise gigantesque, devant la lutte des deux systèmes, les deux molochs: le moloch du capital et le moloch des masses déchaînées qui risque d'abîmer toute civilisation, méchanique ou non? [...] Eh bien je crois, Mesdames et Messieurs, que notre devoir à nous – et je parle de nous personnalistes avoués – est bien d'être des témoins vigilants, des "inquiéteurs", de rester le miroir critique de l'heure actuelle.[26]

Montale engages his own peculiarities, and as such the poet is not simply a clerk but a "convinced personalist" who fears a priori neither the technological progress amplified by consumerism and mass culture nor the so-

---

are assured that, when the exploitation of workers by the capital will no longer be possible nor conceivable, the field will also be ready for the creation of a new moral man. [...] But socialism itself – which is a human movement with merely human goals to accomplish – socialism itself, will it suffice to the man who cares about his own destiny?").

25 J. Benda, *La Trahison des Clercs* (1927, 1946²), Grasset, Les Cahiers Rouges, 2003; see E. Montale, "Si è spento Julien Benda, il filosofo che si oppose a Bergson" (1956), SM 1957-1961.

26 E. Montale, "Je suis un personnaliste convaincu" (1948), SM 729: "What should therefore be the duty of the men of good will? What should be the attitude of the clergy, of the men of culture, of the men of faith, before the gigantic crisis, before the struggle of the two systems, these two Molochs: the Moloch of capital and the Moloch of the raging masses, [two monsters] who may damage every kind of civilization, mechanical or not? [...] Well, I think, ladies and gentlemen, that our duty – and I mean us, staunch personalists – is to be vigilant witnesses, "inquiéteurs", to remain the critical mirror of our time".

cial conquests brought forth by socialism. By confronting himself he also gains the advantage of remaining free – free from ideological constraints and from future political dictatorships.[27] The "vigilant witness", however, is not closed in his own private sanctuary: Montale clearly expresses his own beliefs on the antinomy between isolation and communication. Notwithstanding the isolation that is the natural destiny of the individual, Montale considers the purpose of intellectual activity – whether philosophical or poetic – to be the overcoming of the individual's solitude.[28]

The concern in the prose with the contemporary political situation returns in the poems written in the same span of years. "Piccolo testamento", written in 1953 and the first of the "Conclusioni provvisorie" in *La bufera*, vindicates intellectual liberty with pride. Here, the light of thought, in itself so elusory and evanescent as to be compared to the luminescence resulting from a snail's tracks or refracting from smashed shards of glass, does not come from a church, nor from a workshop:

> Questo che a notte balugina
> nella calotta del mio pensiero,
> traccia madreperlacea di lumaca
> o smeriglio di vetro calpestato,
> non è lume di chiesa o d'officina
> che alimenti
> chierico rosso, o nero.[29]

---

27 E. Montale, "Je suis un personnaliste convaincu" (1948), SM 729: "Ne craignons pas le progrès technique, ne doutons pas de l'avenir moral de l'homme, mais restons libres, Messieurs et Mesdames, dans tous les moments, dans tous les épreuves. Ce n'est pas seulement mon avis personnel, c'est l'avis, je crois, de tous les hommes qui, comme moi, ont passé presque toute leur vie dans l'esclavage", ("We shall not fear the technical progress, nor doubt the moral future of man, yet we shall remain free, ladies and gentlemen, in all times, in all events. This is not only my personal opinion, this is the opinion, I believe, of all the men who, like me, have spent most of their lives in slavery"). The comparison between living under an absolutist regime and the state of slavery recurs in the second introductory poem of *Satura*, "Botta e risposta I" (OV 276), see *infra*.

28 E. Montale, "La solitudine dell'artista" (1952), in AMS 53: "Il tentativo di fermare l'effimero, di rendere comunicante l'io individuale che non è tale per definizione, la rivolta, insomma, contro la condizione umana (rivolta dettata da un appassionato *amor vitae*) è alla base delle ricerche artistiche e filosofiche del nostro tempo" ("The attempt to halt the ephemeral, to render communicative the individual "I", who is by definition not communicative, the revolt, in sum, against the human condition [a revolt dictated by a passionate *amor vitae*] is the heart of the artistic and philosophical inquiries of our time"). See also P.M. Sipala, *Eugenio Montale e l'intellettuale italiano nel dopoguerra*, in *La poesia di Montale*, eds. S. Campailla and C.F. Goffis, Firenze, Le Monnier 1984, p. 318.

29 OV 267, ll. 1-7: "This flickering at night / in the casing of my thoughts, / mother-of-pearl tracing of snail / or glass-grit trampled underfoot, / this is not light of factory or church / fed by cleric / whether red or black", trans. W. Arrowsmith.

The chiasmus linking the lamp in the church to the black clerk and that of the workshop to the red clerk, repeats a polarity reiterated on other occasions.[30] The speaker disdainfully rejects both poles:

> Ognuno riconosce i suoi: l'orgoglio
> non era fuga, l'umiltà non era
> vile, il tenue bagliore strofinato
> laggiù non era quello di un fiammifero.[31]

Intellectual pride is not an escape from reality; the humility that results from recognition of individual impotence in opposing the purge is not cowardliness. The sparkle of intelligence, even if it is not brighter than the light of a match, is the only memento of a possible resistance.

Yet, even if the primary task of an intellectual is to communicate, the electoral disappointments and the lack of faith in the postwar politico-philosophical system had taken a toll on Montale's approach to writing. While, in the earlier books, the changes in stylistic register were motivated by the search for novelty, consonant with Pound's call to "make it new", the search for new expressive means is now linked to the dramatic fracture that Montale notes between the intellectual and society. The article "La solitudine dell'artista" is, at heart, a cry of alarm and a plea for help:

> L'isolamento dell'artista, la sfiducia nel linguaggio e la conseguente ricerca di nuovi mezzi espressivi sono aspetti connessi al progresso meccanico, alla diffusione della cultura media e alla volgarizzazione (in senso etimologico) dell'artista.[32]

The lack of faith in language is an old trope of Montale the modernist, one that we can find verbatim in an essay dated 1925: "Se *i poeti hanno perduto la fiducia nelle parole*, i critici che non vogliono essere da meno si raccomandano quando alla provvidenza, quando a Freud e alla contingenza".[33] He links a lack of faith in the expressive possibilities of poetry to the spirit

---

30 See E. Montale, "Né in Dio né in Marx" (1956), AMS 58-64.

31 OV 267, ll. 27-31: "Each man knows his own: pride / was not flight, humility was not / cowardice, that faint glow catching fire / beneath was not the striking of a match", trans. W. Arrowsmith.

32 E. Montale, "La solitudine dell'artista" (1952), AMS 55: "The isolation of the artist, the mistrust of language, and the subsequent search for new modes of expression are aspects connected to mechanical progress, to the diffusion of middlebrow culture, and to the vulgarization (in the etymological sense) of the artist".

33 E. Montale, "Stile e tradizione" (1925), AMS 10, emphasis mine. "*If poets have lost their faith in words*, the critics who do not wish to be inferior beseech now providence, now Freud and circumstance".

of the times; in 1925 the culprit seems to be the diffuse and barely disguised disrepute in which Italian society holds the man of letters and the intellectual.[34] However in 1952 the culprits are, mechanical progress, the diffusion of mass culture, and the vulgarization of the artists. Whatever the reason, after giving *La bufera e altro* to Neri Pozza for publication, the poet Montale cloaked himself in silence.

When asked, Montale explains his silence by pointing to the constraints of his work as a journalist at the «Corriere della Sera», and to the fact that, for him, writing in prose was incompatible with writing in poetry. If the former reason seems probable, given that from 1955 to 1959 he frequently traveled for reporting assignments and published more than a hundred articles a year, the latter is patently false – the osmosis of themes, cues, and images between the prose and verse is evident over the arc of Montale's career. His poetic silence arouses curiosity because despite this silence his fame as a poet grew and public accolades began to accumulate: in 1959 he was awarded the Légion d'honneur; in 1961 he received the *laurea honoris causa* from the University of Milan; in 1962, the Accademia dei Lincei assigned him the Premio Feltrinelli. In 1966, several volumes celebrating his work were published in celebration of his seventieth birthday; in 1967, he received an honorary degree from Cambridge, and then later in Rome he was nominated a senator for life by President of the Republic, Giuseppe Saragat, "per avere illustrato la patria e per altissimi meriti nel campo letterario e artistico" ("for having illuminated the country and for the highest merits in the field of literature and the arts"). But Montale's "consistent personal reticence", described by the press release that announced the award of the Nobel Prize in Literature in 1975,[35] remains unchanged, and as the number of granted interviews multiplies, the poet shows himself to be annoyed by the intrusions on his privacy.

For Montale, being interviewed meant being repeatedly interrogated about why he stopped writing. In response to these questions he sometimes invoked the usual reasons, and other times changed the subject to avoid giving a response. Sometimes too he seems to delight in responding with puns and wordplay. To the question, "what is the question that irritates you the most?" he replies, "the one about news of my poetic production". When asked "What is the relationship between journalism and

---

[34] E. Montale, "Stile e tradizione" (1925), AMS 11.

[35] "Nobel Prize in Literature 1975 – Press Release", Nobelprize.org. Nobel Media AB 2014. Web. 10 July 2015.
http://www.nobelprize.org/nobel_prizes/literature/laureates/1975/press.html.

literature?" he states, "journalism is to literature as reproduction is to love. In some cases the two can coincide".[36]

Only once, tangentially, in an interview to Corrado Stajano, does Montale say something that helps make the reasons for his poetic silence understandable. When Montale, speaking in Stajano's dictaphone, begins declaring his utmost respect for those who do not feel the need to write, Stajano prods him: "Non è un atteggiamento snobistico, questo, un alibi al suo non scrivere di oggi?" ("Isn't this a snobbish attitude, an alibi for your not writing today"?) Montale replies initially with one of his well-honed arguments, the cliché that life and art are mutually exclusive, just to dismiss the point; but then, perhaps because he likes the young Stajano, who worked at «Il Mondo» (not the bi-weekly founded by Montale immediately after the war, but a weekly inspired by the principles that Benedetto Croce had defined as "radical" and to which Montale occasionally contributed), he gives him a different answer:

> L'arte è la forma di vita di chi veramente non vive, un compenso o un surrogato. Non credo, poi, che il nostro tempo sia favorevole alle arti", continua il poeta mostrandomi un saggio di Cesare Vasoli su Hegel, estratto a fatica da una pila di libri. "Le ragioni del mio silenzio si potrebbero trovare qui.[37]

Stajano is not familiar with the book (which is hardly surprising, since Vasoli is still a young, relatively unknown professor of philosophy at the

---

[36] Both answers are given to Enrico Roda in E. Montale, "Quarantuno domande a Eugenio Montale" (1955), AMS 1597.

[37] E. Montale, "Il profeta dell'apocalisse" (1964), interview by C. Stajano, AMS 1634-1641 (quote from p. 1634), "'Art is the form life takes for those who truly do not live, a compensation or a surrogate. I don't believe, therefore, that our time is favorable to the arts', the poet continues, showing me an essay on Hegel by Cesare Vasoli, extracted with effort from a stack of books. 'The reasons for my silence could be found here'". The topos of the irreconcilability of life and literature in Montale goes back to at least 1917, see QG AMS 1334: "L'uomo più grande sarebbe colui che considerando la miseria di una sua possible immortalità (artistica) fra gli uomini (essere spulciato da professori, citato sbadigliando da chi non l'ha conosciuto, vivere a stento su un pezzo di carta), si condannasse al silenzio e chiudesse in sé i propri tesori", ("The greatest man would be the one who, realizing the affliction of his hypotetical (artistic) immortality among men (to be combed though by professors, quoted absent-mindedly by those who did not know him, barely surviving on a piece of paper) decided to remain silent and kept for himself his treasures"). See also "Intenzioni (Intervista immaginaria)" (1946), AMS 1476, "pensai presto, e ancora penso, che l'arte sia la forma di vita di chi veramente non vive: un compenso o un surrogato", ("I realized early, and I still believe it, that art is the from of life proper of those who do not truly live: a surrogate or a compensation"); and "Per finire", in *Diario del '71 e del '72* (OV 508). It is worth noticing that by 1964 Montale had once more started writing poetry: *Satura*, the chapbook printed by Bodoni in a limited edition for the wedding of Sandra Fagiuoli-Crespi containing the new "Botta e risposta", was out in 1962; Montale obviously decided to not inform his young colleague.

University of Florence), misunderstands the thrust of Montale's clue, and replies off topic: "Ma l'estetica di Hegel era valida anche quando lei scriveva" ("But the aesthetic of Hegel was valid even when you were writing"). Montale understands that he has not been understood and simplifies his original response to the point of a commonplace, "Vede, io non vado alla ricerca della poesia, aspetto di esserne visitato" ("Look, I do not go in search of poetry; I wait to be visited by it"). Their conversation moves on, with Montale's meaning, and the book that could explain his silence, still lost on Stajano.

The book in question is *Tra cultura e ideologia*, a collection of essays that includes a section dedicated to Hegel, one to Kierkegaard, and one to Nietzsche. It is possible that Montale, reading the description that Vasoli gives of the young Nietzsche, felt an impulse to identify with him:

> La prima constatazione che noi faremo parlando di Nietzsche consisterà perciò solo nel notare che egli [...] si era formato in un periodo di profonda crisi ideologica, e per di più, all'indomani di una sconfitta che ha pesato così gravemente sull'evoluzione storica della borghesia tedesca e dei suoi ceti intellettuali. All'origine di questa crisi stanno infatti due eventi distinti, ma intimamente legati tra loro; e, cioé, da un lato la dissoluzione della filosofia hegeliana, della sua concezione della storia e della sua "trama" dialettica, e, dall'altro, il fallimento della rivoluzione liberale tedesca.[38]

The mention of a period of profound ideological crisis in the aftermath of a defeat, and of the failure of a liberal revolution, would have resonated with Montale, who lived through the breakup of the Partito d'Azione and the rise of the two ideological blocs of the Cold War with profound disappointment. But it is mainly the hint to the failure of Hegelian philosophy that would have interested the poet, and that interest would have been multiplied by reprises and thorough analysis of the argument in the final part of the book, which treats the currents in contemporary Italian culture.

Vasoli, having graduated under the direction of Eugenio Garin with a thesis on Nietzsche as a forerunner and cause of the moral crisis of the twentieth century, developed a perspective that enabled him to comprehend

---

[38] C. Vasoli, *Tra cultura e ideologia*, Milano, Lerici, 1961, pp. 85-86: "The first observation that we will make, therefore, while speaking of Nietzsche will consist only in noting that he [...] grew up in a period of profound ideological crisis, and furthermore, during the aftermath of a defeat that weighed so heavily on the historical evolution of the German bourgeoisie and its intellectual classes. At the origins of this crisis, in fact, there are two distinct but intimately connected events; they are, on the one hand, the dissolution of Hegelian philosophy, of his conception of history and its dialectical "narrative", and on the other hand, the failure of the liberal German revolution".

"lo stato di intimo disagio e di profonda inquietudine che non solo domina oggi certe zone avanzate della cultura liberale, ma ha trovato espressione nella stessa crisi permanente dei 'democratici laici'".[39] Through Nietzsche, Vasoli is able to reveal the ethical deficiencies of Hegelian historicism:

> Configurando lo sviluppo storico come un processo dialettico nel quale la "libertà" e la "coscienza" spirituale si realizzano in forme sempre più compiute, sino alla totale conquista della libertà nella pura Autocoscienza, Hegel pervenne alla totale riduzione razionale di tutto il passato alla misura finale del presente ed alla piena giustificazione di tutto il presente quale fine e scopo del passato.[40]

But if, according to Vasoli, idealist historicism is no longer of help in navigating the ethical crisis left by the world wars, Heideggerian existentialist ontology is equally subject to critique, notwithstanding the fact that existentialism comes to be recognized as a position opposed to the dialectics of idealism. In Montale's reading, Vasoli's essays precociously reveal the reasons for the crisis of progressive ideologies in the second half of the twentieth century.[41] Both idealism and existentialism, viewed from the perspective of a society that had lived through the horrors of two world wars, had failed to explain the immanence of evil and ended up justifying it – idealism including it in a historical dialectic of thesis-antithesis-synthesis, existentialism accepting it as a necessary, complementary counterweight to the good. These premises inform the composition of one of *Satura's* most challenging poems, "Dialogo":

> (N) «Se l'uomo è nella storia non è niente:
> la storia è un *marché aux puces*, non un sistema».
> (E) «Provvidenza e sistema sono tutt'uno
> e il Provvidente è l'uomo».
> (N) «Dunque è provvidenziale

---

[39] *Ibid.*, p. 498: "the state of inner discomfort and of profound disquiet that not only dominates certain progressive sectors of today's liberal culture, but has also found expression in the same permanent crisis of the 'secular democrats'". On Eugenio Garin's link between Italian literary production and European philosophical context in the first half of the twentieth century, see E. Garin, *Cronache di filosofia italiana, 1900-1943*, Bari, Laterza, 1955. See also M. Cangiano, *Come si identifica (e come si storicizza) il Modernismo italiano*, «Le parole e le cose», Web http://www.leparoleelecose.it/?p=22632#_ftn1 accessed May 12, 2016.

[40] *Ibid.*, p. 87: "Depicting historical development as a dialectical process in which 'freedom' and spiritual 'consciousness' are realized in ever more complete forms, up to the total conquest of freedom by pure self-consciousness, Hegel arrived at the total rational reduction of the entire past to the final measure of the present and at the full justification of the entire present as the end and aim of the past".

[41] See also M. Maggi, *Cesare Vasoli: Un ricordo*, «Annali del Dipartimento di Filosofia di Firenze (Nuova Serie)», XVIII (2012), p. 257.

anche la pestilenza».
(E) «La peste è il negativo del positivo,
è l'uomo che trasuda il suo contrario».
(N) «Sempre avvolto però nel suo sudario».
(I) «Il sistema ternario
secerne il male e lo espelle,
mentre il binario se lo porta dietro».
(N) «Ma il ternario lo mette sottovetro,
e se vince lo adora».
(I/E) «Vade retro,
Satana!».[42]

In this parody of a Platonic dialogue we can recognize three voices. The first, that I will call "Il nemico della dialettica" (N, enemy of dialectic), following Montale's suggestion, is the voice of the author, or the voice of any reasonable person disillusioned by the overarching philosophical systems. The second is the voice of a "Filosofo esistenzialista" (E, existentialist philosopher), a Manichean ("manicheo"), because he believes in good and evil as two distinct, irreconcilable but inseparable facts. The third is the voice of a neo-Hegelian, a "Filosofo idealista" (I, idealist philosopher) who believes in historical dialectic.

The first to speak is (N), who asserts that history is a flea market, a place where objects are stacked without order or logic. And if the old convention called history does not exist, neither does man, when interpreted historically. (E) responds by declaring the immanence of his own system of thought: man, and not God, is the engine and the interpreter of history. (N), therefore, tries to reveal the intrinsic limitation of existentialist thought – the inseparability of good and evil – which internalizes yet does not solve the

42 OV 327: "If a man is in history, he is nothing: / history is a *marché aux puces*, not a system." / "Providence and system are one and the same, / and Provident is mankind." / "Then, even the plague is providential." / "The plague is the negation of a positive, it is humanity exuding his opposite." / "Always, however, wrapped in its shroud." / "The ternary system excretes evil and expels it, / while the binary system keeps it within." / "But the ternary system puts evil in a shrine, / and if evil wins, it adores it." "Vade retro, / Satan!". The initials of those I propose as participants in the dialogue are not in the text, and I have added them in the original Italian for clarity. The poem appeared as a segue to the "Variazione" published in the «Corriere della Sera» (November 30, 1968), preceded by an introduction: "Il solito anonimo poeta (?) mi manda questa pseudo-poesia che pubblico senz'appulcrarci parola. Penso che sia opera di un nemico della dialettica". ("The usual anonymous poet (?) sends me this pseudo-poem that I am publishing without embellishing even a word of it. I believe it to be the work of an enemy of dialectic"), PR 1108. The title on the manuscript was "Filosofia, ninfa gentile..." (see OV 998), an echo of a short aria by Ippolito Pindemonte set to music by Vincenzo Bellini ("Malinconia, ninfa gentile", in *Sei Ariette, numero 1*).

ethical problem, a fact highlighted by the hypermetric quasi-rhyme *provvidenzia(le) : pestilenza.* (E) then falls into the trap, admitting that negative and positive cannot be separated; the "dermatologic" touch of the argument is clarified by a comment made by Montale in 1968: "Per i manichei, intendo dire chi crede nel bene e nel male come due fatti distinti e inconciliabili, il male sussiste sempre, te lo porti attaccato alla pelle [...]" [43] Thus, (N) does not need to add anything to the logic of his own argument, and he allows himself a play on words: humanity oozes pestilence ("trasuda"), and is wrapped in a "sudario", the funerary shroud, a glaring reference to the devastations caused by the second world war. (I) therefore intervenes, boasting about the efficacy of his own dialectical system over the dichotomy of (E). In a first draft of the poem, the attack was more explicit:

> «Questo non è un sistema perché è binario,
> manicheismo rancido che non approda al meglio».
> «Il sistema ternario produce il male e lo espelle
> mentre il binario se lo porta dietro».[44]

Hegelian dialectics produces evil (antithesis), but is also able to expel it (synthesis), according to (I). No, concludes (N): the dialectical system does not eliminate evil, but makes it part of its ontology; and since the antithesis becomes part of the synthesis, the dialectical movement may end up justifying evil, or "adoring" it. That is consistent with a Hegelian view of history, but does not erase the objections raised by contingentism. The link between Hegelian dialectic and worship is explained in another comment from Montale, where he links the tripartite system to the Christian trinity:

---

43 E. MONTALE, "Discorrendo della fine del mondo" (1968), interview by Manlio Cancogni, AMS 1692: "For the Manicheans, by which I mean those who believe in good and evil as two distinct and irreconcilable affairs, evil always exists, you wear it attached to your skin [...]". For Montale's antiteleological position, see also "Il Montale di *Satura*" (1971), interview by Mario Miccinesi, AMS 1703: "Se la storia è il succedersi dei fatti e lo storico è colui che registra e annota questi fatti, nessuno di noi sfugge alla storia. Se però lo storico vuol dimostrarci che i fatti contengono una finalità, un *telos* provvidenziale, allora il sedicente storico non potrà far altro che giustificare tutto quello che accade, con particolare entusiasmo, e malafede, per i periodi più disastrosi del grande show finalistico", "If history is the progression of events and the historian is the one who records and comments upon these events, none of us escapes history. If, however, the historian wants to show us that the string of events contains a finality, a providential *telos*, then our self-appointed historian will not be able to do anything more than justifying all that happens, with particular enthusiasm – and bad faith – for the most disastrous periods of the great finalistic show").

44 OV 998: "This is not a system because it is binary, / a rancid Manichaeism that does not reach what is best. /" "The ternary system produces evil and ejects it, / while the bynary system keeps it within".

> La forma dialettica, hegeliana, con la tesi, l'antitesi e la sintesi, non so perché mi ricorda il principio trinitario. Trovo che è una formula molto pericolosa, a parte la sua dubbia fondatezza logica. Chi la adotta è come se pretendesse di produrre sì il male ma di espellerlo col superamento. Tesi, il bene, antitesi, il male, sintesi [...] e si è a posto.[45]

At this point (I), or (E), or both, decide to truncate the conversation with the formula used by Jesus Christ to renounce temptation (Mark 8:33), which has become the traditional form to enact an exorcism. The "Nemico della dialettica" (N) has then revealed idealism and existentialism for what they are: systems of belief.

It is important to clarify that Montale's postwar opinions and philosophical intentions are more tentative and nuanced than the simplifications that this poem implies. This short text steeped in abstractions does not leave room for the exposition necessary for the construction of a coherent, unassailable philosophic system. Here the structure of the verses tends toward the final clause, as we see in the rhyme scheme – *dietro : sottovetro : retro* – which produces an enjambment to arrive at a paradoxical, amused comparison between the disillusioned author and the Lord of Darkness, complete with an exclamation point: "Satana!" We are not in a philosophic dialogue here, but in its parody. The only way left to manage incoherence and alienation is "a willingness to live with uncertainty, to tolerate and, in some cases, to welcome a world seen as random and multiple, even, at times, absurd".[46] A small consolation remains: even after the collapse of all philosophical systems, even after the triumph of history's irrationality over the rational principles of the world, humanity and its ethical principles carry on. It may not be much, but it is everything:

> Io credo che l'uomo abbia dei doveri, delle responsabilità, che gli sono stati dettati da un sentimento morale. E credo che questo sentimento possa sopravvivere ai trasformismi religiosi e filosofici. Ma è tutto.[47]

---

45 E. Montale, "Discorrendo della fine del mondo" (1968), interview by Manlio Cancogni, AMS 1692: "The Hegelian dialectic form, with thesis, antithesis, and synthesis, I don't know why, reminds me of the Trinitarian principle. I find it a most dangerous formula, aside from its dubious logical legitimacy. It's as if those who adopt it claim to produce evil in this way but to expel it by overcoming it. Thesis, good, antithesis, evil, synthesis [...] and everything is in its place".

46 A. Wilde, *Horizons of Assent: Modernism, Postmodernism, and the Ironic Imagination*, Baltimore, Johns Hopkins University Press, 1981, p. 45.

47 E. Montale, "La poesia e il resto" (1971), interview by Raffaello Baldini, AMS 1709: "I believe humanity has duties, and responsibilities, that were dictated to it by moral sentiment. And I believe that this sentiment can survive religious and philosophical transformisms. But that's all".

3. *Satura* and the multiple meanings of the text

Understanding the philosophical roots of Montale's postmodern turn allows us to reframe the position of *Satura*, and by and large all of Montale's later period. The author sometimes confirms the congruity of his poetic production, declaring that all of his books of poetry are in reality a single book: "Ho scritto un solo libro, di cui prima ho dato il *recto*, ora do il *verso*";[48] at other times he instead underscores the differences between the new book and its predecessors, claiming to have significantly altered it at a lexical, thematic, and structural level:

> Gli altri miei libri, sia pure non troppo consapevolmente, ancora obbedivano al concetto del canzoniere, una raccolta che tende a una specie di completezza anche formale, senza buchi, senza intervalli, senza nulla di trascurato. Qui invece mi sono più lasciato schiudere, tanto che non prevedevo molto il risultato e accantonavo nel cassetto qualche poesia e ancora due mesi prima di dare il manoscritto all'editore ero dubbioso se farlo o no.[49]

Therefore, the debate between continuity and rupture has understandably engaged Montale's readers, who variously opined for the cohesion of all of Montale's poetic production, or for its discontinuity, or, in some cases, for both.[50] The postmodern perspective reinforces the third option

---

[48] E. Montale, "Ho scritto un solo libro" (1975), interview by Giorgio Zampa, AMS 1724: "I have written only a single book, of which before I gave the *recto* and now I give the *verso*". The metaphor, apt to a bibliophile, reinforces a similar concept expressed four years before, distinguishing between front and backstage: see "Il Montale di *Satura*" (1971), interview by Mario Miccinesi, AMS 1702: "Se il poeta M. fosse morto dopo la *Bufera* nessuno avrebbe parlato di prematura scomparsa. Ma non è morto, e quando ha ripreso a scriver versi, dopo molti anni di prosa-prosa, la necessità di mostrare l'*envers du décor* gli si è imposta inesorabilmente. Così faceva Fregoli quando rivelava ciò che accadeva nel retroscena", "If the poet M. had died after *Bufera* nobody would have spoken of a premature departure. But he did not die, and when he took up writing poems again, after many years of prose, the need to demonstrate *l'envers du décor* imposed itself upon him inexorably. Just so had Fregoli done when he revealed what happened backstage".

[49] E. Montale, "*Satura* di Eugenio Montale" (1971), interview by Maria Corti, AMS 1700: "My other books, even if unconsciously, still obeyed the concept of the canzoniere, a collection that tends toward a type of completeness, even formal, without holes, without intervals, without anything neglected. Here instead I allowed myself to be more open, such that I could not foresee very well the final product and set aside some poems in the drawer, and even two months before giving the manuscript to the editor, I was unsure whether or not to do it".

[50] As is the case with Romano Luperini, who successfully combines all of Montale's periods in an effective synthesis, even while making explicit their differences. See R. Luperini, "Montale e il canone poetico del Novecento italiano", in *Montale e il canone poetico del Novecento*, cit., p. 368: "Rompendo con i modelli chiusi [i.e., with the Petrarchan tradition of the *Canzoniere*], rilanciando la lezione allegorica di Dante e ponendo con forza la questione del signifi-

if we understand literary postmodernism as both a breakthrough from the modernist *Weltanschaaung*, and as a "selective intensification of certain tendencies within modernism itself",[51] as we can similarly understand the *verso* of Montale's poetry as a decisive break with his previous period, as well as the intensification, and more generally modification, of elements already present in his work.

When considered through this postmodern perspective, Montale's *modus componendi* remains remarkably coherent: let's recall that fragment from *Quaderno Genovese* where the teenaged poet annotates a meditation on the composition process extracted from *Les poètes et la poesie*, by his symbolist numen Duhamel:

> Giusta idea del D[uhamel]: non occorre prender notazioni rapide, sul luogo, delle sensazioni provate, per iscoprire nuove immagini e analogie; è anzi dannoso. Occorre digerire, *dimenticare*, le sensazioni; non sono già perdute, così facendo; all'atto della creazione – anche dopo molti anni – scaturiscono in noi, più nuove, più vere, più *necessarie*: il tempo opera una scelta in noi, e tiene le migliori e le profonde.[52]

If we compare this passage with an answer that Montale gives himself in the "Autointervista" of 1971, we get the sense that in his older age the poet has internalized Duhamel's precepts:

> Io pubblico quando si è prodotta in me una certa accumulazione, cioé quando mi accorgo che un certo numero di poesie "fanno" un possibile libro.
>
> *L'accumulazione di cui lei parla è anche di fatti, di episodi che riguardano la sua vita, oppure deve intendersi come una maturazione dei temi che la interessano?* Gli episodi sono sempre stati pochi. Quando accadono non mi dico mai: ecco, ne farò una poesia. Questa riscoperta avviene in me dopo lungo tempo.[53]

---

cato – del suo bisogno (*Ossi*), della sua ricerca (*Occasioni* + *Bufera*) infine della sua mancanza (*Satura* e oltre) –, Montale indica una strada nell'inferno meccanizzato, nel nuovo Medio Evo postmoderno in cui andiamo addentrandoci: più che alla fine di un percorso, sembra al suo inizio". ("Breaking with closed models, reviving Dante's allegorical lesson, and forcefully posing the question of the meaning – of his need (*Ossi*), of his search (*Occasioni* + *Bufera*), and finally of his deficiency (*Satura* and beyond) – , Montale points out a route through the mechanized inferno, through the new postmodern Middle Ages into which we are sinking: more than at the end of a path, he seems to be at its beginning").

51 S. Connor, *Postmodernist Culture*, Oxford, Basil Blacknell, 1989, p. 109.

52 *Quaderno Genovese*, AMS 1326: "Duhamel's got the right idea: it isn't necessary to take rapid notes, on the place, of the sensations experienced, in order to discover new images and analogies; rather, to do so is damaging. It is necessary to overcome, to *forget*, the sensations; they're not lost in the process; in the act of creation – after many years – they well up in us, newer, truer, more *necessary*: time makes a choice for us, retaining the best and most profound".

53 E. Montale, "Autointervista" (1971), AMS 1501: "I publish when a certain accumulation is generated in me, that is to say when I realize that a certain number of poems 'make' a

The writing process is not the only element that does not change in Montale's poetry. To support the concept that already existing elements continue and intensify in later works, one could list thematic, cultural, and stylistic connections; the taste for paradox or linguistic games, for instance, is present in Montale's earlier poems. However, in the second phase of his career they shift from elements that characterize a poem to elements that structure it, as in "Xenia II, 8" (OV 304, "E il Paradiso? Esiste un paradiso? / Credo di sì, signora, ma i vini dolci / non li vuol più nessuno", "And Paradise? Does it exist? / I believe so, Madam, but sweet wines / are not in demand anymore") and in "*Déconfiture* non vuol dire…" (OV 314), where the lucubration over a false friend from French quickly escalates in speculation over the functioning of language.

The quintessentially postmodern ideas of the irreality of the real, or of the world as a representation, are not exclusive to the latter period; rather, they inform some of the early *Ossi*, as in "I limoni" and "Forse un mattino …"[54] Even if expressed in a different way, the compositional and thematic constants of the previous period survive in the latter: the poetry of the object in "Xenia II, 14" (OV 310) intensifies the writing process of "Carnevale di Gerti" (OV 120) and "Ballata scritta in una clinica" (OV 209); the notion of a love that never ends, but in fact grows stronger upon the departure of the beloved – the poetics of a desire motivated and necessitated by absence – that had prompted the cycles of Annetta and Clizia is intensified in the two sections of "Xenia".

Conversely, to support the argument that a decisive break occurs between *recto* and *verso*, one could list (albeit simplistically) the different philosophical and epistemological underpinnings that guide the later poetry not only toward a new understanding of space(s) and time but also toward a radical rethinking of ontology. In *Satura*, a different epistemology leads to a different metaphysics: in the "Xenia II, 8" quoted earlier, heaven and hell are redefined within a context that excludes any reference to medieval patristics – a great distance from "Mottetti", and the *Bufera*, a book that has been interpreted as modeled on Dante's *Vita Nova*. The declaration "Non

---

book possible. *Does the accumulation that you mention also include facts, episodes from your life, or do you mean it as a maturation of themes that interest you?* The episodes have always been few in number. When they happen, I never say to myself: there it is, I'll make a poem from that. This rediscovery occurs in me after a great deal of time".

[54] See E. Montale, "Non ama essere nella storia per qualche verso…", interview by Giulio Nascimbeni (1977), AMS 1727: "Ribadisco qualcosa che ho sempre pensato sulla realtà dell'esistente: che possa essere tutto un sogno che noi stiamo sognando. E che quindi sia un sogno anche tutto quello che ho fatto" ("I repeat something I've always thought about ontological reality: it might simply be a dream we are dreaming. Therefore, all I ever did might also be a dream").

sono sicuro nemmeno che il mondo esista, che la materia esista, che io esista. Non mi stupirei affatto se qualcuno mi dimostrasse che non esiste nulla"[55] extends the doubt about the existence of the real to doubting the existence of the very subject.

The postmodern perspective resolves the logic of noncontradiction without recurring to the dialectic process, and allows the resolution of the differences of a dichotomic division of Montale's corpus through a polysemous approach to the texts. Just as it is true that *Satura* represents both a rupture with and an intensification of the preceding poems, it is also true that the texts that form the fourth collection, as much as and even more than the preceding poems, require a reader attentive to the multiple possibilities of the signifier. Such a disclaimer is useful even when considering the title of the collection. The *Ossi di seppia* were a metaphor with multiple possible explanations: the bones of the cuttlefish could be interpreted as rubbish, or as the result of an attentive *labor limae*, of the sea's long cleaning process, or even as the negation of the very act of writing, according to an ingenious reading by Diego Bertelli.[56] A title with similar metaphorical resonances, *Rete a strascico*, had been considered for the fourth book but was eventually discarded.[57]

Instead of interpretation or misinterpretation of the metaphoric process, *Satura* accumulates possible meanings through the text itself. The title encourages multiple approaches and justifies multiple explanations: or, in the words of the author: "Il titolo ha tre o quattro significati. Escluso quello di appetitosi *avantgoûts*, desidero che li mantenga tutti".[58] The title *Satura* had initially been used in 1962 for a slim chapbook, designed as a wedding gift. On this occasion the title recalled the Latin expression *satura lanx*, a reference to a dish made from ingredients of various origins used during celebratory banquets, to communicate its purpose as a gift composed of material of diverse origin. However, the culinary metaphor is now excluded by the author. And yet, *Satura* maintains the idea of a text composed of material of diversified provenance or, alternatively, of satiric verse. As an attentive reader, Andrea Zanzotto, noticed, *Satura* also refers to the satura-

---

55 E. Montale, "Il mestiere di poeta", interview by Alessandro Camon (1965), AMS 1646: "I'm not even sure that the world exists, that matter exists, that I exist. I would not be at all surprised if someone showed me that nothing exists".

56 See D. Bertelli, *From Lexicon to Symbol: the Role of Petrarch in the Building of Montale's Poetics in* Ossi di seppia, «Modern Languages Notes» 124, 1 (Jan. 2009), p. 202.

57 See OV 973.

58 See E. Montale, "Autointervista" (1971), AMS 1501: "The title has three or four meanings. Excluding that of tasty *avantgoûts*, I would like to preserve them all".

tion of mass-mediatic communication characteristic of the times.[59] It may additionaly imply the saturation of reality, the satiety of the world as an outcome of the consumeristic ideology; a declaration by Montale released after the next volume of verses reinforces this last interpretation: "Nel caso in cui l'uomo sia assediato dalle cose (è la mia attuale situazione) la voce non può dialogare che con esse, magari per tentare di esorcizzarle".[60]

"Il tu", the volume's first poem, bolsters the book's demand for multiple interpretations, as it redefines the relationship between author, characters and readers:

IL TU

I critici ripetono,
da me depistati,
che il mio tu è un istituto.
Senza questa mia colpa avrebbero saputo
che in me i tanti sono uno anche se appaiono
moltiplicati dagli specchi. Il male
è che l'uccello preso nel paretaio
non sa se lui sia lui o uno dei troppi
suoi duplicati.[61]

Instead of fearing the angst of fragmentation, the poem embraces the perspectival play offered by a rapidly multiplying reality; its central trope is multiplication, as the lexicon underscores ("ripetono", "moltiplicati", "duplicati"). The speaker is a figuration of the author, who immediately introduces to his readers an awareness of themselves, and cites their words, which reflect upon an element much contested in his own earlier works: the titular "tu", we are informed, is not an institution. The commentators have been sidetracked by the "I", who had been lying (but now supposedly confesses the truth), and admits to having multiplied the figures of the apostrophe in a hall of mirrors, i.e., in the the poetical texts. Yet this is not a full explanation, since the readers are not in the position to understand to

---

[59] See A. Zanzotto, *In margine a Satura*, «Nuovi argomenti» 23-24, July-December 1971, pp. 215-220.

[60] E. Montale, "Finché l'assedio dura..." (1973), AMS 1503: "In the situation where humanity is besieged by things (my current situation), the voice cannot converse, except with those things, perhaps in an attempt to exorcise them".

[61] OV 273: "My critics repeat, / misguided by me, / that my "you" is an institution. / Without my intervention they would have understood / that in me the many are one even if they appear / multiplied by the mirrors. The problem / is that the bird caught in the trap / does not know if he is he or one of his too / many duplicates".

what exactly the syntagma "in me i tanti sono uno" ("in me the many are one") is referring.[62]

Who are these others? The many muses hidden in the previous books (Anna degli Uberti, Paola Nicoli, Maria Rosa Solari, Irma Brandeis, G.B.H., Maria Luisa Spaziani), now represented as a single person? We cannot exclude this possibility because, if it is true that different objects, locations, or situations usually characterize Montale's muses, it is also true that in some texts we can suppose an overlapping of female figures.[63]

Or the conciliation between "one" and "many" could refer to the figure of the author, yielding as such two distinct possible interpretations: either the author seeing himself reflected in his characters, or the author egotistically asserting the creation of those characters. It could also be a nod to the most famous verses by Walt Whitman, the triplet in section 51

---

[62] When the critic Silvio Guarnieri requested an explanation, Montale replied with a comment so vague that it can not even be considered deceitful (as many comments sent to Guarnieri were), see E. Montale, "Commento a se stesso", S. Guarnieri, ed. (1966), AMS 1521: "io soffro e vivo negli altri e considero gli altri come me", ("I suffer and live in others and consider others like myself").

[63] See E. Montale, "Dialogo con Montale sulla poesia" (1960), AMS 1603: "Mi è accaduto di fondere in me diversi personaggi che per me sono reali" ("It has happened that different characters have blended in me, characters who are real to me"). In *Le occasioni*, for example, Maria Rosa Solari seamlessly transforms into Irma Brandeis at the beginning of the "Mottetti": the fact did not go unnoticed to the dedicatee, who asked for an explanation; Montale answered in a letter dated January 15, 1935. See E. Montale, *Lettere a Clizia*, cit., p. 122: "Mi sono preso filosoficamente la tua furiosa predica del 26 Dic. about la genesi dei *Mottetti*. Ecco: i famigerati *Mottetti* furono scritti *prima* di avere conosciuto I.B. Di quella redazione sopravvisse solo il Mottetto 3°; nel Mottetto n° 2 l'immagine di I.B. (abitante in Costa San Giorgio) andò a coincidere con M.R.S. nata a Genova, "Città di San Giorgio e del Drago". [...] Se rileggo i tre Mottetti ci ritrovo una Miss Gatu [private nickname for Irma Brandeis] che sia stata anche in un Sanatorio dove si gioca a bridge; la verità biografica va a farsi f... ma la verità poetica no. [...] Sono infedele?" ("I took philosophically your reproach dated Dec. 26 about the genesis of the *Mottetti*. Well: the infamous *Mottetti* were written *before* I met you. Of that first draft only N. 3 survived; in N. 2 the figure of I.B. (living in Costa S. Giorgio) coincided with M.R.S. born in Genoa, "the city of S. George and the dragon". [...] If I read the first three *Mottetti* I find in them a Miss Gatu who has been in a Sanatorium where people played bridge; biographical accuracy has f... itself, but poetical truth has not. [...] Have I been unfaithful?". See also P. De Caro, *Invenzioni di ricordi: Vite in poesia di tre ispiratrici montaliane*, Foggia, Centro Grafico Francescano, 2007, pp. 189 *et passim*. Furthermore, in *La bufera e altro* Clizia and Mosca intersect in a poem that apparently narrates a recognizable misadventure shared with Drusilla Tanzi / Mosca, in the only poem in which the figure of the future wife appears before her death, "Ballata scritta in una clinica". It is worth noting that on a textual level Clizia and Mosca will cross paths again in *Satura*, "Le revenant", a text that concludes with the same existential doubt expressed in "Il tu": it is not difficult to see a link between the bird limed in the net and uncertain of its own identity, with the verses "Mi chiedo perché i fili di due rocchetti / si sono tanto imbrogliati; e se non sia quel fantasma / l'autentico smarrito e il suo facsimile io" (OV 340). See, on the subject, I. Antici, *Le revenant di Montale: studio su una duplice assenza*, «RID, Rivista Online di Italianistica», Dipartimento di Italianistica Roma Tre, 2008, pp. 1-13.

of the "Song of Myself" that says: "Do I contradict myself? / Very well then I contradict myself / (I am large, I contain multitudes"), since admittedly what the poetic "I" is doing here is to contradict the assertions of a former self.[64] What becomes clear by the poem's end is that the theme of repetition is connected causally with a loss of identity, but it remains unclear whether the identity is of the "many" or the "one" (which may be precisely the point).

Another thing we do not know is the identity of the "tu": the immediate signification refers to the pronoun itself, as used in the previous texts; but the *pro*noun, intrinsically, is a substitution for a noun. Whose is the name replaced in the poem's title? Perhaps it is Clizia, the person addressed in the provisional conclusions of *La bufera*? This conjecture is intriguing, because it would create a bridge between the old and the new volume, and would connect both with the only poems written within the hiatus of Montale's silence, "Lagunare" (1960) and "Botta e risposta" (later "Botta e risposta I", 1961). It could also be the mysterious interlocutor by whom Montale declares he is "being written" in a self-interview published in the «Corriere della Sera» shortly before the book's release.[65] The reality is that the text wants us to retain the suspicion that the pronoun might address the reader, as common in Montale: be it a generic reader (see "Poesie per Camillo Sbarbaro II", OV 17: "Sii preveggente per lui, tu galantuomo che passi", and "Non chiederci la parola…" OV 27), or a specific one.

Several poems composed by Montale the modernist are messages intended to be read by a very specific "tu", even if the hope that these messages reach their destination is negligible (and in fact "L'onda, vuota, / si rompe sulla punta, a Finisterre", recites a poem emblematically entitled *Su una lettera non scritta*: "The empty wave / breaks over the promontory, in Finisterre," where the wave is "empty" because it does not contain a bottle with a message; OV 191, ll. 14). Again, by the time we reach the closing clause, the only certainty the text has yielded us is the connection between repetition and loss of identity. We do not know who is hidden behind the metaphor of the bird caught in the net. We recognize the situation as an echo from "In limine", the poem opening *Ossi di seppia*, and since "Il tu" is

---

[64] See W. WITHMAN, *Song of Myself* (1855), New York, Dover Publications, 2001, p. 53 (Part 51, ll. 6-8).

[65] E. MONTALE, "Autointervista" (1971), AMS 1502: "In un certo senso io mi lascio scrivere. / *Da chi?* / Da lui, e non è necessario dare un significato mistico al mio interlocutore. Tuttavia è vero che io sottintendo sempre la presenza di qualcuno che il lettore può identificare a piacer suo" ("In a certain sense I let myself be written. / *By whom?* / By him, and it's not necessary to give a mystical significance to my interlocutor. However, it is true that I always imply the presence of someone whom the reader can identify as he pleases").

the proemial poem of the second part, or *verso*, of Montale's poetic career, the connection between the two poems cannot be coincidental. If we believed that metaphors within Montale's corpus are sustained and connected, we should identify the bird with the poet himself, since in "In limine" the "I" remains caught in the net, while the "you" has a hope of flight: "Cerca una maglia rotta nella rete / che ci stringe, tu balza fuori, fuggi!" (OV 5). Yet a similar metaphor recurs elsewhere, and in chronologically closer texts, for example in "La storia (II)", where we read that many animals are able to escape from the holes in the net (fish, in the case at hand).

What is clear is the loss of identity experienced at the end, even if we do not know who is hidden beneath the metaphor of the bird caught in the net. "Il tu" stages its own indeterminacy; it exploits the polysemous possibilities of interpretation while looking back to an earlier season of Montale's poetry, and it does so with a simplicity of rhythm, with a prosaic structure that is emblematic of the whole book. Equally indicative is the playfulness with which the poem introduces the book: the poet is confessing to mischief, yet the metaphor analyzed does not retain the sense of urgency and drama that characterized "In limine". It may well be possible because, as Frederic Jameson notes, "one of the most fateful differences between high modernism and post-modernism" is "the utter extinction of that pathos or even tragic spirit with which the high moderns lived their torn and divided condition, the repression even of anxiety itself".[66]

If *Ossi di seppia* traced the shift from a youthful desire for *corréspondences* to the fragmented and alienated modernist self, *Satura* now encourages, and openly embraces, the multiplying possibilities of interpretation. We remember how important it was to arrive at an individuation and a moral affirmation of subjectivity in texts like "Incontro", "Vasca", "Portovenere". On the contrary, in "Il tu", this need is not felt; the author mirrors without fearing that the looking glasses will multiply. We have transitioned to an "I" who can not only proclaim to "contain multitudes" or "Je est un autre", but to an "I" who actually contains many others while also being himself.

After focusing on the theme of multiplicity in his opening poem, Montale continues with a text that, conversely, presents itself as definitive, as it is very personal and it quotes from texts and situations elaborated in his previous books. "Botta e risposta I", written in 1962, continues the monologue suspended in the poem concluding *La bufera*, "Il sogno del prigioniero". The prisoner segregated in a place where "albe e notti [...] variano

[66] F. Jameson, *Baudelaire as Modernist and Postmodernist*, in C. Hošek – P. Parker (eds.), *Lyric Poetry Beyond New Criticism*, cit., p. 260.

per pochi segni" ("except for a few signs, you can't tell dawn from night", OV 268, l. 1) is the same individual recalling in the new book a metaphoric confinement in King Augia's stables:

> Uscito appena dall'adolescenza
> per metà della vita fui gettato
> nelle stalle d'Augìa.
>
> Non vi trovai duemila bovi, né
> mai vi scorsi animali;
> pure nei corridoi, sempre più folti
> di letame, si camminava male
> e il respiro mancava; ma vi crescevano
> di giorno in giorno i muggiti umani.[67]

To confirm his identity we recognize his memories, or, to remain on the textual level, the self-quotations that connect the verses respectively to "Carnevale di Gerti" (OV 120), "A Liuba che parte" (OV 123), and to the whole cicle of Clizia:

> Un ricciolo
> di Gerti, un grillo in gabbia, ultima traccia
> del transito di Liuba, il microfilm
> d'un sonetto eufuista scivolato
> dalle dita di Clizia addormentata[68]

King Augia's stables are a place made famous by Hyginus's retelling of the labors of Hercules. According to the myth, Euristheus commanded Hercules, as the fifth labor, to clean up in a single day Augia's stables, home to thousands of immortal herds, which had not been cleaned in years. To accomplish the otherwise impossible task, Hercules redirected the bed of the river Alpheus in such a way that it temporarily passed through the stables.[69] Here a flood, a river diverted from its course, inundates the poet's prison and cleanses it, one would believe, of the scatological mountains

---

[67] OV 277, ll. 1-9: "Just out of adolescence / for half of my life I was thrown / in the stables of Augia. // I did not see there two thousand oxen, nor / animals of any kind; / yet in the hallways, increasingly encumbered / with manure, walking was difficult / and breathing was hard; / the human bellows were louder every day".

[68] *Ibid.*, ll. 21-25: "a lock / of Gerti, a cricket in its cage, the last sign / of Liuba's visit, the microfilm / of a euphuist sonnet slipped / from the fingers of a sleeping Clizia".

[69] Hyg. *Fab.* 14. The bovine dimension of the metaphor could also reverberate the passage "L'iddio taurino non era / il nostro" from "Ballata scritta in una clinica" (OV 209, ll. 24-25).

that had been tainting it. Yet, even if in the poem "A liberarci, a chiuder gli intricati / cunicoli in un lago, bastò un attimo / allo stravolto Alfeo" (ll. 33-35; Alpheus is "stravolto" because the river has deviated from its course; another occurrence of the process of re-etymologization so common in the first book), the cleaning does not appear to be final, and the incarceration does not conclude with a liberation:

> A liberarci, a chiuder gli intricati
> cunicoli in un lago, bastò un attimo
> allo stravolto Alfeo. Chi l'attendeva
> ormai? Che senso aveva quella nuova
> palta? e il respirare altre ed eguali
> zaffate? e il vorticare sopra zattere
> di sterco? ed era sole quella sudicia
> esca di scolaticcio sui fumaioli,
> erano uomini forse,
> veri uomini vivi
> i formiconi degli approdi?[70]

The river's intervention, rather than liberating, bears new mud; the stenches are different ("altre"), but they remain. The liberation does not liberate, the sun does not return to shine, and the insects do not become men.[71] The historical process of liberation, the overthrowing of fascism and the monarchy and the proclamation of the Republic, failed to improve their situation, as it did not remedy their uncouth condition.

Curiously, Hercules himself is not mentioned here, despite the poem's metaphorical transformation of a myth involving the demigod. The merit of having stirred the excrement is left to the Alpheus alone. For the Alpheus – like *Satura*'s other rivers, the Euphrates and the Arno – is an image of time. Keeping in mind the anti-Hegelian polemic maintained by Montale, we can see that rivers, in as much as they are images of time, represent an annulment, since "la storia" itself "non è" as the eponymous poem repeats with anaphoric obsessiveness (OV 316).[72] By turning to biblical references,

---

70 OV 277, ll. 33-43: "Liberating us, sealing the mazes / of that hellish warren in a lake, was an instant's work / for the diverted Alpheus. Who expected Him / now? What was the meaning of that new / muck? And the different but no less sickening / stench exhaled? And the wild gyring of shit / over the barges? / And was that the sun, that sweaty / lure of slag and dregs on the smokestacks, / could those be men, / real living men, / those huge ants on the wharfs?", trans. W. Arrowsmith.

71 The exchange of identity between man and "formicone" returns in "Botta e risposta II", OV 347, ll. 1-5.

72 On the logical relationship between the nonexistence of history and the intermittence of reality, see "L'Eufrate," OV 371, ll. 7-9: "Non ripetermi che anche uno stuzzicadenti, / an-

one could suggest that, if the departure from the idealistic world of infancy towards the world of space/time was depicted in "Mediterraneo" as an escape from Eden, then the flood caused by the great rivers represents not the end of the world, but the end of the world as we know it, without even the consolation of an "Arca" (OV 200) of salvation. "Xenia II, 14" can also be read this way, as it is a text entirely constructed around the idea of the flood as a liquidation of now useless historical, social, and literary paradigms.

Written on November 24, 1966, twenty days after the catastrophic overflowing of the Arno that had submerged Florence, "Xenia II, 14" imagines the destiny of the objects that remained in the basement of the house once inhabited by Montale and Drusilla Tanzi:

> L'alluvione ha sommerso il pack dei mobili,
> delle carte, dei quadri che stipavano
> un sotterraneo chiuso a doppio lucchetto.
> Forse hanno ciecamente lottato i marocchini
> rossi, le sterminate dediche di Du Bos,
> il timbro a ceralacca con la barba di Ezra,
> il Valéry di Alain, l'originale
> dei Canti Orfici – e poi qualche pennello
> da barba, mille cianfrusaglie e tutte
> le musiche di tuo fratello Silvio.
> Dieci, dodici giorni sotto un'atroce morsura
> di nafta e sterco. Certo hanno sofferto
> tanto prima di perdere la loro identità.
> Anch'io sono incrostato fino al collo se il mio
> stato civile fu dubbio fin dall'inizio.

---

che una briciola o un niente può contenere il tutto. / È quello che pensavo anch'io quando esisteva il mondo", ("Don't repeat that even a simple toothpick, / even a crumb, a nothing, can contain everything. / It is what I used to believe when the world still existed"). Drawing a parallel between the overflowing of the Alfeo and that of the Arno, I do not intend to claim that the two examples replicate the exact same metaphor. Like the Mediterranean Sea in *Ossi di seppia*, the flood in *Satura* can be interpreted in different ways in different texts, or even in different ways in the same text (on this point, see the notes by Riccardo Castellana on "Botta e risposta I" in the annotated edition of *Satura*, Milano, Mondadori, 2015, pp. 9-19). Between the flood caused by Alfeo and that caused by Arno, the ethical significance is reversed, the public/private dimension changes: in the former, the flood represents a missed opportunity for change, renewal, cleansing; in the latter, the inundation of the entire city is an explanation for the loss of a piece of individual identity. What unites the texts is the idea that water, both when "pensa se stessa" and when it becomes "vortice e rapina", represents, according to the simple Heraclitean analogy, the passage of time, which in the poetics of Montale can provoke the loss of biographical detail (as in "La casa dei doganieri", OV 161), or cause the sudden resurgence after a long settling of the fragment of a memory that then develops into material for poetic activity (as in, one of innumerable examples, the "jackals on the leash" of "La speranza di pure rivederti...", OV 138).

Non torba m'ha assediato, ma gli eventi
di una realtà incredibile e mai creduta.
Di fronte ad essi il mio coraggio fu il primo
dei tuoi prestiti e forse non l'hai mai saputo.[73]

The devastating action of the flood destroys a memorial, a real cellar doubly padlocked, but also the metaphorical resting place of the repertory of Montale's cultural formation. The paintings, books, trinkets, and music that share the author's destiny of being clutched by mud, of losing their identity in a "morsura / di nafta e di sterco", are all objects of significance in the cultural and personal biography of Montale. As Tiziana de Rogatis has noted, "Il desolante catalogo [...] non ha nulla di casuale. [...] Montale rimanda ai temi, i testi e le immagini della *koiné* europea nella quale, tra gli anni Venti e i Trenta, si è formato".[74] Among the books that fought and suffered but in the end surrendered to the flood and lost their value as cultural testimony were the books that Charles du Bos had dedicated to him, and the copy of *Personae Separatae* that Pound had gifted him during their frequentations of Rapallo; the edition that Alain (the pen name of Émile Chartier) had published of Paul Valéry's *Charmes*, a work discussed many times in the editing of *Solaria* with Sergio Solmi, the former comrade-in-arms, now an esteemed companion in literary criticism.[75] The same fate

---

[73] OV 310: "The flood has drowned the clutter / of furniture, papers, and paintings that crammed / the double-padlocked cellar. / Maybe they fought back blindly – the books / in red morocco, Du Bos's endless dedications, / the wax seal with Ezra's beard, Alain's / *Valéry*, the first edition / of the *Canti Orfici*, as well as a couple / of shaving brushes, a thousand knikknacs, and all / the compositions by your brother Silvio. / Ten, twelve days in that awful maw / of gasoline and crap. Clearly they suffered / terribly before loosing their identity. / I must be deep in crud too, up to my neck, since / my civil status was uncertain from the outset. / It's not muck that besets me, but the events / of an unbelievable, and unbelieved, reality. / My courage in facing them was the first / of your loans, and perhaps you never knew". Translation modified from W. Arrowsmith's.

[74] T. De Rogatis, *Montale e il classicismo moderno*, Pisa-Roma, Istituti Editoriali e Poligrafici Internazionali, 2002, p. 36: "The melancholy catalog [...] is far from random. [...] Montale returns to the themes, texts, and images of the European *koiné* in which, during the '20s and '30s, he was formed". A useful analysis of the poem in English is in R. Castellana, "L'alluvione ha sommerso il pack dei mobili (Xenia II, 14)" in *Montale Readings*, eds. Ó.É. Ceallacháin, F. Pedriali, Glasgow, University of Glasgow Press, 2000, pp. 103-125. At the base of the readings of "Xenia II, 14" by de Rogatis and Castellana, as well as of the reading proposed here, is the seminal interpretation offered by R. Luperini in *Montale o l'identità negata*, Napoli, Liguori, 1984, pp. 23-29.

[75] From the fact that the works of Du Bos known by Montale did not contain remarkably long dedications in the printed copies, we can deduce that he is referring to dedications *ad personam*: it is possible, given that Du Bos was a friend of Sergio Solmi, but Montale doesn't mention an encounter. About Montale's writings on Du Bos, see E. Montale, "Giornate di lettura: Charles Du Bos" (1927), SM I pp. 224-231; Id., "Libri (*Le dialogue avec André Gide* e *Journal intime* di Charles Du Bos)" (1930), SM I pp. 398-394; Id., "Libri (*Approximations* di Charles

greeted the edition *intra moenia* of the *Canti orfici* by Dino Campana, which the poet from Marradi personally sold to the clients of the Florentine café Le Giubbe Rosse. The legend goes that Campana would rip from the book the poems that, in his opinion, the buyer would not be able to comprehend, such that F.T. Marinetti would have found in his hands the cover alone. We can conjecture that the edition possessed by Montale had all its pages, because when the Genovese poet arrived in Florence, Campana was already under duress in the mental asylum of Lastra a Signa.

Mentioning these books in the text replicates the mechanism of the objective correlative, as with the rest of the real objects enumerated afterwards; but the books possess a more consistent semiotic weight because they can be read, and thanks to intertextual references, they can be read through Montale's eyes. In this way we realize that, for Montale, Du Bos had been not only a representative critic for comprehending French symbolism but that he had also been a model for shrugging off the certainties of Croce's idealist philosophy. We can read this in a passage that contrasts Du Bos with the Italian critics of 1935:

> I nostri critici che contano sono lontani da [Du Bos], addirittura agli antipodi (e magari qualcuno gli si facesse più vicino...): esaminato un poeta sanno dirvi a quale pagina e a quale rigo nasce, muore, rinasce e rimuore la sua poesia e la sua non-poesia; e che lui, il poeta, è morto tre anni dopo o tre anni prima del necessario, e che il suo "mondo" è più angusto di quello di un predecessore, preceduto questi, a sua volta, da una serie di poeti progressivamente e proporzionalmente più ristretti l'uno dell'altro; finché non si arriva, risalendo una fila indiana di epigoni e di disgraziati, a un "maggiore" che non si discute più per mancanza di interesse o di ossigeno. Nel Du Bos questa paura della vita d'oggi non c'è.[76]

In the same fashion, Alain, the pacifist philosopher who had contradictorily but voluntarily participated in the First World War because he

---

Du Bos)" (1935), SM I pp. 530-535. Pound's gift is mentioned in several occasions by Montale: see E. Montale, "Fronde d'alloro in un manicomio" (1949), SM 793; Id., "Se i biglietti da mille fossero quelli di Ezra Pound" (1955), SM 1886. See also R. Castellana, *L'alluvione ha sommerso il pack dei mobili*, in *Montale Readings*, cit., p. 107 *et passim*. "Il Valéry di Alain" refers to P. Valéry, *Charmes: Poèmes commentés par Alain*, Paris, Gallimard, 1929.

[76] E. Montale, "Libri (*Approximations* di Charles Du Bos)" (1935), SM 531: "Our critics who matter are far from [Du Bos], completely at the antipodes (and perhaps someone ought to bring them closer ...): having studied a poet they know to say of him on which page and line his poetry and his non-poetry is born, dies, is reborn, dies again; and that he, the poet, died three years after or three years before his time, and that his "world" is narrower than that of a predecessor, this one preceded, in his turn, by a series of poets progressively and proportionally more restricted one after the next, until one arrives, climbing a single file line of descendants and disgraces, at a "forefather" who is no longer discussed, for lack of interest or oxygen. In Du Bos this fear of modern life does not exist".

considered it unjust to stand on the sidelines while his friends were sent to the slaughter, represented for Montale not only a genial reader of Valéry, but a role model. Campana's book, positioned at the origin of that Orphic, hermetic tendency in Florentine poetry that Montale had always aimed to avoid, geographically delimits the cultural experience of the young man who had completed his own cultural formation in a city where young anti-fascist intellectuals, meeting in the Giubbe Rosse café, were watched over by the fascists who met in the Paszkowski café across the way.

The shaving brushes included in the poem carry the testimonial value of these objects from a cultural plane to a personal one; furthermore, the "musiche di tuo fratello Silvio",[77] which connect the "I" and the "you", foreshadows the analogy between things and people: "Anch'io sono incrostato fino al collo [...] / non torba mi ha assediato, ma gli eventi / di una realtà incredibile e mai creduta". The peat that precedes and follows Alfeo's intrusion, aside from the metaphor, transforms into the events of reality that besiege Montale, as the verb anticipates "l'assedio delle cose" noted in the aforementioned interview "Finché l'assedio dura..."; this reality is "incredibile e mai creduta", consistent with the unreality explored in *Ossi* and then intensified in the 1950s as a consequence of the philosophical developments we have already considered. The flood of the basement caused by the river and the flood of the old philosophical and cultural certainties both lead to a postmodern identity crisis whose historical consequences are understood by Montale in a way that resonates with the most advanced thinkers of the second half of the century.

4. A New Understanding of History and Geography

> A tormenting thought: as of a certain point, history was no longer *real*. Without noticing it, all mankind suddenly left reality; everything happening since then was supposedly not true; but we supposedly didn't notice.[78]

Quoting this sentence from *The Human Province* by Elias Canetti, Jean Baudrillard substantiates his opinion that at a certain point in time the hu-

---

77 Drusilla Tanzi's brother was a little known composer who died young, as we read in "Xenia I, 13" (OV 293).

78 As quoted in Jean Baudrillard, *The Illusion of the End*, trans. C. Turner, Stanford, Stanford University Press, 1994, p. 1. See also Id., *Forget Foucault*, New York, Semiotext(e), 1987, pp. 67 *et passim*; and S. Best – D. Kellner, *Postmodern Theory: Critical Interrogations*, New York, The Guilford Press, 1991, p. 133.

man race has dropped out of history and entered a posthistorical experience. He could have arrived at the same conclusion by citing texts from Montale's second phase. Baudrillard believes that "at some point in the 1980s, history took a turn in the opposite direction. Once the apogee of time, the summit of the curve of evolution, the solstice of history had been passed, the downward slope of events began and things began to run in reverse".[79] But Montale was ahead of, or perhaps behind, the times: in a poem dated 1968 he had already claimed that time could proceed in reverse, or rather that there are many different times proceeding backward and forward in parallel:

> Non c'è un unico tempo: ci sono molti nastri
> che paralleli slittano
> spesso in senso contrario e raramente
> s'intersecano.[80]

To claim that for Montale the certain point after which history was no longer real was that fateful November 4, 1966 when the river Arno burst its banks, causing the flood of Florence, would be preposterous, unnecessary, and in contrast with the intention of leaving the range of interpretation open to the utmost degree admissible by logic. In fact, Montale does not need a precise moment in time in which to locate the end of time – not because he would fear the contradiction, but because in his most radical analysis history has never existed, and he had never truly believed in it.[81]

If read in its entirety, the poem "Tempo e tempi", the beginning of which is cited above, reveals a point of contact with those brief illuminations, the illusory instants of happiness, an important point because of its ethical relevance:

> Non c'è un unico tempo: ci sono molti nastri
> che paralleli slittano
> spesso in senso contrario e raramente

---

[79] J. Baudrillard, *The Illusion of the End*, trans. C. Turner, Stanford: Stanford University Press, 1994, p. 10.

[80] OV 342, ll. 1-4. For the translation see *infra*.

[81] E. Montale, "Discorrendo della fine del mondo" (1968), interview by Manlio Cancogni, AMS 1693: "[La realtà storica] non esiste, è un'apparenza, un puro fenomeno (io del resto sin da ragazzo ho dubitato della realtà della materia, dello spazio, del tempo), un puro fenomeno dicevo, che peraltro non può sentirsi soddisfatto del suo stato, tranne illusori momenti di felicità, brevi illuminazioni ..." ("[Historical reality] does not exist, it is an illusion, a pure phenomenon – since childhood, in fact, I have doubted the reality of matter, of space, of time) – a pure phenomenon, I was saying, that however cannot be satisfied with its state, except for illusory instants of happiness, brief illuminations ...").

s'intersecano. È quando si palesa
la sola verità che, disvelata,
viene subito espunta da chi sorveglia
i congegni e gli scambi. E si ripiomba
poi nell'unico tempo. Ma in quell'attimo
solo i pochi viventi si sono riconosciuti
per dirsi addio, non arrivederci.[82]

The many possible timelines run in parallel, like treadmill ribbons arranged in rows; they rarely intersect, but when they do their occasional crossing reveals a truth which is unique. This singular truth stands in contrast to the many timelines and is expunged by those who control the system as soon as it is revealed. It is an instant: but an instant of truth is sufficient for those who truly live, those who turn around and see from "Forse un mattino...", those able to recognize one another from "Il sogno del prigioniero", to make contact and acknowledge that the "short illumination" will not be repeated.

The other text in which the Montale of *Satura* expounds his philosophical conception of time is "La storia", a poem that palingenetically divides itself into two parts: one negative and one positive. "La storia" explains what history is not, starting with a self-citation pertaining to the first poem of "Movimenti", "I limoni:"

La storia non si snoda
come una catena
di anelli ininterrotta.
In ogni caso
molti anelli non tengono.
La storia non contiene
il prima e il dopo,
nulla che in lei borbotti
a lento fuoco.[83]

---

[82] OV 342: "There's no unique time, rather many conveyer belts / running parallel / often in the opposite verso and rarely / intersecting. [But when they do,] the sole truth / is disclosed, and immediately / erased by whoever supervises / the wheels and the switches. That's when we fall back / into unique time. But in that instant / only the few people still alive / have recognized each other in time to say, / not be-seeing-you, but good-bye". "Tempo e tempi", (OV 342), translation modified from W. Arrowsmith's. For the hypotext by Jorge Luis Borges that inspired the first four verses, the story "Coleridge's Dream" from *Other Inquisitions* (1952), see Montale's review of the Italian translation of the book, "Ipotesi di Borges" (1963), SM 2605-2607, and the notes by Riccardo Castellana in *Satura*, Milano, Mondadori, 2015, pp. 148-150.

[83] Ov 315, ll. 1-9: "History is not articulated / like an unbroken / link chain. / In any case / many links don't hold. / History has / no before and after, / nothing in it simmers / on a slow fire." Translation modified from W. Arrowsmith's.

A break with the past, or an intensification? If in "I limoni" one hoped to find the ring that failed to hold, here the rings that fail to hold are many, and in any event, history is not a chain. It is not ordered in a sequence; it does not have a before and an after. History is not a judge, nor is it a teacher; the old Latin saying, *historia magistra vitae*, proves false:

> La storia non somministra
> carezze o colpi di frusta.
> La storia non è magistra
> di niente che ci riguardi.
> Accorgersene non serve
> a farla più vera e più giusta.[84]

The second part of the poem, even if it begins with the same negative anaphoric process, is built in the positive, and it tells us what history is and what it does.

> La storia non è poi
> la devastante ruspa che si dice.
> Lascia sottopassaggi, cripte, buche
> e nascondigli. C'è chi sopravvive.
> La storia è anche benevola: distrugge
> quanto più può: se esagerasse, certo
> sarebbe meglio, ma la storia è a corto
> di notizie, non compie tutte le sue vendette.[85]

The lucid, dramatic objectivity of the first part leaves space, in the second, for the *divertissement* of paradox. History, in its benevolence, destroys everything it can. It would be better if it truly destroyed everything, but, in keeping with the paradox, history does not know all the news.

As the first part presented an echo from "I limoni", the second part recycles a metaphor from "In limine:"

> La storia gratta il fondo
> come una rete a strascico
> con qualche strappo e più di un pesce sfugge.

---

[84] *Ibid.*, ll. 22-27: "History administers / neither kind words nor whippings. / History is no teacher / of anything that concerns us. / Awareness of this doesn't make it / more true, or more just", trans. W. Arrowsmith.

[85] Ov 316, ll. 1-8: "So history is not / the destructive steam shovel it's said to be, / leaving tunnels, crypts, manholes, / hiding-places behind. Some survive it. / History is benevolent too, and it destroys as much as it can: it would be better of course / if even more were destroyed, but history is short / on information, and it does not bring to term all its vendettas". Translation modified from W. Arrowsmith's.

> Qualche volta s'incontra l'ectoplasma
> d'uno scampato e non sembra particolarmente felice.
> Ignora di essere fuori, nessuno glie n'ha parlato.
> Gli altri, nel sacco, si credono
> più liberi di lui.[86]

The "rete che ci stringe" of "In limine" has lost all its dramatic power: not only because escaping from history's net no longer seems impossible, but also because the majority of both those inside and outside it fails to even recognize the difference. The crisis sparked by Vasoli's verses in Montale's understanding of history arrives at the reflection that history is a deception, but it ultimately does not matter whether or not we realize that deception. With the collapse of historicism, there is no longer – nor could there be – a hegemonic system in which to orient oneself: even scientific theories, following Einstein's experimental relativization, are no longer posed as touchstones of absolute value:

> Tutti viviamo nella storia senza saperlo. Ma esiste veramente la storia? Fino a trenta, a quarant'anni fa lo storicismo era la filosofia-religione quasi ufficiale in Italia: un po' meno in Germania, il paese dell'esportazione. La storia era il motore immanente dell'universo: eravamo noi tutti uomini viventi e pensanti. Su questo punto fondamentale nel club degli idealisti-storicisti non c'era discordia. Né facevano obiezione ovviamente i marxisti. In seguito, quasi alla chetichella importammo altre idee, senza che esse siano oggi imperanti e abbiano capintesta di autorità indiscussa. Con tali idee dobbiamo fare i conti anche perché sono le sole che offra il mercato ideologico.[87]

At this point our understanding of time is inextricably tied to that of space, but we no longer grapple with the relativization of time and space, which had informed the modernist aesthetic experience, inspiring the idea that space and time are measured differently depending on the different

---

[86] *Ibid.*, ll. 9-16: "History scrapes the bottom / like a punctured trawl / and more than a few fish escape. / At times you meet the ectoplasm / of a survivor, and he doesn't seem specially happy. / He's unaware he's free, nobody's told him. / The others, in the trawl, are convinced to be / more free than he". Translation modified from W. Arrowsmith's.

[87] E. Montale, "Variazioni" (1974), PR 1159: "We all live in history without knowing it. But does this history really exist? Up to thirty, forty years ago, historicism was nearly the official philosophy/religion in Italy: a little less in Germany, the country of its exportation. History was the immanent motor of the universe: we were all living, thinking humans. On this fundamental point there was no discord in the club of the idealist-historicists. Obviously, the Marxists protested it. Then, almost like a thief in the night, we imported other ideas, without them being predominant today and having a leader of indisputable authority. We must reckon with these ideas, also because they are the only ones being offered up by the ideological marketplace".

positions of the individual "I". Now Montale's poetry is engaged with the notion that space and time do not exist in themselves, but must be established, conjured into existence by the poetic "I".

If Montale's conception of time and history is more sophisticated than that of the majority of his contemporaries, the same is true for his appreciation of space. While sociologists of the 1950s had begun to define humans according to the spaces in which they live, the Montale of *Satura* instead maintains that individuals must create the spaces in which they live. When Henri Lefebvre articulated his theory of a "social space", the basic tenets of his thinking quickly became influential outside of the realm of academic sociology. The idea that physical space is emotionally and semiotically empty – and can be transformed into a meaningful social space by the interpretive, economical, political acts of humanity – was compatible with the Marxist understanding of space as a fabricated commodity. It was additionally compatible with the neo-humanist understanding of mankind as maker, as well as the existentialist understanding of a completely immanent reality. Social space, being a constructed item, was consequentially understood as a way to realize self- and collective identification.

A rather simplified version of Lefebvre's theory of social space immediately becomes the justification for the association of a conventionally recognizable place with an individual's whole ideology: Montale, for example, utilizes the concept when he associates the workshop and the church to respectively the "chierico rosso, o nero" (OV 267, l. 7). The idea that social space provides the coordinates for the sociological and ideological identification of the subject who inhabits it is equally at work in Pasolini's review of *Satura*.[88] Pasolini confines Montale the author within a cultural social space as well as a physical social space, both determined by the culture shared with a community of readers. The cultural space to which Pasolini alludes is a novel by Italo Svevo, an author whom Montale had read, appreciated, and helped to popularize. To flatten the first-person speaker of Montale's first three books into the protagonist of *Senilità* or

[88] According to Pasolini, Montale has construed "una figura da romanzo: un romanzo analogo a uno dei pochi che nella vita gli son piaciuti. Egli ha fatto trapelare nei suoi tre libri che chi dice "io" è un uomo grigio, laconico, irreprensibile, romantico ma ironico; che la sua vita, se proprio si vuole dedurlo, si svolge tra un appartamento elegante ma non eccezionale e un soggiorno in qualche albergo di prima categoria", ("a figure from a novel: a novel equal to one of the few that he has enjoyed in his life. He slowly revealed in his three books that the speaker is dreary, laconic, irreprehensible, romantic but ironic, that his life, if one wishes to deduce it precisely, unfolds between an elegant but unexceptional apartment and a stay in some first-class hotel". See P.P. Pasolini, "Satura" (1971), in *Scritti sulla letteratura e sull'arte*, cit., p. 2560.

La coscienza di Zeno is to reduce him to the limited perspective of the typical modernist figure of the blunderer. Such a reduction is not unjustified: Edoardo Sanguineti made the same move when asked to celebrate Montale at the conference honoring the centennial of the poet's birth.[89] But it remains a flattening of the character, and an unflattering one, too, as the adjectives underscore.

The physical space in Pasolini's reading is circumscribed by the apartment (bourgeois but not upper-class, elegant but unexceptional) and by the first-class hotels recounted in the verses. This circumscription of Montale's cultural and social horizon would prove quite influential with regard to the way in which *Satura* was to be read in the decades to come. The thread of place names recurring in the different sections of the book is seen as motivated by a need for a self-definition devoted to the exhibition of attained wealth. In an article published more than thirty years after Pasolini's review, Éanna Ó Ceallacháin confirms that in *Satura*, the localization's overall effect

> is to paint a scenario of understated cosmopolitan elegance as the setting for the shared memories of the poet's persona and Mosca, a setting subjected to a gently corrosive irony on the part of the io as he both distances himself from and includes himself in the surrounding 'blabla / dell'alta societa' (Xenia I, 5).[90]

Pasolini implies that a double movement, distancing and including, denotes the subject's desire to define himself through his evoked social space. References to the Saint James of Paris and the Danieli of Venice and recollections of job transfers and vacations in European cultural capitals pinpoint geographically the "I" who writes, labeling his cultural, economic, and ideological coordinates, situating him in an upper-class setting to which he aspires but does not belong. This mechanism of localization, once established, can take effect even without being anchored to a precise geographical referent.[91]

---

89 E. SANGUINETI, *Montale e la mitologia dell'inetto*, in *Il secolo di Montale: Genova 1896-1996*, ed. Fondazione Mario Novaro, Bologna, il Mulino, 1998, pp. 269-285.

90 É.Ó. CEALLACHÁIN, *Sanguineti and Montale: Traveling Companions in the 1970s*, «The Modern Language Review», vol. 102 n. 1 (Jan. 2007), p. 94.

91 *Ibid.*: "Yet another Venetian hotel room occurs in 'A tarda notte' later in *Satura*. This time, the establishment is unnamed, but significantly again the poem centres on an unsuccessful telephone call, as a mistaken connection leads the protagonist unexpectedly into a transatlantic conversation with an unknown interlocutor. Here the element of what we might call 'cosmopolitan realism' is again provided by the use of place names: 'Vancouver', 'Milano', 'Una voce dal Pacifico / l'altra dalla laguna', two voices whose dialogue in the Babel of the contemporary world is [...] nevertheless welcomed as a minor 'miracle'".

But what would happen if, abandoning this Lefebvrian interpretation, we pursued an analysis based on the application of one of the more interesting ramifications of Lefebvre's argument, i.e., the theory of non-places codified by Marc Augé? We could find that Montale in his second phase is "caught among the echoes and images of a sort of cosmology which, unlike the ones traditionally studied by ethnologists, is objectively universal, and at the same time familiar and prestigious".[92] Railways stations, airports, restaurants, international hotel chains are familiar and prestigious because they are objectively universal – they are spaces where communication exists beyond history and the game of identity. At the same time these are non-places that "subject the individual to entirely new experiences and ordeals of solitude".[93] What if the hotels, restaurants, touristic and cultural locales that we find in *Satura* were not meaningful social spaces in a Lefebvrian sense, but rather non-places, homogeneous and homogenized places, spaces of circulation and consumption, in which an "I" who has lost his identity is forced to construct a space to discover an Other to mirror?

We could then say that the *spaces* of the international jet set – all potentially interchangeable non-places, as Montale demonstrates (the Danieli replicates Byzantium, "Xenia I, 3", OV 283; the Rôtisserie Périgourdine is ideally connected to Israel, "La morte di Dio", OV 319) – are lived in and thus transformed into *places* by the experiences of the protagonists. Therefore, at the Danieli, the operators' closet will be the *space* loaded with significance, and therefore the place where the "I" converges with others, as revealed by the verb "ripartire" used in a transitive sense modeled on the French *répartir*, "to share", rather than the intransitive form commonly used in Italian, "to leave again". Here is the text:

> Al Saint James di Parigi dovrò chiedere
> una camera 'singola'. (Non amano
> i clienti spaiati). E così pure
> nella falsa Bisanzio del tuo albergo
> veneziano; per poi cercare subito
> lo sgabuzzino delle telefoniste,
> le tue amiche di sempre; e ripartire,
> esaurita la carica meccanica,
> il desiderio di riaverti, fosse
> pure in un solo gesto o un'abitudine.[94]

---

[92] M. AUGÉ, *non-places: introduction to an anthropology of supermodernity* (1995), London and New York, Verso, 2000, p. 106.

[93] *Ibid.*, p. 93.

[94] Xenia I, 3, OV 283: "At the St. James in Paris I'll have to ask for / a room for one. (They

"To share the desire to have you back", the sharing of both desire and memory runs counter to the "single occupancy", the widower's solitude. The "I" returns (physically or imaginatively) to the places where he remembers his wife in hopes of finding her there, or at least of finding a shared memory of her.

One could argue at this point that geographical specification is an important element in the book, not because it defines the "I" but because it is evoked and characterized by him. The postmodern era, in addition to having abolished historical progression, has also taken from humanity its spatial points of reference: there is no longer a difference between "aldilà" and "quaggiù";[95] the connection, the possible miraculous encounter, between the living and the dead in *Ossi di seppia* ("Incontro", OV 96) has become the common condition. Rather, the suspicion is that "we are all dead without knowing it".[96] Just as clinging to the chronicle turns out to be the only remaining stance when faced with the end of history, modulating an agreed upon identifying sign (Xenia I, 4, OV 284) remains the only hope of re-locating oneself in a world without cardinal directions. This is the only way to conceive of existence in "uno spazio che non avendo fine / non può neanche avere un senso", ("a space that being endless / is also deprived of a sense", Xenia I, 7, OV 287).

Satura's poems begin a meditation on time and space that, though it sometimes blurs the border between science and science fiction (as is the case in "Laggiù", OV 394), remains a constant theme of Montale's later works. Spatial discoveries, however, always point to a backward reflection, on the earth, on humanity, on the "I" and the "you": as in "Fine del '68" (OV 366), where the images of the earth seen from the moon sent by Apollo 8 point to a reflection on the Vietnam War.

In subsequent collections, time and space remain inextricably intertwined; but every time these categories are mentioned their ontology, or at least their knowability, is cast into doubt, and the reflection becomes a bitter consideration of the human condition:

---

don't like / single guests). Ditto / in the fake Byzantium of your Venetian / hotel; and then, right off, hunting down / the girls at the switchboard, / your friends of a life; to share [with them], having exhausted my rewind, / the desire to have you back, / if only in one gesture, / one habit of yours". Translation modified from W. Arrowsmith's.

95 Cf. "Xenia I, 4" and "Xenia I, 7".

96 "Avevamo studiato per l'aldilà / un fischio, un segno di riconoscimento. / Mi provo a modularlo nella speranza / che tutti siamo già morti senza saperlo". "We had agreed on a tune / to recognize each other in the otherworld. / Now I find myself whistling it, in the hope / we are all dead without knowing it". "Xenia I, 4", OV 284.

Amici, non credete agli anni-luce
al tempo e allo spazio curvo o piatto.
La verità è nelle nostre mani
ma è inafferrabile e sguiscia come un'anguilla.
Neppure i morti l'hanno mai compresa
per non ricadere tra i viventi, là
dove tutto è difficile, tutto è inutile.[97]

Ontological truth, even if it seems to be within reach, is in reality unreachable. Montale's own obsessive desire to understand his origins and destiny makes him return to the argument on various occasions: the circularity of the movement being, in and of itself, a proof and a negation of the existence of temporal and spatial categories.

5. Apocalyptic and Conformist

Is Montale a narcissist, then? Yes, and no. Undoubtedly, the author looks at himself in the mirror of his poetry, as well as in the mirror of his era. But both mirrors return a fragmented, multiplied image, unmoored from the categories of space and time, factors that complicate the identification process instead of certifying it. If narcissism instead implies having knowledge of oneself, as Tiresias prophesied, and consequently expiating such knowledge with death, then Montale could hardly be considered a narcissist: particularly in the 1960s, when he was not sure of his own existence, or of the existence of the world.[98]

But Pasolini believes in the world, and in himself, and informs his neorealist perspective with the conviction that what is in a book "in effetti è" ("effectively is"), that is, has the ontological possibility of coinciding with reality:

Montale ha ricostruito se stesso con ciò che egli in effetti è, perché tutto questo "romanzesco" che ho qui sopra elencato corrisponde né più né meno che alla realtà, e non avrebbe mai potuto offrire alcuna diversa alternativa.[99]

---

[97] Ov 642: "Dear friends, do not believe in light-years / in time or in space curved or flat. / Verity is in our hands / but it is elusive, and it wriggles like an eel. / Even the dead have never understood it, / in order not to fall back among the living, there / where everything is difficult, everything is pointless". See Ov 1145 and 1150.

[98] See Ov. *Meth.* III 345. Montale's assertion here paraphrasized is in "Il mestiere di poeta", interview by Alessandro Camon (1965), AMS 1646.

[99] P.P. Pasolini, "Satura" (1971), in *Scritti sulla letteratura e sull'arte*, Milano, Mondadori, 1999, p. 2561: "Montale has reconstructed himself with that which he effectively is, for ev-

This assessment must have appeared very problematic to Montale: how could the 'reality' Pasolini describes be defined? Whose reality, in which time and place? And how could any reality coincide with the text, if not by updating once more what Montale considered an execrable, symbolist, D'Annuzian union of art and life?

Though Pasolini understands that Montale's poetic seismograph has registered the fall of ideologies and the end of history, his own ideology prevents him from agreeing with it. In his characterization of *Satura* as a "novel", Pasolini reveals his inability to register the perspective of the book. Pasolini's reading interprets Montale the poet as a representative of the reactionary bourgeoisie and flattens *Satura*'s biographical elements in a narcissistic reflection of the author. It fails in comprehending how, precisely by starting with minimal biographical hints, Montale challenges all of reality, in all forms. However, notwithstanding the different perspective, Pasolini, amongst all the contemporary readers of *Satura*, best comprehends Montale's cultural itinerary. He understands that *Satura* is the result of the author's anti-idealist and anti-positivist positions and reads the book as an anti-Marxist pamphlet: something that, logically speaking, it effectively is, even if its distance from Marxism is a consequence, not an objective, of its author's philosophical positions.[100]

erything 'novelistic' that I listed above corresponds to nothing more and nothing less than reality, and it could never have offered another alternative". For a brief summary of the Pasolini-Montale polemic, which neither begins nor ends with the episode recounted here, and for the identification of Pasolini in Montale's character Malvolio, see Massimo Gezzi's commentary on "Lettera a Malvolio" in E. Montale, *Diario del '71 e del '72*, Milano, Mondadori, 2010, pp. 188-198.

100 See P.P. Pasolini, "Satura" (1971), in *Scritti sulla letteratura e sull'arte*, cit., p. 2564: "Tutto il libro non è in fondo che la volgarizzazione – sentita linguisticamente come registro poetico – delle idee della scienza più recente e quindi più attendibile, sul "tempo:" si tratta dunque di un libro anti-positivista e anti-hegeliano. [...] Dagli errori del positivismo e della filosofia hegeliana, Montale deduce "a braccio" gli errori del marxismo, che si fonda appunto filosoficamente sul positivismo ed Hegel. Il marxismo crede nel "tempo" e i suoi critici letterari credono nei "tempi:" la scienza dimostra che sbagliano, che non ci sono né "tempo" né "tempi;" che la logica, oltreché la dialettica, può essere puramente oppositoria, o addirittura monadica: che tutto ritorna, oppure sta fermo, insomma, e non è vero che ci sia un "progredire". Dunque se il marxismo è un'illusione ormai insostenibile, Montale si libera dal marxismo e dal peso che questo può essere sulla coscienza. Tutta *Satura* è in fondo un *pamphlet* antimarxista". ("The whole book is, at heart, nothing more than the vulgarization – signaled linguistically by the poetic register – of the most recent and thus most credible scientific ideas on 'time': it is, therefore, an anti-positivist, anti-Hegelian text. [...] From the errors of positivism and Hegelian philosophy, Montale deduces 'offhand' the errors of Marxism, which is after all philosophically founded on positivism and Hegel. Marxism believes in 'time' and its literary critics believe in the 'times': science demonstrates that they're wrong, that neither time nor the times exists, that logic, as well as dialectics, can be purely oppositional or totally monadic, that everything

Pasolini's is an exceptionally lucid comprehension of Montale's position. We now have the texts needed to complete the portrait of Montale's anti-Hegelian polemic, but the famous quartina:

> Rabberciando alla meglio
> il sistema hegeliano
> si campa da più di un secolo.
> E naturalmente invano.[101]

Though written in 1969, had not yet been published (it will appear in *Poesie disperse*) and Pasolini could not have known it. However, for him the conception of history elaborated by idealist German philosophy is a fundamental, ineluctable aspect of Marxism, the defense of which was so important for him that fourteen years before he had a similar argument with Edoardo Sanguineti. Sanguineti was a university professor and a representative of the neo-avant-garde poetic movement *I Novissimi* and of the prose group *Gruppo '63* who, although a "Chinese" Marxist (such was the designation of the members of the Partito Comunista Italiano influenced by Mao Tse Tung's reading of Marx), was aware of being on the verge of a "nervous breakdown of history", as he calls it.[102] Certainly Sanguineti was aware of the fact that Marx, since the Bruxelles period, had himself been a harsh critic of the Hegelian vision of history as "pure spirit".[103] In a poem entitled "Una polemica in prosa", published in Pasolini's journal *Officina* (no. 11, Nov. 1957) Sanguineti combatively disputes Pasolini's faith in history – a faith which, according to Sanguineti, may be self-serving.

---

returns, or stands still, and in sum it's not true that there is a 'progression'. Thus if Marxism is an illusion that can no longer be sustained, Montale liberates himself from Marxism and from the weight that it can place upon the conscience. All of *Satura* is, at heart, an anti-Marxist pamphlet".

101 Ov 802, dated 20/4/69: "Repairing as we can / the Hegelian system / we have survived for over a century. / But obviously in vain". See OV 1177.

102 *I novissimi, poesie per gli anni '60*, ed. A. Giuliani, Milano, Rusconi e Paolazzi, 1961, p. 170. On the Pasolini-Sanguineti dispute and on other connections between the poetic careers of Montale and Sanguineti, which are more than either of them would care to admit, see G. Gazzola, *Ernst Hoffmann o Marty Feldman? La poesia di Edoardo Sanguineti prima e dopo* Laborintus, «Romance Languages Annual», X (1999), pp. 265-268.

103 See K. Marx, *The German Ideology*, in *The Marx-Engels Reader*, ed. R. Tucker, New York and London: Norton, 1978, p. 166: "The Germans move in the realm of 'pure spirit,' and make religious illusion the driving force of history. The Hegelian philosophy of history is the last consequence, reduced to its 'finest expression', of all this German historiography, for which it is not a question of real, not even of political, interests, but of pure thoughts".

Ma, dicevo, Lei crede nella Storia [...]

io che non sono né eroico né solo
sto fuori della storia e della grazia
di quello sperimentalismo vero

e autentico, che già non può, Lei dice
non caratterizzarLa, se sta sempre
'al punto in cui il mondo si rinnova'.

E come non starebbe, se Lei stesso
lo ha collocato lì? Felice Lei,
Pasolini felice, se la storia,

se la sua Storia, sempre, si capisce
lavora proprio per Lei [...]![104]

Following the example, Montale also replies to Pasolini's criticism with a poem entitled "Lettera a Malvolio" published in the book that followed, *Diario del '71 e del '72* (1974). The poem presents intertextual ties to Pasolini's review: replying to accusations of fleeing historical responsibilities to take refuge in and advantage of capitalist, bourgeois society, Montale returns these imputations to their sender. It was not a question of flight, he says, taking up again the subject-matter and terminology of "Piccolo testamento": "l'orgoglio / non era fuga, l'umiltà non era / vile" (Ov 267, ll. 27-29). The detached air of the *personnaliste avoué* is not a symptom of cowardice. Back then the horror of Fascism was clearly distinguishable, and the "I" could only object to it with "decency", intended as propriety and suitability of behavior, a sentiment that in its etymological meaning indicates an ethics of conduct towards society. *Decet / addecet* indicates what is proper when dealing with the community; the verb shares its semantic field with the noun *decus*, indicating honor, distinction, dignity. It is an attitude that can necessitate heroic acts, like risking one's life for one's country;[105] it is an ethical stance independent of fideistic, philosophical,

104 "Yet, as I was saying, you believe in History [...] I, not heroic nor alone, am located outside / of history and of the grace of that true and authentic // experimentalism which can not fail, as you say, to characterize you, / since it belies / 'at the point where the world renovates itself.' // And how could it not be there, since it was you / who decided its position? Happy you, / happy Pasolini, if history // (your private history, of course) / is at work expressly for you". See E. SANGUINETI, *K ed altre cose*, Milano, All'insegna del pesce d'oro, 1962, pp. 39-40.

105 See HOR. *Odes* III.2.13 : "dulce et decorum est pro patria mori".

and even scientific constructions, in which Montale had little faith, as he observes in an interview shortly after the book's publication: "Il mondo è nato da un'esplosione (il big bang di una mia poesia) o da un'intenzione? Nessuna delle due ipotesi soddisfa. Tuttavia una volta elaborato il concetto di decenza, io ho accettato come un obbligo questo concetto".[106]

Decency is obliged to take its distance from horror, and thus withdrawal is not an escape. To explain his own position Montale again divides his life into "prima" and "dopo", before and after the flood caused by the river Alpheus. Before, Montale says, the distinction between right and wrong was clear, and to behave ethically was not at all difficult:

> [...] No,
> non si trattò mai d'una fuga
> ma solo di un rispettabile
> prendere le distanze.
>
> Non fu molto difficile dapprima,
> quando le separazioni erano nette,
> l'orrore da una parte e la decenza,
> oh solo una decenza infinitesima
> dall'altra parte. No, non fu difficile,
> bastava scantonare scolorire,
> rendersi invisibili,
> forse esserlo. Ma dopo.[107]

After the flood, in the society of the permanent oxymoron, it is no longer possible to tell up from down, or worthy from worthless. The revision of the myth of Hercules' fifth labor returns to signify that "after", according to the morals of the speaker, is no better than "before". Rather, "la nuova palta", the "altre ed eguali zaffate" (Ov 278, ll. 36-38) are worsened

---

106 "Was the world born from an explosion (the big bang of my poem) or from an intention? Neither of these hypotheses satisfies. However, the concept of decency having once been formulated, I accepted this concept as an obligation". E. Montale, "Ho scritto un solo libro" (1975), interview by G. Zampa, AMS, p. 1724. The poem to which montale refers is "Big bang o altro", recently published in the literary magazine *Nuovi argomenti*, where he repeats his doubt regarding human knowledge, either of the scientific or the religious kind: "Mi pare strano che l'universo / sia nato da un'esplosione, / mi pare strano che si tratti invece / del formicolìo di una stagnazione. // Ancora più incredibile che sia uscito / dalla bacchetta magica / di un dio che abbia caratteri / spaventosamente antropomorfici". (OV 531 ll. 1-8; see OV 1115).

107 "Lettera a Malvolio", OV 456, ll. 5-16: "No, / it was never a matter of taking flight, / simply a dignified / option of distance. // It was easy enough at the start / when the divisions were so marked / horror on one side, and decency, / well, only an infinitesimal decency, / on the other. No, it wasn't so hard. / All it took was avoidance, fading away, / becoming invisible, maybe / being invisible. But later...", trans. W. Arrowsmith.

by the fact that the world has lost, together with the coordinates of space and time, its ethical compass:

> Ma dopo che le stalle si vuotarono
> l'onore e l'indecenza stretti in un solo punto
> fondarono l'ossimoro permanente
> e non fu più questione
> di fughe e di ripari. Era l'ora
> della focomelia concettuale
> e il distorto era il diritto, su ogni altro
> derisione e silenzio.[108]

Montale's new work is premised on the end of history, and it tries to come to terms with its ethical consequences opposing the "decenza infinitesima" of the "I" (l. 12) to the "indecenza" of the age (l. 18). But this claim from Pasolini's perspective, is a denial of history's persistence and a negation of its necessity as a precondition for ethical judgment. Montale ends the poem accusing Pasolini of masterfully cashing in on the new epoch, "l'ora della focomelia concettuale" ("the time of conceptual phocomelia"):

> Fu la tua ora e non è finita.
> Con quale agilità rimescolavi
> materialismo storico e pauperismo evangelico,
> pornografia e riscatto, nausea per l'odore
> di trifola, il denaro che ti giungeva.[109]

He attacks Pasolini, reproaching him for prospering from this contradiction, for wanting it both ways. This reverses the initial charge, since Pasolini also accuses Montale of having it both ways, positioning himself as both a nihilist who lacks faith in history and an accomodationist intellectual who colludes with the powers that be to his own advantage.[110]

---

[108] *Ibid.*, ll. 17-24: "But later when the stables had emptied, / honor and indecency bound in a single pact / established the permanent oxymoron / and the question was no longer one / of flight and refuge. It was the age / of the conceptual phocomele, / and the crooked was straight, and ridicule and silence / about everything else", trans. W. Arrowsmith.

[109] *Ibid.*, ll. 25-29: "It was your age, and it isn't over. / With what dexterity you made your mishmash / of historical materialism and biblical pauperism, pornography and redemption, disgust for the smell / of truffles, the money that came your way", trans. W. Arrowsmith.

[110] The polemics with Pasolini concerning Montale's supposed integration within the system of power reemerges in another poem of *Diario del '71 e del '72*, "Il cavallo", (OV 470) written on January 3, 1972, where the poet compares his nomination as *Senatore a vita* to the nomination of his horse in the Roman Senate by "Caracalla" (but the emperor in question was Caligula, see *Suet. De Vita Caes. Vita Gai*, 55). On the topic see also the short poem "Non so se quello che annuso" in E. Montale, *La casa di Olgiate e altre poesie*, Milano, Mondadori

If considered against the dichotomy Eco proposed in 1964 in *Apocalittici e integrati*, Montale was guilty of being both apocalyptical and conformist. The documents he authored in this period (journal articles, interviews, the poetic texts themselves) all contain an array of evidence for those who would accuse him of apocalypticism. Montale's reactionary postures are evident: he did not trust the student movements of 1968; he supported neither new poetry nor new poets, unless they were admirers of his; he disdained television, film, pop music; he believed semiotics pointlessly complicate otherwise simple concepts. Montale's anti-positivist and anti-historical ideas and his refusal to believe in an ontology of time and space are crucial conditions sufficient, *stricto sensu*, to number him among the apocalyptics' ranks. A mistrust in the new Political elite and a blossoming ecocritical spirit prevent him from having any hope in the future:

> Ho dei profondi motivi per dubitare del futuro della nazione: credi davvero che questo paese sarà in grado, sempre, di far vivere cinquanta o sessanta milioni di persone? Stiamo sopprimendo un mestiere come quello dell'agricoltore che era importante, molto importante. E anche se incominciamo a capirlo non sappiamo reagire, non sappiamo autogovernarci. L'industria è in crisi, nelle grandi città non c'è più posto, eppure guarda la televisione, leggi i giornali: la lode della città e dell'industria continua, sistematica, ossessiva, e continua la distruzione della vita agreste, della provincia. Il progresso! [111]

And yet Pasolini is also not entirely wrong when he accuses Montale of being a conformist. Aside from the stream of recognitions, honors, con-

---

2006, p. 5. As a senator Montale remained a consistent radical liberal: he voted in favor of and then defends the divorce law, he was anti-Catholic, and he supported the abolition of the Concordat. In politics he was definitively not a nihilist; rather, he believed in the coexistence of the principles of personal liberty and social justice. See E. Montale, "La poesia e il resto" (1971), interview by Raffaello Baldini, AMS 1709: "Probabilmente la socialdemocrazia [...] è ancora l'unica strada, se non l'unico partito: unire quelle due difficili cose che sono il massimo di libertà individuale e il massimo di decisione collettiva per eliminare ciò che è ingiusto, che è contrario non solo alla Costituzione, ma alla dignità umana". ("Social democracy is probably [...] still the only path, if not the only party, to unite those two difficult things that are the maxim of individual liberty and the maxim of joint decision-making in order to eliminate whatever is unjust, whatever is contrary not only to the Constitution, but to human dignity").

[111] E. Montale, "Spero nel meglio ma vedo il peggio" (1972), interview by Giorgio Bocca, AMS 1719: "I have profound reasons to doubt the future of our nation: do I really believe that this country will be equipped, forever, to sustain fifty or sixty million people? We are eliminating a trade like that of the farmer, which was important, very important. And even if we begin to understand it, we don't know how to react, we don't know how to govern ourselves. Industry is in crisis, there's no more room in the big cities, and yet, watch the television, read the newspapers: the praise for the city and for industry persists, systematically, obsessively, and the destruction of rural life, of provincial life, persists too. Progress!".

ferences dedicated to his work, and the nomination as senator for life for cultural achievements, one notes the fact of greatest symbolic importance: the column "Variazioni" took the spot in the cultural page of the «Corriere della Sera» that had once belonged to Gabriele D'Annunzio's "Faville del maglio". But the real proof that Montale conforms to his postmodern times lies in the very existence of *Satura* and of subsequent books: the crisis of the philosophical system does not prevent him from writing, rather it gives him material on which to write. To the end of history he responds with chronicles; to the end of pre-interpreted space he responds by giving new meanings to the places in which he lives. To the end of univocal meaning he responds with manifold possibilities of interpretation. To the end of certainties he responds with the irony of old age.

However, Montale, even equipped with good reasons to consider himself both an apocalyptic and a conformist, prefers to consider himself neither one nor the other, so as not to abdicate his own role of *personnaliste avoué*. We can understand his take on Eco's book in the review he prepared for the August 2, 1964 edition of the «Corriere della Sera». It is no surprise that Montale reviews the just-released work: the theme of mass culture and the role of art in a world dominated by machines is close to his heart. Precisely because of this interest of his, the book does not unsettle him: the attention that Eco grants to comic strips, television, and advertising makes him write that at base "l'arte per tutti è sempre esistita e non ha affatto bisogno di nuovi ritrovati tecnici e meccanici".[112] Instead, profiting from simple wordplay (the "means" that lead to an "end" / the "means" of mass communication), he points his and our attention towards the importance of ends:

> Nel suo nuovo e ricco libro, *Apocalittici e integrati*, Umberto Eco ci ripete quanto ci viene detto da più parti: posto che la civiltà di massa e i suoi mezzi di comunicazione sono uno stato di fatto irreversibile è vano chiudersi nella sterile negazione (mistica e reazionaria) dei così detti apocalittici. I mezzi sono quel che sono: l'uomo deve dominarli e piegarli ai suoi fini. Ma quali sono questi fini? Qui si naviga nel buio.[113]

112 E. MONTALE, "Di bene in meglio" (1964), AMS 299: "Art for everyone has always existed, and it has no need at all for new technical and mechanical inventions".

113 *Ibid.*: "In his new, rich book, *Apocalyptics and Conformists*, Umberto Eco repeats to us that which is being told to us from all quarters: given that mass culture and its means of communication are an irreversible, established fact, it is pointless to close oneself in the sterile negation (mystical and reactionary) of the so-called apocalyptics. The means are what they are: humankind must dominate them and bend them to its ends. But what are these ends? Here one navigates in the dark". On the reservation Montale had about the concept of dividing the Italian cultural system in "apocalittici" and "integrati", see also "Soltanto inventariare" (1965),

Montale's critical reflection in this text is not directed toward Eco, or at least not solely at him. Montale is considering the failure of teleological systems, and thus those "navigating in the dark" include not only Eco but also himself. From this perspective there is no difference between apocalyptics and conformists. In the postmodern age we all, like Montale's poetic "I", are bereft of ethical, historical, and geographical bearings.[114]

AMS 375-377 where, while defining Eco a "brilliant author", he affirms that "l'operazione di arbitraggio e equidistanza tra apocalittici e integrati" ("the process of arbitration and neutrality between apocalyptics and conformists") ultimately concedes to Eco the right to judge who's what and at best describes the present situation, without offering a way forward. Eco, for his part, described Montale's attitude as one of a man "pronto ad affrontare curioso la novità, pronto a dichiararsene inquieto, pessimista ma non dogmatico" ("ready to face innovation with curiosity, ready to declare himself disturbed and pessimistic as a result, but not dogmatic"). U. Eco, *Apocalittici e integrati* (1964), Milano, Bompiani, 2003, p. VII.

[114] See E. Montale, "Il mestiere di poeta" (1965), interview by Alessandro Camon, AMS 1647-1648: "Tra ottimisti e pessimisti del resto la diagnosi è identica: varia la prognosi. Voglio dire, il risultato è lo stesso, varia il segno algebrico premesso. [...] Il problema è questo: che il materiale non sarà mai più storicizzabile. L'idealismo è stato battuto in breccia proprio da questa impossibilità di storicizzazione" ("Moreover, for both optimists and pessimists the diagnosis is the same: it's the prognosis that varies. I mean to say, the result is the same, it's the given algebraic sign that varies. [...] The problem is that the material will no longer be historicizable. Idealism has been vanquished precisely by this impossibility of historicization").

Chapter VII

EPILOGUE

1. In Search of Time Past

Paris change! mais rien dans ma mélancolie
N'a bougé! palais neufs, échafaudages, blocs,
Vieux Faubourgs, tout pour moi devient allégorie,
et mes chers souvenirs sont plus lourds que des rocs.[1]

After all, the idea that Montale positioned himself both as an apocalyptic and as a conformist is evident from the end of the 1940s, a period that saw Italy working towards the reconstruction detailed in the Marshall Plan, but not yet enjoying the outcome of the economic boom. In 1949, Montale proclaimed confidence in the neo-humanistic possibilities of post-war Western civilization, precisely because of its reacquired ability to embrace in a single perspective both the past and the future: "J'envisage donc l'humanisme comme une conscience du lien qui relie le passé à l'avenir".[2] But then, in apparently schizophrenic fashion, he lamented how the modern era risked falling victim to excessive fragmentation of time and space and thereby losing the sentiment of the eternal: "L'époque de la technique, l'époque de la vitesse est en train de perdre le sentiment de l'éternel. Il faut qu'elle le retrouve".[3]

The way out of this apparent contradiction, unsurprisingly, is represented by the work of art, considered a natural antibody to *le temps de la*

---

1 Ch. Baudelaire, "Le Cygne", ll. 29-32 : "Paris changes! But nothing in my melancholy / has budged. New buildings, scaffoldings, blocks, / old quartiers, everything becomes allegory / and my dear memories are heavier than rocks."

2 E. Montale, "Le futur sur les genoux de Dieu" (1949), SM 784: "I understand humanism as an awareness of the bond that ties the past and the future".

3 E. Montale, "Le temps de la vitesse" (1949), SM 782: "The epoch of the technical, the epoch of velocity, is about to lose its sentiment of the eternal. It must find it back".

vitesse méchanique: "Le temps de la vitesse a déjà créé un art qui résiste a la vitesse. [...] Il faut le chercher, l'éncourager, le faire connaître, avant que le sentiment de l'art disparaisse, submergé par le sentiment nouveau de la vie méchanique".[4] Art – and specifically the art of writing – can serve as an antidote to the accelerating rhythm of collective life, for the production of literature, as Montale understands it, is capable of controlling time. He found an excellent execution of the theme at the very beginning of *À la recherche du temps perdu*, and before that he found it in the verses of two beloved poets from the Italian tradition, Petrarch and Leopardi; but if for the latter poets, writing is a means of balancing the impermanence of the "I", building for it a landscape to inhabit in the permanence of the page, for Montale the modernist, the process of writing is the only way to return to the places where everything began, to proceed in his own search of time past.

In the aftermath of World War II, after realizing that the political hope of a nation redeemed by the best minds was no longer possible, Montale inaugurates a myth of return to the primal landscape of Liguria. In pages akin to Walter Benjamin's *Berlin Childhood around 1900* (1938), he reflects on the meaning of memory and imagination and demonstrates that his writing is capable of travelling in both directions of the timeline, equally capable of connecting the past and the future. Travelling in time substitutes (actual) travelling in space, since Eugenio, from the end of World War II to 1976, refused to return to either Genoa or Monterosso. There might be a parallel between a Montale who writes of his familiar places without practicing them, and a Benjamin who writes of his native Berlin while exiled in Bonomo, or a Joyce who could only have written *Ulysses* while not in Dublin, because he appreciated his absence as a most complete form of presence; but for Montale, since the 1950s, the choice not to physically return to his place of departure was also instrumental in avoiding a confrontation with a landscape that was being progressively destroyed by real estate speculation. The landscape Eugenio knew is doubly removed from him because of its distance in time as well as the devastation of the space. The old scenery does not exist anymore and return is no longer possible, except in the way Baudelaire had indicated: the allegorical way, a return by way of writing embedded in the writing about a return. This approach to eco-criticism is a direct consequence of Montale's modernist conscience: Remo Ceserani revealed how the awareness of the consumption of landscape is a symptom of the transition from modernism to postmodernism:

---

[4] *Ibid.*: "The time of velocity has already created an art that resists velocity. [...] We must search for it, encourage it, before the sentiment of art disappears, overwhelmed by the new sentiment of the mechanical life".

After so many efforts to change the world and to make it new and human, in the end it was discovered that nature [...] had been so widely colonized by men, so conquered and placed in service of machines, production, commerce, and the design of power, that nothing remained of it.[5]

Returning to the point of departure is also a process of measuring the distance already travelled and the pathway left to be traversed, an idea that Montale sets forth in poems and in correspondence, where the represented journey can be seen as an allegory of his poetic career. Janus's door, the threshold between land and sea marked by the rail tracks between Genoa and Monterosso, becomes the landmark against which he measures all distances.

Every myth of return entails a precondition: a strategic departure. When he finally abandoned the city of Janus in order to begin his Florentine life, Montale wrote to his *maestro* and friend Larbaud that the parting was painful to him:

Dès le 1er Janvier 1927 j'irai demeurer à Florence pour gagner ma vie chez l'éditeur Bemporad; laisser Gênes pour une ville à Baedecker m'est pénible; mais Gênes n'est pas, heureusement et malheureusement, une ville où un homme de letters puisse trouver un travail ad hoc.[6]

Montale knew he would encounter a sympathetic ear in his reader, given that Larbaud adored Genoa and visited frequently; however, his displeasure at abandoning familiar places is believably sincere. Initially, Montale returned often, and a record of one of his trips from Florence to Genoa exists in a note written in 1929 to his friend Piero Gadda Conti: "Sono passato da Levanto e la riviera era formidabile. *Credo non esista nulla di simile*

[5] R. Ceserani, *Italy and Modernity: Peculiarities and Contradictions*, in *Italian Modernism. Italian Culture Between Decadentism and Avant-Garde*, eds. L. Somigli, M. Moroni, Toronto, University of Toronto Press, 2002, p. 38. See I. Calvino, "Natura" (1959), in *Saggi 1945-1985*, ed. M. Barenghi, Milano, Mondadori, 1995, II, p. 2684: "Ho capito questo: che la natura è mortale; non è quell'eterno termine antitetico all'uomo, l'altro da sé cui continuamente contrapporci: è un fragile bene, periturо, un'irripetibile giovinezza del mondo, e appena se ne è visto un frammento morire, è già come se tutto fosse perso" ("I have come to understand that nature is mortal; it is not an eternal limit antithetical to humanity, not the Other with which we continually contrast ourselves: it is a fragile good, fleeting, an unrepeatable youth of the world, and as soon as we see a fragment of it perish, it is as though all were already lost").

[6] E. Montale, *Caro maestro e amico: carteggio con Valery Larbaud (1926-1937)*, ed. M. Sonzogni, Milano, Archinto, 2003, p. 39 (12 November 1926): "I will be moving to Florence after the first of January, 1927, to work at the Bemporad publishing house; to leave Genoa for such a tourist city is distressing me, but Genoa is not, for better and for worse, the kind of city where a man of letters can find a fitting employment". The journey from Liguria to Florence is described in the poem "Accellerato" (OV 130).

al mondo".[7] The beauty of the Riviera is still capable of reaching his heart. Soon, however, as Montale's circle of Florentine friends widened, his visits home became less frequent. He returned consistently for Christmas and Easter; for St. Stephen's Day and for the Monday after Easter he regularly visited the Rodocanachi villa in Arenzano, where he met with Camillo Sbarbaro, Angelo Barile, and Adriano Grande.[8] Nevertheless, in the letters from the years 1927-1928 addressed to his friend Angelo Barile, there are several mentions of his relief at having left Genoa behind.[9] He began to travel instead, an activity that interested him and that intensified after his move to the Gabinetto Vieusseux in 1929. Consistently, he wrote to Sergio Solmi about his desire to live, to travel, and to gain new experiences, in order to rejuvenate his poetic inspiration.[10]

In 1931 he returned to Monterosso due to the death of his father Domingo;[11] it would be the last visit to the "Casa delle due palme" until seven years later, and by then a letter to Irma Brandeis attests that he considered the old landscape a part of his past, a place to avoid: a place that, though beautiful, reeked of putrescence:

Darling,

Sono qui a risalutare mia madre, ormai vecchia di 76 anni e poco riconoscibile. Questa è la villa dove sono nati i cuttle fish bones; quella che hai visto più o meno dal treno. Una pagoda a tre piani con grandi palme davanti, un giardino in decadenza e un orto. [...] È un luogo bellissimo, ma ormai per me non sa che di putredine e mi fa misurare meglio i pochi passi che ho fatti da allora e quelli che *devo* ancora fare per essere solamente me stesso, senza più contatti con un passato che non mi appartiene.[12]

---

7 See P. Gadda Conti, *Montale nelle Cinque Terre (1926-1928)*, «Letteratura», XX (1966), 79-81: "I went by Levanto, and the Riviera was extraordinary. *I don't believe there is anything like it in the world*". Italic in the original.

8 See L. Rodocanachi, *Amici poeti degli anni Trenta*, in *La poesia di Angelo Barile, Atti del convegno di studi*, ed. D. Astengo, Genova, Edizioni di «Resine», 1978, pp. 54-57.

9 E. Montale, *Giorni di libeccio. Lettere ad Angelo Barile (1920-1957)*, eds. D. Astengo, G. Costa, Milano, Archinto, 2002: "Quando verrai a trovarmi? Io sto discretamente, e certo meglio che a Genova, città dov'è una disgrazia vivere" ("When will you visit? I am quite well, and certainly I feel better [here] than in Genoa, a city where it is a disgrace to live"), p. 71 (June 8, 1927); "Io sto così così ma non rimpiango la Liguria che m'era diventata troppo inospite" ("I am so-so but do not miss Liguria, which had become too inhospitable to me"), p. 74 (October 17, 1927); "La mia vita genovese era *horrid* davvero" ("My life in Genoa was truly horrid"), p. 76 (October 21, 1927); "Io non rimpiango molto la Liguria, dove ho sofferto troppo" ("I hardly regret Liguria, [a place] where I suffered too much"), p. 80 (October 3, 1929).

10 See the letter to S. Solmi dated September 29, 1929 in "Cronologia", SM LX.

11 See the poem "Voce giunta con le folaghe", OV 250.

12 E. Montale to Irma Brandeis, in *Lettere a Clizia*, cit., p. 237 (September 7, 1938): "Darling, / I am here to see my mother, now an old woman of 76 and hardly recognizable. This is

The great bitterness Eugenio felt on account of that which his niece Bianca labeled the "uprooting from his land" had become transformed into a love-hate relationship with the region, the seeds of which we can see *a posteriori* in the *Ossi di seppia*.[13] Montale started to return to Liguria only for the funerals of close relatives; his beloved sister Marianna died prematurely in 1938, and his mother in 1942, during the war. After the war the visits ceased completely: [14] from 1945 on, the poet spent his summer vacations with Drusilla Tanzi at the seaside town of Forte dei Marmi, in Versilia. In 1948, finally employed by the daily newspaper «Corriere della Sera», he moved with Tanzi/Mosca from Florence to Milan. The Casa delle due palme was sold around 1954, and it could not have been an easy decision for the Montale family. Eugenio wrote a letter in April 1954 to his remaining cousins in Genoa, pronouncing his decision to no longer take the train on the Genoa-La Spezia line, so as not to run the risk of seeing through the tunnel openings the house that had now been sold: "Cercherò di non passare più sulla linea Genova-La Spezia, e pazienza. Per voi sarà più duro".[15]

According to Luciano Rebay, when Montale returned again to Monterosso in 1963 for his brother Ugo's funeral, it was his first time there after twenty-five years of absence. He found the places of his childhood and his poetic youth so changed that he made his stay as short as possible, swearing never to return there again.[16] By then Montale's disappointment at the changes his territory had undergone had transformed into sorrow. A similar consternation moved another Ligurian, Italo Calvino, to write a novel

---

the house where the cuttlefish bones were born, the one you more or less saw from the train. A three-floored pagoda with huge palm trees out front, a lawn in decline, and a garden. [...] It is an extremely beautiful place, but now for me it reeks only of putrescence, and it makes me measure better the few steps I have taken since then and those I *must* still take in order to be purely myself, without further contacts with a past that does not belong to me".

13 B. MONTALE, "Montale: cronache e luoghi familiari", in *La Liguria di Montale*, eds. F. Contorbia and L. Surdich, Savona, Sabatelli, 1996, p. 25: "Eugenio ha provato grande amarezza per lo sradicamento dalla sua terra e ha conservato gelosamente nella memoria quanto col tempo è andato distrutto", ("Eugenio has felt great bitterness because of having been uprooted from his land, and he has jealously conserved in his memory what has been destroyed over time").

14 *Ibid*.

15 See B. MONTALE, "Montale: cronache e luoghi familiari", in *La Liguria di Montale*, eds. F. Contorbia and L. Surdich, Savona, Sabatelli, 1996, p. 31: "I will try to no longer use the Genoa-La Spezia line. Oh well. For you it will be harder".

16 See L. REBAY, "Montale per amico", in *La Liguria di Montale*, eds. F. Contorbia e L. Surdich, Savona, Sabatelli, 1996, p. 265. Rebay's calculation is approximate, as Montale had certainly returned to Monterosso in 1942, but he effectively did not return to Liguria for at least twenty years.

entitled *La speculazione edilizia*, coincidentally published in 1963.[17] In Calvino's book, as in reality, indiscriminate building along the coast destroys the region's most beautiful nooks and crannies. The market for second homes and mass vacations had democratized vernal leisure, but it had also devastated the territory, with irreparable consequences. The village of Rapallo, appreciated by Pound for its rugged beauty, was developed so rapidly and in such a disorganized fashion that since then the term "rapallizzazione" in Italian has become a synecdoche for the devastation of territory caused by the indiscriminate cementification that occurred during and after the economic boom.

The words of Montale's niece Bianca confirm, from a private familial point of view, Rebay's testimony:

> Profonda amarezza ha provato Eugenio per il massacro di quell'angolo di riviera aspro, solitario, pittoresco in cui è nata la sua prima ispirazione. Pochi ormai, e si tratta ovviamente di persone non più giovani, si rendono esattamente conto della devastazione avvenuta in quella parte di Monterosso tra la stazione ferroviaria e le pendici del Mesco in cui si trovavano gli orti, il giardino, le vigne, il bosco della Villa Montale.[18]

Bianca Montale speaks of massacre and devastation of the landscape; to be jealous of the beauty of the Riviera was a family tradition, if Bianca's great-aunt Marianna could complain about the ruin of Monterosso as early as 1916: "Me lo rovinano Monterosso: lavorano per il doppio binario e dappertutto son pietre, mucchi di terra, rotaie…".[19] Eugenio did not represent an exception and magnified his sister's worries fifty years later: "il paesaggio tipico che esisteva una volta in Liguria sta per essere distrutto".[20]

Gianfranco Contini and Maria Luisa Spaziani – two important figures for Montale in the 1950s (though for different reasons, and though Contini,

---

17 I. Calvino, *La speculazione edilizia*, Torino, Einaudi, 1963.

18 B. Montale, "Montale: cronache e luoghi familiari", in *La Liguria di Montale*, eds. F. Contorbia and L. Surdich, Savona, Sabatelli, 1996, p. 26: "Eugenio felt profound bitterness on account of the massacre of that rugged, solitary, picturesque corner of the Riviera in which his first inspiration was born. Now there are few people, obviously people who are no longer young, who realize exactly what devastation occurred in that part of Monterosso between the train station and the slopes of the Mesco in which one found the gardens, lawn, vineyards, and forest of the Villa Montale".

19 M. Montale, *Lettere da casa Montale (1908-1938)*, cit., p. 292 (April 17, 1916): "They are ruining my Monterosso! They are adding a second track for the train and there are stones, piles of dirt, rails everywhere".

20 E. Montale, "Cinquant'anni di poesia" (1966), interview by Leone Piccioni, AMS 1675: "The tipical Ligurian landscape is about to be destroyed". See also "La riviera di Ciceri (e la mia)" (1970), AMS 1459.

a friend of Drusilla Tanzi, did not look kindly upon the poet's relationship with the young heiress) – also vouched for Montale's desire never to return to the places of his first literary inspiration. During a funeral oration for Montale, Contini recalled a dialogue that, in its scatological brevity, reflects the tones of the two men's epistolary: "Perché non tornava mai in una città così stupenda? Perché, mi disse un giorno, non si torna in una città dove si riconoscono i paracarri dove si fece pipì da bambini".[21] Maria Luisa Spaziani instead tells of having had to visit Monterosso by herself because Montale refused to accompany her, an unexpected move on the part of the poet, who usually made a point to behave chivalrously:

> A Monterosso si rifiutava assolutamente di ritornarci, anche quando decisi di andarci io per la prima volta. Il paesaggio era cambiato, ritocchi forse poco significativi per chi non c'era mai stato ma devastanti per lui. Al posto degli scogli che quarant'anni prima si prestavano a giochi, salti e "imboscate o arrembaggi di pirati" c'era un parcheggio di cemento, e per colpa delle nuove costruzioni nemmeno dal terrazzino più alto della villa si vedeva più l'arco completo del mare.[22]

Thus, in the years between the Second World War and the death of his brother Ugo, Montale, according to those who knew him and according to the statements we find in his writings, refused to return to Genoa or Monterosso. And yet it is precisely in that period that he began to write consistently about Liguria again, returning to the places of his youth through memory and imagination. He certainly had to write, out of necessity or contractual obligation: in the period between the liberation of Florence and the move to Milan, articles and translations constituted his only source of income, and later his position with the «Corriere della Sera» required him to deliver a minimum of five articles a month. Although the newspaper's director, Guglielmo Emanuel, kept Montale's byline on the third page – the page then reserved for culture in Italian newspapers – he refused

---

21 Citation from the text of the funeral oration given by Gianfranco Contini on the occasion of death of Eugenio Montale, printed under the title "Addio Eusebio, addio Arsenio", in *Mantova per Montale. Immagini e documenti*, ed. Vanni Scheiwiller, Milano, Scheiwiller, 1983, n.p.: "Why did he never return to such a stupendous city? Because, he told me one day, you should not return to a city where you recognize the curbstones where you peed as a child".

22 M.L. Spaziani, *Montale e la Volpe. Ricordi di una lunga amicizia*, Milano, Mondadori, 2011, pp. 33-34: "He absolutely refused to return to Monterosso, even when I decided to go there for the first time. The landscape had changed – changes that were hardly meaningful, perhaps, for someone who had never been there but devastating for him. In place of the rocks that forty years prior had lent themselves to games, leaps, and "ambushes or the boarding of pirates", there was a parking lot. Additionally, due to the new construction, you could no longer see the full arc of the sea, not even from the highest balcony of the villa".

to entrust Montale with literary criticism assignments, the only prose genre with which Montale was familiar. We have a recollection of this situation directly from the author:

> A un grande quotidiano approdai solo dopo la liberazione di Milano e in quella nuova sede mi si fece intendere che lo spazio era ristretto e che la critica letteraria doveva entrare, almeno provvisoriamente, in quarantena. [...] D'altra parte mi mancava la fantasia del narratore nato e non potevo contare che su ricordi personali, su esperienze vissute. Non disponevo certo del pozzo di S. Patrizio avendo sempre condotto una vita appartata, dopo il '40 semiclandestina. In compenso quelle poche memorie erano andate lievitando e di giorno in giorno mi sembravano sempre più irreali. Non potevo fonderle in un tutto omogeneo, in un continuo. Si rifiutavano di organizzarsi secondo un ordine e una prospettiva. Dovevo lasciarle sorgere a piacer loro e così fu. Nacquero così i racconti-non racconti, le poesie non-poesia che anni dopo raccolsi sotto il titolo *La farfalla di Dinard*.[23]

Montale explains how he began his second profession and why he needed to draw from the book of memory in order to meet his contractual obligations. Not knowing how to write anything that did not proceed from an occasion (a theme that recurs often in both the stories themselves and in his meta-literary prose), he was forced to build his articles on lived experiences, and these experiences inevitably brought him back to the scenery of Liguria. Interestingly, the non-stories stories gathered in *La farfalla di Dinard* are organized according to their geographical setting: from its first edition on, the book began with "Racconto d'uno sconosciuto" ("Story of a Stranger"), in which the narrating "I" eavesdrops on the story of a stranger, who tells of having tried, as a boy, to flee both his father's home and a city that was oppressing him. [24] The attempt ends in failure: "Nulla

---

[23] E. MONTALE, *Trentadue variazioni, 14* (1969), PR 575-576: "I arrived at a large newspaper only after the liberation of Milan, and in that new place I came to understand that space was tight and that literary criticism had to be quarantined, at least provisionally. [...] Meanwhile I was missing the imagination of the born narrator; I could only count on personal memories and lived experiences. I certainly did not have at my disposal a deep well of material, having always led a solitary life, practically a clandestine one after 1940. In compensation those few memories had been growing, and day by day they seemed more and more unreal to me. I could not blend them into a homogeneous whole, into a continuum. They refused to organize themselves according to an order and a perspective. I had to let them rise up as they wished, and so they did. Thus were born the non-stories stories and the non-poetry poetry that I collected years later under the title *La farfalla di Dinard*". See E. MONTALE, *La farfalla di Dinard*, Venezia, Neri Pozza, 1956[1]; Milano, Mondadori, 1960[2].

[24] See E. MONTALE, *Racconto d'uno sconosciuto* (1946), PR 10: "Avendo così tutto preveduto, mi sentivo al sicuro da ogni insidia, e mi compiacqui di prolungare la vigilia della partenza e di assaporarla con dolcezza. Ripercorsi a una a una le vecchie strade dell'infanzia, rifeci gli itinerari che avevo seguito per anni recandomi a scuola; non avevo amici, ma non trascurai qualche

da fare! La catena che m'ero illuso di voler fare a pezzi era più forte di prima".[25] Yet even if the Montale-as-stranger character failed to abandon the familiar city, Montale the author succeeded in his attempt to produce a text to submit to the newspaper.

Eugenio will recur to memory many other times: the edition of *Farfalla di Dinard* published in 1956 includes a section entirely set in Monterosso.[26] In the second edition of the same book, the allocation of the stories according to their geographical setting becomes even more precise. "Parte prima" includes all the stories set in Liguria, with only two apparent exceptions: the first is found in the story "Le rose gialle" ("The Yellow Roses"), set in Florence and Milan but tied by narrative demands to the following story; the second exception is the story that concludes the section, "La piuma di struzzo" ("The Ostrich Feather"), published in the «Corriere della Sera» the month after Montale's arrival in Milan (Feb. 2, 1948). The detail about the date is not impertinent; rather, it is essential to understanding the tale's unfolding. For once, the author does not hide himself behind a heteronym, and writes directly in the first person singular. He says he was visited, by night, by the ghosts of a tenor from Genoa (Marcello) and a basso from Florence (Astorre). The two singers perform various arias from Verdi's *Forza del destino* and Gounod's *Faust* in Montale's living room, and they seem to wake the whole building. Then they vanish, leaving the narrator in a state of great confusion, a feeling that increases when the next door neighbor is interrogated and claims never to have heard any nocturnal noises. The narrator is left alone with his questions:

> Avevo assistito all'appuntamento di un morto con un vivo o all'escursione serale di due defunti? E se i due non sapevano nulla di me, come mai avevano trovato la mia casa? E se, infine, dovevo considerarli come un frutto del mio subcon-

---

visita di congedo, senza accennare ad alcuna partenza e meravigliando tutti con i miei strani discorsi", ("Having thus foreseen everything, I felt safe from every trap, and I was pleased to prolong the eve of my departure, to savor it with sweetness. I retraced one by one the old streets of my youth, I traveled once more the paths that I had followed for years on my way to school; I had no friends, but I did go on some leave-taking visits, never hinting at a departure and astonishing everyone with my strange talk").

25 *Ibid.*, PR 11: "Nothing could be done! The chain I wanted to break was now stronger than ever".

26 The second section includes: "La regata" (1948), "La casa delle due palme" (1948), "Le rose gialle" (1943; set between Florence and Milan, but connected to the following one by the figure of Clizia/the interviewer), "Donna Juanita" (1948). At the beginning of the section the author noted: "Questi racconti, senza essere forse i migliori, sono nati insieme e stanno un poco a sè perché hanno qualche rapporto d'ambiente con la mia prima poesia" ("These short stories, not necessarily my best, were born together and remain slightly apart from the others because of their setting, which is related to my early poetry"). See PR 1171.

scio, un'allucinazione, perché non avevo partorito qualche personaggio di maggior peso nella mia vita? Poi riflettei che un nesso tra le due figure esisteva in me: incontrando Marcello avevo sperato, un giorno di emularne la gloria, di battere la sua pista; dividendo il digiuno di Astorre, trent'anni dopo, ho ringraziato Iddio di avermi salvato dai rischi della sua vita, sebbene per incorrere in guai anche più umilianti. I due uomini erano il principio e la fine di un arco, di una parabola mia personale, privata.[27]

Montale, having just arrived in Milan, reflects on his own past through the figures of the two opera singers. The Genoese Marcello recalls the years Montale spent in lessons with Maestro Sivori and his youthful ambition of becoming a professional opera singer. The Florentine Astorre, with whom he remembers having spent the days prior to the liberation of Florence ("Peloso e affamato, sempre in pigiama [...] aveva saltato i pasti per parecchi giorni, lui e la sua numerosa famiglia"),[28] concludes the cycle of his "personal and private parable".

The first section of the definitive edition of *La farfalla di Dinard* opens with an episode involving Montale's adolescence in Genoa and concludes with a short story that sums up the main stages of his life, written during or immediately after his move to Milan. The second section, on the contrary, includes stories set in Florence: the city is sometimes mentioned directly, as in "I nemici del Signor Fuchs" (PR 74), and at other times with a periphrasis, as in "Il Signor Stapps" ("Una città ch'era stata uno dei polsi della civiltà europea", "A city that had been one of the pulses of European civilization", PR 78); sometimes one must deduce the geographical setting from the dialect terms used by the characters, as in "Visita di Alastor" (PR 86-89): but the episodes, the initial occasions, are always tied to the Florentine period. The third and fourth parts, instead, are set in various European locales: Paris, Edinburgh, Zurich, and also Florence and Milan. Aside from the textual ties between these stories and Montale's postwar

---

[27] E. MONTALE, "La piuma di struzzo" (1948), PR 68: "Was it the rendezvous between a living man and a dead one that I had witnessed, or was it just two ghosts on their nocturnal round? And if the two knew nothing about me, how could they have found out my address? And if they were merely the product of my subconscious, why could it not have produced someone more significant? Then I reflected that there was after all some link between these two. Having met Marcello once I had hoped that one day I would be able to emulate his glory, to follow in his footsteps. And as far as Astorre was concerned, having shared his hunger thirty years later, I was thankful that I had been spared the hazards of his life, although I had to face some which were even more humiliating. The two men were the beginning and the end of an arc, of a personal and private parable". Transl. modified from G. Singh.

[28] *Ibid.*, PR 66: "Hairy, famished, always in pajamas [...] he and his numerous family had gone without meals for days", trans. G. Singh.

poems, it seems that Montale wants to replicate, in the book's geographical organization, the settings described in the three poetry books published up to that point. The new beginning, the beginning of a second career, is meaningfully connected to the memory, themes, and places of his youth. The shared geographical identity at the beginning and the end, the return to the narrative topoi of the outset, is not an original idea from a modernist perspective: after all, it was T.S. Eliot who said, "What we call the beginning is often the end / And to make an end is to make a beginning / The end is where we start from".[29] However, Montale's return to his origins is not simply a fresh start. As Walter Benjamin had already come to see by studying Baudelaire's descriptions of Paris, places from the past can only be revisited in an allegorical mode. Benjamin intended allegory as a reaction to the disorientation that followed the industrial revolution, redefining the classical and medieval trope for his modern times: "Allegory arises from an apprehension of the world as no longer permanent, as passing out of being: a sense of its transitoriness, an intimation of mortality".[30] Montale's assorted returns to the places of his youth, first imagined returns and then also real ones, reflect this modernist idea of allegory quite well.

2. The Heads of Janus

Janus "biceps" is not just the god of beginnings, but also the god of endings; not only the god of departures, but also of returns. The myth of Janus is a myth of return, and returning to the myth in this conclusion will help to clarify another modernist attribute of Montale's work. First of all, the convergence of spatial and temporal dimensions in the figure of Janus facilitates the understanding that a journey into the past is a journey into the distance, and vice versa: for a modern writer, spatial and temporal dimensions are inextricable.

When Montale physically returned to Genoa, invited by local authorities who wanted to celebrate his appointment as Senator for Life, he

---

[29] T.S. Eliot, *Four Quartets*: V, "Little Gidding", ll. 1-3, in *The Complete Poems and Plays, 1909-1950*, cit., p. 144.

[30] B. Cowan, *Walter Benjamin's Theory of Allegory*, «New German Critique» 22 (Winter 1981), p. 110. For the canonical definition of "allegory" see Isidore of Seville, *Etymologiae* I, 37, 22: "Allegoria est alieniloquium, aliud enim sonat, alium intelligitur", ("Allegory is to talk about something else, since one thing is said and a different thing is understood"). See also Th. Aquinus, *Summa Theologiae*, Prima, Q. 2, 10.

wished to revisit the places of his childhood; we have a description of that visit from his niece Bianca, who accompanied him:

> Nel '67 Eugenio a Genova ha voluto rivisitare con me angoli di città lasciati quarant'anni prima: dall'Istituto Vittorino da Feltre dei padri Barnabiti, che aveva frequentato bambino, sino alla stazione superiore della Funicolare di S. Anna [...] Corso Dogali, dove era nato, e via Privata Piaggio, in circonvallazione a monte, dove aveva abitato a lungo, non erano e non sono troppo mutate. Ed è stato un errare a caccia di fantasmi.[31]

It would seem that Eugenio too left a recollection of that visit: the short story "La donna barbuta" ["The Bearded Lady"] has numerous parallels with Bianca's narrative. From the story we learn that the ghost that the author was anxious to encounter was that of his old family servant, Maria, who took him to school when he was a child:

> Il maturo signore vestito correttamente di grigio che assisteva all'uscita degli scolaretti dal collegio dei Barnabiti non aveva destato, dapprima, alcuna attenzione fra i pochi adulti ch'erano in attesa fuori. [...] I bimbi uscivano a gruppetti di due o tre, o anche soli; pochi trovavano qualche «grande» che li prendesse per mano. Ma fra questi grandi il signore maturo non vide, con disappunto, alcuna serva. Il signore maturo – chiamiamolo il signor M. per brevità – disse a fior di labbro «me l'aspettavo» e si mosse lentamente verso i portici di via XX Settembre. I portici erano press'a poco quelli di quarant'anni prima, e anche l'edifizio della scuola non era molto mutato. Il signor M. era mutato assai e lo sapeva, ma siccome evitava di guardarsi nelle vetrine dei negozi, poteva anche dimenticare che quarant'anni non erano passati invano per lui.[32]

---

31 B. Montale, *Montale: cronache e luoghi familiari*, in *La Liguria di Montale*, eds. F. Contorbia and L. Surdich, Savona, Sabatelli, 1996, p. 26: "In '67 Eugenio wanted to revisit with me corners of the city of Genoa that he had left behind forty years prior: from the Barnabite fathers' Istituto Vittorino da Feltre, which he had attended as a child, to the upper station of the Sant'Anna Funicular [...] Corso Dogali, where he was born, and Via Privata Piaggio, which circles the mountain, where he lived for a long time, were not and are not much changed. We wandered in search of ghosts".

32 E. Montale, "La donna barbuta" (1948), PR 43: "The elderly man in an elegant grey suit, standing by the gate of the Collegio dei Barnabiti and watching the pupils come out, hadn't at first attracted any attention from the few grown ups who were also waiting there. [...] The children came out in twos and threes and sometimes alone. Very few found anyone waiting to take them home. But among those present, the elderly man, much to his disappointment, didn't see any maidservant. A couple of maids with hats on, yes – but no maidservant. The elderly man – let us call him M. – murmured: 'I'm not surprised', and walked slowly away towards the arcades of Via XX Settembre. The arcades were much the same as they had been forty years ago and the school building itself hadn't changed much. Signor M., on the other hand, had changed a great deal and he knew it. But since he avoided looking at his own reflection in shop windows, he managed to persuade himself that the past forty years hadn't

This initial disappointment notwithstanding, the ghost ultimately materializes and the encounter occurs:

Il signor M. sapeva perfettamente di non esser più un batuso (un monello), non ignorava che la vecchia Maria era morta trent'anni prima nell'ospizio a pagamento dove l'avevano messa quando in casa non era più stato possibile ospitare un'ottantenne in pieno sfacelo, per non dire in putrefazione. Lo sapeva, ma poiché strade e case erano quasi eguali fra l'istituto dei Barnabiti e la sua casa di quarant'anni fa, egli pensava che non fosse pazzesco da parte sua aver evocato in corpo e spirito la defunta guardiana delle sue passeggiate infantili.[33]

Eugenio confirms his niece's story, adding some details, like the identity of the ghost he sought. What has not yet been said, however, is that the story in question was published in 1948, nearly twenty years prior to the real visit described by Bianca Montale – during the period in which, as we know, Eugenio categorically refused to return to Genoa. The fact that this story of the visit precedes – and by no small span – the actual event brings us back to the allegorical nature of the visit itself and of the story that the author tells of it. Recounting in detail an event that will not take place for another twenty years, Montale provides an example of how the act of writing is capable of controlling time, "une conscience du lien qui relie le passé à l'avenir": the article "Le future sur les genoux de Dieu" arrives only a few months after "La donna barbuta", and almost simultaneously with other stories contained in the Genoese portion of *Farfalla di Dinard*. The short stories in the first part of the book actualize the lost past and the uncertain future; they re-present past and future in the eternal present of the page.

Montale's return to the place of origin happens in a (modernist) allegorical form that relates to the movement from symbolism to modernism examined in the preceding chapters. A symbol is the expression of the agreement between the semantic function and the representative function of language; it is structured as a synecdoche because it is inevitably a part of the whole that it represents.[34] Modernist allegory instead implies a disjunction between the narrative self and the phenomenal world, which is

---

touched him at all", trans. G. Singh. The figure of Maria returns in the poem "Quel che resta (se resta)", OV 587.

[33] E. Montale, "La donna barbuta" (1948), PR 44: "Signor M. knew perfectly well that he was not a scamp anymore, and that the woman Maria had died some thirty years ago in an old people's home. All this he knew – but since the streets and the houses between the elementary school and his home of forty years ago were almost the same, he didn't find it all that strange that he should evoke, in detail, the woman who had guided his infant steps", trans. G. Singh.

[34] See P. De Man, *Blindness and Insight. Essays in the Rhetoric of Contemporary Criticism* (1971), Minneapolis, University of Minnesota Press, 1983, p. 207.

the reason why attempts to use a work of art to stop time are ultimately doomed to failure. The imperfect circularity of stories demonstrates the distance between the time past and the present, further revealing the disjunctive tendency of the modernist allegory, as Paul De Man explained it:

> Allegory designates primarily a distance in relation to its own origin, and, renouncing the nostalgia and the desire to coincide, it establishes its language in the void of this temporal difference. In so doing, it prevents the self from an illusory identification with the non-self, which is now fully, and painfully, recognized as a non-self.[35]

Properly, "Signor M. knew perfectly well that he was not a scamp anymore, and that the woman Maria had died some thirty years ago in an old people's home", and he also knew that places and people may reappear exactly as they were only by virtue of the combined yet ephemeral power of memory and art. Montale the author avoided returning to his familiar landscape for the very same reason why "Signor M." avoids the mirror image reflected in the shop windows: to stay away from the curbstones bearing a trace of his passage, to evade the signs that would force him to acknowledge the transience of time, the devastation of the self and of his landscape. The "non-stories stories" are at once the embodiment of a quest for origins, and the admission of the failure of such a quest in modern times. Is that a contradiction? Absolutely.

---

[35] *Ibid.*

BIBLIOGRAPHY

Consulted Primary Sources

1. *Poetry*

Ossi di seppia, Torino, Gobetti, 1925[1]; Torino, Ribet, 1928[2]; Lanciano, Carabba, 1931[3].

Le occasioni, Torino, Einaudi, 1939; reprinted in 1940, 1942, 1943, 1945.

La bufera e altro, Venezia, Neri Pozza, 1956.

Satura (1962-1970), Milano, Mondadori, 1971.

Diario del '71 e del '72, Milano, Mondadori, 1973.

Quaderno di quattro anni, Milano, Mondadori, 1977.

L'opera in versi (= OV), eds. R. Bettarini, G. Contini, Torino, Einaudi, 1980. It includes the six previous collections plus *Altri Versi*; *Quaderno di traduzioni*; *Poesie disperse edite e inedite*

Tutte le poesie, ed. G. Zampa, Milano, Mondadori, 1984[1]; 2011[25].

La casa di Olgiate e altre poesie, eds. R. Cremante, G. Lavezzi, Milano, Mondadori, 2006.

2. *Prose*

Quaderno Genovese, ed. Laura Barile, Milano, Mondadori, 1983.

Prose e Racconti (= PR), ed. M. Forti, Milano, Mondadori, 1995; it includes the collections of short stories *Farfalla di Dinard* (1956[1]; 1960[2]); *Fuori di casa* (1969); *La poesia non esiste* (1971); *Trentadue variazioni* (1973); *Prose varie di fantasia e di invenzione* (not yet collected in a volume).

Il secondo mestiere. Prose 1920-1979 (= SM), ed. G. Zampa, Milano, Mondadori, 1996, 2 voll.

Il secondo mestiere. Arte, musica, società (= AMS), ed. G. Zampa, Milano, Mondadori, 1996; it includes the collections of articles *Auto da fé* (1966); *Prime alla Scala* (1981); *Altri scritti musicali* (articles written for the daily «Corriere della Sera» but not included in the previous collection); *Quaderno Genovese* (written 1917; published 1983); *Scritti sull'arte*; *Monologhi, colloqui* (non before collected in a volume).

3. *Epistolaries*

I. Svevo – E. Montale, Carteggio, ed. G. Zampa, Milano, Mondadori 1976.

Eugenio Montale – Giuseppe Prezzolini: Cinque lettere, ed. L. Rebay, «Forum Italicum» vol. 17 n. 2 (Fall 1983).

"Lettere a Nino Frank", ed. F. Bernardini Napoletano, Almanacco dello Specchio 12, Milano, Mondadori, 1986, pp. 17-64.

Lettere e poesie a Bianca e Francesco Messina 1923-1925, ed. L. Barile, Milano, Scheiwiller, 1995.

Eusebio e Trabucco. Carteggio di Eugenio Montale e Gianfranco Contini, ed. D. Isella, Milano, Adelphi, 1997.

Caro Maestro e Amico. Carteggio con Valery Larbaud (1926-1937), ed. M. Sonzogni, Milano, Archinto, 2003.

Lettere a Clizia, eds. R. Bettarini, G. Manghetti, F. Zabagli, Milano, Mondadori, 2006.

Giorni di libeccio. Lettere ad Angelo Barile (1920-1957), eds. D. Astengo, G. Costa, Milano, Archinto, 2002.

4. *Annotated Editions*

Ossi di seppia, eds. P. Cataldi, F. d'Amely, Milano, Mondadori, 2002.

Le occasioni, ed. D. Isella, Torino, Einaudi, 1996.

Le occasioni, ed. T. De Rogatis, Milano, Mondadori, 2011.

La bufera e altro, ed. G. Mazzoni, Milano, Mondadori, 2011.

Satura, ed. R. Castellana, Milano, Mondadori, 2009.

Diario del '71 e del '72, ed. M. Gezzi, Milano, Mondadori, 2010.

Quaderno di quattro anni, eds. A. Bertoni, G.M. Gallerani, Milano, Mondadori, 2015.

5. *Translations into English*

A somewhat dated but useful evaluative catalogue of Montale's translations into English is in T. Parks, *A Prisoner's Dream: Eugenio Montale in Translation*, «The New York Review of Books», 4 February 1999.

"Arsenio," trans. M. Praz, «Criterion», VII (June 1928), pp. 54-57.

Bones of the Cuttlefish, trans. A. Mazza, Oakville, Ontario, Mosaic Press, 1984.

Cuttlefish Bones, trans. W. Arrowsmith, New York, London, Norton & Co., 1993.

The Occasions, trans. W. Arrowsmith, New York, London, Norton & Co., 1987.

The Coastguard's House, English Versions of the Poetry of Eugenio Montale, trans. J. Reed, Newcastle upon Tyne, Bloodaxe Books, 1990.

The Storm and Other Things, trans. W. Arrowsmith, New York, London, Norton & Co., 1987.

Satura, trans. W. Arrowsmith, New York, London, Norton & Co., 1998.

The Collected Poems of Eugenio Montale 1925-1977, trans. W. Arrowsmith, ed. R. Warren, New York, London, Norton & Co., 2012.

Poets in Our Time, trans. A. Hamilton, New York, Urizen Books, 1976.

Collected Poems 1920-1954, trans. J. Galassi, New York, Farrar, Straus and Giroux, 2000.

New Poems, trans. G. Singh, New York, New Directions, 1972.

"Poems", trans. W. Balzano, J. Holdridge, «Italian Poetry Review» VIII, 2013, pp. 123-127.

The Butterfly of Dinard, trans. G. Singh, Lexington, KY, The University Press of Kentucky, 1971.

Selected Essays, trans. G. Singh, Manchester, Carcanet, 1978.

The Second Life of Art: Selected Essays, ed. and trans. J. Galassi, New York, Ecco Press, 1982.

Posthumous Diary, ed. and trans. J. Galassi, New York, Turtle Point Press, 2001.

Selected Secondary Sources

W. Adamson, *Avant-Garde Florence. From Modernism to Fascism*, Cambridge (MA), Harvard University Press, 1993.

S. Agosti, *Il testo poetico. Teoria e pratiche d'analisi*, Milano, Rizzoli, 1972.

J. Ahern, *Out of Montale's Cavern: A Reading of Calvino's* Gli amori difficili, «Modern Language Studies», 12, 1 (Winter 1982), pp. 3-19.

G. Alfano, *Paesaggi, mappe, tracciati. Cinque studi su letteratura e geografia*, Napoli, Liguori Editore, 2010.

G. Allegri, *The Long Twentieth Century*, London, Verso, 1994.

G. Almansi – B. Merry, *Eugenio Montale: The Private Language of Poetry*, Edinburgh, Edinburgh University Press, 1977.

L. Anceschi, *Nuovi studi pascoliani*, Bolzano-Cesena, Centro di Cultura dell'Alto Adige-Società di Studi Romagnoli, 1963.

I. Antici, *Le revenant di Montale: studio su una duplice assenza*, «RID, Rivista Online di Italianistica», Dipartimento di Italianistica Roma Tre, 2008, pp. 1-13.

T. Arvigo, *Guida alla lettura di Montale. Ossi di seppia*, Roma, Carocci, 2001.

M. Augé, *non-places: introduction to an anthropology of supermodernity (1995)*, London and N.Y., Verso, 2000.

M. Bacigalupo, *Pound and Montale*, «Journal of Modern Literature», 23.1 (1999), pp. 45-58.

— *Ezra Pound, un poeta a Rapallo*, Genova, Edizioni S. Marco dei Giustiniani, 1985.

K. Baedeker, *Baedecker's Northern Italy*, Leipsic, Baedeker, 1899.

Z. Baranski – R. West (eds.), *The Cambridge Companion to Modern Italian Culture*, Cambridge, Cambridge University Press, 2003.

G. Bardazzi, *Schopenhauer tra Montale e Sbarbaro*, «Studi novecenteschi», 15 n. 35 (1988) pp. 63-107.

L. Barile, *Adorate mie larve. Montale e la poesia anglosassone*, Bologna, il Mulino, 1990.

J. Baudrillard, *The Illusion of the End*, trans. C. Turner, Stanford, Stanford University Press, 1994.

R. Bazlen, *Scritti*, ed. R. Calasso, Milano, Adelphi, 1984.

R. Beasley, *Theorists of Modernist Poetry: T.S. Eliot, T.E. Hulme, Ezra Pound*, London and N.Y., Routledge, 2007.

J. Benda, *La Trahison des Clercs* (1927, 1946[2]), Grasset, Les Cahiers Rouges, 2003.

R. Ben-Ghiat, *Mapping Squadrist Violence*, «Contemporary European History», 22/4, November 2013, pp. 579-583.

C. Benes, *Urban Legends. Civic identity and the Classical Past in Northern Italy, 1250-1350*, University Park, Pennsylvania State University Press, 2011.

W. Benjamin, *Reflections*, ed. and trans. P. Demetz, New York, Schocken Books, 1986.

— *The Origin of German Tragic Drama* (1963), trans. J. Osborne, New York and London, Verso, 2009.

B. Bergonzi, *War Poets and Other Subjects*, Brookfield (VT), Ashgate, 1999.

H. Bergson, *Time and Free Will: an Essay on the Immediate Data of consciousness* (1889), trans. F.L. Pogson, New York, Harper and Row, 1910.

— *Matter and Memory* (1896), trans. N.M. Paul, W.S. Palmer, London, G. Allen, New York, MacMillan, 1912.

— *An Introduction to Metaphysics* (1903), trans. T.E. Hulme, London, G. Allen, New York, MacMillan, 1913.

— *Durée et simultaneité. A propos de la théorie d'Einstein*, Paris, Alcan, 1922.

— *L'Énergie spirituelle* (1919), Middletown, DE, FB Editions, 2015.

D. Bertelli, *From Lexicon to Symbol: the Role of Petrarch in the Building of Montale's Poetics in* Ossi di seppia, «Modern Languages Notes» 124, 1 (Jan. 2009), pp. 195-212.

G. Bertone, *Letteratura e paesaggio. Liguri e no*, Lecce, Manni, 2001.

S. Betocchi, *Gli anni di Montale al Vieusseux di Firenze*, «Italica», 71, n. 3 (Autumn 1994), pp. 331-324.

R. Bettarini (ed.), *Lettori di Montale*, Torino, Aragno, 2013.

— *Scritti montaliani*, Firenze, Le Lettere, 2009.

G.P. Biasin, *Montale, Debussy, and Modernism*, Princeton, Princeton University Press, 1989.

P. Bigongiari, *Montale tra Boutroux e M.lle de Scudéry*, «Il Bimestre», n. 6, gennaio-febbraio 1970, pp. 11-20.

L. Blasucci, *Gli oggetti di Montale*, Bologna, il Mulino, 2002.

G. Boine, *Il peccato, Plausi e Botte, Frantumi, Altri scritti*, ed. D. Puccini, Milano, Garzanti, 1983.

P. Bonfiglioli, *Pascoli, Gozzano, Montale e la poesia dell'oggetto*, «Il Verri», a. II, n° 4, 1958, pp. 34-54.

— *Pascoli e il Novecento*, «Palatina», a. II, no. 7, luglio-settembre 1958, pp. 14-39.

A. Bonsanti, *La nuova stazione di Firenze*, Milano, Mondadori, 1965.

E. Bonora, *Conversando con Montale*, Milano, Rizzoli, 1983.

E. Boretti, *Montale e Bergson*, «Le lingue del mondo», 50, n. 2 (1985), pp. 103-116.

M. Borio, *Satura. Da Montale alla lirica contemporanea*, Pisa-Roma, Serra, 2013.

É. Boutroux, *De la contingence des lois de la nature* (1874), Paris, Alcan, 1902.

M. Bradbury – J. McFarlane (eds.), *Modernism. A Guide to European Literature 1890-1930*, London, Penguin Books, 1991.

D. Bradshaw, *A Concise Companion to Modernism*, Oxford, Blackwell, 2003.

I. Brandeis, *Una musa di Montale*, eds. J. Cook and M. Sonzogni, Balerna (CH), Edizioni Ulivo, 2008.

D. Brown, *The Modernist Self in Twentieth-Century English Literature. A Study in Self-Fragmentation*, London, Macmillan, 1989.

C.J. Brook, *The expression of the inexpressible*, Oxford, Clarendon Press, 2002.

B. Burwick – P. Douglass (eds.), *The Crisis in Modernism, Bergson and the Vitalist Controversy*, Cambridge, Cambridge University Press, 1992.

M. Cacciari, *Krisis: saggio sulla crisi del pensiero negativo da Nietzsche a Wittgenstein*, Milano, Feltrinelli, 1978.

M. Calinescu, *Five Faces of Modernity*, Durham, Duke University Press, 1987.

I. Calvino, *La speculazione edilizia*, Torino, Einaudi, 1963.

— *Saggi 1945-1985*, ed. M. Barenghi, Milano, Mondadori, 1995.

G. Cambon, *The Privacy of Language: A Note on Eugenio Montale's Obscurity*, «Modern Language Notes», 78, n. 1, Italian Issue (Jan. 1963), pp. 75-79.

E. Campailla – C.F. Goffis (eds.), *La poesia di Eugenio Montale: Atti del Convegno Internazionale tenuto a Genova dal 25 al 28 novembre 1982*, Firenze, Le Monnier, 1984.

M. Cangiano, *Tra due modernismi. La versione di Boine della 'Morte di Dio'*, «Rivista di Letteratura Italiana», 3, 2015, pp. 37-52.

— *Come si identifica (e come si storicizza) il Modernismo italiano*, «Le parole e le cose», Web http://www.leparoleelecose.it/?p=22632#_ftn1 accessed May 12, 2016.

L. Caretti, *T.S. Eliot in Italia*, Bari, Adriatica Editrice, 1968.

P. Carravetta, *Del postmoderno. Critica e cultura in America all'alba del duemila*, Milano, Bompiani, 2009.

R. Caserio, *The Novel in England, 1900-1950*, New York, Twayne, 1999.

M. Cataldi, *Montale*, Palermo, Palumbo, 1991.

M. de Certau, *L'invention du quotidien. Vol. I, L'art de faire*, Paris, Union Générale d'Éditions, 1980.

É.Ó. Ceallacháin, *Eugenio Montale: The Poetry of the Later Years*, Oxford, Legenda, 2001.

— *Sanguineti and Montale: Traveling Companions in the 1970s*, «The Modern Language Review», vol. 102 n. 1 (Jan. 2007).

É.Ó. Ceallacháin – F. Pedriali (eds.), *Montale Readings*, Glasgow, University of Glasgow Press, 2000.

R. Ceserani, *Raccontare il postmoderno*, Torino, Bollati Boringhieri, 1997.

S. Chessa – M. Tortora (eds.), *Interazioni montaliane*, «L'Ellisse», monographic issue, VII, 2012.

A. Cima – C. Segre (eds.), *Eugenio Montale* (1977), Milano, Bompiani, 1997.

A. Comparini, *Iride: l'Alcesti di Montale*, Borgomanero (No), Ladolfi, 2014.

F. Condello, *I filologi e gli angeli. È di Eugenio Montale il* Diario postumo?, Bologna, Bononia University Press, 2014.

S. Connor, *Postmodernist Culture: An Introduction to Theories of the Contemporary*, Oxford, Basil Blackwell, 1989.

G.F. Contini, *Una lunga fedeltà. Scritti su Eugenio Montale*, Torino, Einaudi, 2002.

F. Contorbia, *Montale, Genova, il modernismo, e altri saggi montaliani*, Bologna, Pendragon, 1999.

F. Contorbia (ed.), *Eugenio Montale: immagini di una vita*, Milano, Mondadori, 1996.

F. Contorbia – L. Surdich (eds.), *La Liguria di Montale*, Savona, Sabatelli, 1996.

A. Cortellessa (ed.), *Le notti chiare erano tutte un'alba. Antologia dei poeti italiani nella Prima guerra mondiale*, Milano, Bruno Mondadori, 1998.

M. Corti – M.A. Grignani (eds.), *Autografi di Montale, Fondo dell'Università di Pavia*, Torino, Einaudi, 1976.

B. Croce, *Breviario di estetica* (1913), Bari, Laterza, 1969.

— *Filosofia, Poesia, Storia*, Milano-Napoli, Ricciardi, 1951.

F. Croce, *La primavera hitleriana e altri saggi su Montale*, Genova, Marietti, 1997.

— *La storia della poesia di Eugenio Montale*, Genova, Costa & Nolan, 2005.

P. De Caro, *Invenzioni di ricordi. Vite in poesia di tre ispiratrici montaliane*, Foggia, Centro Grafico Francescano, 2002.

— *Journey to Irma. Una approssimazione all'ispiratrice Americana di Eugenio Montale*, Foggia, De Meo, 1999.

M. DeKoven, *Rich and Strange: Gender, History, Modernism*, Princeton, Princeton University Press, 1991.

G. Deleuze, *Proust and Signs* (1972), trans. R. Howard, London, The Athlone Press, 2000.

P. De Man, *Blindness and Insight. Essays in the Rhetoric of Contemporary Criticism* (1971), Minneapolis, University of Minnesota Press, 1983.

K. DeMeester, *Trauma and Recovery in Virginia Woolf's* Mrs. Dalloway, «Modern Fiction Studies», 44, no. 3, 1998, pp. 649-673.

H.M. Dennis (ed.), *Ezra Pound and Poetic Influence*, Amsterdam, Rodopi, 2000.

T. De Rogatis, *Montale e il classicismo moderno*, Pisa-Roma, Istituti Editoriali e Poligrafici Internazionali, 2002.

— *Mappe del tempo: Eugenio Montale e T.S. Eliot*, Ospedaletto, Pisa, Pacini Fazzi, 2012.

D. Donaghue, *The Old Moderns*, New York, Knopf, 1994.

P. Douglass, *Bergson, Eliot & American Literature*, Lexington, KY, University Press of Kentucky, 1986.

G. Duhamel, *Les poètes et la poésie*, Paris, Mercure de France, 1912.

T. Eagleton, *Culture and the Death of God*, New Haven and London, Yale University Press, 2014.

K. Ebury, *Modernism and Cosmology*, N.Y., Palgrave Macmillan, 2014.

U. Eco, *Apocalittici e integrati* (1964), Milano, Bompiani, 2003.

M. Eksteins, *Rites of Spring: The Great War and the Birth of Modern Age*, Boston, Houghton Mifflin, 1989.

A. Einstein, *Relativity. The Special and General Theory*, trans. R.W. Lawson, New York, Crown, 1961.

— *The Meaning of Relativity* (1953), London, ElecBook, 2001. ProQuest ebrary. Web (16 July 2015).

T.S. Eliot, *A Sermon Preached in Magdalene College Chapel, 7 March 1948. Cambridge*, Cambridge University Press, s.d.

— *The Waste Land. A Facsimile and Transcript*, ed. V. Eliot, New York, Harcourt Brace, 1971.

— *The Complete Poems and Plays, 1909-1950*, New York, Harcourt, 1980.

— *To Criticize the Critic and Other Writing*, Lincoln and London, University of Nebraska Press, 1991.

— *The Sacred Wood and Major Early Essays*, Mineola, N.Y., Dover Publications, 1998.

V. Faggi, *Montale a Brescia*, Brescia, La Quadra, 1993.

G. Ficara, *Montale sentimentale*, Venezia, Marsilio, 2012.

Fondazione Mario Novaro (ed.), *Il secolo di Montale: Genova 1896-1996*, Bologna, il Mulino, 1998.

L. Fontanella, *La parola aleatoria. Avanguardia e sperimentalismo nel Novecento italiano*, Roma, Le Lettere, 1992.

M. Forti, *Eugenio Montale. La poesia, la prosa di fantasia e d'invenzione*, Milano, Mursia, 1973.

— *Svevo Romanziere*, Milano, All'Insegna del Pesce d'Oro, 1966.

S. Foster, *Relativity and the* Waste Land*: A Postulate*, «Texas Studies in Literature and Language», 7, n. 1 (1965), pp. 77-95.

M. Foucault, *The Foucault Reader*, ed. P. Rabinow, New York, Random House, 1984.

A. Francini, *Cronaca di una lunga fedeltà: il caso dei poeti statunitensi*, «Semicerchio» XVI-XVII (1997), pp. 11-16.

U. Friedman, *A Brief History of the Wristwatch: the Military Origins of Wearable Tech, a Century Before the Apple Watch*, «The Atlantic», May 27th, 2015. Web: http://www.theatlantic.com/international/archive/2015/05/history-wristwatch-apple-watch/391424/ (June 15, 2015).

A. Friedman – C.C. Donley, *Einstein as Myth and Muse*, Cambridge, Cambridge University Press, 1989.

N. Frye, *The Modern Century*, Toronto, Oxford University Press, 1967.

P. Fussel, *The Great War and Modern Memory*, London, Oxford University Press, 1975.

C.E. Gadda, *Giornale di guerra e di prigionia*, Firenze, Sansoni, 1965.

P. Gadda Conti, *Montale nelle Cinque Terre (1926-1928)*, «Letteratura», XX (1966), pp. 79-81.

P. Galison, *Einstein's Clocks, Poincaré's Maps*, New York and London, Norton, 2003.

A. Gareffi, *Montale antinomico e metafisico*, Firenze, Le Lettere, 2014.

— *I ritmi della mente di Montale*, «Sincronie», VII, 13, 2003, pp. 93-94.

E. Garin, *Cronache di filosofia italiana, 1900-1943*, Bari, Laterza, 1955.

P. Gathercolle, *Two Kindred Spirits: Eugenio Montale and T.S. Eliot*, «Italica», XXXIII, 3, 1955, pp. 170-179.

G. Gazzola, *Ernst Hoffmann o Marty Feldman? La poesia di Edoardo Sanguineti prima e dopo Laborintus*, «Romance Languages Annual», X, (1999), pp. 265-268.

E. Giachery, *La metamorfosi dell'orto*, Roma, Bonacci, 1985.

M.A. Gillies, *Henri Bergson and British Modernism*, Montreal, McGill-Queen's University Press, 1996.

A. Giuliani (ed.), *I novissimi: poesie per gli anni '60*, Milano, Rusconi e Paolazzi, 1961.

F. Giusti, *Il meriggio e la poesia. L'ora meridiana nella poesia italiana della prima metà del Novecento*, «Otto/Novecento», Anno XXIX, n. 2 (maggio/agosto 2005), pp. 161-169.

— *Nove indizi di postmodernismo in* Satura, «Contemporanea, Rivista di studi sulla letteratura e la comunicazione», 7, 2009, pp. 49-69.

J. Goldman, *Modernism, 1910-1945: Image to Apocalypse*, New York, Palgrave MacMillan, 2004.

L. Greco, *Montale commenta Montale*, Parma, Pratiche Editrice, 1990.

M.A. Grignani, *La costanza della ragione. Soggetto, oggetto e testualità nella poesia italiana del Novecento*, Novara, Interlinea, 2002.

— *Dislocazioni. Epifanie e metamorfosi in Montale*, Lecce, Piero Manni, 1998.

M.A. Grignani – R. Luperini (eds.), *Montale e il canone poetico del Novecento*, Roma, Laterza, 1998.

A. Guglielmi, *Avanguardia e sperimentalismo*, Milano, Feltrinelli, 1964.

— *Vero e falso*, Milano, Feltrinelli, 1968.

— *La linea Svevo-Pirandello*, Milano, Mursia, 1972.

G. Guglielmi, *L'invenzione della letteratura. Modernismo e avanguardia*, Napoli, Liguori, 2001.

R. Gullón, *Direcciones del modernismo*, Madrid, Gredos, 1971.

R. Hamilton – H. Herwig (eds.), *The Origins of WWI*, Cambridge, Cambridge University Press, 2003.

T. Harrison, *1910: The Emancipation of Dissonance*, Berkeley, The University of California Press, 1996.

I. Hassan, *The Dismemberment of Orpheus, Towards a Postmodern Literature (1973)*, New York, Oxford University Press, 1982.

P. Hégy, *L'autorité dans le catholicisme contemporain: du Syllabus à Vatican II*, Paris, Éditions Beauchesne, 1975.

D.M. Hertz, *Eugenio Montale, the Fascist Storm, and the Jewish Sunflower*, Toronto, University of Toronto Press, 2013.

R. Holmes, *Firing Lane*, London, Jonathan Cape, 1985.

C. Hošek – P. Parker (eds.), *Lyric Poetry Beyond New Criticism*, Ithaca, Cornell University Press, 1985.

C. Huffmann, *T.S. Eliot, Eugenio Montale and the Vagaries of Influence*, «Comparative Literature», 27 (1975), pp. 193-207.

— *Montale, Eliot and the Poetic Object*, «Italian Quarterly», XXI, no. 81, Summer 1980, pp. 63-82.

L. Hutcheon, *A Poetics of Postmodernism. History, Theory, and Fiction*, New York, Routledge, 1988.

— *The Politics of Postmodernism*, New York, Routledge, 1989.

A. Huyssen, *After the great Divide: Modernism, Mass Culture, and Postmodernism*, London, MacMillan, 1988.

A. Huyssen – K. Scherpe (eds.), *Postmoderne. Zeichen eines kulturellen Wandels*, Hamburg, Rowolht, 1986.

S. Hynes, *A War Imagined: The First World War and English Culture*, London, Bodley Head, 1990.

G. Ioli, *Montale*, Roma, Salerno, 1991.

M. Isnenghi, *Il mito della Grande Guerra*, Bologna, il Mulino, 1989.

Jacobus da Vargine, *Cronaca della città di Genova dalle origini al 1297*, ed. S. Bertini Guidetti, Genova, ECIG, 1995.

R. Jakobson, *Language in Literature*, Canbridge (MA), Harvard University Press, 1987.

F. Jameson, *The Cultural Turn. Selected Writings on the Postmodern, 1983-1998*, London and New York, Verso, 1998.

— *Postmodernism. Or, the Cultural Logic of Late Capitalism*, Durham, Duke University Press, 1993.

— *Fables of Aggression. Wyndham Lewis, The Modernist as Fascist*, Berkeley, University of California Press, 1979.

J. Joyce, *Gens de Dublin*, Paris, Plon, 1926.

— *Stephen Hero* (1906), New York, New Directions, 1963.

A. Kadarkay (ed.), *The Lukács Reader*, Oxford, Blackwell, 1995.

D. Kadlec, *Pound, BLAST, and Syndicalism*, «ELH», 60.4 (1993), pp. 1015-1031.

P. Kalliney, *Modernism in a global context*, New York and London, Bloomsbury, 2015.

I. Kant, *Prolegomena to Any Future Metaphysics that Will Be Able to Come Forward as Science* (1783), trans. G. Hatfield, Cambridge, Cambridge University Press, 2005.

H. Kenner, *The Invisible Poet: T.S. Eliot*, London, Methuen, 1979.

S. Kern, *The Culture of Time and Space (1880-1918)*, Cambridge, Harvard University Press, 1983.

M. Kolb, *Nietzsche, Freud, Benn, and the Azure Spell of Liguria*, Toronto, University of Toronto Press, 2013.

K. Kraus, *Die letzten Tage der Menschheit* (1922), Frankfurt am Main, Suhrkamp, 1992.

S. Kumar, *Bergson and the Stream-of-Consciousness Novel*, London, Blackie, 1962.

A. Lafon, *La camaraderie au front*, Paris, Armand Colin, 2014.

N. Lagioia, *Svevo, Joyce: storia di un'amicizia* (2012), «Minima&Moralia», Web http://www.minimaetmoralia.it/wp/svevo-joyce-storia-di-unamicizia/ accessed 9 September 2015.

R. Lampugnani, *Immanenza e trascendenza di Montale: l'esempio di Bergson*, «Spunti e ricerche», 6, n. 1 (1990), pp. 57-75.

G. La Piana, *A Review of Italian Modernism*, «Harvard Theological Review», IX, 4, October 1916, pp. 351-375.

S. Latham – G. Rogers, *Modernism: Evolution of an Idea*, London and New York, Bloomsbury, 2015.

D.H. Lawrence, *The Cambridge Edition of the Works of D.H. Lawrence*, Cambridge, Cambridge University Press, 2012.

S. Leblanc (a.k.a. H. Bremond), *Une Oeuvre Clandestine d'Henri Bremond*, ed. E. Poulat, Roma, Edizioni di Storia e di Letteratura, 1972.

E.J. Leed, *No Man's Land: Combat and Identity in World War I*, Cambridge, Cambridge University Press, 1979.

H. Lefebvre, *The Social Production of Space* (1958), Oxford, Blackwell, 1974.

R. Leporatti (ed.), *«Le occasioni» di Eugenio Montale 1928-1939*, Giornata di Studi, Università di Ginevra, 9 dicembre 2011, Lecce, Pensa MultiMedia, 2014.

É. Le Roy, *A New Philosophy: Henri Bergson* (1913), Web: Project Gutenberg http://www.gutenberg.org/files/1347/1347-h/1347-h.htm accessed 14 August 2015.

M. Levenson (ed.), *The Cambridge Companion to Modernism*, Cambridge, Cambridge University Press, 1999.

A. Levi, *L'indeterminismo nella filosofia francese contemporanea. La filosofia della contingenza*, Firenze, Seeber, 1904.

C. Levi, *The Watch*, New York, Farrar, Straus & Young, 1951.

H. Levin, *What Was Modernism?*, «The Massachusetts Review», Vol. 1, No. 4 (Summer 1960), pp. 609-630.

P. Lewis (ed.), *The Cambridge Companion to European Modernism*, Cambridge, Cambridge University Press, 2011.

G. Lonardi, *Il fiore dell'addio. Leonora, Manrico e altri fantasmi del melodramma nella poesia di Montale*, Bologna, il Mulino, 2003.

J. Lowney, *The American Avant-Garde Tradition. Williams Carlos Williams, Postmodern Poetry, and the Politics of Cultural Memory*, Lewisburg (PA), Bucknell University Press, 1997.

G. Lukács, *Soul and Form* (1910), New York, Columbia University Press, 2010.

R. Luperini, *Montale e l'allegoria moderna*, Napoli, Liguori, 2012.

— *Montale o l'identità negata*, Napoli, Liguori, 1984.

— *L'allegoria del moderno. Saggi sull'allegorismo come forma artistica del moderno e come metodo di conoscenza*, Roma, Editori Riuniti, 1990.

— *La fine del postmoderno*, Napoli, Guida, 2005.

— *L'autocoscienza del moderno*, Napoli, Liguori, 2006.

— *Gli esordi del Novecento e l'esperienza della «Voce»*, Bari, Laterza, 1976.

R. Luperini – M. Tortora (eds.), *Sul modernismo italiano*, Napoli, Liguori, 2012.

A. Lyttelton, *The Seizure of Power: Fascism in Italy 1919-1929*, New York and London, Routledge, 2004.

F. Madox Ford, *It Was the Nightingale*, London, Heinemann, 1933.

R. Mancini, *Liturgie totalitarie. Apparati e feste per la visita di Hitler e Mussolini a Firenze (1938)*, Firenze, Le Cariti, 2010.

S. Mancini, *Montale ed Eliot attraverso La Bufera e i Four Quartets: tempo, trascendenza e storia*, «Quaderni del '900», II, 2002, pp. 71-88.

G. Marcenaro, *Eugenio Montale*. Milano, Bruno Mondadori, 1999.

R. March – Tambimuttu (eds.), *T.S. Eliot. A Symposium*, Chicago, Henry Regnery Company, 1949.

A. Marchese, *Amico dell'invisibile. La personalità e la poesia di Eugenio Montale*, Torino, SEI, 1996.

— *Montale. La ricerca dell'Altro*, Padova, Edizioni Messaggero, 2000.

— *Visiting Angels: interpretazione semiologica della poesia di Montale*, Torino, SEI, 1977.

V. Marchesi, *Eugenio Montale critico letterario*, Roma, Edizioni di storia e letteratura, 2013.

C. Marshik (ed.), *The Cambridge Companion to Modernist Literature*, Cambridge, Cambridge University Press, 2015.

K. Marx, *The Marx-Engels Reader*, ed. R. Tucker, New York and London, Norton, 1978.

A. Marzola, *Guerra e identità. Percorsi nella letteratura inglese del Novecento*, Roma, Carocci, 2005.

S. Matthews, *Modernism*, London, Arnold, 2004.

F.O. Matthiessen, *The Achievement of T.S. Eliot*, Oxford, Oxford University Press, 1959.

M. Maggi, *Cesare Vasoli: Un ricordo*, «Annali del Dipartimento di Filosofia di Firenze (Nuova Serie)», XVIII (2012), p. 257.

P. Melli, *Genova preromana*, Genova, Fratelli Frilli, 2007.

P. McCormick, *Aspects yellowing darkly: Ethics, Intuition, and the European High Modernism*, Kraków, Jagiellonian University Press, 2010.

P.V. Mengaldo, *La tradizione del Novecento*, Torino, Bollati Boringhieri, 1996.

R. Meoli Toulmin, *Shakespeare e Eliot nelle versioni di Montale*, «Belfagor», n. 26, 1981, pp. 453-471.

F. Meriano, *Arte e vita*, eds. G. Manghetti, C.E. Meriano, V. Scheiwiller, Milano, Scheiwiller, 1982.

M. Millan, *The Institutionalization of Squadrismo: Disciplining paramilitary Violence in the Italian Fascist Dictatorship*, «Contemporary European History», 22/4, November 2013, pp. 551-573.

S. Miller (ed.), *Military strategy and the Origins of the First World War*, Princeton, Princeton University Press, 1985.

M. Montale, *Lettere da casa Montale, 1908-1938*, ed. Z. Zuffetti, Milano, Àncora, 2006.

I. Montanelli, *Qui non riposano*, Milano, Tarantola, 1945.

F. Moretti, *Segni e stili del moderno*, Torino, Einaudi, 1987.

— *Atlas of the European Novel 1800-1900*, London and New York, Verso, 1998.

— *Signs Taken for Wonders. On the Sociology of Literary Forms*, London and New York, Verso, 1983.

— *La letteratura vista da lontano*, Torino, Einaudi, 2005.

M. Morrisson, *Modernism, Science, and Technology*, New York and London, Bloomsbury, 2016.

R. Mosena, *Le affinità di Montale. Letteratura ligure del Novecento*, Roma, Studium, 2006.

G. Nascimbeni, *Montale nello zaino di Strehler*, «Corriere della Sera», February 10, 1996, p. 25.

I. Newton, *The Mathematical Principles of Natural Philosophy* (1687), trans. A. Motte, New York, Daniel Adee, 1846.

F. Olsen, *Eliot's Objective Correlative. Tradition or Individual Talent*, Brighton, Sussex Academic Press, 2012.

T. O'Neill, *Montale's Fishy Petrarchism*, «Modern Language Notes», 106, no.1, Italian Issue (Jan. 1991), pp. 78-116.

M. Onfray, *Le désir d'être un volcan. Journal hédoniste*, Paris, Grasset, 1996.

R. Orlando, *Applicazioni montaliane*, Lucca, Pacini Fazzi, 2001.

C. Ott, *Torso-Göttin Sprache. Eugenio Montales Poetik im Medium seiner Lyrik*, Heidelberg, Universitätsverlag Winter, 2003.

T. Pagano, *The Making and Unmaking of Mediterranean Landscape in Italian Literature*, Madison, Fairleigh Dickinson University Press, 2015.

P. Pancrazi, *Scrittori d'oggi*, Serie III, Bari, Laterza, 1946.

S. Pannella, *E. Montale e T. S. Eliot*, «Galleria», IV, 5-6 (December 1954), pp. 244-256.

G. Pascoli, *Studi per il centenario della nascita di Giovanni Pascoli pubblicati nel cinquantenario della morte*, Bologna, Commissione per i testi di lingua, 1962.

— *Atti del Convegno nazionale di studi pascoliani: San Mauro Pascoli, 11-12-13 maggio 1962*, Santarcangelo di Romagna, S.T.E.M., 1965.

P.P. Pasolini, *Scritti sulla letteratura e sull'arte*, Milano, Mondadori, 1999.

E. Pasquini, *La memoria culturale nella poesia di Eugenio Montale*, Modena, Mucchi, 1991.

G. PELL, *Memorial Space, Poetic Time. The Triumph of Memory in Eugenio Montale*, Leichester, Troubadur Publishing, 2005.

M. PERLOFF, *The Futurist Moment*, Chicago, University of Chicago Press, 1986.

A. PIPA, *L'influence de Boutroux et de Bergson sur Montale*, «Revue des Études Italiennes», 22 (1976), pp. 193-204.

R. POGGIOLI, *Essays in European Literature*, Cambridge, Harvard University Press, 1965.

P. POLITO – A. ZOLLINO (eds.), *Paesaggio ligure e paesaggi interiori nella poesia di Eugenio Montale*, Atti del convegno internazionale (11-13 dicembre 2009), Firenze, Olschki, 2011.

E. POUND, *New Selected Poems and Translations*, ed. R. Sieburth, New York, New Directions, 2010.

— *A Memoir of Gaudier-Brzeska*, New York, New Directions, 1970.

— *Literary Essays of Ezra Pound*, ed. T.S. Eliot, London, Faber, 1960.

R. POUND, *The Lost Generation of 1914*, N.Y., Coward-McCann, 1965.

M. PRAZ, *The House of Life*, London, Methuen, 1964.

— *Machiavelli and the Elizabethans, Annual Italian Lecture of the British Academy*, London, Humphrey Milford, 1928.

G. PREZZOLINI, *Del linguaggio come causa di errore (H. Bergson)*, Firenze, Spinelli, 1904.

S. PRICE, *James Joyce and Italo Svevo, The Story of a Friendship*, London, Somerville Press, 2016.

M. QUAINI, *L'ombra del paesaggio: Orizzonti di un'utopia conviviale*, Reggio Emilia, Diabasis, 2006.

T. QUIRK, *Bergson and American Culture: The Worlds of Willa Cather and Wallace Stevens*, Chapel Hill, University of North Carolina Press, 1990.

P. RAE (ed.), *Modernism and Mourning*, Lewisburg, Bucknell University Press, 2007.

L.S. RAINEY, *The Creation of the Avant-Garde: F.T. Marinetti and Ezra Pound*, «Modernism/ Modernity», 1.3 (1994), pp. 195-220.

S. RAMAT, *Montale*, Firenze, Vallecchi, 1965.

— (ed.), *Omaggio a Montale*, Milano, Mondadori, 1966.

— *Il libro come «opera»: la strada di Arsenio*, «Italianistica», 11, 1973, pp. 268-304.

G. RENSI, *La scepsi estetica*, Bologna, Zanichelli, 1920.

— *Interiora rerum*, Milano, Unitas, 1924.

W. RENZI, *In the Shadow of the Sword. Italy's neutrality and Entrance into the Great War, 1914-1915*, New York, Peter Lang, 1987.

C. RICCARDI, *Montale dietro le quinte. Fonti e poesie dagli Ossi alla Bufera*, Novara, Interlinea, 2014.

G. ROGANTE, *La frontiera della parola. Poesia e ricerca di senso da Pascoli a Zanzotto*, Roma, Studium, 2007.

E. ROSADA, *Il contingentismo di Montale*, «Studi novecenteschi», X, 1983, 5-56.

R. RUBINI, *The Other Renaissance. Italian Humanism Between Hegel & Heidegger*, Chicago, The University of Chicago Press, 2014.

E. SANGUINETI, *Tra liberty e crepuscolarismo*, Milano, Mursia, 1961.

— *Ideologia e linguaggio*, Milano, Feltrinelli, 1965.

M.C. Santini, *La farfalla di Dinard e la memoria montaliana*, La Spezia, Agorà, 1999.

F.M. Sardelli, *L'affare Vivaldi*, Palermo, Sellerio, 2015.

T. Sauer, *Albert Einstein's 1916 Article on the General Theory of Relativity*, Web http://arxiv.org/abs/physics/0405066v1 (28 Aug. 2015).

C. Sbarbaro, *L'opera in versi e in prosa*, eds. G. Lagorio and V. Scheiwiller, Milano, Garzanti, 2016.

C. Scarpati, *Sulla cultura di Montale*, Milano, Vita e Pensiero, 1997.

P.A. Schilipp (ed.), *Albert Einstein*, LaSalle, IL, Open Court, 1992.

A. Schopenhauer, *The World as Will and Idea*, trans. R.B. Haldane and J. Kemp, London, Kegan, Paul, Trench, Trübner & Co., 1909.

S. Schwartz, *The Matrix of Modernism: Pound, Eliot, and early Twentieth Century Thought* (1988), Princeton, Princeton University Press, 2014.

A. Seroni, *Ragioni critiche*, Firenze, Vallecchi, 1944.

P. Sica, *Modernist Forms of Rejuvenation: Montale and T.S. Eliot*, Firenze, Olschki, 2003.

— *Il fanciullo invecchiato, la poesia fisiologica e la civiltà meccanica: il senso dell'età umana, dell'arte e della società negli Ossi di seppia di Eugenio Montale*, «Modern Language Notes», 116, no. 1, Italian Issue (Jan. 2001), pp. 150-161.

G. Simmel, *The Philosophy of Landscape* (1913), Josef Bleicher, trans., «Theory, Culture & Society», vol. 24 (7-8) 2007, pp. 20-29.

G. Simonetti, *Dopo Montale. Le «Occasioni» e la poesia italiana del Novecento*, Lucca, Pacini Fazzi, 2002.

S. Slataper, *Il mio Carso* (1912), ed. Giani Stuparich, Milano, Mondadori, 1958.

S. Solmi, *Poesie complete*, Milano, Adelphi, 1974.

— *Saggi sul fantastico*, Torino, Einaudi, 1978.

L. Somigli – M. Moroni (eds.), *Italian Modernism. Italian Culture Between Decadentism and Avant-Garde*, Toronto, University of Toronto Press, 2002.

L. Somigli – S. Storchi (eds.), *The Great War and the Modernist Imagination in Italy*, «Annali d'Italianistica», Vol. 33, 2015.

M. Sonzogni, *Debiti e doni della tradizione poetica: Montale tra T.S. Eliot e Samuel Beckett. Appunti su Montale traduttore e tradotto*, «The Italianist», 25 (2005), pp. 173-207.

— *La speranza di pure rivederti... Clizia, Montale e l'impossibilità di dirsi addio*, Milano, Archinto, 2013.

M.L. Spaziani, *Montale e la Volpe*, Milano, Mondadori, 2011.

S. Spender, *The Struggle of the Modern*, London, Hamish Hamilton, 1963.

S. Stanford Friedman, *Definitional Excursions. The meaning of Modern / Modernity / Modernism*, «Modernism/modernity», Vol. 8, No. 3 (September 2001), pp. 493-513.

D. Stevenson, *The First World War and International Politics*, Oxford, Oxford University Press, 1988.

— *Armament and the Coming of War*, Oxford, Clarendon Press, 1996.

L. Surdich, *Le idee e la poesia. Montale e Caproni*, Genova, Il Melangolo, 1998.

I. Svevo, *Una vita*, Trieste, Ettore Vram, 1892.

— *Senilità*, Trieste, Ettore Vram, 1898.

— *La coscienza di Zeno* (1923), eds. E. Montale, B. Maier, Milano, Dall'Oglio, 1986.

P. Szondi, *On Textual Understanding and Other Essays*, trans. H. Mendelsohn, Manchester, Manchester University Press, 1978.

G. Talbot, *Montale's Mestiere Vile. The Elective Translations from English of the 1930s and 1940s*, Dublin, Irish Academy Press, 1995.

H. Thomas, *Montale in English*, New York, Handsel Books, 2004.

M. Tortora, *«Ogni apparenza dintorno vacille s'umilia scompare». Lettura di* Corno Inglese, «Allegoria», 65-66, gennaio-dicembre 2012, pp. 134-153.

C. Ubaldini, *Arsenio e la profezia del* forse *(tra Prufrock e Isaia)*, «Sincronie», X, 20, 2006, pp. 231-242.

G. Ungaretti, *Selected Poems*, ed. and trans. A. Frisardi, New York, Farrar, Strauss and Giroux, 2002.

P. Valéry, *Charmes: Poèmes commentés par Alain*, Paris, Gallimard, 1929.

C. Vasoli, *Tra cultura e ideologia*, Milano, Lerici, 1961.

S. Verdino, *L'ultimo paesaggio di Montale*, «Nuova corrente», 58 (2011), pp. 27-44.

M. Veronesi, *Fra oscurità e autocoscienza: Nota su Montale poeta-critico*, «Atelier», IX, 36 (December 2004), pp. 40-49.

R.S. Virgillito, *La luce di Montale*, Milano, Edizioni Paoline, 1990.

E. Vittorini, *Arsenio*, «Circoli», 6, 1931, pp. 79-101.

R. West, *Eugenio Montale: Poet on the Edge*, Cambridge, MA, Harvard University Press, 1981.

E. Wilson, *Alex's Castle: A Study in Imaginative Literature of 1870-1930*, New York and London, Scribner, 2004.

K. Wilson, *Modernism*, London, Continuum, 2007.

H. Witemeyer (ed.), *The Future of Modernism*, Ann Arbor, University of Michigan Press, 1997.

W. Withman, *Song of Myself* (1855), New York, Dover Publications, 2001.

M.H. Withworth, *Einstein's Wake*, Oxford, Oxford University Press, 2002.

V. Woolfe, *Collected Essays*, London, Chatto & Windus, 1966.

— *Mrs. Dalloway* (1925), London, Urban Romantics, 2012.

W.B. Yeats, *The Poems*, ed. D. Albright, London, Everyman's Library, 1992.

A. Wilde, *Horizons of Assent: Modernism, Postmodernism, and the Ironic Imagination*, Baltimore, Johns Hopkins University Press, 1981.

Q. Wright, *A study of War*, Chicago and London, University of Chicago Press, 1965.

A. Zanzotto, *In margine a Satura*, «Nuovi argomenti», 23-24, July-December 1971, pp. 215-220.

A. Zollino, *I paradisi ambigui. Saggi su musica e tradizione nell'opera di Montale*, Piombino, Il Foglio, 2008.

CONTENTS

FINITO DI STAMPARE
PER CONTO DI LEO S. OLSCHKI EDITORE
PRESSO ABC TIPOGRAFIA • SESTO FIORENTINO (FI)
NEL MESE DI NOVEMBRE 2016

BIBLIOTECA DELL'«ARCHIVUM ROMANICUM»

Serie I: Storia - Letteratura - Paleografia

1. Bertoni, G. *Guarino da Verona fra letterati e cortigiani a Ferrara (1429-1460)*. 1921. (esaurito)
2. —— *Programma di filologia romanza come scienza idealistica*. 1922. (esaurito)
3. Verrua, P. *Umanisti ed altri «studiosi viri» italiani e stranieri di qua e di là dalle Alpi e dal mare*. 1924, 234 pp., 2 tavv.
4. Cino da Pistoia, *Le rime*. 1925. (esaurito)
5. Zaccagnini, G. *La vita dei maestri e degli scolari nello Studio di Bologna nei secoli XIII e XIV*. 1926. (esaurito)
6. Jordan, L. *Les idées, leurs rapports et le jugement de l'homme*. 1926, X-234 pp.
7. Pellegrini, C. *Il Sismondi e la storia della letteratura dell'Europa meridionale*. 1926, 168 pp.
8. Restori, A. *Saggi di bibliografia teatrale spagnola*. 1927, 122 pp., 3 cc.
9. Santangelo, S. *Le tenzoni poetiche nella letteratura italiana dalle origini*. 1928. (esaurito)
10. Bertoni, G. *Spunti, scorci e commenti*. 1928, VIII-198 pp.
11. Ermini, F. *Il «dies irae»*. 1928, VIII-158 pp.
12. Filippini, F. *Dante scolaro e maestro. (Bologna - Parigi - Ravenna)*. 1929, VIII-224 pp.
13. Lazzarini, L. *Paolo de Bernardo e i primordi dell'Umanesimo in Venezia*. 1930. (esaurito)
14. Zaccagnini, G. *Storia dello Studio di Bologna durante il Rinascimento*. 1930, X-348 pp., 42 ill.
15. Catalano, M. *Vita di Ludovico Ariosto*. 2 voll. 1931. (esaurito)
16. Ruggieri, J. *Il canzoniere di Resende*. 1931, 238 pp.
17. Döhner, K. *Zeit und Ewigkeit bei Chateaubriand*. 1931. (esaurito)
18. Troilo, S. *Andrea Giuliano politico e letterato veneziano del Quattrocento*. 1932. (esaurito)
19. Ugolini, F. A. *I Cantari d'argomento classico*. 1933. (esaurito)
20. Berni, F. *Poesie e prose*. 1934. (esaurito)
21. Blasi, F. *Le poesie di Guilhem de la Tor*. 1934, XIV-78 pp.
22. Cavaliere, A. *Le poesie di Peire Raimond de Tolosa*. 1935. (esaurito)
23. Toschi, P. *La poesia popolare religiosa in Italia*. 1935. (esaurito)
24. Blasi, F. *Le poesie del trovatore Arnaut Catalan*. 1937. (esaurito)
25. Gugenheim, S. *Madame d'Agoult et la pensée européenne de son époque*. 1937. (esaurito)
26. Lewent, K. *Zum Text der Lieder des Giraut de Bornelh*. 1938. (esaurito)
27. Kolsen, A. *Beiträge zur Altprovenzalischen Lyrik*. 1938. (esaurito)
28. Niedermann, J. *Kultur. Werden und Wandlungen des Begriffs und seiner Ersatzbegriffe von Cicero bis Herder*. 1941. (esaurito)
29. Altamura, A. *L'Umanesimo nel mezzogiorno d'Italia*. 1941. (esaurito)
30. Nordmann, P. *Gabriel Seigneux de Correvon, ein schweizeri-scher Kosmopolit. 1695-1775*. 1947. (esaurito)
31. Rosa, S. *Poesie e lettere inedite*. 1959. (esaurito)
32. Panvini, B. *La leggenda di Tristano e Isotta*. 1952. (esaurito)
33. Messina, M. *Domenico di Giovanni detto il Burchiello. Sonetti inediti*. 1952. (esaurito)
34. Panvini, B. *Le biografie provenzali. Valore e attendibilità*. 1952. (esaurito)
35. Moncallero, G. L. *Il Cardinale Bernardo Dovizi da Bibbiena umanista e diplomatico*. 1953. (esaurito)
36. D'Aronco, G. *Indice delle fiabe toscane*. 1953, 236 pp.
37. Branciforti, F. *Il canzoniere di Lanfranco Cigala*. 1954. (esaurito)
38. Moncallero, G. L. *L'Arcadia*. Vol. I: *Teorica d'Arcadia*. 1953. (esaurito)
39. Galanti, B. M. *Le villanelle alla napolitana*. 1954. (esaurito)
40. Crocioni, G. *Folklore e letteratura*. 1954. (esaurito)
41. Vecchi, G. *Uffici drammatici padovani*. 1954, XII-258 pp., 73 tavv. esempi mus.
42. Vallone, A. *Studi sulla Divina Commedia*. 1955. (esaurito)
43. Panvini, B. *La scuola poetica siciliana*. 1955. (esaurito)
44. Dovizi, B. *Epistolario di Bernardo Dovizi da Bibbiena*. Vol. I (1490-1513). 1955. (esaurito)
45. Collina, M. D. *Il carteggio letterario di uno scienziato del Settecento (Janus Plancus)*. 1957, VIII-174 pp., 5 tavv. f.t.
46. Spaziani, M. *Il canzoniere francese di Siena (Biblioteca Comunale HX 36)*. 1957. (esaurito)
47. Vallone, A. *Linea della poesia foscoliana*. 1957. (esaurito)
48. Crinò, A. M. *Fatti e figure del Seicento anglo-toscano. (Documenti inediti sui rapporti letterari, diplomatici e culturali fra Toscana e Inghilterra)*. 1957. (esaurito)
49. Panvini, B. *La scuola poetica siciliana. Le canzoni dei rimatori non siciliani*. Vol. I. 1957. (esaurito)
50. Crinò, A. M. *John Dryden*. 1957, 406 pp., 1 tav. f.t.
51. Lo Nigro, S. *Racconti popolari siciliani. (Classificazione e Bibliografia)*. 1958. (esaurito)
52. Musumarra, C. *La sacra rappresentazione della Natività nella tradizione italiana*. 1957. (esaurito)
53. Panvini, B. *La scuola poetica siciliana. Le canzoni dei rimatori non siciliani*. Vol. II. 1958. (esaurito)
54. Vallone, A. *La critica dantesca nell'Ottocento*. 1958, 240 pp. Ristampa 1975.
55. Crinò, A. M. *Dryden, poeta satirico*. 1958. (esaurito)
56. Coppola, D. *Sacre rappresentazioni aversane del sec. XVI, la prima volta edite*. 1959, XII-270 pp., ill.
57. Piramus et Tisbè. *Introduzione - Testo critico - Traduzione e note a cura di F. Branciforti*. 1959. (esaurito)
58. Gallina, A. M. *Contributi alla storia della lessicografia italo-spagnola dei secoli XVI e XVII*. 1959, 336 pp.
59. Piromalli, A. *Aurelio Bertola nella letteratura del Settecento. Con testi e documenti inediti*. 1959. Ristampa 1998.
60. Gamberini, S. *Poeti metafisici e cavalieri in Inghilterra*. 1959, 270 pp.
61. Berselli Ambri, P. *L'opera di Montesquieu nel Settecento italiano*. 1960. (esaurito)

62. *Studi secenteschi*, vol. I (1960). 1961, 220 pp.

63. VALLONE, A. *La critica dantesca del '700*. 1961. (esaurito)

64. *Studi secenteschi*, vol. II (1961). 1962, 334 pp., 7 tavv. f.t.

65. PANVINI, B. *Le rime della scuola siciliana*. Vol. I: Introduzione - Edizione critica - Note. 1962, LII-676 pp. Rilegato.

66. BALMAS, E. *Un poeta francese del Rinascimento: Etienne Jodelle, la sua vita - il suo tempo*. 1962, XII-876 pp., 12 tavv. f.t.

67. *Studi secenteschi*, vol. III (1962). 1963, IV-238 pp. 4 tavv. f.t.

68. COPPOLA, D. *La poesia religiosa del sec. XV*. 1963, VIII-150 pp.

69. TETEL, M. *Étude sur la comique de Rabelais*. 1963. (esaurito)

70. *Studi secenteschi*, vol. IV (1963). 1964, VI-238 pp., 5 tavv.

71. BIGONGIARI, D. *Essays on Dante and Medieval Culture*. 1964. (esaurito)

72. PANVINI, B. *Le rime della scuola siciliana* - Vol. II: Glossario. 1964, XVI-180 pp. Rilegato.

73. BAX, G. *«Nniccu Furcedda», farsa pastorale del XVIII sec. in vernacolo salentino*, a cura di Rosario Jurlaro. 1964, VIII-108 pp., 12 tavv.

74. *Studi di letteratura, storia e filosofia in onore di Bruno Revel*. 1965, XXII-666 pp., 3 tavv.

75. BERSELLI AMBRI, P. *Poemi inediti di Arthur de Gobineau*. 1965, 232 pp., 3 tavv. f.t.

76. PIROMALLI, A. *Dal Quattrocento al Novecento. Saggi critici*. 1965, VI-190 pp.

77. BASCAPÈ, A. *Arte e religione nei poeti lombardi del Duecento*. 1964, 96 pp.

78. GUIDUBALDI, E. *Dante Europeo, I. Premesse metodologiche e cornice culturale*. 1965. (esaurito)

79. *Studi secenteschi*, vol. V (1964). 1965, 192 pp., 2 tavv. f.t.

80. VALLONE, A. *Studi su Dante medioevale*. 1965, 276 pp.

81. DOVIZI, B. *Epistolario di Bernardo Dovizi da Bibbiena*. Vol. II (1513-1520). 1965. (esaurito)

82. *La Mandragola* di Niccolò Machiavelli per la prima volta restituita alla sua integrità. 1965. (esaurito)
Edizione di lusso numerata da 1 a 370, su carta grave, con 2 tavv. f.t.

83. GUIDUBALDI, E. *Dante Europeo, II. Il paradiso come universo di luce (la lezione platonico-bonaventuriana)*. 1966, VIII-462 pp., 2 tavv. f.t.

84. LORENZO DE' MEDICI IL MAGNIFICO, *Simposio*, a cura di Mario Martelli. 1966, 176 pp., 2 riproduzioni.

85. *Studi secenteschi*, vol. VI (1965). 1966, IV-310 pp., 1 tav. f.t.

86. *Studi in onore di Italo Siciliano*. 1966, 2 voll. di XII-1240 pp. compless. e 6 tavv. f.t.

87. ROSSETTI, G. *Commento analitico al "Purgatorio" di Dante Alighieri*. Opera inedita a cura di Pompeo Giannantonio. 1966, CIV-524 pp.

88. PIROMALLI, A. *Saggi critici di storia letteraria*. 1967. (esaurito)

89. *Studi di letteratura francese*, vol. I. 1967, XVI-176 pp.

90. *Studi secenteschi*, vol. VII (1966). 1967, VI-166 pp., 6 tavv. f.t.

91. PERSONÈ, L. M. *Scrittori italiani moderni e contemporanei. Saggi critici*. 1968, IV-340 pp.

92. *Studi secenteschi*, vol. VIII (1967). 1968, VI-230 pp., 1 tav. f.t.

93. TOSO RODINIS, G. *Galeazzo Gualdo Priorato, un moralista veneto alla corte di Luigi XIV*. 1968, VI-226 pp., 9 tavv. f.t.

94. GUIDUBALDI, E. *Dante Europeo, III. Poema sacro come esperienza mistica*. 1968, VIII-736 pp., 24 tavv. f.t. di cui 1 a colori.

95. DISTANTE, C. *Giovanni Pascoli poeta inquieto tra '800 e '900*. 1968, 212 pp.

96. RENZI, L. *Canti narrativi tradizionali romeni. Studi e testi*. 1969, IV-170 pp.

97. VALLONE, A. *L'interpretazione di Dante nel Cinquecento. Studi e ricerche*. 1969, 306 pp.

98. PIROMALLI, A. *Studi sul Novecento*. 1969. (esaurito)

99. CACCIA, E. *Tecniche e valori dal Manzoni al Verga*, 1969, X-286 pp.

100. GIANNANTONIO, P. *Dante e l'allegorismo*. 1969. (esaurito)

101. *Studi secenteschi*, vol. IX (1968). 1969, IV-384 pp., 9 tavv. f.t.

102. TETEL, M. *Rabelais et l'Italie*. 1969, IV-314 pp.

103. REGGIO, G. *Le egloghe di Dante*. 1969, X-88 pp.

104. MOLONEY, B. *Florence and England. Essays on cultural relations in the second half of the eighteenth century*. 1969, VI-202 pp., 4 tavv. f.t.

105. *Studi di letteratura francese*, vol. II (1969). 1970, VI-360 pp., 11 tavv. f.t.

106. *Studi secenteschi*, vol. X (1969). 1970, VI-312 pp.

107. *Il Boiardo e la critica contemporanea* a cura di G. Anceschi. 1970, VIII-544 pp.

108. PERSONÈ, L. M. *Pensatori liberi nell'Italia contemporanea. Testimonianze critiche*. 1970, IV-290 pp.

109. GAZZOLA STACCHINI, V. *La narrativa di Vitaliano Brancati*. 1970, VIII-160 pp.

110. *Studi secenteschi*, vol. XI (1970). 1971, IV-292 pp. con 9 tavv. f.t.

111. BARGAGLI, G. (1537-1587), *La Pellegrina*. Edizione critica con introduzione e note di F. Cerreta. 1971, 228 pp. con 2 ill. f.t.

112. SAROLLI, G. R. *Prolegomena alla Divina Commedia*, 1971, LXXII-454 pp. con 9 tavv. f.t. Ristampa 2002.

113. MUSUMARRA, C. *La poesia tragica italiana nel Rinascimento*. 1972, IV-172 pp. Ristampa 1977.

114. PERSONÈ, L. M. *Il teatro italiano della «Belle Époque». Saggi e studi*. 1972, 410 pp.

115. *Studi secenteschi*, vol. XII (1971). 1972, IV-516 pp. con 2 tavv. f.t.

116. LOMAZZI, A. *Rainaldo e Lesengrino*. 1972, XIV-222 pp. con 2 tavv. f.t.

117. PERELLA, R. *The critical fortune of Battista Guarini's «Il Pastor Fido»*. 1973, 248 pp.

118. *Studi secenteschi*, vol. XIII (1972). 1973, IV-372 pp. con 11 tavv. f.t.

119. DE GAETANO, A. *Giambattista Gelli and the Florentine Academy: the rebellion against Latin*. 1976, VIII-436 pp. e 1 ill.

120. *Studi secenteschi*, vol. XIV (1973). 1974, IV-300 pp. con 4 tavv. f.t.

121. DA POZZO, G. *La prosa di Luigi Russo*. 1975, 208 pp.

122. PAPARELLI, G. *Ideologia e poesia di Dante*. 1975, XII- 332 pp.

123. *Studi di letteratura francese*, vol. III (1974). 1975, 220 pp.

124. COMES, S. *Scrittori in cattedra*. 1976, XXXII-212 pp. con un ritratto e 1 tav. f.t.

125. Tavani, G. *Dante nel Seicento. Saggi su A. Guarini, N. Villani, L. Magalotti*. 1976, 176 pp.

126. *Studi secenteschi*, vol. XV (1974). *Indice generale dei voll. I-X(1960-1969)*. 1976, 188 pp.

127. Personè, L. M. *Grandi scrittori nuovamente interpretati: Petrarca, Boccaccio, Parini, Leopardi, Manzoni*. 1976, 256 pp.

128. *Innovazioni tematiche, espressive e linguistiche della letteratura italiana del novecento* - Atti dell'VIII Congresso dell'Associazione internazionale per gli studi di lingua e letteratura italiana. 1976, XII-300 pp.

129. *Studi di letteratura francese*, vol. IV (1975). 1976, 180 pp. con 2 ill.

130. *Studi secenteschi*, vol. XVI (1975). 1976, IV-244 pp.

131. Caserta, E. G. *Manzoni's Christian Realism*. 1977, 260 pp.

132. Toso Rodinis, S. *Dominique Vivant Denon. I fiordalisi, Il berretto frigio, La sfinge*. 1977, 232 pp. con 10 ill. f.t.

133. Vallone, A. *La critica dantesca nel '900*. 1976, 480 pp.

134. Fratangelo, A. e M. *Guy De Maupassant scrittore moderno*. 1976, 180 pp.

135. Cocco, M. *La tradizione cortese e il petrarchismo nella poesia di Clément Marot*. 1978, 320 pp.

136. Mastrobuono, A. C. *Essays on Dante's Philosophy of History*. 1979, 196 pp.

137. *Primo centenario della morte di Niccolò Tommaseo (1874-1974)*. 1977, 224 pp.

138. Siciliano, I. *Saggi di letteratura francese*. 1977, 316 pp.

139. Schizzerotto, G. *Cultura e vita civile a Mantova fra '300 e '500*. 1977, 148 pp. con 9 ill. f.t.

140. *Studi secenteschi*, vol. XVII (1976). 1977, 184 pp., con 5 tavv. f.t.

141. Gazzola Stacchini, V. - Bianchini, G. *Le Accademie dell'Aretino nel XVII e XVIII secolo*. 1978, XVIII-598 pp. con 18 ill. n.t. e 24 f.t.

142. Friggieri, O. *La cultura italiana a Malta. Storia e influenza letteraria e stilistica attraverso l'opera di Dun Karm*. 1978, 172 pp. con 5 ill. f.t.

143. *Studi secenteschi*, vol. XVIII (1977). 1978, 276 pp.

144. Vanossi, L. *Dante e il «Roman de la Rose» Saggio sul «Fiore»*. 1979, 380 pp.

145. Ridolfi, R. *Studi Guicciardiniani*. 1978, 344 pp.

146. Allegretto, M. *Il luogo dell'Amore. Studio su Jaufre Rudel*. 1979, 104 pp.

147. Misan, J. *L'Italie des doctrinaires (1817-1830). Une image en élaboration*. 1978, 204 pp.

148. Toaff, A. *The Jews in medieval Assisi 1305-1487. A social and economic history of a small Jewish community in Italy*. 1979, 240 pp. con 14 ill. f.t.

149. Trovato, P. *Dante in Petrarca. Per un inventario dei dantismi nei «Rerum vulgarium Fragmenta»*. 1979, X-174 pp.

150. Fiorato, A. C. *Bandello entre l'histoire et l'écriture. La vie, l'expérience sociale, l'évolution culturelle d'un conteur de la Renaissance*. 1979, XXII-686 pp.

151. *Studi secenteschi*, vol. XIX (1978). 1979, 260 pp.

152. Bosisio, P. *Carlo Gozzi e Goldoni. Una polemica letteraria con versi inediti e rari*. 1979, 444 pp.

153. Zanato, T. *Saggio sul «Comento» di Lorenzo de' Medici*. 1979, 340 pp.

154. *Studi di letteratura francese*, vol. V. 1979, 204 pp.

155. Piromalli, A. *Società, cultura e letteratura in Emilia Romagna*. 1980, 180 pp.

156. Accademici Intronati di Siena, *La Commedia degli Ingannati*. 1980, 248 pp.

157. *Studi di letteratura francese*, vol. VI. 1980, 176 pp.

158. Harran, D. *«Maniera» e il Madrigale - Una raccolta di poesie musicali del Cinquecento*. 1980, 124 pp.

159. *Studi secenteschi*, vol. XX (1979). 1980, VI-214 pp.

160. Ussia, S. *Carteggio Magliabechi. Lettere di Borde, Arnaud e associati lionesi ad A. Magliabechi*. 1980, 244 pp.

161. Da Col, I. *Un romanzo del Seicento. La Stratonica di Luca Assarino*. 1981, 244 pp. con 24 tavv. f.t.

162. *Studi secenteschi*, vol. XXI (1980). 1981, 294 pp.

163. *Studi di letteratura francese*, vol. VII. 1981, 224 pp.

164. Castelletti, C. *Stravaganze d'amore. «Comedia»*. 1981, 172 pp.

165. *Carteggio inedito fra N. Tommaseo e G. P. Vieusseux*. I: (1835-1839). A cura di V. Missori. 1981, 688 pp.

166. *Studi secenteschi*, vol. XXII (1981). *Indice generale dei voll. XI-XX (1970-1979)*. 1981, 184 pp.

167. *Il Rinascimento. Aspetti e problemi attuali*. Atti del X Congresso dell'Associazione internazionale per gli studi della lingua e letteratura italiana. 1982, VI-700 pp.

168. *Stendhal e Milano*. Atti del XIV Congresso internazionale Stendhaliano. 1982, 2 tomi di complessive XXVI-972 pp. e 2 tavv. a colori.

169. *Studi secenteschi*, vol. XXIII (1982). 1982, 328 pp. con 1 tav. f.t.

170. *Studi di letteratura francese*, vol. VIII. 1982, 208 pp.

171. *Studi di letteratura francese*, vol. IX. 1983, 274 pp.

172. Aonio Paleario, *Dell'economia o vero del governo della casa*. 1983, 120 pp. con 4 tavv. f.t.

173. Dalla Palma, G. *Le strutture narrative dell'«Orlando Furioso»*. 1984, 228 pp.

174. *Studi secenteschi*, vol. XXIV (1983). 1983, 324 pp.

175. Raugei, A. M. *Bestiario valdese*. 1984, 362 pp. con ill. n.t.

176. Da Pozzo, G. *L'ambigua armonia. Studio sull'«Aminta» del Tasso*. 1983, 336 pp.

177. *Studi di letteratura francese*, vol. X. 1983, 208 pp.

178. *Miscellanea di studi in onore di V. Branca*. Vol. I: *Dal Medioevo al Petrarca*. 1983, XII-492 pp. con 1 tav. f.t.

179. —— Vol. II: *Boccaccio e dintorni*. 1983, VI-450 pp.

180. —— Vol. III: *Umanesimo e Rinascimento a Firenze e Venezia*. 1983, 2 tomi di complessive XII-848 pp.

181. —— Vol. IV: *Tra Illuminismo e Romanticismo*. 1983, 2 tomi di complessive XII-900 pp.

182. ——Vol. V: *Indagini Otto-Novecentesche*. 1983, VI-390 pp.

183. Rizzo, G. *Tommaso Briganti. Inedito poeta romantico*. 1984, 274 pp.

184. Poliaghi, N. F. *Stendhal e Trieste*. 1984, VI-202 pp. con 22 ill.

185. Michelangelo Buonarroti il giovane, *La Fiera. Redazione originaria (1619)*. 1984, 162 pp. con 4 tavv. f.t.

186. *I cantari. Struttura e tradizione*. 1984, 200 pp.

187. Bianchini, G. *Federico Nomi. Un letterato del '600. Profilo e fonti manoscritte*. 1984, XVI-338 pp. con 11 tavv. f.t.

188. *Studi secenteschi*, vol. XXV (1984). 1984, 304 pp.

189. Zambon, F. *Robert De Boron e i segreti del Graal*. 1984, 132 pp.

190. *Fenoglio a Lecce*. 1984, 248 pp.

191. Schettini Piazza, E. *Giuseppe Chiarini. Saggio biobibliografico di un letterato dell'Ottocento*. 1984, X-158 pp. con 1 tav. f.t.

192. *Studi di letteratura francese*, vol. XI. 1985, 362 pp. con 9 tavv. f.t.

193. Misan, J. *Les lettres italiennes dans la presse française (1815-1824)*. 1985, 210 pp.

194. Cairns, C. *Pietro Aretino and the Republic of Venice. Researches on Aretino and his circle in Venice, 1527-1556*. 1985, 272 pp.

195. Bertelà , M. *Stendhal et l'Autre. L'homme et l'oeuvre à travers l'idée de féminité*. 1985, 352 pp.

196. Piglionica, A. M. *Dalla realtà all'illusione*: The Tempest *o la parola preclusa*. 1985, 146 pp.

197. *Studi secenteschi*, vol. XXVI (1985), 1985, 352 pp.

198. Cervigni, D. S. *Dante's poetry of dreams*. 1986, 230 pp.

199. *Studi di letteratura francese*, vol. XII. 1986, II-282 pp. con 4 tavv. f.t.

200. Marco Polo, *Il milione*. Edizione del testo toscano («ottimo»). 1986, XII-418 pp.

201. Delmay, B. *I personaggi della «Divina Commedia». Classificazione e regesto*. 1986, LVI-414 pp.

202. *Patronage and Public in the Trecento*. 1986, 180 pp. con 36 ill. f.t.

203. Mitchell, B. *The Majesty of the State. Triumphal Progresses of Foreign Sovereigns in Renaissance Italy, 1494-1600*. 1986, VIII-240 pp. con 8 ill. f.t.

204. *Ugo Angelo Canello e gli inizi della filologia romanza in Italia*. 1987, 276 pp. con 4 tavv. f.t.

205 *Studi secenteschi*, vol. XXVII (1986). 1986, IV-348 pp.

206. Dé dé yan, C. *Diderot et la pensée anglaise*. 1986, IV-366 pp.

207. *La letteratura e i giardini*. 1987, 436 pp. con 9 tavv. f.t.

208. *Letteratura italiana e arti figurative*. 1988, 3 voll. di complessive VIII-1438 pp. con 60 ill. f.t.

209. *Studi secenteschi*, vol. XXVIII (1987). 1987, IV-332 pp. con 2 ill. f.t.

210. *Dante e la Bibbia*. Atti del convegno internazionale. 1988, 372 pp.

211. *Veronica Gàmbara e la poesia del suo tempo nell'Italia Settentrionale*. Atti del convegno. 1989, 442 pp.

212. *Studi di letteratura francese*, vol. XIII. 1987, 194 pp.

213. Colombo, A. *I «Riposi di Pindo». Studi su Claudio Achillini (1574-1640)*, 1988, 228 pp.

214. *Letteratura e storia meridionale. Studi offerti a Aldo Vallone*. 1989, 2 tomi di complessive XVI-960 pp. con 7 tavv. f.t.

215. Sabbatino, P. *La «Scienza» della scrittura. Dal progetto del Bembo al manuale*. 1988, 256 pp.

216. *Studi di letteratura francese*, vol. XIV. 1988, 144 pp.

217. Pirro Schettino, *Opere edite e inedite*. Edizione critica. 1989, 410 pp. con 4 tavv. f.t.

218. *Giorgio Pasquali e la filologia classica del '900*. Atti del convegno. 1988, VI-278 pp.

219. *Studi secenteschi*, vol. XXIX (1988). 1988, IV-328 pp.

220. Landoni, E. *La teoria letteraria dei provenzali*. 1989, XXXIV-168 pp.

221. *Il meraviglioso, il verosimile tra antichità e medioevo*. 1989, 360 pp. con 5 tavv. f.t.

222. Procaccioli, P. *Filologia ed esegesi dantesca nel Quattrocento. L'«Inferno» nel «Comento sopra la Comedia» di Cristoforo Landino*. 1989, 266 pp.

223. Santarcangeli, P. *Homo Ridens. Estetica, filologia, psicologia, storia del comico*. 1989, VI-452 pp.

224. *Filologia e critica dantesca. Studi offerti a Aldo Vallone*. 1989, XVI-660 pp. con 2 tavv. f.t.

225. *Dantismo russo e cornice europea*. 1989, 2 voll. indivisibili di XXXVI-880 pp. complessive.

226. *Studi di letteratura francese*, vol. XV. 1989, 284 pp. con 1 tav. f.t.

227. *Studi secenteschi*, vol. XXX (1989). 1989, IV-316 pp.

228. *Il tema della fortuna nella letteratura francese e italiana del Rinascimento. Studi in memoria di Enzo Giudici*. 1990, XX-550 pp. con 1 tav. f.t.

229. Sebastio, L. *Strutture narrative e dinamiche culturali in Dante e nel «Fiore»*. 1990, 320 pp.

230. *Studi di letteratura francese*, vol. XVI. 1990, 248 pp. con 1 tav. f.t.

231. *Studi di letteratura francese*, vol. XVII. 1990, 156 pp.

232. *Studi di letteratura francese*, vol. XVIII. 1990, 332 pp. con 1 tav. f.t.

233. Dozon, M. *Mythe et symbol dans la «Divine Comédie»*. 1991, XVI-634 pp.

234. Vallone, A. *Strutture e modulazioni nei canti della «Divina Commedia»*. 1990, 226 pp.

235. Comollo, A. *Il dissenso religioso in Dante*. 1990, 154 pp.

236. Bendinelli Predelli, M. *Alle origini del «Bel Gherardino»*. 1990, 362 pp.

237. Guerin Dalle Mese, J. *Egypte: La mémoire et le rêve. Itineraires d'un voyage, 1320-1601*. 1990, 656 pp. con 7 tavv. f.t.

238. Sorella, A. *Magia, lingua e commedia nel Machiavelli*. 1990, 264 pp.

239. *Studi secenteschi*, vol. XXXI (1990). 1990, XXVIII-296 pp. con 6 tavv. f.t.

240. *Miscellanea di studi in onore di Marco Pecoraro*. 1991. Vol. I: *Da Dante al Manzoni*, X-398 pp. con 7 tavv. f.t.; Vol. II: *Dal Tommaseo ai contemporanei*, IV-414 pp.

241. *Lingua e letteratura italiana nel mondo oggi*. 1991, 2 tomi di XVI-732 pp. complessive.

242. Sabbatino, P. *L'Eden della nuova poesia. Saggi sulla «Divina Commedia»*. 1991, 232 pp.

243. *Alfonso M. De Liguori e la società civile del suo tempo*. 1990, 2 tomi di VIII-682 pp. complessive.

244. *Famiglia e società nell'opera di Giovanni Verga*. 1991, VI-494 pp.

245. *Studi secenteschi*, vol. XXXII (1991). 1991, IV-332 pp. con 4 tavv. f.t.

246. Hein, J. *Enigmaticité et messianisme dans la «Divine Comédie»*. 1992, II-654 pp.

247. Sanguineti White, L. *Dal detto alla figura. Le tragedie di Federico Della Valle*. 1992, 162 pp.

248. Grossvogel, S. *Ambiguity and allusion in Boccaccio's* Filocolo. 1992, 254 pp.

249. *Studi di letteratura francese*, vol. XIX. 1992, 526 pp. con 4 ill. f.t. e figg. n.t.

250. Padoan, G. *Il lungo cammino del «Poema sacro». Studi danteschi*. 1992, IV-310 pp.

251. *Studi secenteschi*, vol. XXXIII (1992). 1992, IV-210 pp. con 4 tavv. f.t.

252. Ankli, R. *Morgante iperbolico. L'iperbole nel* Morgante *di Luigi Pulci*. 1993, 422 pp.

253. *Studi secenteschi*, vol. XXXIV (1993). 1993, IV-476 pp. con 1 tav. ripiegata f.t.

254. Sabbatino, P. *Giordano Bruno e la "mutazione" del Rinascimento*. 1993, 230 pp. con 6 figg. f.t. Ristampa 1998.

255. *Studi secenteschi*, vol. XXXV (1994). 1994, IV-286 pp. con 4 tavv. f.t.

256. *Studi di letteratura francese*, vol. XX. 1994, 294 pp. con 1 tav. f.t.

257. Sabbatino, P. - Scorrano, L. - Sebastio, L. - Stefanelli, R. *Dante e il Rinascimento. Rassegna bibliografica e studi in onore di Aldo Vallone*. 1994, 212 pp.

258. *Italo Svevo scrittore europeo*. A cura di N. Cacciaglia e L. Fava Guzzetta. 1994, VIII-574 pp.

259. Sebastio, L. *Il poeta e la storia. Una dinamica dantesca*. 1994, 264 pp.

260. *Le feste dei pastori del Rubicone per Napoleone I Re d'Italia*. Opera inedita a cura di A. Piromalli e T. Iermano. 1994, 152 pp.

261. *Studi secenteschi*. Vol. XXXVI (1995). 1995, IV-302 pp. con 6 tavv. f.t.

262. *Geografia, storia e poetiche del fantastico*. A cura di M. Farnetti. 1995, 244 pp. con 4 ill. f.t.

263. *Studi secenteschi*. Vol. XXXVII (1996). 1996, IV-406 pp.

264. Iermano, T. *Il melanconico in dormiveglia. Salvatore Di Giacomo*. 1995, 270 pp.

265. Ardissino, E. *L'«aspra tragedia». Poesia e sacro in Torquato Tasso*. 1996, 236 pp.

266. Zangheri, L. *Feste e apparati nella Toscana dei Lorena (1737-1859)*. 1996, 332 pp. con 115 ill. f.t.

267. *Letteratura e industria*. Atti del XV Congresso dell'Associazione internazionale per gli studi di lingua e letteratura italiana. 1997, 2 tomi di XVIII-1288 pp. complessive con 76 ill. f.t.

268. Angiolillo, G. *La nuova frontiera della tanatologia. Le biografie della Commedia*. Vol. I: *Inferno*. 1996, 182 pp.

269. Angiolillo, G. *La nuova frontiera della tanatologia. Le biografie della Commedia*. Vol. II: *Purgatorio*. 1996, 308 pp.

270. Angiolillo, G. *La nuova frontiera della tanatologia. Le biografie della Commedia*. Vol. III: *Paradiso*. 1996, 270 pp.

271. *Studi secenteschi*. Vol. XXXVIII (1997). 1997, IV-444 pp.

272. Benporat, C. *Cucina italiana del Quattrocento*. 1996, 306 pp. con 4 figg. f.t. in b. e n. e 8 tavv. f.t. a colori. Ristampa 2001.

273. *Studi di letteratura francese. Rivista europea*, vol. XXI (1996). 1996, 238 pp. con 2 figg. n.t.

274. Fratnik, M. *Enrico Pea et l'écriture du moi*. 1997, 402 pp.

275. Montevecchi, F. *Il potere marittimo e le civiltà del Mediterraneo antico*. 1997, 596 pp. con 85 figg. n.t.

276. Rossetto, S. *Per la storia del giornalismo. Treviso dal XVII secolo all'unità*. 1996, 222 pp. con 10 tavv. f.t.

277. Girardi, R. *Incipitario della lirica meridionale e repertorio generale degli autori di lirica nati nel Mezzogiorno d'Italia (secolo XVI)*. 1996, 458 pp.

278. Sabbatino, P. *La bellezza di Elena. L'imitazione nella letteratura e nelle arti figurative del Rinascimento*. 1997, 270 pp. con 1 grafico n.t. e 12 tavv. f.t. Ristampa 2001.

279. Panicara, V. *La nuova poesia di Giacomo Leopardi. Una lettura critica della* Ginestra. 1997, 148 pp.

280. *Torquato Tasso e la cultura estense*. A cura di G. Venturi, indice dei nomi e bibliografia generale a cura di A. Ghinato e R. Ziosi. 1999, 3 tomi di VIII-1462 pp. complessive con 101 ill. f.t.

281. Gavioli, E. *Filologia e nazione: l'«Archivum romanicum» nel carteggio inedito di Giulio Bertoni*. 1997, 202 pp. con 4 ill. f.t.

282. *Studi di letteratura francese. Rivista europea*, vol. XXII (1997). 1997, 330 pp.

283. *Studi secenteschi*. Vol. XXXIX (1998). 1998, IV-368 pp. con 4 tavv. f.t.

284. *Studi secenteschi*. Vol. XL (1999). 1999, IV-390 pp.

285. *Studi di letteratura francese. Rivista europea*, vol. XXIII (1998). «Lire le roman». 1998, 270 pp.

286. *Alfonso M. de Liguori e la civiltà letteraria del Settecento*. Atti del Convegno internazionale per il tricentenario della nascita del Santo (1696-1996). Napoli 20-23 ottobre 1997. A cura di P. Giannantonio. 1999, XX-476 pp.

287. *Leopardi e Bologna*. Atti del Convegno di studi per il Secondo Centenario Leopardiano (Bologna 18-19 maggio 1998). A cura di M. A. Bazzocchi. 1999, XVI-316 pp. con 4 tavv. f.t.

288. *Studi secenteschi*. Vol. XLI (2000). 2000, IV-502 pp.

289. *Studi di letteratura francese. Rivista europea*, vol. XXIV (1999). «L'estranéité». 1999, 246 pp.

290. Smith, G. *The Stone of Dante and later florentine celebrations of the Poet*. 2000, X-72 pp. con 16 ill. f.t.

291. *L'immaginario contemporaneo*. Atti del Convegno letterario internazionale, Ferrara, 21-23 maggio 1999. A cura di R. Pazzi. 2000, XII-198 pp.

292. *The Poetics of Place. Florence Imagined*. Edited by I. Marchegiani Jones and T. Haeussler. 2001, XIV-220 pp.

293. Lawson Lucas, A. *La ricerca dell'ignoto. I romanzi d'avventura di Emilio Salgari*. Traduzione di S. Rizzardi e F. Rusciadelli. 2000, XVI-208 pp. con 1 tav. f.t.

294. *Il castello, il convento, il palazzo e altri scenari dell'ambientazione letteraria*. A cura di M. Cantelmo. 2000, VI-326 pp.

295. *Studi secenteschi*. Vol. XLII (2001). 2001, IV-472 pp. con 20 ill. f.t.

296. *Studi di letteratura francese. Rivista europea*, vol. XXV (2000). 2001, 192 pp.

297. *La lingua e le lingue di Machiavelli*. Atti del Convegno internazionale di studi, Torino 2-4 dicembre 1999. 2001, 352 pp.

298. *Studi secenteschi*. Vol. XLIII (2002). 2002, IV-372 pp. con 9 ill. f.t.

299. *Umanisti bellunesi fra Quattro e Cinquecento*. Atti del Convegno di Belluno, 5 novembre 1999. A cura di P. Pellegrini. 2001, XIV-296 pp. con 24 tavv. f.t.

300. Sodini, C. *L'Ercole tirreno. Guerra e dinastia medicea nella prima metà del '600*. 2001, VI-326 pp. con 16 tavv. f.t. in b. e n. e 9 a colori.

301. *Il tragico e il sacro dal Cinquecento a Racine*. Atti del Convegno internazionale, Torino e Vercelli, 14-16 ottobre 1999. A cura di D. Cecchetti e D. Dalla Valle. 2001, X-330 pp.

302. Benporat, C. *Feste e banchetti. Convivialità italiana fra Tree Quattrocento*. 2001, 290 pp. con 12 tavv. f.t. a colori.

303. *Studi di letteratura francese. Rivista europea*, vol. XXVI (2001). «Théâtre et société au XVIIe siècle». 2002, 254 pp.

304. *La «liquida vertigine»*. Atti delle giornate di studio su Tommaso Landolfi. Prato, Convitto Nazionale Cicognini, 5-6 febbraio 1999. A cura di I. Landolfi. 2002, XXVI-266 pp.

305. *Studi secenteschi*. Vol. XLIV (2003). 2002, IV-340 pp. con 3 tavv. f.t.

306. LEUSHUIS, R. *Le Mariage et l'"amitié courtoise' dans le dialogue et le récit bref de la Renaissance*. 2003, XIV-286 pp.

307. FRATNIK, M. *Paysages. Essai sur la description de Federico Tozzi*. 2002, XVI-182 pp.

308. *Alfieri e il suo tempo*. Atti del Convegno internazionale, Torino - Asti, 29 novembre - 1 dicembre 2001. A cura di M. Cerruti, M. Corsi, B. Danna. 2003, XII-488 pp. con 3 figg. n.t. e 5 tavv. f.t. di cui 4 a colori.

309. *Robert Davidsohn (1853-1937). Uno spirito libero tra cronaca e storia*. Tomo I: *Atti della giornata di studio*. Tomo II: *Gli scritti inediti*. Tomo III: *Catalogo della biblioteca*. A cura di W. Fastenrath Vinattieri e M. Ingendaay Rodio. 2003, XXX-812 pp. complessive con 1 fig. n.t. e 30 tavv. f.t.

310. *Studi di letteratura francese. Rivista europea*, vol. XXVII (2002). 2003, 286 pp.

311. *Il volto e gli affetti. Fisiognomica ed espressione nelle arti del Rinascimento*. Atti del Convegno di studi, Torino, 28-29 novembre 2001. A cura di A. Pontremoli. 2003, 314 pp. con 14 tavv. f.t.

312. SICA, P. *Modernist Forms of Rejuvenation. Eugenio Montale and T.S. Eliot*. 2003, X-156 pp.

313. *Studi secenteschi*. Vol. XLV (2004). 2004, IV-484 pp. con 6 tavv. f.t.

314. *Sabba da Castiglione (1480-1554). Dalle corti rinascimentali alla Commenda di Faenza*. Atti del Convegno, Faenza, 19-20 maggio 2000. A cura di A.R. Gentilini. 2004, X-496 pp. con 16 figg. n.t. e 54 tavv. f.t. di cui 6 a colori.

315. SABBATINO, P. A l'infinito m'ergo. *Giordano Bruno e il volo del moderno Ulisse*. 2003, XVI-212 pp. con 15 tavv. f.t.

316. MASTROIANNI, M. *Le* Antigoni *sofoclee del Cinquecento francese*. 2004, 264 pp.

317. *Francesco di Giorgio alla corte di Federico da Montefeltro*. Atti del Convegno internazionale di studi, Urbino, monastero di Santa Chiara, 11-13 ottobre 2001. A cura di F.P. Fiore. 2004, 2 tomi di complessive XXIV-710 pp. con 296 figg. n.t.

318. *Relazioni letterarie tra Italia e Penisola Iberica nell'epoca rinascimentale e barocca*. Atti del primo Colloquio Internazionale, Pisa, 4-5 ottobre 2002. A cura di S. Vuelta Garcı´a. 2004, X-178 pp. con 2 figg. n.t.

319. BOZZOLA, S. *Tra Cinque e Seicento. Tradizione e anticlassicismo nella sintassi della prosa letteraria*. 2004, VIII-168 pp.

320. BALMAS, E. *Studi sul Cinquecento*. 2004, XXX-666 pp. con 11 figg. n.t. e 11 tavv. f.t.

321. *Studi di letteratura francese. Rivista europea*, vol. XXVIII (2003). 2004, 138 pp.

322. FURLAN, F. *La donna, la famiglia, l'amore tra Medioevo e Rinascimento*. 2004, 122 pp.

323. ALFIERI, V. *Esquisse du Jugement Universel*. A cura di G. Santato. 2004, 128 pp. con 2 figg. n.t.

324. *Studi secenteschi*. Vol. XLVI (2005). 2005, IV-386 pp. con 13 tavv. f.t.

325. *Il Capitolo di San Lorenzo nel Quattrocento*. Convegno di studi, Firenze, 28-29 marzo 2003. A cura di P. Viti. 2006, XII-360 pp. con 8 tavv. f.t.

326. MARTELLOTTI, A. *I ricettari di Federico II. Dal «Meridionale» al «Liber de coquina»*. 2005, 284 pp. Ristampa 2011.

327. FOSCOLO, U. *Dell'origine e dell'ufficio della letteratura. Orazione*. 2005, 172 pp.

328. RUGGIERO, R. *«Il ricco edificio». Arte allusiva nella* Gerusalemme Liberata. 2005, XXII-194 pp.

329. *Studi secenteschi*. Vol. XLVII (2006). 2006, IV-368 pp.

330. POZZI, M. - MATTIODA, E. *Giorgio Vasari storico e critico*. 2006, XXII-438 pp.

331. *Leonis Baptistae Alberti Descriptio Vrbis Romae*. Edizione critica di Jean-Yves Boriaud e Francesco Furlan. 2005, 164 pp. con 10 tavv. f.t.

332. *Resultanze in merito alla vita e all'opera di Piero Jahier. Saggi e materiali inediti*. A cura di F. Giacone. 2007, XII-368 pp. con 4 tavv. f.t.

333. CEVOLINI, A. *De arte excerpendi. Imparare a dimenticare nella modernita`*. 2006, 460 pp. con 9 figg. n.t.

334. *Studi secenteschi*. Vol. XLVIII (2007). 2007, IV-432 pp.

335. MONTINARO, G. *L'epistolario di Ludovico Agostini. Riforma e utopia*. 2006, 294 pp.

336. *Il mito d'Arcadia. Pastori e amori nelle arti del Rinascimento*. Atti del Convegno internazionale di studi, Torino, 14-15 marzo 2005. A cura di D. Boillet e A. Pontremoli. 2007, XXII-266 pp. con 8 figg. n.t. e 14 tavv. f.t.

337. SEBASTIO, L. *Il Poeta tra Chiesa ed Impero. Una storia del pensiero dantesco*. 2007, 214 pp.

338. *Studi di letteratura francese. Rivista europea*, voll. XXIXXXX (2004-2005). «Il viaggio francese in Italia». 2007, 226 pp. con 1 fig. n.t.

339. *I linguaggi dell'Altro. Forme dell'alterità nel testo letterario*. Atti del Convegno *I Linguaggi dell'Altro/altro*, Università di Lecce, 21-22 aprile 2005. A cura di A.M. Piglionica, C. Bacile di Castiglione, M.S. Marchesi. 2007, XXIV-228 pp. con 2 figg. n.t.

340. BENPORAT, C. *Cucina e convivialita` italiana del Cinquecento*. 2007, 344 pp. con 16 tavv. f.t.

341. *Il cantare italiano fra folklore e letteratura*. Atti del Convegno internazionale di Zurigo, Landesmuseum, 23-25 giugno 2005. A cura di M. Picone e L. Rubini. 2007, XIV-528 pp. con 6 figg. n.t.

342. COVINO, S. *Giacomo e Monaldo Leopardi falsari trecenteschi. Contraffazione dell'antico, cultura e storia linguistica nell'Ottocento italiano*. 2009, I tomo XVI-328 pp. II tomo VI-392 pp. con 2 tavv. f.t.

343. *Studi secenteschi*. Vol. XLIX (2008). 2008, IV-434 pp. con 8 tavv. f.t.

344. *Traduzioni, imitazioni, scambi tra Italia e Portogallo nei secoli*. Atti del primo Colloquio internazionale, Pisa, 15-16 ottobre 2004. A cura di M. Lupetti. 2008, X-172 pp. con 2 figg. n.t. e 15 tavv. f.t. di cui 12 a colori.

345. *L'identità italiana ed europea tra Sette e Ottocento*. A cura di A. Ascenzi e L. Melosi. 2008, XIV-184 pp. con 5 figg. n.t.

346. WILSON, R. *Prophecies and prophecy in Dante's* Commedia. 2007, X-228 pp.

347. *Writing Relations: American Scholars in Italian Archives. Essays for Franca Petrucci Nardelli and Armando Petrucci*. Edited by D. Shemek and M. Wyatt. 2008, XII-242 pp. con 13 figg. n.t. e 2 tavv. f.t.

348. IOLY ZORATTINI, P. *I nomi degli altri. Conversioni a Venezia e nel Friuli Veneto in età moderna*. Con prefazione di M. Massenzio. 2008, XX-388 pp. con 4 tavv. f.t.

349. Urraro, R. *Giacomo Leopardi: le donne, gli amori*. 2008, VIII-378 pp.

350. Rabboni, R. *Speculare sodo, ragionar sostanzioso. Studi sull'abate Conti*. 2008, X-336 pp.

351. Tiozzo, E. *La letteratura italiana e il premio Nobel. Storia critica e documenti*. 2008, VIII-358 pp. con 29 tavv. f.t.

352. Capecchi, G. - Marzi, M. G. - Saladino, V. *I granduchi di Toscana e l'antico. Acquisti, restauri, allestimenti*. 2008, VIII-342 pp. con 78 tavv. f.t. di cui 16 a colori.

353. *Studi secenteschi*. Vol. L (2009). 2008, IV-346 pp. con 2 figg. n.t. e 13 tavv. f.t.

354. *In assenza del re. Le reggenti dal secolo XIV al secolo XVII (Piemonte ed Europa)*. A cura di F. Varallo. 2008, XXXII-610 pp. con es. mus. n.t. e 7 tavv. f.t.

355. Celli, C. *Il carnevale di Machiavelli*. 2009, IV-218 pp.

356. *Iacopo Sannazaro. La cultura napoletana nell'Europa del Rinascimento*. Convegno internazionale di studi, Napoli, 27-28 marzo 2006. A cura di P. Sabbatino. 2009, VIII-430 pp. con 5 figg. n.t. e 14 tavv. f.t.

357. *«La bourse des idées du monde». Malaparte e la Francia*. Atti del Convegno internazionale di studi su Curzio Malaparte, Prato-Firenze, 8-9 novembre 2007. A cura di M. Grassi. 2008, XII-234 pp.

358. *La metafora in Dante*. A cura di M. Ariani. 2009, VI-286 pp.

359. Coen, P. *Il mercato dei quadri a Roma nel diciottesimo secolo. La domanda, l'offerta e la circolazione delle opere in un grande centro artistico europeo*. I. Con una prefazione di E. Castelnuovo. II. Appendice documentaria. 2010, LX-816 pp. con 32 tavv. f.t. a colori.

360. *Saggi di letteratura architettonica, da Vitruvio a Winckelmann*. I. A cura di F.P. Di Teodoro. 2009, VI-372 pp. con 67 figg. n.t. e 21 tavv. f.t.

361. *Don Giovanni nelle riscritture francesi e francofone del Novecento*. Atti del Convegno internazionale di Vercelli, 16-17 ottobre 2008. A cura di M. Mastroianni. 2009, XIII-330 pp.

362. Marchesi, M.S. *Eliot's Perpetual Struggle. The Language of Evil in* Murder in the Cathedral. 2009, XXXVIII-144 pp.

363. *Studi di letteratura francese. Rivista europea*, voll. XXXIXXXII (2006-2007). «Dictionnaires et écrivains». 2009, 130 pp.

364. *Studi secenteschi*. Vol. LI (2010). 2010, IV-394 pp.

365. *Saggi di letteratura architettonica, da Vitruvio a Winckelmann*. II. A cura di L. Bertolini. 2009, VI-254 pp. con 66 figg. n.t. e 5 tavv. f.t. a colori.

366. Frenquellucci, C. *Dalla Mancha a Siena al Nuovo Mondo. Don Chisciotte nel teatro di Girolamo Gigli*. 2010, XVI-334 pp.

367. *Giuseppe Ungaretti - Jean Lescure. Carteggio (1951-1966)*. A cura di R. Gennaro. 2010, XXVI-252 pp.

368. Testa, F. *Winckelmann e l'architettura antica*. In preparazione.

369. *Saggi di letteratura architettonica, da Vitruvio a Winckelmann*. III. A cura di H. Burns, F.P. Di Teodoro e G. Bacci. 2010, VI-392 pp. con 126 figg. n.t.

370. Barsella, S. *In the Light of the Angels: Angelology and Cosmology in Dante's* Divina Commedia. 2010, XVI-214 pp.

371. Durante, E. - Martellotti, A. *«Giovinetta peregrina». La vera storia di Laura Peperara e Torquato Tasso*. 2010, VI-352 pp. con 2 tavv. f.t. a colori, con CD contenente "Madrigali per Laura Peperara".

372. Squillace, G. *Il profumo nel mondo antico. Con la prima traduzione italiana del «Sugli odori» di Teofrasto*. Prefazione di L. Villoresi. 2010, XX-282 pp. con 8 tavv. f.t. a colori.

373. Cerocchi, M. *Funzioni semantiche e metatestuali della musica in Dante, Petrarca e Boccaccio*. 2010, XII-160 pp. con 6 es. mus. n.t.

374. *La Ronde. Giostre, esercizi cavallereschi e* loisir *in Francia e Piemonte fra Medioevo e Ottocento*. Atti del Convegno internazionale di Studi, Museo storico dell'Arma di Cavalleria di Pinerolo, 15-17 giugno 2006. A cura di F. Varallo. 2010, XIV-276 pp. con 37 figg. n.t. e 19 tavv. f.t. a colori.

375. *La parola e l'immagine. Studi in onore di Gianni Venturi*. A cura di M. Ariani, A. Bruni, A. Dolfi, A. Gareffi. 2010, 2 tomi di complessive VIII-892 pp. con 42 figg. n.t. e 35 tav. f.t. di cui 10 a colori.

376. Bertelli, S. *La tradizione della «Commedia»: dai manoscritti al testo*. I. *I codici trecenteschi (entro l'antica vulgata) conservati a Firenze*. Presentazione di P. Trovato. 2011, XVI-446 pp. con 68 figg. n.t. e 32 tavv. f.t. a colori.

377. *Nascita della storiografia e organizzazione dei saperi*. Atti del Convegno internazionale di studi, Torino, 20-22 maggio 2009. A cura di E. Mattioda. 2010, XII-346 pp. con 1 tav. f.t. a colori.

378. *Studi secenteschi*. Vol. LII (2011). 2011, VI-446 pp. con 6 figg. n.t.

379. Ardizzone, M.L. *Dante: il paradigma intellettuale. Un'*inventio *degli anni fiorentini*. 2011, XXVI-264 pp.

380. Fenech Kroke, A. *Giorgio Vasari. La culture de l'allégorie*. Préface de P. Morel. 2011, XXII-556 pp. con 24 figg. n.t. e 16 tavv. f.t. a colori.

381. *Gabriele d'Annunzio. Inediti 1922-1936. Carteggio con Maria Lombardi e altri scritti*. A cura di F. Caburlotto, prefazione di P. Gibellini. 2011, XLVI-80 pp. con 3 figg. n.t. e 8 tavv. f.t.

382. Bertozzi, R. *L'immagine dell'Italia nei diari e nell'autobiografia di Paul Heyse*. 2011, XVI-822 pp. con 4 figg. n.t. e 1 tavv. f.t. a colori.

383. Leonardi, M. *L'Età del Vespro siciliano nella storiografia tedesca (dal XIX secolo ai nostri giorni)*. 2011, X-148 pp.

384. *Un trattato universale dei colori. Il ms. 2861 della Biblioteca Universitaria di Bologna*. Edizione del testo, traduzione e commento a cura di Francesca Muzio. 2012, XXIV-300 pp.

385. *Beniamino Dal Fabbro, scrittore*. Atti della giornata di studi, Belluno, 29 ottobre 2010. A cura di R. Zucco. 2011, X-164 pp. con 20 tavv. f.t. a colori.

386. Carnevale Schianca, E. *La cucina medievale. Lessico, storia, preparazioni*. 2011, XLVI-758 pp.

387. Remigi, G. *Cesare Pavese e la letteratura americana: «una splendida monotonia»*. 2012, XVIII-226 pp.

388. Segatori, S. *Forme, temi e motivi della narrativa di Ippolito Nievo*. 2011, VIII-188 pp.

389. *I* Marmi *di Anton Francesco Doni: la storia, i generi e le arti*. A cura di G. Rizzarelli. 2012, XVIII-430 pp. con 35 figg. n.t.

390. *Paesaggio ligure e paesaggi interiori nella poesia di Eugenio Montale*. Atti del Convegno internazionale, «Credo non esista nulla di simile al mondo», Parco Nazionale delle Cinque Terre, Riomaggiore-Monterosso, 11-13 dicembre 2009. A cura di P. Polito e A. Zollino. 2011, VIII-284 pp. con 7 figg. n.t.

391. Fumagalli, E. *Il giusto Enea e il pio Rifeo. Pagine dantesche*. 2012, VIII-266 pp.

392. *Dialogo & conversazione. I luoghi di una socialità ideale dal Rinascimento all'Illuminismo*. A cura di M. Høxbro Andersen e A. Toftgaard. 2012, IV, 264 pp.

393. Payne, A. *The Telescope and the Compass. Teofilo Gallaccini and the Dialogue between Architecture and Science in the Age of Galileo*. 2012, XX-242 pp. con 96 figg. n.t.

394. *Teofilo Gallaccini. Selected Writings and Library*. Edited by A. Payne, with the Contribution of G.M. Fara. 2012, X-414 pp. con 102 figg. n.t.

395. Buccini, S. *Francesco Pona. L'ozio lecito della scrittura*. 2013, XIV-228 pp. con 37 figg. n.t.

396. *Studi di letteratura francese. Rivista europea*, voll. XXXII-IXXXIV (2008-2009). «La poésie de langue française contemporaine». 2011, 154 pp.

397. D'Elia, A. *La* peregrinatio *poietica di David Maria Turoldo*. Prefazione di D. Della Terza. 2012, XIV-182 pp.

398. Battisti, E. *Michelangelo: fortuna di un mito. Cinquecento anni di critica letteraria e artistica*. A cura di G. Saccaro Del Buffa. 2012, XVIII-248 pp. con 19 tavv. f.t. di cui 15 a colori.

399. *Studi secenteschi*. Vol. LIII (2012). 2012, IV-404 pp. con 4 figg. n.t.

400. Addesso, C.A. *Teatro e festività nella Napoli aragonese*. 2012, X-172 pp.

401. Bellorini, G. *Il magnifico Signor Cavallier Luigi Cassola Piacentino. Edizione critica dei* madrigali. *Censimento e indice dei capoversi di tutte le rime*. 2012, XVI-222 pp.

402. Martellotti, A. *Linguistica e cucina*. 2012, XIV-172 pp.

403. Marselli, N. *L'architettura in relazione alla storia del mondo*. A cura di D. Iacobone. 2012, IV-90 pp.

404. *«Legato con amore in un volume». Essays in honour of John A. Scott*. Edited by John J. Kinder and Diana Glenn. 2013, XX-350 pp. con 6 figg. n.t. e 3 tavv. f.t.

405. Buckstone, J.B. *Robert Macaire, or, the Exploits of a Gentleman at Large*. Edited and with an introduction by M.S. Marchesi. 2012, LII-64 pp.

406. Capecchi, G. - Pegazzano, D. - Faralli, S. *Visitare Boboli all'epoca dei Lumi. Il giardino e le sue sculture nelle incisioni delle 'Statue di Firenze'*. 2013, VI-244 pp. con 228 ill. n.t. e 1 pieghevole.

407. *Studi di letteratura francese. Rivista europea*, voll. XXXVXXXVI (2010-2011). «Henri Meschonnic entre langue et poésie». 2012, 210 pp. con 12 figg. n.t. e 8 tavv. f.t.

408. Doni, A.F. *I Marmi*. A cura di G. Rizzarelli e C.A. Girotto.In preparazione.

409. Del Gatto, A. Quel punto acerbo. *Temporalità e conoscenza metaforica in Leopardi*. 2012, X-116 pp.

410. Giambonini, F. *Bernardino Lanino ritrattista e l'ambiente artistico politico del suo tempo*. 2013, VI-334 pp. con 9 tavv. f.t. a colori.

411. *Studi secenteschi*. Vol. LIV (2013). 2013, X-372 pp. con 5 figg. n.t.

412. Butti de Lima, P. *Il piacere delle immagini. Un tema aristotelico nella riflessione moderna sull'arte*. 2012, VIII-202 pp. con 3 tavv. f.t. a colori.

413. Mocca, C. *Discorsi Preservativi e curativi delle peste Col modo di purgare le Case, & Robbe Appestate*. A cura di R. Scarpa. 2012, XXX-54 pp.

414. Tordella, P.G. *Il disegno nell'Europa del Settecento. Regioni teoriche ragioni critiche*. 2012, XIV-284 pp. con 16 tavv. f.t.

415. *Regionis forma pvlcherrima. Percezioni, lessico, categorie del paesaggio nella letteratura latina*. Atti del Convegno di studio, Palazzo Bo, Università degli studi di Padova, 15-16 marzo 2011. A cura di G. Baldo e E. Cazzuffi. 2013, VIII-278 pp. con 6 figg. n.t.

416. *Lo «Zibaldone» di Leopardi come ipertesto*. Atti del Convegno internazionale, Barcellona, 26-27 ottobre 2012. A cura di M. de las Nieves Muñiz Muñiz. 2013, X-506 pp. con 5 figg. n.t. e 9 tavv. f.t. a colori.

417. Viglione, M. *Le insorgenze controrivoluzionarie nella storiografia italiana. Dibattito scientifico e scontro ideologico (1799-2012)*. 2013, XII-132 pp.

418. Burlamacchi, M. *Nobility, Honour and Glory. A brief Military History of the Order of Malta*. Translated from the Italian by M. Roberts. 2013, X-76 pp. con 13 tavv. f.t. di cui 9 a colori.

419. Petrioli Tofani, A. *L'inventario settecentesco dei disegni degli Uffizi di Giuseppe Pelli Bencivenni*. 2014, 4 tomi di complessive XXX-1826 pp.

420. Marzi, M.G. *Il Gabinetto delle Terre di Luigi Lanzi nella Galleria degli Uffizi. Vasi, terrecotte, lucerne e vetri dalle Collezioni medicee-lorenesi al Museo Archeologico Nazionale di Firenze*. In preparazione.

421. *L'*Iconologia *di Cesare Ripa. Fonti letterarie e figurative dall'antichità al Rinascimento*. Atti del Convegno internazionale di studi, Certosa di Pontignano, 3-4 maggio 2012. A cura di M. Gabriele, C. Galassi, R. Guerrini. 2013, XXVIII-236 pp. con 58 figg. n.t.

422. Aricò, N. *Architettura del tardo Rinascimento in Sicilia. Giovannangelo Montorsoli a Messina (1547-57)*. 2013, XIV-226 pp. con 60 figg. n.t. e 16 tavv. f.t. a colori.

423. Modesti, P. *Le delizie ritrovate. Poggioreale e la villa del Rinascimento nella Napoli aragonese*. 2014, X-272 pp. con 1 fig. n.t. e 64 tavv. f.t. di cui 15 a colori.

424. *Architettura e identità locali*. Vol. I. A cura di L. Corrain e F.P. Di Teodoro. 2013, X-586 pp. con 161 figg. n.t. e 3 tavv. f.t. a colori.

425. *Architettura e identità locali*. Vol. II. A cura di H. Burns e M. Mussolin. Con la collaborazione di Clara Altavista. In preparazione.

426. Fara, G.M. *Albrecht Dürer nelle fonti italiane antiche: 1508-1686*. 2014, XII-590 pp.

427. *Studi secenteschi*. Vol. LV (2014). 2014, IV-330 pp. con 4 figg. n.t.

428. Fara, A. *L'arte della scienza. Architettura e cultura militare a Torino e nello stato sabaudo 1673-1859*. 2014, XII-272 pp. con 1 fig. n.t. e 64 tavv. f.t.

429. *Studi di letteratura francese. Rivista europea*, voll. XXXVI-IXXXVIII (2012-2013). «La langue de la poésie française contemporaine». 2014, 168 pp.

430. Felici, A. *Michelangelo a San Lorenzo (1515-1534). Il linguaggio architettonico del Cinquecento fiorentino*. Premessa di G. Frosini. 2015, X-378 pp. con 64 figg. n.t.

431. Ceccherini, I. *La biblioteca di Sozomeno*. In preparazione.

432. *Traiano Boccalini tra satira e politica*. Atti del Convegno, Macerata-Loreto, ottobre 2013. A cura di Laura Melosi, Paolo Procaccioli. 2015, XII-482 con 3 figg. n.t.

433. Durante E. - Martellotti, A. *"Amorosa fenice". La vita, le rime e la fortuna in musica di Girolamo Casone da Oderzo (c. 1528-1592)*. 2015, VI-482 pp. con 4 figg. n.t.

434. *Incontri di civiltà nel Mediterraneo. L'Impero Ottomano e l'Italia del Rinascimento. Storia, arte e architettura*. A cura di Alireza Naser Eslami. 2014, 184 pp. con 75 figg. n.t. di cui 56 a colori.

435. Rossi, M., *Unione e diversità. L'Italia di Vasari nello specchio della Sistina*. 2014, 184 pp. con 48 figg. n.t. e 16 tavv. f.t. a colori.

436. *L'architettura militare di Venezia in terraferma e in Adriatico fra XVI e XVII secolo*. A cura di Francesco Paolo Fiore. 2014, XXVIII-462 pp. con 185 figg. n.t. e 16 tavv. f.t. di cui 8 a colori.

437. *Studi di Letteratura Francese. Rivista europea*, vol. XXXIX (2014). 2015, 172 pp.

438. *Studi secenteschi*. Vol. LVI (2015). 2015, 458 pp.

439. Urraro, R. *Questa maledetta vita. Il "romanzo autobiografico" di Giacomo Leopardi*. 2015, X-446 pp.

440. Platina, B. De honesta voluptate et valitudine. *Un trattato sui piaceri della tavola e la buona salute*. Nuova edizione commentata con testo latino a fronte a cura di Enrico Carnevale Schianca. 2015, VI-590 pp.

441. Morabito, R. *L'Evo e il tempo del* Canzoniere. 2015, IV-72 pp.

442. *Studi linguistici e letterari tra Italia e mondo iberico in età moderna*. A cura di M. Graziani e S. Vuelta García. 2015, VI-140 pp.

443. Lia, P. *Poetica dell'amore e conversione. Considerazioni teologiche sulla lingua della* Commedia *di Dante*. 2015, XIV-324 pp.

444. Gabriele, M. *La* Porta Magica *di Roma simbolo dell'alchimia occidentale*. 2015, X-222 pp. con 45 figg. n.t. e 12 tavv. f.t. a colori.

445. Blanco, M. *Edipo non deve nascere. Lettura delle* Poésies *di Mallarmé*. 2016, XII-248 pp. con 4 tavv. f.t.

446. *Studi di letteratura francese. Rivista europea*, vol. XL (2015). 2016, 126 pp.

447. McLaughlin, M. *Leon Battista Alberti. La vita, l'umanesimo, le opere*. 2016, XXII-174 pp. con 9 tavv. f.t.

448. Bertelli, S. *La tradizione della «Commedia» dai manoscritti al testo*. II. *I codici trecenteschi (oltre l'antica vulgata) conservati a Firenze*. 2016, VIII-610 pp. con 89 figg. n.t. e 64 tavv. f.t. a colori.

449. Villani, G. *Il convitato di pietra. Apoteosi e tramonto della linea curva nel Settecento*. 2016, X-120 pp. con 8 tavv. f.t. a colori.

450. Valignano, A. *Dialogo sulla Missione degli ambasciatori giapponesi alla curia romana e sulle cose osservate in Europa e durante tutto il viaggio basato sul diario degli ambasciatori e tradotto in latino da Duarte de Sande, sacerdote della Compagnia di Gesù*. A cura di M. Di Russo, traduzione di P.A. Airoldi, presentazione di D. Maraini. 2016, XVI-670 pp. con 79 figg. n.t., 3 cartine e 32 tavv. f.t. a colori.

451. Tordella, P.G. *Hugo von Hofmannsthal e la poetica del disegno tra Otto e Novecento*. 2016, VIII-256 pp. con 8 tavv. f.t. a colori.

452. *Studi secenteschi*. Vol. LVII (2016). 2016, IV-362 pp. con 13 figg. n.t.

453. Aricò, N. *La fondazione di Carlentini nella Sicilia di Juan de Vega*. 2016, XII-280 pp. con 37 figg. n.t. e 16 tavv. f.t. a colori.

454. *Traduzioni, riscritture, ibridazioni: prosa e teatro fra Italia, Spagna e Portogallo*. A cura di M. Graziani e S. Vuelta García. 2016, VI-142 pp.

455. Caputo, G. *L'aurora del Giappone tra mito e storiografia. Nascita ed evoluzione dell'alterità nipponica nella cultura italiana, 1300-1600*. 2016, XX-352 pp. con 19 figg. n.t.

456. Lawson Lucas, A. *Emilio Salgari. Fantasia e verità*. Vol. I. In preparazione.

457. Lawson Lucas, A. *Emilio Salgari. Fantasia e verità*. Vol. II. In preparazione.

458. Lawson Lucas, A. *Emilio Salgari. Fantasia e verità*. Vol. III. In preparazione.

459. Lawson Lucas, A. *Emilio Salgari. Fantasia e verità*. Vol. IV. In preparazione.

460. *Ius Leopardi. Legge, natura, civiltà*. A cura di L. Melosi. 2016, VI-114 pp.

461. *La* Comedia Nueva *e le scene italiane nel Seicento*. A cura di F. Antonucci e A. Tedesco. 2016, 340 pp.

462. Morabito, R. *Le virtù di Griselda. Storia di una storia*. 2016, 302 pp.

463. *Studi di letteratura francese. Rivista europea*, vol. XLI (2016). 2016, 302 pp. con 8 tavv. f.t.

464. Gazzola, G., *Montale, the modernist*. 2016, VIII-234 pp. con 4 figg. n.t.

465. *Pasquino in estasi*. A cura di S. Prandi. In preparazione.

466. Cappozzo, V., *Dizionario dei sogni nel medioevo. Il* Somniale Danielis *in manoscritti letterari*. In preparazione.

Serie II: Linguistica

1. Spitzer, L. *Lexikalisches aus dem Katalanischen und den übrigen ibero-romanischen Sprachen*. 1921. VIII-162 pp.

2. Gamillscheg, E. und Spitzer, L. *Beiträge zur romanischen Wortbildungslehre*. 1921, 230 pp., 3 cc.

3. [Schuchardt, U.]. *Miscellanea linguistica dedic. a Ugo Schuchardt per il suo 80° anniv*. 1922, 121 pp., 2 cc.

4. Bertoldi, V. *Un ribelle nel regno dei fiori (I nomi romanzi del «colchicum autunnale L.» attraverso il tempo e lo spazio)*. 1923, VIII-224 pp. con ill.

5. Bottiglioni, G. *Leggende e tradizioni di Sardegna*. (Testi dialettali in grafia fonetica). 1922. (esaurito)

6. Onomastica - I. Paul Aebischer, *Sur la formation des noms de famille dans le canton de Fribourg (Suisse)*. - II. Dante Olivieri, *I cognomi della Venezia Euganea*. Saggio di uno studio storico-etimologico. 1924, 272 pp.

7. Rohlfs, G. *Grichen und Romanen in Unteritalien* Ein Beitrag zur Geschichte der unteritalienischen Gräzität. 1923. (esaurito)

8. *Studi di dialettologia alto italiana*. - I. Gualzata, M. *Di alcuni nomi locali del Bellinzonese e Locarnese*. - II. Bläuer-Rini, A. *Giunte al «vocabolario di Bormio»*. 1924, 166 pp.

9. Pascu, G. *Romänische elemente in den Balkansprachen*. 1924, IV-112 pp.

10. Farinelli, A. *Marrano* (Storia di un vituperio). 1925, X-80 pp.

11. Bertoni, G. *Profilo storico del dialetto di Modena. (Con appendice di «Giunte al Vocabolario Modenese»)*. 1925, 88 pp.

12. Bartoli, M. *Introduzione alla neolinguistica* (Principi - Scopi - Metodi), 1926. (esaurito)

13. Migliorini, B. *Dal nome proprio al nome comune*. 1927, VI-358 pp. con LXXVIII pp. di supplemento. Seconda ristampa 1999.

14. Keller, O. *La flexion du verbe dans le patois genevois*. 1928, XXVIII-216 pp., 1 c. ripiegata.

15. Spotti, L. *Vocabolarietto anconitano-italiano*. 1929. (esaurito)

16. Wagner, M. L. *Studien über den sardischen Wortschatz. (I. Die Familie - II. Der menschliche Körper)*. 1930, XVI-156 pp., 15 cc.

17. Soukup, R. *Les causes et l'évolution de l'abreviation des pronoms personnels régimes en ancien français*. 1932, 130 pp.

18. Rheinfelder, H. *Kultsprache und Profansprache in den romanischen Ländern*. 1933. (esaurito)

19. Flagge, L. *Provenzalisches Alpenleben in den Hochtälern des Verdon und der Bléone*. Ein Beitrag zur Volkskunde des Basses-Alpes. 1935. (esaurito)

20. Sainéan, L. *Autour des sources indigènes*. Etudes d'étymologie française et romaine. 1935. (esaurito)

21. Seifert, E. *Tenere «Haben» im Romanischen*. 1935, 122 pp., 4 tavv.

22. Tagliavini, C. *L'Albanese di Dalmazia*. 1937. (esaurito)

23. Bosshard, H. *Saggio di un glossario dell'antico Lombardo*. 1938. (esaurito)

24. Vidos, B. E. *Storia delle parole marinaresche italiane passate in francese*. 1939. (esaurito)

25. Alessio, G. *Saggio di Toponomastica calabrese*. 1939. (esaurito)

26. Folena, G. *La crisi linguistica del 400 e l'«Arcadia» di I. Sannazaro*. 1952. (esaurito)

27. *Miscellanea di studi linguistici in ricordo di Ettore Tolomei*. 1953. (esaurito)

28. Vidos, B. E. *Manuale di linguistica romanza*. Prima edizione italiana completamente aggiornata dall'Autore. 1959, XXIV-440 pp. Terza ristampa 1975.

29. Ruggieri, R. *Saggi di linguistica italiana e italo-romanza*. 1962, 242 pp.

30. Mengaldo, P. V. *La lingua del Boiardo lirico*. 1963, VIII-380 pp.

31. Vidos, B. E. *Prestito espansione e migrazione dei termini tecnici nelle lingue romanze e non romanze*. 1965, VIII-424 pp., 3 ill.

32. Altieri Biagi, M. L. *Galileo e la terminologia tecnico-scientifica*. 1965. (esaurito)

33. Polloni, A. *Toponomastica romagnola*, Prefazione di Carlo Tagliavini. 1966. Ristampa 2002.

34. Ghiglieri, P. *La grafia del Machiavelli studiata negli autografi*. 1969, IV-364 pp.

35. *Linguistica matematica e calcolatori*. A cura di A. Zampolli. 1973, XX-670 pp.

36. *Computational and mathematical linguistics*. Vol. I. A cura di A. Zampolli e N. Calzolari. 1977, 2 voll. di XLVI-796 pp. complessive.

37. *Computational and mathematical linguistics*. Vol. II. A cura di A. Zampolli e N. Calzolari. 1980, 2 voll. di VIII-906 pp. complessive.

38. Semerano, G. *Le origini della cultura europea. Rivelazioni della linguistica storica*. 1984, 2 voll. di LXX-956 pp. complessive. Ristampa 2010.

39. *Fonologia etrusca, fonetica toscana. Il problema del sostrato*. 1983, 204 pp. con 1 tav. f.t.

40. La Stella, T. E. *Dizionario storico di deonomastica*. 1984, 236 pp.

41. Rando, G. *Dizionario degli anglicismi nell'italiano contemporaneo*. 1987, XLII-256 pp.

42. *Lessicografia, filologia e critica*. 1986, 204 pp.

43. Semerano, G. *Le origini della cultura europea*. Vol. II. *Dizionari etimologici. Basi semitiche delle lingue Indeuropee*. I tomo: *Dizionario della lingua greca*. II tomo: *Dizionario della lingua latina*. 1994, 2 voll. di C-726 pp. complessive. III ristampa 2007.

44. Scavuzzo, C. *Studi sulla lingua dei quotidiani messinesi di fine Ottocento*. 1988, 208 pp.

45. Agostiniani, L. - Hjordt-Vetlesen, O. *Lessico etrusco cronologico e topografico dai materiali del «Thesaurus Linguae Etruscae»*. 1988, XXXVI-224 pp.

46. O'Connor, D. *A history of Italian and English bilingual dictionaries*. 1990, 188 pp.

47. Boselli, P. *Dizionario di toponomastica bergamasca e cremonese*. 1990, 346 pp.

48. Delmay, B. *Usi e difese della lingua*. 1990, 154 pp. con 1 tav. f.t.

49. Catenazzi, F. *L'italiano di Svevo. Fra scrittura pubblica e scrittura privata*. 1994, 202 pp.

50. Facchetti, G. M. *Frammenti di diritto privato etrusco*. 2000, 116 pp.

51. *La scrittura professionale: ricerca, prassi, insegnamento*. Atti del I Convegno di studi, Perugia, Università per Stranieri, 23-25 ottobre 2000. A cura di S. Covino. 2001, XXIV-454 pp. con 29 figg. n.t. e 1 pieghevole.

52. Leone, A. *Conversazioni sulla lingua italiana*. 2002, 160 pp.

53. Natella, P. *La parola 'Mafia'*. 2002, 172 pp.

54. Facchetti, G. M. *Appunti di morfologia etrusca. Con un'appendice sulla questione delle identità genetiche dell'etrusco*. 2002, 160 pp.

55. Facchetti, G. M. - Negri, M. *Creta minoica. Sulle tracce delle più antiche scritture d'Europa*. 2003, 200 pp. con 21 figg. n.t. e 2 tavv. f.t.

56. Prandi, M. - Gross, G. - De Santis, C. *La finalità. Strutture concettuali e forme d'espressione in italiano*. 2005, 366 pp.

57. Ferguson, R. *A Linguistic History of Venice*. 2007, 322 pp. con 3 figg. n.t.

58. *L'italiano parlato di Firenze, Perugia e Roma*. A cura di L. Agostiniani e P. Bonucci. 2011, 206 pp. con 8 figg. n.t.

59. Medina Montero, J.F. *El verbo, el participio y las clases de palabras "invariables" en las gramáticas de español para extranjeros de los siglos XVI y XVII*. 2015, VIII-192 pp.

60. *Digital Texts, translations, lexicons in a multi-modular web application: methods and samples*. A cura di A. Bozzi. 2015, X-146 pp. con 38 figg. n.t.

61. Parenti, A. *Parole strane. Etimologie e altra linguistica*. 2015, VI-158 pp. con 2 figg. n.t.